Toxic Masculinity in the Ancient World

Intersectionality in Classical Antiquity
Series Editors: Mark Masterson, Victoria University of Wellington, and Fiona McHardy, University of Roehampton

This series focuses on the intersection of gender and sexuality, in the Greco-Roman world, with a range of other factors including race, ethnicity, class, ability, masculinity, femininity, transgender and post-colonial gender studies. The books in the series will be theoretically informed and will sit at the fore-front of the study of a variety of outsiders – those marginalised in relation to the 'classical ideal' – and how they were differently constructed in the ancient world. The series is also interested in the ways in which work in the field of classical reception contributes to that study.

Editorial Advisory Board
Patty Baker, Alastair Blanshard, Susan Deacy, Jacqueline Fabre-Serris, Cristiana Franco, Genevieve Liveley, Mark Masterson, Amy Richlin, Carisa R. Showden

Books available in the series
Women in the Law Courts of Classical Athens, Konstantinos Kapparis
Exploring Gender Diversity in the Ancient World, edited by Allison Surtees and Jennifer Dyer
Marginalised Populations in the Ancient Greek World: The Bioarchaeology of the Other, Carrie L. Sulosky Weaver
Toxic Masculinity in the Ancient World, Melanie Racette-Campbell and Aven McMaster
Believing Ancient Women, Megan E. Bowen, Mary H. Gilbert and Edith G. Nally
Age, Gender and Status in Macedonian Society, 550–300 BCE, Elina M. Salminen
Visit the series web page at: edinburghuniversitypress.com/series-intersectionality-in-classical-antiquity

Toxic Masculinity in the Ancient World

Melanie Racette-Campbell and Aven McMaster

EDINBURGH
University Press

Edinburgh University Press is one of the leading university presses in the UK. We publish academic books and journals in our selected subject areas across the humanities and social sciences, combining cutting-edge scholarship with high editorial and production values to produce academic works of lasting importance. For more information visit our website: edinburghuniversitypress.com

Edinburgh University Press Ltd
13 Infirmary Street,
Edinburgh, EH1 1LT

First published in hardback by Edinburgh University Press 2024

Typeset in 11/13 Adobe Garamond by
by Manila Typesetting Company

A CIP record for this book is available from the British Library

ISBN 978 1 3995 2053 9 (hardback)
ISBN 978 1 3995 2054 6 (paperback)
ISBN 978 1 3995 2055 3 (webready PDF)
ISBN 978 1 3995 2056 0 (epub)

Contents

To those who persevere

Acknowledgements

Aven McMaster

First, let me thank my co-editor, Melanie, without whom this book would have never made it past the 'fun idea on Twitter' stage. Your expertise, diligence and energy have been essential to this process, and I'm so lucky to have you as both a colleague and a friend. Also, to the many contributors – your enthusiasm for this project and your patience with us as the months turned into years are very much appreciated. Next, in the spirit of the anti-acknowledgement, I must say that this book would have been much easier to produce had it not been for the insolvency of Laurentian University that led to the closure of my programme and the loss of my job and academic career, not to mention the minor detail of a global pandemic that hit just after we received everyone's first drafts. But I will always be deeply grateful for the extensive and generous support I received from friends and colleagues throughout this difficult period, both emotional and practical, in person and, especially, online. Finally, thank you to my family for your encouragement and love, and for your patience with my fascination for the obscure, eccentric and sometimes downright disreputable details of the Roman world. And to my wonderful husband, Mark Sundaram: thank you. I love you.

Melanie Racette-Campbell

First, I'd like to thank my co-editor for thinking of me for this project. It's been an exciting and educational experience and I'm so pleased to have worked with you! Thanks are also due to all our contributors for their patience with the long process of bringing the book to fruition amidst *waves hands* all this. Like Aven, I would like to specifically NOT thank the global pandemic that slowed down everything; I also faced the challenge of moving from the eastern edge of Canada to the centre of it during the pandemic. When we started this project, I was in a contingent position at the very lovely and supportive Department of Classics at Memorial University of Newfoundland; by the time we finished, I had won the academic lottery by getting a tenure-track position at the equally lovely and supportive Department of Classics at the University of Winnipeg. Thanks to all my colleagues at both! And thank you to my partner, Dayvid Racette-Campbell, who provides the stability and love that keeps our life running smoothly even when all else is chaos.

Finally, we both thank the editors and the anonymous referees at Edinburgh University Press, who offered many helpful suggestions to improve this book, as well as the series editors, Mark Masterson and Fiona McHardy.

Notes on Contributors

Samuel Agbamu is a Leverhulme Early Career Fellow in Classics at Royal Holloway, University of London. From January 2023 he will be at the University of Reading. His research focuses on Latin literature and its reception, especially in post-classical imperial contexts. He is working on a monograph on Petrarch's Latin epic, the *Africa*, and its role in shaping ideas of nationhood, imperialism and ethnicity for early Renaissance Humanism. He is also working on a book based on his PhD thesis, which he submitted in 2019, on modern Italian imperialism's reception of the Roman Empire in Africa.

Britta Ager specialises in ancient magic, agriculture and the senses, and especially the intersections of these areas. Her first book, *The Scent of Ancient Magic*, was published in 2022.

Jessica Penny Evans received her PhD from Trinity College Dublin and is a senior lecturer in Classics at the University of Vermont, where she teaches in the programmes for Gender, Sexuality and Women's Studies, and Critical Race and Ethnic Studies. Her research focuses on the intersections of masculinity and historiography.

Rhiannon Evans is Associate Professor of Classics and Ancient History at La Trobe University in Melbourne, Australia, as well as the co-host of the popular podcast *Emperors of Rome*. She is interested in new pedagogies for Classics, and is a Senior Fellow of the Higher Education Academy.

T. H. M. Gellar-Goad is Associate Professor of Classics at Wake Forest University. He specialises in Latin poetry, especially the funny stuff: Roman comedy, Roman erotic elegy, Roman satire and – if you believe him – the allegedly philosophical poet Lucretius. He is author of *Laughing Atoms, Laughing Matter:*

Lucretius' De Rerum Natura *and Satire, Plautus: Curculio, A Commentary on Plautus'* Curculio (forthcoming), and *Masks* (forthcoming). He is a long-time member of the steering committee of the Women's Classical Caucus and organised the Feminism & Classics 2022 international conference.

Charles Goldberg is Associate Professor of History at Bethel University in Minnesota. His primary research is on the nexus between Roman politics and masculinity. His book *Roman Masculinity and Politics from Republic to Empire* was published in 2021. His other research and teaching interests include ancient imperialism, ancient religion and the digital humanities.

Michael Goyette is an Instructor of Classics and Ancient Studies at Eckerd College in St Petersburg, Florida. His research and teaching interests include ancient science and ancient medicine, the health humanities, gender, tragedy, reception and pedagogy. These interests frequently stem from his fascination with conceptualisations of health, illness and embodiment in the ancient world, along with their implications for lived experience. He is highly enthusiastic about interdisciplinary inquiry, and in both his research and teaching he strives to demonstrate how the ancient world can illuminate present-day issues and topics in fields ranging from the humanities to the sciences.

Kendell Heydon holds a PhD in Classics from the University of Nottingham and MA and BA (Hons) degrees in Greek and Roman Studies from the University of Calgary. His research interests include Spartan history and culture, gender and sexuality studies, and sociological approaches to Classics. Kendell is a sessional instructor with the Department of Classics and Religion at the University of Calgary. He also serves as Writing Support Coordinator with the University of Calgary's Student Success Centre, where he utilises his passion for language to support students on their journeys towards becoming excellent academic writers.

Tristan K. Husby wrote his dissertation on manumission in the Roman Republic. He has taught at both the college and high school level and has an interest in using role playing as a form of pedagogy to teach history. While living in New Hampshire, he is currently writing a game for the consortium Reacting to the Past.

Joanna Kenty is an expert in Cicero's speeches and Roman political oratory. Her book *Cicero's Political Personae* was published in 2020. She earned her PhD from the University of Pennsylvania in 2014. She has written on gender in the ancient world for *Eidolon*, including articles on Hillary Clinton's rhetorical ethos and teaching the story of Lucretia.

Jayne Knight is Lecturer in Classics at the University of Tasmania. She received her PhD from the University of British Columbia. She researches Latin literature and Roman cultural history, with particular interests in rhetoric, politics and emotions. She is preparing a monograph on anger and politics in late republican and early imperial Rome.

Elizabeth A. Manwell is the Sally Appleton Kirkpatrick Chair of Classics at Kalamazoo College. Her current research interests concern improving Latin and Ancient Greek language pedagogy and assessment, and investigating how gender identity is expressed through ancient agricultural writings. She makes a *libum* that would make Cato swoon.

Simona Martorana is an Alexander von Humboldt Research Fellow at Kiel University and the University of Hamburg. She completed her PhD in July 2021 at Durham University (UK), after spending some time at Harvard University as a Visiting Fellow. She is a scholar in classical and medieval Latin literature, who combines a rigorous philological reading of the texts with modern theoretical approaches, particularly from gender, posthumanism, medical humanities and ecocriticism. Her publications include several articles on Latin poetry and medieval Latin philology. She is working on a monograph that explores motherhood within Ovid's *Heroides* through feminist readings.

Melissa Marturano is an Assistant Professor of Classical Languages and Literature at Bard High School Early College, Queens, where she teaches spoken ancient Greek and Latin and ancient literature in translation. She graduated in 2017 from the Graduate Center, City University of New York, where her dissertation focused on sexualised violence and lateral violence among women in Ovid's poetry. She has recently published book reviews on works of feminist scholarship, literature and reception, and an article on feminist pedagogy and teaching Ovid with the American journal *Classical Outlook*. A portion of her dissertation will soon be published in a volume on rape in antiquity.

Mark Masterson is Associate Professor of Classics at Te Herenga Waka/ Victoria University of Wellington, New Zealand. His has written two books: *Between Byzantine Men: Desire, Homosociality, and Brotherhood in the Medieval Empire* (2022) and *Man to Man: Desire, Homosociality and Authority in Late-Roman Manhood* (2014). He was one of three editors of *Sex in Antiquity: Gender and Sexuality in the Ancient World* (2014). He is also author of a number of articles and book chapters on sex and desire between men in history and other topics.

Aven McMaster is Professor Emerita of Ancient Studies from Thorneloe University at Laurentian. Her research interests are Latin poetry, gender and sexuality, and reception. She is also a co-host of the podcast *The Endless Knot*.

Jordan D. G. Mitchell is a PhD Candidate in Ancient History at the University of North Texas. His main areas of research are Roman imperial literature, gender and sexuality, and Augustan literature. He is working on his dissertation *Artifex Patriae: The Specter of Augustus in Petronius' Satyrica*.

Davide Morassi is an MSCA Fellow at the Universidad Complutense of Madrid, having recently completed a DPhil in ancient history at the University of Oxford. His thesis discusses the role and responsibilities of the Classical Athenian *strategoi*, arguing that they had substantial independence on the field. His other research interests include Greek and Roman military history, theories of leadership, archaic tyrannies and, obviously, gender and sexuality in Classical Athens.

Jaclyn Neel is Assistant Professor of Greek and Roman Studies in the College of Humanities at Carleton University. Her research interests include Roman intellectual history, mythography, and modern interpretations of these myths. She has published *Early Rome: Myth and History and Legendary Rivals: Collegiality and Ambition in the Tales of Early Rome*, as well as several articles spanning Etruscan myth, Tarpeia and Roman Republican history. Her public scholarship includes articles for *The Conversation* and Khan Academy's *Smarthistory*.

Kimberly Passaro took her MA in Classics from the University of Cincinnati and has published on gender diversity in the ancient world. She has since changed professional tracks, but remains interested in late antique literature and early Christianity. She lives in Ohio with her three cats and spends her time baking and adding to an already endless reading list.

Melanie Racette-Campbell is an Assistant Professor of Classics at the University of Winnipeg. She works on Roman masculinity, Augustan literature and classical reception in the Renaissance and in modern pop culture. Her book *The Crisis of Masculinity in the Age of Augustus* was published in 2023 and she is working on the next one, on Cicero, masculinity and the city of Rome.

Brian P. Sowers is an Associate Professor of Classics at Brooklyn College and the Graduate Center of the City University of New York. Interested in a wide range of subjects, including gender and sexuality in late antique literature, he is the author of *In Her Own Words: The Life and Poetry of Aelia Eudocia*. He lives in Brooklyn and can frequently be found reading or writing in a local café.

Jonathan Wallis is Senior Lecturer in Classics at the University of Tasmania. He received his PhD from the University of Cambridge. He is the author of *Introspection and Engagement in Propertius: A Study of Book 3* (2018). He researches literary culture and genre in the Roman world and the modern reception of Latin literature.

Abbreviations

CIL	*Corpus Inscriptionum Latinarum*. Berlin 1863–.
CTRP	Meyer, M., and R. Smith, eds. *Ancient Christian Magic: Coptic Texts of Ritual Power*. San Francisco: Princeton University Press, 1994.
DT	Audollent, A., ed. *Defixionum Tabellae*. Paris: Luteciae Parisiorum, 1904.
LIMC	*Lexicon Iconographicum Mythologiae Classicae*. Zürich: Artemis Verlag, 1981–.
OCD	*Oxford Classical Dictionary*. Oxford: Oxford University Press.
OLD	Glare, P. G. W. *Oxford Latin Dictionary*. 2nd ed. Oxford: Oxford University Press, 2012.
PDM	*Papyri Demoticae Magicae*, in the edition of Betz, H. D., ed. *The Greek Magical Papyri in Translation, Including the Demotic Spells*. 2nd ed. Chicago: University of Chicago Press, 1992.
PGM	Preisendanz, K., and A. Henrichs, eds. *Papyri Graecae Magicae: Die griechischen Zauberpapyri*. 2nd ed., 2 vols. Stuttgart: Teubner, 1973–4.
SuppMag	Daniel, R. W., and F. Maltomini. *Supplementum Magicum*, vol. 1. Cologne: Westdeutscher Verlag, 1990.
TLL	*Thesaurus Linguae Latinae*. Berlin: DeGruyter.

Foreword

Donna Zuckerberg

When I sent my editor the first draft of my manuscript for *Not All Dead White Men*, she responded the next day telling me that it wasn't quite ready to send to readers for peer review. She asked me to first go through, do a search for the word 'toxic', and then replace at least half of its instances. Or, alternatively, she suggested that I could dedicate some space to interrogating how I was using the word and what a heavily loaded term like 'toxic masculinity' meant to me in the context of the manosphere – or Ovid, for that matter. What were the stakes of viewing classical antiquity and its reception in male-dominated spaces through the lens of such a fraught concept, one that is so often debated, dismissed and misrepresented? The exploration of what toxic masculinity meant in the context of the study and reception of ancient Greece and Rome seemed too complex for a paragraph or a footnote – it deserved its own, in-depth study. It seemed easier to think of a handful of synonyms and go with the find-and-replace option instead.

The essays in this volume take the time to explore the topic with the nuance it deserves. When I was studying the manosphere, I saw how flawed and over-simplified their conceptualisation of ancient masculinity was: Sparta and Rome, in particular, are seen by far-right online communities as a time when men were 'really' men, not the beta cuck white knights they are now. The scholars who have contributed to this volume have done us a great service in exploring the edge cases that show how difficult it was for men in antiquity to stay within the rigid confines of normative, hegemonic masculinity. Often, men risked going too far or not far enough in their gender performance and being seen as brutes or weaklings.

Unfortunately, fact-checking and scholarship won't have much of an impact in the communities where toxic masculinity thrives and is valorised. Even the term 'toxic masculinity' itself is derided there and misunderstood as an argument that all men, always, are toxic. (As the editors of this volume note, this argument is nonsensical: if all masculinity were toxic, there would be no need for 'toxic masculinity' as a term to describe a subset of behaviour. But, like I said, fact-checking won't do us much good here.) But even though we might not convince them, we can work as scholars to problematise and complicate their claims. We can challenge the idea that there was a single, monolithic concept of 'masculinity' in antiquity and that it was always seen as unquestionably positive.

Masculinity is a difficult concept to pin down. Definitions of it can tend to be circular: masculinity is the set of traits that make one seem to be performing a male role, which is then itself defined through masculine gender performance. But many widely held beliefs about masculinity associate it with wielding power. Real men, according to one belief, are confident, assertive and dominant. In that system, good men use that dominance responsibly and conscientiously to take care of their communities, while toxic men use that power to hurt others and force them into submissive social roles.

Toxic masculinity has proven to be a useful and durable concept because it helps us understand how gendered power dynamics can be used for harm. It is important to keep that understanding in mind, especially when looking at societies where behaviours we would find abhorrent – such as enslaving others or subjecting them to sexual violence – were considered acceptable and normative as a way of expressing one's gender performance and social role. Toxic masculinity can be easier to notice and identify in ancient literature than it is in our own society. And we can use that understanding to deepen our own awareness of how easy it is for hegemonic masculinity to become toxic.

I wish that this book had already existed for me to cite back when I was writing *Not All Dead White Men*, but I'm glad that we have it now. The thoughtful approaches to the concept in this volume show that, while toxic masculinity is an evergreen problem, naming it and studying it can be a form of resistance.

Introduction: Toxic Masculinity and Classics

Melanie Racette-Campbell and Aven McMaster

In the *Iliad*, Ajax (the 'greater' Ajax, that is) is the 'bulwark of the Achaeans', the greatest warrior on the Greek side after Achilles, and a prominent figure in both council and war. But the story for which he is most famous is his quarrel with Odysseus over the armour of Achilles and his subsequent madness and suicide. Confident that he, as the greatest fighter in the Greek ranks, deserves to inherit Achilles' divine armour after the hero's death, Ajax is enraged and humiliated when the Greek army decides to award the armour to Odysseus instead, a reaction that mirrors Achilles' own rage when he suffered the loss of his war prize (the enslaved woman Briseis) at the beginning of the *Iliad*. Ajax tries to take revenge for this humiliation – just as Achilles initially wanted to do when confronting Agamemnon – but the goddess Athena, instead of preventing violence and counselling restraint, as she did with Achilles in that earlier episode, facilitates Ajax's violence but turns it against the flocks and herds of the Greeks instead of the Greek leaders by driving Ajax temporarily mad. This further humiliates the hero, whose ability as a fighter is used against him. His reputation, in his own eyes, is irreparably damaged, and there is only one way he can live up to his own ideal of manhood: as he puts it in Sophocles' play *Ajax*, 'A truly noble man must live with honour/or die with honour' (*Ajax* 479–80). And so Ajax kills himself. The very things that made Ajax a great hero – his strength, his pride, his anger and his drive to win glory at any cost – are also the cause of his self-destruction.

This paradox – that the qualities that are required for ideal manhood might also have harmful and even tragic effects – is an illustration of the high stakes of masculinity in the ancient world. Ajax stands as an example of the cost of male competition, the drawbacks of an honour-based culture and the dangers of a world in which violence is an acceptable answer to most problems; the Sophocles play, along with many other ancient references to his story, presents him as a cautionary tale to its contemporary audience of elite citizen men. But

Ajax also seems to be a perfect demonstration of a much more modern concept: toxic masculinity.

When we use the term 'toxic masculinity' we are not saying that all masculinity is or must be toxic, but rather that there are some specific aspects of some kinds of masculinity that harm not only others but also the toxically masculine men themselves. Opponents of this terminology often miss this point and choose to see those who use it as claiming that all masculinity is toxic. Yet the addition of the adjective 'toxic' implies that masculinity is not inherently toxic and that there are therefore 'non-toxic' masculinities that are healthy and positive: the existence of a negative term requires an opposite positive.[1] And while the term may be new, the behaviours and attitudes it describes are not: this is an example of language taking time to catch up to action. This book is meant to contribute to this 'catch up' by asking if the concept is useful for describing and interrogating the masculinities of the ancient Mediterranean. It is also not alone in testing the usefulness of 'anachronistic' formulations for learning more about the past: for example, Dugan (2005) uses seemingly anachronistic theories and terminology to talk about the ancient past; he notes that Cicero and other Roman authors were well aware that the self presented to others was a product of 'deliberate strategies of fashioning', so that it is not an anachronistic imposition to talk about the Romans engaging in self-fashioning. Similarly, as both Sophocles' treatment of Ajax and numerous examples throughout this book show, Greeks and Romans were aware of the behaviours and attitudes that we classify as 'toxic masculinity' even if they did not have a specific term for it. A useful general discussion can be found in Halberstam (2018), who uses the term 'scavenger methodologies' for using different methods to collect information on those excluded from traditional studies of behaviour. Even though many of the men who are studied in this collection have been included in traditional scholarship, so much of the ancient past is lost, even most of the dominant culture, that we have to be scavengers to get anything approaching a full picture.

On the academic side, theorisation of 'toxic masculinity' arose in the 1990s in the social sciences, especially sociology and psychology.[2] Toxic masculinity is closely related to another concept, 'hegemonic masculinity'. Hegemonic masculinity refers to a set of values, activities and attitudes that are associated with the most acceptable fulfilment of a mainstream style of manhood in any given society or culture.[3] There is not one unchanging set of hegemonic values, activities and attitudes, since they are culturally specific, but in modern Western cultures they often include such things as being passionate about sports, confident, successful in one's work, a provider for one's family, and self-reliant. They can also include the belief that men are superior to and dominant over women and other groups perceived as lesser; a willingness to use violence; a lack of emotional openness; and avoidance of displays of emotions other than anger. Hegemonic masculinity is not necessarily toxic, but its elements can encourage toxic behaviour. Toxicity often arises when hegemonic masculinity is taken to extremes or practised by men who lack other forms of hegemonic power, usually due to their class, race, ethnicity, religion or some other part of their life experience, such as addiction, imprisonment or homelessness.[4] As such, in modern studies it is often, though not always, associated with men from groups that are (or believe they are) disenfranchised in some ways. Hegemonic masculinity is perceived as a problem when it harms those it is not supposed to, but not when it harms those it is supposed to,[5] categories of people that are subject to change over time: it becomes 'toxic' when it is harmful to other (protected) individuals, to one's community or to oneself. Examples of each of these include: violence against women predicated on beliefs of male superiority and control, and the belief that violence is a legitimate means for asserting these; economic disruption caused by powerful men who think that their own success outweighs any responsibility to the success and health of their community; and lower life expectancy caused by unwillingness to deal with mental or physical health issues due to reluctance to show weakness or to rely on others.[6] This last category received a great deal of the early and formative attention in scholarly literature.

The theoretical formulation of toxic masculinity has been used to study populations and individuals enacting behaviours at the extreme edges of those glorified by hegemonic masculinity. Kupers, in a study that sees toxic masculinity as an explanation for the reluctance of some men in prison to seek mental health treatments, suggests that one of the roots of toxicity is situations where men do not receive the rewards and recognition to which they believe they are entitled.[7] Kupers focuses on the idea of respect: there is nothing toxic about wanting respect, but men who are repeatedly denied respect, or believe that they have been, may act out in ways destructive to themselves and others out of frustration.[8] The connection between such feelings of frustration and another aspect of toxic and hegemonic masculinity, control over women, can be seen in cases of violence against women, perhaps most obviously in the case of the spree-killer in Santa Barbara who claimed to be motivated by his belief that he was being unfairly deprived of access to women's bodies.[9] This man's core beliefs about his right to use violence and the validity of his anger and desire to control others are not far removed from mainstream attitudes about manhood. He took them to extremes, but the toxicity of these attitudes was always there, as can even be seen in the specific targets of his aggression, members of groups he deemed 'inferior' or considered competition.[10]

Another example of toxicity arising when men believe they are denied respect is in the work of Karner on American veterans of the Vietnam War.[11] The men in this study are trying to regain a kind of power and masculinity that they feel was withheld from them, especially in comparison to the 'status and economic rewards' that their fathers had received as Second World War veterans.[12] Karner theorises that because the Vietnam veterans did not feel that they were rewarded and acknowledged, they kept acting like adolescents, using violence and antisocial acts to try to assert dominance and control. But ultimately these attempts are toxic to both their societies and to themselves, as their actions harm their mental and physical health, sometimes lead to imprisonment, and create further barriers to the kinds of successful masculine achievements that their fathers displayed, such as fatherhood, career success and home ownership. Their lack of status within larger hegemonic systems results in the qualities that these men value becoming harmful to their own self-interest. A connection between the experiences of Vietnam veterans and the ancient Mediterranean world has been made in Jonathan Shay's 1994 volume *Achilles in Vietnam: Combat Trauma and the Undoing of Character*, which compares the soldiers of the *Iliad* and of Vietnam to examine and better understand the effects of post-traumatic stress disorder.

The formulation 'hegemonic masculinity', upon which toxic masculinity draws, has received a number of challenges. One of the most relevant ones for this volume is its potential to oversimplify and over-generalise what is hegemonic. In order to stay hegemonic, masculinity will change with the times, so that, for instance, a certain amount of pro-feminist speech and behaviour may be incorporated with the goal of upholding the legitimacy of masculine power and control.[13] Another vital issue is that most societies have a wide variety of subcultures and countercultures, all of which have their own, more or less different, version of masculinity. These other masculinities can be powerful in their own contexts even if they lack the broader force of mainstream hegemonic masculinity: indeed, men such as the prisoners studied by Kupers may be conforming to their own most relevant 'hegemonic' masculinity. Debbie Ging's recent work on the online 'manosphere' argues that its masculinities decentre elements like sports and homophobia but maintain elements like beliefs about male superiority and the value of control over women, especially their bodies. She finds in them an example that shows that there is no single way for toxic or hegemonic masculinity to manifest.[14] Cornwall and Lindisfarne argue that hegemonic masculinity produces these subordinate masculinities by its act of setting boundaries and making exclusions.[15] Building upon this point, we can see toxic masculinity as not exactly a subordinate masculinity, but rather a version of hegemonic masculinity that is produced by it. All these ideas provide an interesting gateway into 'countercultures' like those seen in Latin love elegy, which even as it rejects some elements of mainstream Roman masculinity still operates in a format of male control, even when the male appears to submit to the female.[16]

In addition to the scholarship on hegemonic and toxic masculinity, this collection builds on the emergence of the study of masculinity in the ancient world as a significant subcategory of gender and sexuality studies. The study of men as gendered individuals lagged behind that of women, but since the 1990s has begun to catch up.[17] It is vital to the larger feminist project of disrupting the traditional equation of men as representative of humanity, with all other genders as deviations from the norm.[18] Much of this scholarship has focused on how men in antiquity understood their identities as men and on the ideologies around manhood and masculinity in the cultures of the ancient Mediterranean world and beyond, including a number of edited collections, such as Foxhall and Salmon's *Thinking Men: Masculinity and its Self-Representation in the Classical Tradition* (1998) and *When Men were Men: Masculinity, Power, and Identity in Classical Antiquity* (2011) and Rosen and Sluiter's *Andreia: Studies in Manliness and Courage in Classical Antiquity* (2003). The general consensus on the conception of masculinity in these cultures is that it was not viewed as a permanent and inviolable state.[19] As in many cultures, manhood did not come automatically with adulthood, but had to be both learned and earned. Once gained, it could still be lost again, since a man's identity was not based solely on his anatomical sex (for one could be male but not a man) but rather on his projection of masculinity via his body, words and actions and on the acceptance of that projection by others.[20] Because of this, masculinity was fragile and apt to be undermined or lost. Another type of masculinity, however, can be seen in the Priapic model, theorised by Richlin in 1983 as significant for Roman men. This type prioritises an aggressive, penetrative masculinity that threatens others with domination and is rooted in the possession of the phallus. Priapic masculinity is projected in some of the work of the Roman poet Catullus, although many scholars now view this poet's performances of manhood as drawing on a variety of models.[21]

There were plenty of examples in ancient society of males who were not men and who could be held up as warnings for those who sought a masculine identity. Among these, perhaps the most prominent was the figure of the κίναιδος/ *cinaedus*, a male who deviated from masculine deportment in any number of ways, including sexual habits, dress and public behaviour.[22] In a general sense, the *cinaedus* was believed to indulge in pleasure at the cost of his manly self-control, but the specifics of this indulgence could take many forms.[23] This very difficulty in defining what a *cinaedus* did made him a scare-figure for other men: the behaviours that indicated someone was a *cinaedus* were so many and varied that every man had to be vigilant lest he display them.[24] It was even possible to accuse someone of being a *cinaedus* because he was too masculine and therefore must be hiding something![25] It seems that the desire to appear manly and the fear of not appearing manly continued to influence the lives of Roman men, especially but not only the elite, even during the rise of Christianity. Koefler argues that Christianity made itself mainstream when it was able to offer a way of appearing manly that was acceptable to the Roman elite, and eventually replaced the previous hegemonic masculinity with a new one based on the superiority of the previously subordinate Christian man.[26]

This volume is thus part of the growing field of masculinity studies;[27] at the same time, it also joins a conversation currently happening in Classics, especially in its public-facing sectors, about the use of Greek and Roman material to justify and support misogyny and white supremacy. Since at least the release of the movie *300*, some versions of the masculinities of the ancient Mediterranean have been in the public consciousness.[28] These popular images forefront the warrior in his most popular variations: Spartan, Homeric, Roman soldier, even gladiator. But they often have more to say about modern ideas of manhood than ancient ones, even when they get some of the details right. More worrying is the use of ancient texts, images and ideas to support modern bigotry. A significant subset of those in groups identifying or identified as men's rights activists, pickup artists and incels (involuntary celibates) explicitly cite ancient authors or historical figures as inspirations or models for their ideology and behaviour, which raises the question of whether these are drawing on toxic elements in ancient masculinity, and if so, how such elements affected the ancient world and influenced later understandings of gender.[29]

Online fora such as *Eidolon* and *Pharos* have been leading the way towards uncovering, acknowledging and combating the connections between hate groups and bigotry and the ancient world, as have books like Donna Zuckerberg's *Not All Dead White Men*. All of these initiatives take a two-pronged approach. First, they challenge distortions and inaccuracies about the ancient world put forth by hate groups and suggest effective ways to combat them. Second, they acknowledge and analyse the classical past and historical and current scholarship about that past for elements that not only passively enable but even actively contribute to the hate. This public discourse adds to a more general discussion in the popular press about the idea of toxic masculinity, especially with respect to mass shootings and high-profile cases of sexual harassment or assault.[30] People are already using the ancient world as justification for their toxic beliefs and behaviours: ignoring them will not make them go away. As scholars working on the ancient Mediterranean, we have a responsibility to acknowledge and interrogate the aspects of our material that lend support to these readings. We also must look seriously at that which troubles us, instead of focusing only on the positive. There is much to be censured in the ancient world, but there is also a need to apply careful interpretation: our toxicity is not the same as theirs. There is significant intersection between the popular and the scholarly use of the terminology around toxic masculinity, much as there is intersection between scholarly and popular studies of Classics. In this book, we aim to interrogate both the scholarly and the popular conceptions of the term.

As editors, we have encouraged the authors in this volume to investigate the utility of this modern theoretical concept for their work. It is not enough to refer to masculinity or men or even misogyny: the aim is to apply this specific theoretical formulation to words, actions or ideas that appear to be toxic by the modern definition, and then to consider how useful this approach is for studying the ancient world. Some authors have found the concept of toxic masculinity to be illuminating, some have found that the idea was already there in the material they study, even if the ancient world did not have a precise term for it, and some have found that it needs to be modified to apply to the different cultural context or even that it simply is not a concept that makes sense for the material under their consideration. It is important to us that the evidence not be forced to fit the theory, but rather that the theory be used to provide a different way of looking at the evidence and be freely modified or discarded if it is found lacking. The authors also take on the issue of the culturally conditional nature of both hegemonic and toxic masculinity. Behaviours that seem toxic from a modern point of view might not have seemed so at the time, and so every author needs to be specific about the viewpoint(s) they are adopting. The chapters in this volume also limit themselves to male masculinity and to gender as the primary lens for examining their evidence. Some of the authors consider status, ethnicity, race or sexuality in addition, but we realised early on that this book should not attempt to cover everything; the focus on gender also suited the editors' expertise. This book is a beginning and not an end, and we hope many others will build on the work presented here.

We chose not to use culture or era as the organising factor for this volume.[31] Instead, we took two common elements from the definitions of toxic masculinity, violence against others and violence against self, to organise the first section. The second section directly addresses the issue of anachronism with chapters that examine ancient critiques of characteristics and behaviours that look like toxic masculinities. The final section brings together the ancient Mediterranean and toxic masculinities in modern North America, Europe and Australia. These chapters consider how the ancient world is used as an inspiration or justification for toxic beliefs and behaviours by later groups. We wanted the pervasive nature of the themes of each section, regardless of place or time, to stand out, and to give the authors the opportunity to meaningfully interact with those working in other subfields.

The most obviously destructive aspect of toxic masculinity comes in the harm that men cause to other individuals, often those closest to them, and to society as a whole. This kind of violence is rooted in the misogyny and homophobia that come from the sense of control and superiority, a central part of hegemonic masculinity that can easily turn toxic, especially when taken to extremes. It also is a result of the high value that hegemonic masculinity puts on aggression and the suppression of emotions other than anger. These characteristics turn toxic when directed against inappropriate targets or when men lose their self-control. Yet sometimes activities that might seem like toxic violence against others would not have been recognised as such at the time: epic heroism, for instance, is built on violence against the enemy, as is historical military success. But even here, there are limits: Achilles' abuse of the dead Hector (Hom. *Il.* 22. 367–404), the brutal execution of a former ally who betrayed Rome, Mettius Fufetius (Livy 1.23–8), and Octavian's ruthless suppression of the rebellious city of Perugia, for example, seem to have been recognised as 'too far' even in antiquity.

The first chapters in the first section of the volume examine instances of this violence against others. Tristan K. Husby uses a story from Aulus Gellius about Plutarch beating a slave while claiming that he does not feel any anger to examine the utility of the concept of 'toxic masculinity' for discussions of ancient masculinity, in particular the role that anger plays in definitions of masculinity in the ancient world and today. Kimberly Passaro and Brian Sowers look at the stories of Thecla and Saint Justina to outline the development of late antique toxic masculinity by tracing its perpetuation in the early Christian male imagination, a precursor for the continuity of themes of sexual assault in medieval, Renaissance and modern literature. Jessica Evans explores the relationship between masculinities and justice in the Melian Dialogue and Thucydides' history, arguing that competing masculinities produce toxic forms of justice by erasing others' claims to manhood. Davide Morassi assesses how the ideal of masculinity was perceived in relation to its power as a motive for action and comments upon the influence of this paradigm on the actions of Athenian men. Mark Masterson uses our notion of toxic masculinity to shed light on the life of Emperor Nikephoros II Phokas and Byzantine perspectives on him, in a chapter which also deals with toxic masculinity that harms the self, and is therefore a bridge to the second part of this section.

Harm against the self is prevalent in much of the modern scholarly literature coming from the social sciences. It can be divided into two types: a violence against self that arises from a perceived failure to live up to the ideals of hegemonic masculinity, and another that is a result of meeting those very ideals. The first type is that which we see in studies of antisocial and self-destructive behaviour of men in prison or Vietnam war veterans, as well as in Ajax's suicide, with which this Introduction opened. The second type is perhaps most visible in the harsh fact of men's lower life expectancy, which is in part a result of subscribing to ideas about extreme self-reliance, being too tough to seek help for ailments (both physical and mental), self-medicating with alcohol or unregulated drug use, the stress of repressing most emotions, and the behaviours that result from channelling all one's emotional life into anger.

The precise ways that toxic masculinity harms men are culturally specific, and thus do not look the same in antiquity as they do in modern Europe or North America. And yet there are hints that even in antiquity such toxicity was recognised. Joanna Kenty explores a heteronormative trope of Roman political rhetoric which reflects a toxic understanding of power as not only masculine, but also sexually dominant, arguing that Cicero's sense of political virtue is strongly associated with a narrow sense of virility as domination over others and predicated on the exclusion of women from the political sphere. Jaclyn Neel uses a case study of late Republican receptions of the lack of grief shown by Romulus and by Brutus (cos. 509 BCE) after killing close family members, on the basis of which she argues that both the murders and the emotional reactions to them were viewed as toxic behaviours.

When scholars use a theory formulated in modern times to try to better understand the past, a common critique from those who are dedicated to so-called objective readings is that the theoretically oriented approaches are anachronistic. Our second section aims to anticipate such objections in a productive way by analysing texts that clearly show that ancient authors recognised and critiqued the toxic potential in certain aspects of masculinity. Neel's chapter acts as a bridge to this section, in that she argues that at least some of the authors who dealt with these stories felt the need to explain to their audiences the seemingly cold or even inhuman behaviour of these exemplary Roman figures. Jordan Mitchell argues that Petronius subverted traditional social and literary norms in order to show their impracticality and absurdity when applied to 'lived experience'. In the *Satyricon*, subordinate and marginalised individuals and groups of men engage in compensatory manhood acts and displays of exaggerated masculinity in order to emulate the most dominant form of masculinity in society, one result of which is the continual re-establishment of gender stereotypes as policing mechanisms and the re-affirmation of the subordination of women. Elizabeth Manwell examines the Roman virtue of *disciplina*, as exemplified by Cato the Elder in Plutarch's biography, and an instance of resistance in the way that Plutarch interrupts his biography to critique Cato for his adherence to a Roman masculinity that Plutarch finds not only unseemly, but immoral. Simona Martorana demonstrates how Briseis' description of Achilles in Ovid's *Heroides* helps us to reassess the sociological concept of toxic masculinity according to a more fluid, and less binary, view of gender relationships. Rhiannon Evans considers the nexus of gender, ethnicity and social order to explore Caesar's depiction of the Germani and Tacitus' renegotiation of it, arguing that in each context the Germani allow the author to comment on how outrageous masculinity breaches the limits of *libertas* and damages society irreparably. Kendell Heydon analyses Xenophon's account of the trial of Sphodrias in accordance with the understanding of toxic masculinity, to demonstrate that the episode illuminates several ways in which Spartan masculine values, and the practices and institutions which promote them, prove detrimental to both individual Spartan men and Spartan society as a whole. Charles Goldberg examines criticism of the conduct of Roman elite men in the political and military spheres during the 160s BCE, and argues that the discussion of the conduct of Scipio Aemilianus acknowledges the validity of critiques of ancient toxic masculinity while distinguishing him as singularly worthy of political power.

The final section takes on the question of why all this matters in the here and now. Long before scholars began tracing the connections between ancient and modern toxic masculinity, some people were finding inspiration and justification for their toxic attitudes and actions in their (mis)readings of ancient sources. These are not always or only misreadings: one thing classicists must reckon with is the negative impact of the valorisation of these particular ancient cultures in modern times. The chapters in this section investigate places where this meeting of ancient and modern occurs, whether intentionally or not, and suggest ways to interrogate toxicity in the ancient sources and the modern world. Samuel Agbamu discusses the reception of the figure of Scipio Africanus in the formulation of an idealised, Fascist Italian masculinity, in Carmine Gallone's 1937 film *Scipione l'Africano*, arguing that it propagated a toxic masculinity informing and informed by Italy's colonial policy, but mythologised through the lens of classical antiquity. Michael Goyette examines Seneca's philosophical writing and argues that his rhetoric exposes an attitude towards both the emotions and the body that was and is toxic in its sexist tropes, its misogyny and its repression and shaming of the emotions; he then identifies parallels in present-day media, politics and popular culture, such as the derisive use of the phrase 'special snowflake', and shows how the gendered, regressive rhetoric of Senecan Stoicism still resonates with disturbing familiarity. Melissa Marturano explores the role in Ovid's work of the 'nice guy', men who style themselves as chivalrous, generous and even compassionate towards the women they pursue sexually and expect to be rewarded for this behaviour, arguing that Ovid's poetry can help us better discern the origins and survival of misogyny and its ally, toxic masculinity, as it reflects ourselves and our own world's violence against women. Britta Ager examines the rhetoric of love curses and argues that comparisons to modern manifestations of toxic masculinity suggest that the main benefit of erotic *defixiones* was that they offered their users an emotional outlet through which to voice their sense of grievance and sexual entitlement. T. H. M. Gellar-Goad situates modern pseudo-scientific ideas about women's bodies in a tradition dating back at least to the first/second-century CE Greek medical writer Soranus of Ephesus, comparing the 2012 comments by Todd Akin, the Republican Senate candidate for Missouri, about 'legitimate rape' to ancient medical thought and arguing that modern manifestations of this sort of misogynistic misinformation are even more harmful than ancient ones. Finally, Jayne Knight and Jonathan Wallis consider how teachers might use the concept of toxic masculinity to facilitate student engagement with ancient texts and topics in a first-year Classics classroom, using case studies from their first-year Roman civilisation course taught at the University of Tasmania.

This volume is intended to encourage conversations in classrooms and among scholars. We do not claim to cover every possible angle; indeed we have deliberately kept quite a tight focus as to approach and lens of examination, in order to balance the wide range of topics, genres, dates and places. As the complex connections between ancient and modern conceptions of gender continue to change and evolve, our terminology and understanding must evolve along with them. If the chapters in this collection can cast new light on the ancient world or equip us with a clearer understanding of current ideologies and better arguments against hatred, violence and extremism, then we will consider our job well begun.

A final note: this book started on the internet. Specifically, it started on Twitter, when I (Aven) saw a tweet from Anastasia Salter celebrating the release of her new book. Looking at it quickly, I read the title as *Toxic Greek Masculinity in the Medea* and thought 'wow, that sounds like a fantastic book!' But as I looked again, I realised that the title was actually *Toxic GEEK Masculinity in the MEDIA*. I tweeted about my misreading, thinking it was a rather amusing indication of my disciplinary blinkers. And then I started thinking about my misreading, and in conversations on Twitter I realised that my misread title, or a version of it, could make a pretty interesting topic for a collection – so I reached out to Melanie, and our project was born. In a way, the origin of this collection has informed our methodology and theoretical approach throughout the process. The misreading of the original title opened up a new way of looking at the ancient world, and the immediate positive and interested reaction of other scholars (and non-scholars) on Twitter demonstrated how productive critical anachronism and speculative methodologies can be. Our call for contributors was also widely shared on Twitter, and many of the connections we made with the authors in this book were formed through social media or elsewhere online. So thank you to the wonderful community of scholars on Twitter and online for your inspiration and support!

NOTES

1. This point may seem obvious but seems to be lost on a number of the 'opponents' of the use of this concept, e.g. Havrilesky 2017.
2. We have chosen to focus on male masculinities, while recognising the important work done by Halberstam in complicating the connection of masculinity to the dominant white male middle-class body. There may be evidence for toxic female masculinity in the ancient world: Martial's poem on the hypermasculine woman Philaenis (*Epigram* 7.67) and the critiques, preserved in the works of Cicero, Valerius Maximus and Appian, about the behaviour of Fulvia, wife of Mark Antony, during the late 40s BCE could be places to start looking, but the patchy evidence for women in antiquity makes it difficult to examine such a phenomenon. See Boehringer 2018 on Philaenis, Hallett 2015 on Fulvia.
3. The seminal work is Connell 1995.
4. As laid out in Karner 1996, Kupers 2005 and Thomkins-Jones 2017. Harrington (2021) addresses perceived issues with studies such as these but seems to ignore that these theorists are not blaming individual marginalised men whose masculinity can turn toxic; instead they are arguing that the potential for toxicity is always present, but reveals itself in men who lack access to other elements of

masculinity or power structures. Harrington's article also omits any discussion of theorisations of toxic masculinity as societal rather than individualistic, which leads to her criticisms that the concept is individualistic and essentialising.

5. This definition implicitly accepts that harming others is not in itself necessarily toxic; while many today might argue against this view, societies throughout history have always permitted harm against certain categories of people, such as enemy soldiers, condemned criminals, enslaved people, heretics, etc. And contemporary societies still define certain types of harm as acceptable, at least legally.

6. Addis and Cohane 2005; for a reception of these ideas in the popular press, see Holloway 2015.

7. Kupers 2005.

8. Kupers 2005, 717.

9. See Bucholz 2016. The choice not to print his name here is a deliberate one.

10. The Pulse Nightclub shooting of 2016 is another relevant example.

11. Karner 1996.

12. Karner 1996, 66.

13. See Demetriou 2001 for these critiques.

14. Ging 2017.

15. Cornwall and Lindisfarne 1994, 18–19.

16. See especially James 2003.

17. E.g. Foxhall and Salmon 1998; Williams 1999; Graziosi and Haubold 2003.

18. Masterson (2014, 19) begins his survey of studies of ancient masculinity with this very point: 'When we study possessors of the male body in the ancient world and ancient masculinity, when we study ancient men as "men", we call into question the assumption, widely extant in ancient sources, that man is synonymous with humanity *in toto*.'

19. For succinct discussion, see Gleason 1999.

20. These ideas have been well developed in the scholarship on Roman masculinity, such as Edwards 1993, Williams 1999 and Gunderson 2000.

21. Wray (2001) argues that Catullus is performing manhood for a male audience as part of the homosocial competition for social mastery. He uses the anthropology of Mediterranean masculinity in the twentieth century to triangulate with critical literary theory in order to more fully understand what we are seeing in Catullus.

22. Although Masterson (2014, 23) has suggested that in the context of Classical Athens, at least, it is difficult to tell how much of the characterisation of the κίναιδος is a construction of modern scholarship from scattered and difficult-to-synthesise ancient sources. Sapsford (2015, 115) notes that, at least in the documentary evidence from Hellenistic and Roman Egypt, the meaning of κίναιδος as 'passive partner in same-sex intercourse' is absent.

23. For an overview of the *cinaedus*, see Williams 1999, 172–81 and now Sapsford 2022.

24. Gleason 1999, 78. See Halperin (2002, 33) and Skinner (2005, 212) on the difficulty of achieving and maintaining masculinity.

25. Williams (1999, 188) cites a number of epigrams by Martial (1.24, 1.96, 7.58, 7.62, 9.27, 9.47, 11.88) as well as Juvenal's second satire as illustrations of this fear of a crypto-cinaedus.
26. Koefler 2001, 6.
27. For a recent look at the state of the field, see Masterson 2014.
28. Lytle 2007 and Turner 2009.
29. Zuckerberg 2018.
30. Banet-Weiser and Miltner 2015; Hamblin 2016; Marcotte 2016; Soloway 2016.
31. Similar to Dinshaw (1999, 2), for whose study it was important that texts that would not usually be read together are placed in juxtaposition, we found that disrupting the Greek/Roman divide or groupings of authors by era helped to make connections that might not otherwise be made.

PART I

Violence against Others and Self

CHAPTER 1

Plutarch and Punishment: Slavery and Toxic Masculinity in Aulus Gellius 1.26

Tristan K. Husby

The antiquarian Aulus Gellius preserves an account by the Roman Platonist L. Calvenus Taurus, in which he describes how Plutarch acts as a slave-owner when one of his slaves challenges his authority and his conduct as a philosopher. The slave's challenge prompts Plutarch to oversee a cruel beating of the slave. What interests Taurus as a Platonist is whether or not Plutarch is angry as he administers this punishment: the story concludes with Plutarch listing certain physical attributes to prove that he is not angry, but instead serenely detached. Because this story depicts Plutarch as detached both from the pain that he causes to others and from his own emotions, his conduct appears to be an example of what psychologist Terry Kupers terms toxic masculinity. Indeed, Plutarch fits a number of Kupers' required attributes, such as disregard for others' pain, the need to dominate, and a casual attitude towards the use of violence.

However, Kupers also insists that anger is fundamental to toxic masculinity, writing that the code followed by many toxically masculine men requires that they never display emotions other than anger. Kupers, who provided one of the initial academic definitions of toxic masculinity, was exploring masculinity in the American prison system. Kupers argues that toxic masculinity is a tactic for prisoners, for when these men become enraged at the slightest disrespect from other prisoners or prison staff, they signal the cost of disrespecting them. Similarly, Plutarch signals both to the beaten slave and the slaves beating him the costs of disrespecting their owner.

After reviewing Kupers' definition of toxic masculinity, I use the term to argue that readers can understand Plutarch as angry in this passage, despite the evidence he provides. As a Platonist, Taurus is interested in the question of whether or not Plutarch's anger has overridden his control of his senses. Kupers' definition of toxic masculinity decentres the physical attributes that Plutarch himself offers as evidence of his tranquillity and instead focuses on the cruelty that he calmly administers against the slave. Then I contextualise Taurus' story about Plutarch within the larger debate between Stoics and Platonists on the question of the virtue of anger. Taurus, as a Platonist himself, sees in this story an example of how a virtuous and self-controlled man like Plutarch can do the right thing even when incited by his slave. Next, I examine the extent to which Plutarch's actions accord with hegemonic masculinity, a normative type of masculinity to which Kupers contrasts toxic masculinity. I conclude that Plutarch does not neatly fit into either of these descriptions of masculinity, but that these terms are useful for explaining why readers should understand Plutarch as truly angry, despite his protestations to the contrary.

KUPERS AND TOXIC MASCULINITY

Kupers defined toxic masculinity in the context of his examination of why American male prisoners were reluctant to use the therapeutic treatments offered to them in prison.[1] For Kupers, toxic masculinity is distinct from hegemonic masculinity, that is, the masculinity that a society judges to be healthy and worthy of imitation. Instead, toxic masculinity is a way for male prisoners to survive the degrading conditions of incarceration. The word 'toxic' in the phrase 'toxic masculinity' seeks to expose how this strategy is ultimately unhealthy.

As a therapist who treats male prisoners, Kupers is not attempting to describe how all men in prison act. Rather, his goal is to group together some of the men in prison as practitioners of the same type of masculinity. He writes that the following seven proclivities are indicators of toxic masculinity: '[1] extreme competition and greed, [2] insensitivity to or lack of consideration of the experiences and feelings of others, [3] a strong need to dominate and control others, [4] an incapacity to nurture, [5] a dread of dependency, [6] a readiness to resort to violence, [7] and the stigmatization and subjugation of women, gays, and men who exhibit feminine characteristics'.[2] In addition to these attributes, Kupers insists that anger is also a fundamental emotion.[3]

Anger is a way these prisoners can feel free: their anger makes them uncontrollable, that is, temporarily outside of the control of the prison staff and fellow prisoners. Kupers provides the example of a prisoner in solitary confinement who refuses to return his meal tray to the guards. This refusal leads to the threat of the guards reclaiming the tray by force. Rather than backing down, the prisoner welcomes the opportunity for a 'fight'. It is not a real fight as the guards easily overwhelm and wound him with superior numbers, but when the prisoner is taken to the infirmary: 'A nurse examines the shackled prisoner and asks if he was hurt: He responds that they hardly scratched him.'[4] Anger and altercation is a weapon that prisoners use against those higher up on the hierarchy, a method for them to gain the respect that they crave but are denied. But it is a double-edged weapon. Commitment to toxic masculinity prevents prisoners from seeking therapeutic treatment and furthermore prevents them from making best use of the treatment that therapists offer.

PLUTARCH BEATS AN ANONYMOUS SLAVE

Taurus' story about Plutarch is tripartite. The first part is a description of the slave's beating. In the second part, the slave gives two arguments about why the beating should cease. The first argument is that he is actually innocent. When that fails, he argues that because philosophers do not act in anger, Plutarch is not acting like a philosopher. The third part of the story is Plutarch's rebuttal, which consists of his evidence that he is not angry. Because he is not angry, the slave's beating therefore is consistent with the behaviour of a philosopher. The story concludes with Plutarch's command for the beatings to continue. I quote the episode in full:

> 'Plutarchus' inquit 'servo suo, nequam homini et contumaci, sed libris disputationibusque philosophiae aures inbutas habenti, tunicam detrahi ob nescio quod delictum caedique eum loro iussit. Coeperat verberari et obloquebatur non meruisse, ut vapulet; nihil mali, nihil sceleris admisisse. Postremo vociferari inter vapulandum incipit neque iam querimonias aut gemitus eiulatusque facere, sed verba seria et obiurgatoria: non ita esse Plutarchum, ut philosophum deceret; irasci turpe esse; saepe eum de malo irae dissertavisse, librum quoque Περὶ Ἀοργησίας pulcherrimum conscripsisse; his omnibus, quae in eo libro scripta sint, nequaquam convenire, quod provolutus effususque in iram plurimis se plagis multaret. Tum Plutarchus lente et leniter: "quid autem", inquit "verbero, nunc ego tibi irasci videor? ex vultune meo an ex voce an ex colore an etiam ex verbis correptum esse me ira intellegis? mihi quidem neque oculi, opinor, truces sunt neque os turbidum, neque inmaniter clamo neque in spumam ruboremve effervesco neque pudenda dico aut paenitenda neque omnino trepido ira et gestio. Haec enim omnia, si ignoras, signa esse irarum solent." Et simul ad eum, qui caedebat, conversus: "interim", inquit "dum ego atque hic disputamus, tu hoc age".'

'Plutarch', said he [L. Calvisius Taurus], 'once gave orders that one of his slaves, a worthless and insolent fellow, but one whose ears had been filled with the teachings and arguments of philosophy, should be stripped of his tunic for some offence or other and flogged. They had begun to beat him, and the slave kept protesting that he did not deserve the flogging; that he was guilty of no wrong, no crime. Finally, while the lashing still went on, he began to shout, no longer uttering complaints or shrieks and groans, but serious reproaches. Plutarch's conduct, he said, was unworthy of a philosopher; to be angry was shameful: his master had often descanted on the evil of anger and had even written an excellent treatise Περὶ Ἀοργησίας; it was in no way consistent with all that was written in that book that its author should fall into a fit of violent rage and punish his slave with many stripes. Then Plutarch calmly and mildly made answer: "What makes you think, scoundrel, that I am now angry with you. Is it from my expression, my voice, my color, or even my words, that you believe me to be in the grasp of anger? In my opinion my eyes are not fierce, my expression is not disturbed, I am neither shouting madly nor foaming at the mouth nor getting red in the face; I am saying nothing to cause me shame or regret; I am not trembling at all from anger or making violent gestures. For all these actions, if you did but know it, are the usual signs of angry passions". And with these words, turning to the man who was plying the lash, he said: "In the meantime, while this fellow and I are arguing, do you keep at it".'

   Aulus Gellius, *Noctes Atticae,* 1.26.5–9, trans. J. C. Rolfe.

In this passage, Plutarch displays five of the attributes that Kupers lists as being evidence of toxic masculinity. First and second, 'incapacity to nurture' and 'insensitivity to or lack of consideration of the experiences or feelings of others': Plutarch commands the beating of a slave for an unspecified reason. Third, 'need to dominate others': by commanding the first and second rounds of the beating, while continuing to debate with the slave, Plutarch reveals a need for domination. Fourth, 'readiness to resort to violence': Plutarch, despite being a renowned philosopher, refuses to debate his slave without his other slaves beating him. Finally, Plutarch also exhibits extreme competition. Plutarch is determined to prove his slave wrong, and does so by listing his physical attributes as evidence that he is not angry.

  Reading this story through the lens of toxic masculinity emphasises how the philosopher is ready to resort to violence and focused on maintaining his domination over the slave rather than protecting him. That is, this lens refuses to centre Plutarch's emotional control and instead focuses on how he orders the beating of a slave. In the story, Plutarch refuses to respond to the slave's initial argument that the beating is unjust, and instead only responds to the slave's claim that his anger is unworthy of a philosopher. Plutarch responds by listing a variety of his physical attributes, such as his colour and the volume of his voice, as evidence that the slave's diagnosis is incorrect. By focusing on the issue of Plutarch's readiness for violence and desire to dominate, the lens of toxic masculinity suggests that the catalogue of physical symptoms that Plutarch offers is insufficient proof that he is not angry. Because anger is fundamental to Kupers' definition of toxic masculinity, Plutarch's display of self-control may initially appear to distance him from this term. This is not the case. Instead, Kupers' definition of toxic masculinity provides an alternative way of understanding anger to the one Plutarch proposes in the story. Plutarch's definition in the story frames anger as a physiological response, but Kupers analyses anger as a performance of masculinity, that is, it is a question of how one interacts with others.

TAURUS AND ANGER

Like Kupers, Taurus is interested in anger, especially the question of whether displays of anger are virtuous. Indeed, Taurus is not interested in any moral questions about how well Plutarch treated his slaves, but instead focuses on the presence and quality of Plutarch's anger. Unfortunately, due to the fragmentary nature of Taurus' surviving work, it is not clear to what extent he was interested in how anger displays itself on the human body, which is what Plutarch himself recounts in this story.[5] But the surviving evidence about Taurus does make clear that he was interested in how Platonists and Stoics disagreed about the virtues of anger.

Taurus was a Platonist who had studied under Plutarch and in turn became a famous teacher.[6] Gellius, the source of this story, is also an important source for information about his philosophical work, as very few of Taurus' own words survive.[7] In this passage, Gellius reports that Taurus wrote a treatise on anger.[8] Indeed, it is possible that Gellius had that treatise in mind when he asked Taurus the question that prompted the philosopher to reminisce about Plutarch in the first place. For Gellius begins this chapter by writing, 'Interrogavi in diatriba Taurum, an sapiens irasceretur'; 'I once asked Taurus in his lecture-room whether a wise man got angry.'[9] After Taurus recounts the anecdote about Plutarch, he defends his Platonist interpretation of how a wise man uses anger.

While both Platonists and Stoics advocated for strict control over emotions, they disagreed on what the goal of such control should be.[10] The Stoics argued that the virtuous person was one who practised ἀπαθεία (*apatheia*), that is, their rationality had such control that they were unmoved by their emotions. While Platonists like Plutarch were sceptical of anger's usefulness to guide people towards virtue, they argued against *apatheia* as a goal because Plato wrote positively of anger in his dialogues. In the *Republic*, Plato makes θυμός (*thumos*) that which differentiates the guardians from other inhabitants of the ideal city.[11] Nonetheless, Taurus sees no reason to praise anger, but instead takes such passages as evidence of how a Platonist ought to practice *metriopatheia*, that is, the practice of a moderate amount of emotion. Gellius, given his philological interests, focuses on the Greek and Latin vocabulary in his summary of Taurus' interpretation of the Plutarch story:

> Summa autem totius sententiae Tauri haec fuit: non idem esse existimavit aorgesian et analgesian aliudque esse non iracundum animum, aliud analgeton et anaistheton, id est hebetem ac stupentem. Nam sicut aliorum omnium, quos Latini philosophi 'affectus' vel 'affectiones', Graeci 'pathe'

appellant, ita huius quoque motus animi, qui, cum est ulciscendi causa saevior, 'ira' dicitur, non privationem esse utilem censuit, quam Graeci 'steresin' dicunt, sed mediocritatem, quam metrioteta illi appellant.

Now the sum and substance of Taurus' whole disquisition was this: he did not believe that ἀοργησία or 'freedom from anger', and ἀναλγησία, or 'lack of sensibility', were identical; but that a mind not prone to anger was one thing, a spirit ἀνάλγητος and ἀναίσθητος, that is, callous and unfeeling, quite another. For as of all the rest of the emotions which the Latin philosophers call *affectus* or *affectiones*, and the Greeks πάθη, so of the one which, when it becomes a cruel desire for vengeance, is called 'anger', he did not recommend as expedient a total lack, στέρησις as the Greeks say, but a moderate amount, which they call μετριότης.

Aulus Gellius, *Noctes Atticae*, 1.26.10, trans. J. C. Rolfe.

By arguing against the Stoics' absolutes, Taurus recreates the Aristotelian mean in Platonist language.[12] In doing so, Taurus follows what Plutarch himself had done in *On Moral Virtues* when he argued against the Stoics and Pythagoreans.[13]

PLUTARCH AND HEGEMONIC MASCULINITY

Because Plutarch's performance of masculinity is bound up in his status as an aristocratic slave-owner, and because aristocracy and slave-ownership was normative in the Greco-Roman world, it is necessary to examine whether Plutarch's masculinity was hegemonic. In this section, I review the history of the theorisation of the term 'hegemony' and then examine how R. W. Connell and James Messerschmidt apply this theorisation to the term 'hegemonic masculinity'. I argue that in the context of the Roman Principate, Plutarch fulfils some of the requirements of hegemonic masculinity. But because of his role as a philosopher, Plutarch also had social licence to explore alternative masculinities. Indeed, in his story about Plutarch and the anonymous slave, Taurus is interested in Plutarch's reaction precisely because it is unusual and the result of Plutarch's philosophically cultivated masculinity.

The word 'hegemonic' in the phrase 'hegemonic masculinity' derives from Antonio Gramsci's theorisation of hegemony. Thucydides had used the word ἡγεμονία (*hegemonia*) to describe the power that fifth-century Athens had over other city-states that it had not conquered.[14] Likewise, Gramsci, a Marxist, used the Italian word *egemonia* to describe how in capitalist societies, the bourgeoisie dominated the proletariat not just through the state and the economy, but also through the church, social clubs and other organisations that make up civil society.[15] Terry Eagleton summarises Gramsci's thought on hegemony as 'the

ways in which a governing power wins consent to its rule from those it subjugates – though it is true that he occasionally uses the term to cover both
consent and coercion together'.[16] Political thinkers continue to find Gramsci's
term fruitful, most especially the idea that common sense is the result of political struggle. In his book *Hegemony How-To*, the political organiser Jonathan
Smucker argues that his readers can change what counts as twenty-first-century
American common sense by strategically contesting current political and economic structures.[17]

Kessler and others coined the term 'hegemonic masculinity' in 1982 to
describe the hierarchy of multiple masculinities that they found while examining Australian high school students.[18] Other scholars, such as Connell, then
began to apply the concept to the practices of masculinity within societies as
a whole.[19] In their history of how scholars have used this term, Connell and
Messerschmidt highlight the fundamental aspects of hegemonic masculinity:

Hegemonic masculinity was not assumed to be normal in the statistical
sense; only a minority of men might enact it. But it was certainly normative [1]. It embodied the currently most honored way of being a man [2],
it required all other men to position themselves in relation to it [3], and it
ideologically legitimated the global subordination of women to men [4].[20]

Connell and Messerschmidt conclude their review of this term by defending its
usefulness, as it correctly describes a plurality of masculinities and a hierarchy
of masculinities.[21] However, they also encourage researchers to reject the fourth
attribute, that hegemonic masculinity is fundamental to the global subjection of
women. For in their research they conclude that hegemonic masculinities differ
sufficiently across time and cultures that it is not feasible to analyse them as col-
laborating on a common project. They also encourage more rigorous research
into the dynamics and geographies of hegemonic masculinity in specific times
and places.[22]

Understanding Plutarch's own historical context is therefore key to understanding to what extent he performed hegemonic masculinity, most especially
the first two requirements, being honoured and being normative. That Plutarch
was an honoured man is clear: during his life he was given honorary Roman
citizenship and after his death the people of Chaeronea memorialised him with
a bust.[23] That Plutarch's actions as a man were normative is harder to prove. The
surviving evidence reveals that Plutarch was a local aristocrat, born to a prominent family in the town of Chaeronea in Boeotia.[24] The extent to which Greek
aristocrats during the Roman Principate were normative in their localities is the
extent to which Plutarch fulfils the first requirement of hegemonic masculinity.

Through Plutarch's own writings, he partially fulfils the third attribute:
requiring other men to position themselves in relation to this aristocratic

masculinity. Throughout his *Moralia*, Plutarch explains how aristocratic men should behave in a variety of situations, including how much wine to drink, how to study poetry and how to talk about oneself in the audience of a powerful official.[25] In writing these prescriptions for aristocratic men, Plutarch simultaneously reveals the assumptions of how other men are expected to act towards aristocrats. Plutarch's character Fundanus in *On the Control of Anger*[26] reveals the type of subservient masculinity he expects from his slaves. In describing how a slave-owner ought to manage his slaves, Fundanus explains that he expects his slaves to be cheerful and mindful of the small details necessary for the slave-owner to carry out his routine.[27] Through his character, Plutarch quite literally orientates the subservient masculinity of slaves to cater to aristocratic slave-owners like himself.

However, because of his status as a philosopher, Plutarch simultaneously does not fulfil the third attribute of hegemonic masculinity. As a philosopher, Plutarch practised values that were not associated with aristocratic men.[28] For instance, Plutarch valorised husbandly fidelity and vegetarianism.[29] In this way, Principate philosophers like Plutarch were similar to Principate sophists. Maud Gleason demonstrates that second-century sophists used particular clothing, bodily deportment and tones of voice to fortify their own intellectual authority by distinguishing themselves from other men.[30] Likewise, the entire point of Taurus' story is that Plutarch's way of reacting to his slave's insubordination is unusual and worthy of comment. That is, just as in *On the Control of Anger* Fundus demonstrates the control that he has over his emotions as the result of philosophical training,[31] so too does Plutarch. By highlighting how Plutarch maintains self-control in the face of his disobedient slave, Taurus is presenting his readers with the benefits of this alternative type of masculinity. Specifically, Taurus is interested in how Plutarch's suppression of his anger allows him to ask philosophical questions while also ordering his other slaves to continue beating the upstart. The result is a vicious spectacle that combines the authoritative command associated with aristocratic men and the cool withdrawal associated with philosophers.

Plutarch partially fulfils the requirements of performing hegemonic masculinity, since as a member of the Greek aristocracy he performs that masculinity which was honoured in the Greek and Roman world. However, his status as a philosopher prevents him from being easily identified as practising hegemonic masculinity, since his pursuit of wisdom requires him to experiment with emotional self-control that goes beyond what was expected of aristocratic men.

CONCLUSION

That Plutarch's masculinity is so similar to hegemonic masculinity is further demonstration that Kupers' definition of toxic masculinity is not sufficient to describe Plutarch's actions. For Kupers' toxic masculinity is not hegemonic, but rather a strategy that men use in extreme environments while separated from the rest of society. My solution to this dilemma is not to ignore Kupers' research, but rather to historicise it. Plutarch was not a prisoner, he was a free man who sought to control his slave. Plutarch's lack of anger therefore has a different context than the toxic masculinity that Kupers described. The story of Plutarch and the slave is a case study for how freedom and class status are essential to any description of the connection of anger and toxic masculinity. Kupers' definition is indeed useful, as it clarifies that Plutarch's readiness for violence and his need to dominate are extensions of his identity as a man, not simply his identity as a philosopher. Simultaneously, the definition falls short: for Plutarch, despite fulfilling so many aspects of Kupers' definition, is more similar to the prison guard than the prisoner. His anger management therefore has to be understood as his participation in two conflicts: Platonists against Stoics and slave-owners against slaves.

NOTES

1. Notably, Kupers (2017) does not use the term in his later analysis of rape in prison.
2. Kupers 2005, 717.
3. Kupers 2005, 718.
4. Kupers 2005, 719.
5. Lakmann (1995, 39) compares Plutarch's list of physical attributes in this passage to all earlier relevant philosophical treatises that he could have consulted. Fitzgerald (2000, 34–6) contextualises this story among others of slaves' failed attempts to use their owner's philosophy against them.
6. For the question of the precise chronology of the relationships of Plutarch, Taurus and Gellius, see most recently Dillon 1996. Tarrant (2007, 457) remains open to the idea that there may have been more than one Platonist Taurus during this time.
7. The *Suda* records two treatises attributed to Taurus, including one (*Tau* 166) on the differences between Platonism and Aristotelianism.
8. 8.6.
9. 1.26.1.
10. For an introduction to these concerns, see Nussbaum 1994.
11. *Republic*, 411c.
12. Dillon 1996, 242.
13. Dillon 1996, 193–8.
14. 1.76.1.
15. Gramsci 1971, 268, 348, 350, 370 and 376.
16. Eagleton 1991, 112.
17. Smucker 2017.
18. Kessler et al. 1982.

19. Connell 1982 and 1983.
20. Connell and Messerschmidt 2005, 832.
21. Connell and Messerschmidt 2005, 846–7.
22. Connell and Messerschmidt 2005, 847–53. Cf. Messerschmidt 2018, 25–46.
23. His Roman citizenship through his connections to Roman aristocrats: *Life of Otho*, 14.1.
24. Plutarch's memory about his great-grandfather Nicarchus establishes that Nicarchus had been a leader in Chaeronea: *Life of Antony* 68.4.
25. Studying poetry: *How the Young Man Should Study Poetry*, Πῶς δεῖ τὸν νέον ποιημάτων ἀκούειν (*Quomodo adulscens audire debeat*). Talking about one's self: *On Praising Oneself Inoffensively*, Περὶ τοῦ ἑαυτὸν ἐπαινεῖν ἀνεπιφθόνως (*De laude ipsius*).
26. Περὶ Ἀοργησίας (*De Cohibenda Ira*).
27. 462a and 464a. Cf. Hoof 2007, 75.
28. Cf. Dressler 2016, though Dressler is more concerned with the role of the feminine in Roman philosophers' thought rather than their lives.
29. Fidelity: 'Very fortunate is the man who in the entire span of his life knows from the beginning only one woman, the one whom he marries.' (*Life of Cato the Younger*, 7.3). Vegetarianism: *On the Eating of Meat*, Περὶ σαρκοφαγί (*de esu carnium*), cf. Newmyer 2005, 85–105.
30. Gleason 2010.
31. Περὶ Ἀοργησίας (*De Cohibenda Ira*) 453d–454b.

CHAPTER 2

Attempted Rape as Rite of Passage: Constructing the Christian Feminine Ideal

Kimberly Passaro and Brian P. Sowers

Male late antique Christian authors frequently used female characters as a means to further their own ideological ends.[1] This essay explores how early Christian novels exploited rape culture, or the socially normalised sexual violence that is symptomatic of toxic masculinity, as a vehicle for depicting ideal Christian women and, by association, the ideal Christian community.[2] Our analysis begins with Thecla, the apostle Paul's fictional female counterpart in the second-century *Acts of Paul and Thecla* (hereafter *APT*). As itinerant preacher and wonder-worker, Thecla rivals Paul, but it is her ability to resist sexual assault that marks her as his superior. One of the most popular female saints in late antiquity, Thecla and her story captured the imaginations of subsequent authors who used Thecla as a model for other female protagonists. The fourth-century *Acts of Cyprian and Justina* (hereafter *ACJ*), for example, uses Thecla as a prototype for Justina. Like Thecla, who singlehandedly overpowers her attacker, Alexander, Justina defends herself against her assailant, Aglaidas, in the *ACJ*. Aglaidas then hires the magician Cyprian to seduce her with erotic magic, and Justina's ability to resist the demons Cyprian summons leads not only to Cyprian's conversion, but to the conversion of all of Syrian Antioch. In the ensuing centuries, Christian authors, such as Cyril of Scythopolis and Palladius, continued to depict women falling victim to sexual assault and erotic magic. Unlike Thecla and Justina, these later female characters became increasingly passive, portrayed instead as victims requiring the protection of male church leaders.

As late antique Christianity evolved from a counter-cultural movement into a religion of empire and dominance, its use of sexual assault as a figurative representation of its relationship with the wider Mediterranean society evolved as well. By depicting sexual assault as perpetrated by individuals hostile to Christianity, the *APT* and *ACJ* relieve early Christian communities of any responsibility for toxic masculinity by projecting it onto their ideological rivals.

At the same time, they reinforce the very patriarchal structures of oppression that earlier texts called into question. As a manifestation of toxic masculinity, rape represents not only sexual desire but also a desire for dominance. In the *APT*, Alexander serves as the embodiment of Greco-Roman oppression and injustice, which Christianity, through Thecla, unmans. Symbolically, this demonstrates paganism's inability to overcome Christianity: in failing to dominate a Christian woman, the pagan Alexander is effeminised and proven inferior. The effeminisation of Christianity's rivals continues in the *ACJ* through Justina's defeat of Aglaidas and Cyprian, who represent those outside Christian society, either pagan holdouts or magical practitioners. While these texts do not show Christian men engaging in overtly toxic behaviour, the success of the rhetoric of Christian superiority nevertheless relies on the same sexist beliefs which, when challenged, triggered the violent events in these narratives. They therefore reinforce the principles underlying toxic masculinity and rape culture, and serve to perpetuate them. This trend persists into the fifth century and beyond, as imperial Christianity increasingly projected society's toxic masculinity onto the fringes, able to be countered only by the Christian male establishment, which was no less problematic. Our essay outlines the development of late antique toxic masculinity by tracing its evolution in the early Christian male imagination, a precursor for the continuity of attitudes about sexual assault in medieval, Renaissance and modern literature.

THECLA

The *Acts of Paul and Thecla*, a stand-alone apocryphal adventure story later appended to the much longer *Acts of Paul*, recounts Thecla's conversion to Christianity and her attempt to join the first-century itinerant preacher, Paul, on his pan-Mediterranean missionary journey. Because Paul promoted asceticism with a strong emphasis on sexual renunciation, Thecla, as an aspiring convert, breaks off her engagement to a local Iconian aristocrat, Thamyris. She then barters away her bracelets and a silver mirror to gain access to Iconium's jail where Paul had been imprisoned for corrupting the local youth, Thecla in particular. When she and Paul are discovered together, Paul is flogged and banished from Iconium and Thecla is condemned to be burned alive. During her public execution, a miraculous rain extinguishes the pyre's flames, an auspice interpreted favourably by the Iconian elite. Freed, Thecla cuts her hair in a masculine style and leaves Iconium in search of Paul, who refuses to admit her to his apostolic entourage lest she suffer some unexpressed ordeal. This ordeal – an attempted sexual assault – occurs in Pisidian Antioch, where another local aristocrat, Alexander, takes notice of the unknown Thecla upon her arrival in his city. He approaches Paul with money and gifts, questioning him about Thecla, but Paul denies any relationship with her.[3] Emboldened, Alexander attempts to rape Thecla, but she fights him off, tears his clothing and throws his civic regalia to the ground. As punishment for disrespect against an Antiochene official, Thecla is condemned to the beasts, but she is twice preserved: first by a protective lioness who defends her from the ravenous male animals, and second by a bolt of lightning that kills the carnivorous seals swimming in a nearby pool where Thecla – assuming her death was imminent – had baptised herself. Legitimised through her miraculous survival, Thecla converts some Antiochenes to Christianity and is welcomed by Paul into his entourage. The manuscript tradition here contains a wide range of pseudepigraphical episodes about Thecla's subsequent adventures, in which she thrives as an itinerant evangelist performing miracles and converting people to Christianity before her eventual death late in life.

Throughout late antiquity Thecla's cult claimed a prominence among other female saints that rivalled and, indeed, was eclipsed only by that of Mary Theotokos. The *APT* was also disseminated across Mediterranean Christendom at a very early date, certainly by the fourth century. Considering the popularity of ancient devotion to Thecla, scholarly interest in the *APT* has emerged remarkably recently. Only within the past fifty years or so have scholars seriously and critically engaged it, primarily as a reliable historical source for early Christian women.[4] More recently, some critics have interpreted Thecla as a metaphoric projection of the community and author behind the *APT*.[5]

Our essay fits within this recent and growing tradition, and argues that Thecla's character advances what we conceptualise as a second-century feminine ideal, intertextually contrasted with Thecla's biblical predecessors, Ruth and Mary Magdalen, and internally superior to at least three of the story's male characters: Paul, Thamyris and Alexander.[6] As the literary product of a male author operating within an increasingly male-dominated second-century Christian hierarchy, the *APT* is not primarily (or at all) a story of feminine liberation. In our view, the feminine ideal inter- and intra-textually modelled by Thecla functions as a critique of second-century competitors of or (real or imaginary) threats to early Christianity. It is also a subtle means to reorient the socio-religious and domestic/sexual mobility of early Christian women around a hyper-ascetic ideology marked by sexual and marital renunciation.[7] To more forcefully juxtapose Thecla against her male antagonists, however, their interactions with her are characterised by toxic masculinity.[8] Thamyris and Alexander in particular are metaphorically charged characters who depend on toxic masculinity to maintain patriarchal control and Roman imperial authority respectively. By systematically overcoming their toxic threats, Thecla advances Christian alternatives to Greco-Roman sexual, marital and political mores.

Thamyris learns about Thecla's desire for conversion when he visits her at home only to discover that she has locked herself in her bedroom and remains fixed to the window through which she had heard Paul preach. Thamyris urges

Thecla to return to the vibrant life of the family and honour their engagement. In so doing, he reinforces his perceived possession of Thecla with strong possessive pronouns (Θέκλα μοι, τὸν σὸν Θάμυριν). When his attempt proves unsuccessful, Thecla's household mourns as if she has died. Their collective grief underscores how deeply Thecla's marriage, that is, her sexual availability to Thamyris, was associated with her identity and the long-term stability of the household. Thamyris responds to Thecla's rejection by leveraging his social privilege to have Paul arrested for undermining the city's mores through his repudiation of marriage. Thamyris' refusal to acknowledge Thecla's nuptial agency, albeit an agency influenced by Paul's gospel message, facilitates his attempted reassertion of marital control over Thecla and incites the first set of threats against her life.

Alexander advances a more pernicious form of toxic masculinity that triggers the second set of threats against Thecla's life. Unlike earlier perils which occasioned divine assistance, Thecla alone is responsible for defending herself against his sexual assault. First, she asserts her social status as an Iconian aristocrat, a declaration operating within an ancient (and modern) ideology that affords well-born women just enough social privilege to exempt their bodies from the gaze and grasp of rapacious men. Second, because her claim for such social protection falls on deaf ears, she fights off Alexander by tearing his clothes and throwing his civic regalia to the ground. Alexander experiences social shame as a result of Thecla's physical dominance – the narrator says that she made him a public spectacle (ἔστησεν αὐτὸν θρίαμβον) – and he responds by leveraging his social standing to have Thecla condemned to a public execution. When the first stage of the execution fails because a lioness defends Thecla against the male lion and bear set against her, Alexander devises an even more sexually charged way to punish her: tying her legs to a pair of bulls and setting their genitals on fire.

In our view, Thecla's conflicts with Thamyris and Alexander and the men's toxic behaviour can be interpreted within the *APT*'s proto-orthodox context(s) rather than simply through a proto-feminist lens. Accordingly, the *APT* exploits Thecla's exceptional femininity, already anticipated in the story through her rejection of traditional markers of femininity, to set second-century Christian communities against the wider Greco-Roman cultural milieu, here symbolised by two representatives of elite male authority: the paterfamilias and the municipal archon.

Thamyris, scorned by the newly celibate Thecla, represents those social structures that incite (male) violence/power to crush perceived (female) threats to patriarchal hegemony. This patriarchal hegemony is primarily contested around Thecla's engagement and anticipated marriage to Thamyris. Thecla ignores Thamyris' first assertion of patriarchal authority, that is, Paul's imprisonment, by leaving the safety of her house and pursuing Paul to the jail cell, a space marked as socially transgressive and absent of patriarchal control. Thamyris then invokes the city's officials to defend the civic institution of marriage and his right to patriarchal authority over Thecla. Thamyris' toxic reactions to Thecla's multiple rejections of his domestic authority therefore shift from his use of possessive adjectives to the governor's insistence that their marriage falls under the jurisdiction of Iconian law (κατὰ τὸν Ἰκονιέων νόμον). By challenging patriarchal mores, Thecla had, in effect, violated civic institutions and, as a result, was subject to the unmitigated force and violence of the Iconian state.

By contrast, Alexander represents the rapacious tendencies inherent to Greco-Roman civic authority that respond to any challenge to their social authority – Thecla's disrespect to Alexander's regalia, for example – with murderous rage. For that reason, once the Antiochene government resolves to execute Thecla, they maintain this decision even after Thecla's life has been miraculously spared multiple times. Alexander's central role in commissioning additional and increasingly wild beasts underscores the profound malignance and injustice of these civic institutions and their representatives. In fact, the Antiochene authorities abandon their attempted execution of Thecla only when a female relative of the emperor Claudius faints and causes fear among the city that Thecla's execution could elicit imperial displeasure. In the face of a larger and more powerful authority, the leading men of Antioch stay her execution.

Taken together, Thamyris and Alexander represent two major social power structures explicitly challenged by second-century Christianity. On the one hand, inasmuch as the proto-orthodox community responsible for the *APT* advanced an ascetic and celibate lifestyle for men and especially for women, it stood at odds with traditional forms of ancient Mediterranean patriarchy. Providing women with the option of not marrying posed a threat to this system, although it should be noted that early Christianity quickly replaced one form of patriarchy with another. On the other hand, as second-century Christian communities disassociated themselves from the ideologies of diasporic Judaism from which many of these communities had originated, their refusal to participate in civic institutions, particularly religious events, marked them as potential threats to civic life. For that reason, it is during the second century that occasional acts of violence against Christians simply for being Christian enter the historical record. The *APT*'s depiction of an exceptional female character defeating male representatives of patriarchal and civic authority despite their repeated threats to her life and body symbolises the eventual and inevitable victory of Christianity over those Greco-Roman social institutions, from *oikos* to *polis*, that presented the most consistent challenge to its message. Within the rhetorical framework of the text, Christianity wins and the pagan enemy, so weak as to be beaten by a girl, is emasculated. This deeply problematic mindset of Christian communities, who downplay their own investment in toxic masculinity while pointing fingers at their opponents, will be further exemplified in the *ACJ*.

JUSTINA

Two hundred years after the *APT* was written, Christianity emerged victorious over its ideological competitors. By the fourth century, thanks in large part to the patronage of Constantine (r. 306–337 CE) and his successors, Christianity became a legitimate religious option in the late Roman empire; under Theodosius I (r. 379–395 CE), Christianity became the empire's only legally recognised religion.[9] During this transitional century, Christian authors continued to use sexual assault and the motif of toxic masculinity to rhetorically discredit their ideological competitors. In this way, fourth-century Christian prose fictions were building on an established literary foundation. But now that Christianity was rapidly becoming the religion of empire, as it were, those social forces, domestic and civil, that received the hostile attention of earlier authors had either conformed to Christian values or transformed Christianity into their own image. In other words, fourth-century imperial Christianity had to direct its literary opprobrium elsewhere, towards different ideological competitors.

The *Acts of Cyprian and Justina*, a stand-alone account subsequently expanded and eventually versified in epic metre by the fifth-century poet Aelia Eudocia, recounts the conversion of its two titular fictitious characters with a particular focus on Justina. Intertextually linked to Thecla, Justina hears the gospel from her bedroom window and chooses to convert. Whereas Thecla's mother does not convert until the end of the *APT*, Justina's parents have a vision of Christ in their sleep, prompting her father to lead his household to the Antiochene church so they can all convert together. For this reason, the newly converted Justina is not alienated from her household after deciding to join the rank of Christian virgins.[10] During one of her daily church visits, she receives the attention of Aglaidas, a local aristocrat who, like Alexander in the *APT*, finds the story's female ascetic desirable. After first proposing marriage, an offer summarily rejected, Aglaidas decides to sexually assault Justina during another trip between her house and church. Justina's successful and complete defeat of Aglaidas' assault is explicitly compared to Thecla's defeat of Alexander, but it is more physically dominant: she throws him on the ground, pulls out his hair and tears his clothing. Humiliated, Aglaidas hires the local magician, Cyprian, to use his power to seduce Justina. Cyprian's erotic magic takes the form of three demonic assaults against Justina, who remains within the safety of her home and uses the sign of the cross to defeat her now demonic assailants. After the third demon flees the *signum crucis*, Cyprian acknowledges God's superior power and converts to Christianity. Quickly rising through the ranks, he is eventually appointed bishop of Antioch, where he makes Justina mother superior to the city's growing cohort of virgins. In a later account, Cyprian and Justina are executed in Nicomedia during the so-called Great Persecution under Diocletian and the tetrarchs.

Aside from critical editions and preliminary analyses of details useful for the history of magic and Greco-Roman cults, Justina and the *ACJ* have received less scholarly attention than Thecla and the *APT*.[11] More recently, some attention has been directed to the fifth-century epic version of the hagiography by Aelia Eudocia.[12] Nuanced treatments of Justina as a literary character or of the influence of her cult on late antique-medieval Christianity remain woefully few. In this section, we highlight Justina's role as a literary survivor of sexual/spiritual assault to contextualise the *ACJ* within an early Christian tradition of thinking with toxic masculinity and to model a corrective regarding the Cyprian and Justina legend. In our view, the *ACJ* is first and foremost a story about Justina and those hostile attempts against her body. Cyprian's conversion, while a focus of later accounts about the two saints, is a secondary feature of the text.

One way the *ACJ* centralises Justina's character is by intertextually linking her with Thecla, whose legend was growing in popularity and complexity and whose cult in central Anatolia welcomed Christian pilgrims from across the Mediterranean. Of those textual details shared between Thecla and Justina, two are essential for our analysis. First, the story opens with Justina sitting at her window where she, like Thecla, hears the gospel message and desires conversion. The rather obvious borrowing of this scene links Justina to Thecla and anticipates the overall trajectory of her story: like Thecla, Justina will convert to an ascetically oriented Christianity which will precipitate multiple threats to her life, all of which she will overcome. Second, one of these threats, Aglaidas' attempted rape, is marked in the narrative as a direct parallel to Alexander's attempted rape of Thecla (ἀκόλουθα πράξασα τῇ διδασκάλῳ Θέκλῃ).

Justina's ability to overcome multiple threats to her body and soul distinguish her as a remarkable late antique woman, paving the way for her eventual veneration as a saint. From a textual perspective, however, while built on a pre-existing foundation laid by Thecla, Justina quickly deviates from and, in many ways, eclipses her literary model. The differences between these two women indicate how features of toxic masculinity in the *ACJ* advanced uniquely fourth-century Christian interests, distinct from those relevant to the second-century community/author responsible for the *APT*. Most of the substantial changes in the *ACJ* are therefore limited to the sociocultural backdrop of the story. In other words, the ideological objectives behind the toxic attacks on Justina are different from those in comparable scenes involving Thecla. As we argued above, Thecla can be seen as a foil for second-century Christian anxieties when the religion was still small and outlawed, but these anxieties were no longer applicable to the religion of empire that Christianity gradually became during the middle decades of the fourth century.

For instance, although her conversion parallels Thecla's, Justina's is marked by less domestic anxiety and no toxic patriarchy, although elements of patriarchal control remain present within the text. In the *APT*, Thecla's desire to convert forces her to break off her engagement to Thamyris, which in turn fractures her relationship with the members of her household and the people of her hometown. Justina, by contrast, converts alongside her parents under the oversight of her father and the Antiochene bishop. The narrative focus of this scene is so centred on Justina's father that she herself is effectively absent until the family returns home. Post conversion, Justina remains within the confines and safety of her house; she is vulnerable to Aglaidas' assault only while travelling to and from church.

The domestic and civic anxieties elicited by Thecla's conversion were no longer operative within the literary conceit of the *ACJ*. Rather than creating an ideological landscape in which its protagonist experiences a rupture in her domestic and civic communities, the *ACJ* reinforces and maintains Justina's social system. It is as if the Antioch in which Justina converts had already become Christian, despite the fact that the story ostensibly occurs at the end of the third century, decades before Constantine would issue the Edict of Milan. The time when Thecla's challenge to domestic patriarchy, articulated through her refusal to marry, had social value for Christianity had come and gone. By the fourth century, domestic patriarchy had gradually become Christian patriarchy.

If, as we maintain, fourth-century urban Christianity no longer imagined itself at odds with the Greco-Roman domestic power structure, its relationship to civic systems was even closer, especially in light of the growing influence of urban bishops and clerics.[13] For that reason, while Aglaidas and Cyprian still pose real threats to Justina's safety, they no longer represent local civic authority able to wield the sort of political might held by the urban magistrate Alexander in the *APT*. Instead, Aglaidas and Cyprian are positioned at the fringes of Antiochene society and represent urban aristocratic pagans, the final holdouts against Christianity.[14] Their connection to traditional religions is explicit: the first thing we are told about Aglaidas is that he comes from the Antiochene aristocracy and that he remained dedicated to 'idol worship'. Cyprian is an even more marginal character. While his social status is never mentioned in the *ACJ*, based on details from the wide Cyprian legend, he came from Athens and, after studying traditional Greek cults, he travelled to Egypt and Babylon to study magic. From there, he settled in Antioch, where he gained notoriety as an accomplished magician. Unlike Alexander, who mobilises his city against Thecla, Aglaidas and Cyprian effectively work alone, without any explicit civic support. This makes sense only if the urban landscape of Antioch is imagined by its author to already be predominantly Christian.

These changes to the domestic and civic landscape of the fourth-century Christian literary imagination are also reflected in the different types of violence depicted in the *APT* and *ACJ*. Attacks on Thecla were more straightforward and strictly physical and occurred prior to her baptism, after her family had rejected her but before she was accepted by Paul. Her perseverance and rejection of traditional femininity emphasises her own exceptionality as much as the strength of Christianity. For Justina, the narrative trajectory is somewhat different. Beginning with Aglaidas' attempted rape, the level of sexual violence escalates as the story progresses, and it becomes increasingly difficult to determine whether it is Aglaidas or Cyprian who wants to rape Justina. At some point, Aglaidas disappears from the narrative altogether, making it fairly clear that Cyprian is her assailant. At the end of the story, when Cyprian decides to convert to Christianity, Satan attempts to physically force himself on Cyprian, and the language used in that scene echoes that of Aglaidas' original assault against Justina. In addition, because Justina has a model to follow as well as the support of her community, the focus here begins to skew towards Christian rather than personal resistance to domination, and the close relationship between sexual and spiritual violation is made more explicit by the fact that her assailants (and ultimately Cyprian's as well) are not merely non-Christians, but demonic. In other words, despite the altered social context, the *ACJ* still articulates contemporary ideological competition between imperial Christianity and the vestiges of traditional religions in terms of sexual assault and toxic masculinity. The fourth-century literary imagination of early Christian authors was therefore still centred around rape culture, projecting heinous actions onto their perceived competitors whom they increasingly outlawed and dehumanised as time went on.

CODA

Our admittedly cursory analysis of these two early Christian texts has argued that one strategy behind early Christianity's rhetoric of religious competition and dominance was to project sexual assault onto its perceived enemies. In the second century when the *APT* was written, Christianity competed with the domestic and civil power structures of the Greco-Roman Mediterranean. Christianity slowly gained imperial legitimacy and by the fourth century it no longer viewed domestic and civic institutions with the same hostility. Rather, it characterised individuals and groups outside its community as effectively on the margins of society where, by the end of the fifth century, they might well have been. In both instances, however, the competitors of Christianity within these stories consistently exhibit toxic masculinity. Most obvious are the multiple attempts to rape Thecla and Justina; less obvious is Thamyris' hostile reaction to his broken engagement to Thecla.

This literary motif took on a life of its own in subsequent centuries. Later accounts regarding Thecla contain an episode in which some local physicians, jealous of the now elderly Thecla's ability to heal the sick, hire a gang of young men to sexually assault her.[15] After these men gain entry to her house, Thecla prays for God to protect her and is saved. Other fifth- and sixth-century stories build on the stock narrative of the young Christian woman and the unsolicited advances she receives from a local pagan man who resorts to magic to seduce her.[16] While obviously part of the same literary milieu as that of the Cyprian-Justina legend, the Christian women in these later accounts are incapable of fighting off their assailants.[17] As a result, their fathers or husbands must bring the young women to the local bishops, who, after protecting the women from erotic magic, chastise them for failing to attend church regularly. Here, not only do these authors employ sexual assault narratives, they do so in ways that blame the female victims and cede religious power into the hands of the male power structure. By the fifth century, Christian patriarchy was so fully re-established that all the male characters advance toxic behaviours. This demonstrates how problematic the Christian mindset truly was. By projecting toxic behaviours onto their ideological rivals, Christian authors sought not to detoxify masculinity or equalise power structures, but to legitimise their own communities and gain prominence. Women such as Thecla and Justina are pawns in this game. Once Christianity has asserted dominance over its external competitors – both using exceptional women as a means to this end and employing rhetoric which relies upon sexist beliefs about male superiority for its effectiveness – it then begins to turn inward and exert control over the women themselves. Thus the desire for dominance which fuels rape culture and which is exhibited by Alexander's and Aglaidas' acts of sexual violence was equally present within the Christian community itself; it simply manifested differently. Christian projection of toxic masculinity onto non-Christians was not so much an attempt to change the system or expose its many evils as to co-opt the system to their own benefit.

NOTES

1. Kraemer (2011), Schenk (2017) and Nortjé-Meyer (2018) address some of the challenges inherent in reconstructing the lived experiences of early Christian women vis-à-vis depictions of women in early Christian literature.
2. See Glendinning 2013. Franiuk and Shain (2011) explore comparable uses of sexual assault in non-Western religious texts.
3. On Paul's denial, see Narro 2019, 127–8.
4. A couple of representative examples are Davies 1980 and MacDonald 1983.
5. Streete 2009, 73–102; Cooper 2013; and Hylen 2015.
6. This essay only contains our reading of Thecla's relationship with her male antagonists. For our reading of Thecla's gender ambiguity and her intertextual competition with Ruth and Mary, see Sowers and Passaro 2020. Our methodology complements that modelled by Narro 2019.
7. On the issue of sexual renunciation in early Christianity, see Castelli 1986.
8. Our analysis of toxic masculinity, especially in religious texts, builds on the work of hooks 2004; Connell 2005; and Posadas 2017.
9. For more on the impact of Constantine and his heirs on Christianity, see Brown 2013 and Lenski 2016.

10. Justina's continued role within her house is discussed in more detail in Sowers 2012 and 2020.
11. A few representative examples are Nock 1927; Nilsson 1947; and Festugière 1950.
12. Bevegni 2006 and Sowers 2020.
13. See Brown 1992 and Rapp 2013.
14. Quiroga (2018) advances a slightly different view of this dynamic period and highlights the similarities between late antique 'pagan' and Christian elite.
15. Streete 2009, 98–9.
16. Palladius' *Historia Lausiaca* 17.6, Cyril's *Life of Euthymus* 57, and Jerome's *Life of Hilarion* 12 most clearly reflect this literary tradition, although *Life of Symeon Stylites the Younger* 49 and Jerome's *Life of Hilarion* 11 are also related.
17. This motif is discussed by Dickie (1999), Frankfurter (2001) and Sowers (2017).

CHAPTER 3

Engendering Justice in a Gendered World: The Case of Thucydides' Athenians

Jessica Penny Evans

Thucydides' history is first and foremost a story of men. While masculinity's role in political culture has been recognised by sociologists and political scientists,[1] its role in shaping both men's behaviour and the structure of Thucydides' history remains relatively unexplored. As Gregory Crane has observed, Thucydides' focus on military and political events ensured their prominence in history as a discipline.[2] If Thucydides' history, the story of the war fought between Athens, Sparta and their respective allies, is, in fact, a story of men, it stands to reason that the text has much to offer our understanding of masculinity. As sociologists have warned, conflating women and gender has led to analyses that overlook how politics is shaped by masculinity and men's interests,[3] and, perhaps most importantly, by competition between a plurality of masculinities.[4] Recently focus has shifted from hegemonic – the 'masculinity that occupies the hegemonic position in a given pattern of gender relations, a position always contestable'[5] – to toxic masculinity – those qualities of hegemonic masculinity that are 'socially destructive, such as misogyny, homophobia, greed, and violent domination'.[6] While the qualities associated with hegemonic masculinity represent the ideal in accordance with which 'men organize their lives, either by aspiring to the hegemonic ideal or deviating from it', hegemonic masculinity need not be toxic.[7] As Connell and Messerschmidt note, a future in which a 'more humane, less oppressive' version of manhood becomes the hegemonic norm is possible.[8]

Historically and culturally contingent, masculinity only seems transhistorical because patriarchy engenders inequality, thereby producing identities similar enough across times and cultures to appear natural. Take, for example, 'heteronormativity', a defining feature of both hegemonic and toxic masculinity.[9] A fifth-century Greek man who penetrated the body of a male slave would not be heteronormative by modern standards, yet penetration of bodies – be they women or male slaves – did not necessarily mitigate his hegemonic status.[10]

The salient markers of masculinity in ancient Greece operated quite differently, albeit in ways that still ensured a select group of men remained in power.

Toxic masculinity's central feature – that it is socially destructive and encourages violent domination – offers an important lens through which to evaluate masculinity in Thucydides' history: it allows us to consider how policy decisions leading to acts of violent domination are driven by identity. Thucydides discusses the shifting norms of masculinity, *andreia*, in his analysis of civil war in Corcyra, where conflicts between democrats and oligarchs led to unimaginable acts of violence that violated the shared norms of the community. In this paper I argue that Thucydides' theory of masculinity in the Corcyra episode can help us better understand how identity operates in the Mytilenean Debate. In this debate two speakers, Diodotus and Cleon, present opposing views regarding the fate of the Mytileneans, who, fearing they would eventually be subjugated, had rebelled against Athens. Those who have examined the role of identity in these speeches have focused on class issues: the exclusively male space of the assembly renders gender's operations invisible. Using Thucydides' theory of masculinity, I identify language coded masculine and effeminate in the speeches of Diodotus and Cleon, each of whom appeals to a particular masculine demographic in his speech. These speeches are as much about masculinity as they are about class.

Diodotus and Cleon appeal to voters' identities as men. Diodotus' speech, therefore, is a response to Cleon's hypermasculine rhetoric. The careful balance struck by Diodotus between a more traditional, restrained masculinity – as identified by Thucydides in the Corcyra episode – and Cleon's hypermasculinity leads to a new, hypercalculating rhetoric of manhood. I suggest that this new masculinity, disguised as 'human nature', engenders a logic of war that results in the slaughter of thousands in Melos: simultaneously fragile and invisible, this hyperrational masculinity drives men to engage in acts of violence for fear of being perceived as weak. By attributing their actions to 'human nature', men render invisible the homosocial mechanism at play while absolving themselves of responsibility for their actions. While theorists today identify misogyny, homophobia, greed and violent domination as the social mechanisms producing toxic acts of manhood, in Thucydides' narrative the most socially destructive discourse of manhood is the one masquerading as human nature, which renders masculinity's operations silent, unmarked and invisible. Not only does it erase the social mechanisms that ensured peace among men, offering men a pretext for unbridled violence, it destroys the efficacy of language to avert armed conflict.

Thucydides teases out the vicissitudes of masculinity in the Corcyra episode precisely because its destabilisation renders visible what had been regarded as natural. Thucydides' analysis, however, falls short: he is blind to the ways that masculine culture defines the boundaries of what constitutes human nature.

Today Thucydides' beliefs about 'human nature' are deployed not only in theories of political realism but in conversations about modern politics. A gendered reading of Thucydides provides insight into the ways the past is deployed to justify social and political inequalities today.

CORCYRA, CONFLICT AND MASCULINITY'S DESTABILISATION

According to Thucydides, the conflict in Corcyra between democratic Athenian allies and oligarchs, supported by Sparta, came to a head: so bloody was the revolution that suppliants killed each other on sacred ground to avoid trial, some even hanging themselves from trees; fathers killed their sons; men killed one another not for political reasons but out of personal hatred (3.81.3–5). This was not the only time during the Peloponnesian War that political divisions within a city-state resulted in such violence, but it was the first. Drawing upon the conflict in Corcyra, Thucydides seeks to identify a universal theory of war's effects on men, believing that such events 'have occurred and always will occur so long as the nature of people remains the same' (3.82.2).[11] While Thucydides uses ἀνθρώπων, a non-gender-specific word, to qualify 'nature', the events and circumstances that led to this observation concern men, the primary agents of war. Here Thucydides defines the nature of people – or rather, human nature – as the nature of men. In the analysis that follows, Thucydides explores the relationship between civil war and words,[12] but does so in language that points to masculinity's instability.[13] He states, 'they changed the customary opinion of words (or labels) in accordance with their judgement of actions' (3.82.4).[14] Thucydides provides the following examples of this discursive shift:

> τόλμα μὲν γὰρ ἀλόγιστος ἀνδρεία φιλέταιρος ἐνομίσθη, μέλλησις δὲ προμηθὴς δειλία εὐπρεπή, τὸ δὲ σῶφρον τοῦ ἀνάνδρου πρόσχημα, καὶ τὸ πρὸς ἅπαν ξυνετὸν ἐπὶ πᾶν ἀργόν, τὸ δ' ἐμπλήκτως ὀξὺ ἀνδρὸς μοίρα προσετέθη, ἀσφαλείᾳ δὲ τὸ ἐπιβουλεύσασθαι ἀποτροπῆς πρόφασις εὔλογος.

> Thoughtless daring was considered manliness for a partisan cause, a delay shaped by forethought was an appealing disguise for cowardice, self-control was a pretext for unmanliness, intelligence with regard to the whole was laziness in everything, rash haste was attributed to the part of man, while aiming at safety was a sensible pretext for hindering. (3.82.4)

Stasis (internal conflict or civil war) shifts the spectrum of masculine behaviour: men who encouraged 'thoughtless daring' and 'rash haste' embodied a hyper-masculinity. Those who encouraged 'delays based on forethought' and whose actions were checked by self-control, intelligence and safety exercised a restrained masculinity. While considered masculine during times of peace, the restrained man was rendered unmanly by the hypermasculinity of his peers.[15]

The conditions of *stasis*, according to Thucydides, swept through the Greek world. Athens was no exception. War was the perfect arena for men to prove their intellectual acumen and physical prowess as citizens. From a young age, men defined themselves in relation to their peers through competition. Through a zero-sum system of competition, men demonstrated both self-control and control over others. Expressing this control was central to Athenian manhood.[16] Masculinity's zero-sum calculus meant that men must constantly surveil and prove their manhood.[17] War offered men opportunities to distinguish themselves in bold, reckless ways, opening the floodgates to an ever-escalating redefining and reinscribing of masculinity.

THE COMPETING MASCULINITIES OF THE MYTILENEAN DEBATE

According to Thucydides, in 428 BCE nearly the entire island of Lesbos, led by the city of Mytilene, revolted from Athens, which was suffering from the plague. The Athenian response was swift and brutal: adult men would be put to death; women and children would be enslaved (3.36.2). Regretting the rashness of this decision almost immediately, the Athenians meet a second time to discuss Mytilene. Thucydides provides two speeches, one by Cleon, who argues the Mytileneans deserve the harshest penalty, and the other by Diodotus, who believes the original plan to be contrary to Athenian interests. Thucydides' theory of masculinity provides a lens through which to evaluate the rhetorics of masculinity in the speeches of Cleon and Diodotus, revealing the extent to which policy decisions – in particular those regarding the lives of individuals – are shaped by masculine identities.

Described by Thucydides as a most violent man and most persuasive among the people, Cleon privileges qualities associated with hypermasculinity in the Corcyra episode, in particular the depreciation of intelligence in favour of ignorance. To make this new hypermasculinity more credible, Cleon pairs it with qualities associated with restrained manhood. Cleon constructs the ignorance of the lower classes as a virtue by pairing ignorance (ἀμαθία) with moderation (σωφροσύνη). In addition to praising the ignorance of the masses, Cleon develops a discourse of anti-intellectualism by combining cleverness (δεξιότης) and intemperance (ἀκολασίας) (3.37.3).[18] For Cleon those whose ignorance is tempered by moderation, people whom he refers to as the *phauloteroi* – the lower classes, the poor – are better citizens (3.37.3). According to Cartledge, despite the prevalence of the lower classes who served in the Athenian navy, 'Athens' dominant military ideology remained a hoplite ideology,' while those specialising in non-hoplite warfare – those who could not afford the hoplite armour – were considered less Athenian.[19] If the hoplite who mastered his body and emotions was the ideal, then the masculinity of anyone less than a hoplite would always be precarious.[20] The *phauloteroi*'s service in the Athenian military compromised their claims to hegemonic manhood, the central tenets of which were qualities associated with a more restrained manhood. They perceived their peers' exercise of restraint in the form of 'cleverness' as a slight to their own equality.

Cleon exploits the precarity of this demographic's masculinity by framing policy in terms of identity. He states that making concessions to allies conveys softness, *malakia*, a word associated with femininity (3.37.2).[21] The Athenians, he says, conduct themselves in daily life without fear or suspicion, but giving allies the same leeway is a sign of softness or effeminacy.[22] The Athenian empire, he says, is tyrannical: obedience can only be maintained through the superiority that comes from being stronger and not by loyalty (3.37.2). Cleon's zero-sum framing of war in the language of softness or effeminacy rendered 'war intelligible':[23] war was a man's game because the protocols of domination on which masculinity was predicated shaped the logic of war.[24] Although Cleon exercises power over the audience by persuading them, this exercise of power, though emasculating the audience, is tempered by the hardness of imperialism he advocates.[25] A vote for Cleon is an expression of dominance reaffirming citizens' masculinity.

Cleon constructs Mytilene as a city-state which 'ranks force ahead of justice',[26] rendering a subject state an enemy to be feared and thus vanquished (3.39.3). Not punishing the Mytileneans, Cleon argues, must mean that they revolted justly and that the Athenians were wrong to rule (3.40.4). By constructing Mytilene as an unjust aggressor, Cleon suggests that the Athenians must be the victims. In doing so Cleon redirects narratives of victimhood: rather than being victims of social-class inequality, Cleon's supporters become empowered subjects of an empire avenging injustice. The Mytileneans' refusal to recognise the Athenians as masters threatens Athenian power and, consequently, the masculinity of citizen men, for whom anything less than domination was slavery. Cleon ends his speech as he began, urging the Athenians not to 'soften or weaken' (μαλακισθέντες) (3.40.7).

Cleon's opposition to the delay (3.38.1) and his belief that the best decisions are rash ones are both qualities associated with hypermasculinity according to Thucydides' theory of masculinity in the Corcyra episode. Rather than addressing the entire citizen body, Cleon exploits masculinity's fragility, tapping into the vulnerabilities of the poor, whose class position made them susceptible to such concerns.[27] In doing so, Cleon offers men alternative means of expressing their manhood as citizens of an empire exercising power over the bodies of subjects. By framing concessions to subject city-states as effeminate, Cleon renders policy personal, linking it to the identities of citizen men whose masculinity was always already compromised, and assimilating the fate of Athens' empire to individual men's perception of self. Cleon's hypermasculine rhetoric threatened the perceived masculinity of those who privileged intelligence, moderation and caution. His direct appeal to the poor points to the partisan nature of his speech.[28] Cleon's rhetoric is shaped, therefore, by the intersections of gender and class.

While Cleon argues that the Athenians must kill all adult men and enslave the women and children, for Diodotus the initial verdict was too harsh and did not align with Athenian interests. Diodotus frames his speech in language associated with restrained masculinity. He begins by addressing Cleon's excursus on speech acts in language calculated to appeal to a restrained, masculine audience.[29] He says that those who contend that words are not the teachers of deeds must be void of understanding (ἀξύνετος) or self-interested. He deems the anger informing the initial decision thoughtlessness or folly (ἄνοια). Haste is the result of ignorance (ἀπαιδευσία) and a deficiency of knowledge (3.42.1). The similarities between the masculinities identified by Thucydides at 3.82.4 and Cleon's and Diodotus' opening remarks on rhetoric point to the importance of identity, in particular, masculinity. The debate may be a 'contest of words', as Ober suggests, but it is also a contest of masculinities.[30]

Diodotus' position on justice is informed not by anger, haste or a reckless daring, all qualities associated with hypermasculinity in the Corcyra episode, but by a careful calculation of interest based on the superiority of the Athenians. According to Diodotus, a punishment both just and advantageous is impossible: 'it will be much more expedient for keeping empire if we pursue this strategy, namely of agreeing to suffer an injustice, as opposed to annihilating – however justly – those whom we should not' (3.47.5).[31] Diodotus' position signals a discursive shift in Athenian attitudes regarding justice's role in mediating conflict. Whereas in Book One the Athenians claimed to settle disputes with allies in accordance with laws despite their greater strength – a sign of their moderation (1.76.3–4) – Diodotus rejects the premise that conflicts can be settled in a court of law, embracing instead the benefits of their superior power. Cleon's argument feels rhetorically more aggressive, but his conceptualisation of justice establishes Athens and Mytilene as equals, thereby weakening Cleon's argument despite his aggressive assertions to the contrary. Given the zero-sum stakes of Cleon's vision of Athenian empire – that any concession would weaken, *malakisthentes*, the Athenians – to even consider justice would be to admit defeat. Diodotus points out that if the Athenians were sensible (σωφρονοῦμεν), they would understand that the debate is not concerning justice but the good counsel of the Athenians (3.44.2). In war, the sensible, moderate man understands punishment must be exacted in accordance with partial interest rather than rash anger.

Diodotus' commitment to long-term strategy is based on intelligence and careful calculation, but his success hinges on his ability to discipline the emotions roused by Cleon. To achieve this, Diodotus reveals how moderate punishment serves the interest of empire and thus taps into men's identities as rational subjects. The language of expediency informed by reason tames the anger of men, reminding them, as Pericles once did, that war requires restraint, and sometimes winning means inaction.[32] Diodotus' position only seems moderate in comparison to Cleon's, but both speeches construct decisions regarding the life and death of Athenian subjects as inextricable from the masculine identities of voters. Men who might otherwise have been persuaded by Cleon's hypermasculine rhetoric are persuaded by Diodotus because his long-term strategy ensured Athenian domination, thus securing the masculine identities of voters.

The Athenians reversed their initial decision, putting to death only those implicated in the rebellion. The vote, however, was close: Cleon nearly won. The language of the debate suggests that Thucydides saw the conflict as a defining moment in what we might call 'identity politics'.[33] Cleon and Diodotus each speak to a particular demographic. The competition between these duelling discourses of masculinity results in a new discourse of manhood appealing to both camps. In his critique of hegemonic masculinity, Demetriou notes the importance of dialectical processes in reformulating configurations of hegemonic masculinity: hegemonic masculinity appropriates from other masculinities whatever is necessary for domination.[34] Hegemonic masculinity does not exist in isolation but in conversation with marginal masculinities. Diodotus, in responding to Cleon's rash, angry, retributive justice, constructs an argument imbued with what Debnar calls 'merciless rationality'.[35] Responding to the hypermasculinity of Cleon and his audience, Diodotus elaborates a masculinity which was hyper to the extent that its commitment to calculation in the interest of domination overrides any moral imperatives. The unequal dynamics of war meant that concerns of interest superseded justice. This new hyperrational, calculating masculinity – informed by the dominance of hypermasculine men and the cool calculation of Diodotus' more traditional masculinity – gave rise to a discourse of expediency, a hyperrational masculinity, that would be fully realised in the Melian Dialogue.

THE TOXIC NATURE OF THE MELIAN DIALOGUE

In 416 the Melians asserted their right to neutrality despite Athenian demands that they pay tribute to Athens. Eventually all the men living on the island of Melos were executed and the women and children enslaved. Thucydides constructs a dialogue between the Athenian and Melian ambassadors that would earn him a reputation as the 'father' of political realism, according to which men pursue their interests regardless of law or morality in accordance with nature.[36] A gendered reading of the Melian Dialogue, however, suggests that Athenian ideologies of nature – as depicted by Thucydides – were defined by a hyperrational masculinity that was itself a product of masculinity's crisis.

At the very beginning of the dialogue the Athenians request that negotiations between themselves and the Melians be based on fact: the Athenian forces outnumber the Melians, making surrender the only logical recourse. Furthermore, the Athenians reject the Melians' appeal to justice:

> τὰ δυνατὰ δ' ἐξ ὧν ἑκάτεροι ἀληθῶς φρονοῦμεν διαπράσσεσθαι, ἐπισταμένους πρὸς εἰδότας ὅτι δίκαια μὲν ἐν τῷ ἀνθρωπείῳ λόγῳ ἀπὸ τῆς ἴσης ἀνάγκης κρίνεται, δυνατὰ δὲ οἱ προύχοντες πράσσουσι καὶ οἱ ἀσθενεῖς ξυγχωροῦσιν.

We need to accomplish what we can on the basis of what we both really think, each side fully aware that justice is only a factor in human decision when the parties are on equal footing. (5.89.1)[37]

The Athenians' rejection of justice – like Diodotus' (3.44.4) – is framed as a rational response to the fundamental inequality of war and the hypermasculine belief that yielding is tantamount to effeminacy.

The Melians, however, reject Athenian realism. The Melians' response to realism is based not on the model of a rational state-actor but their own identity as men: if such desperate measures are being taken by the Athenians, who perceived Melos' neutrality as a threat to their power, then 'it would be incredibly contemptible (πολλὴ κακότης) and cowardly (δειλία) for free people such as ourselves to accept enslavement over any other option' (Thuc. 5.100.1).[38] The Melians reject the subjectivity that their weakness relative to the Athenian position of strength suggests. Cowardice would undermine the Melians' masculinity as much as a loss of sovereignty would if they were to surrender. By framing the stakes in the language of cowardice, the Melians imply that the Athenians' position is not shaped merely by power, but also by honour and manhood.

The Athenians' response to this argument reveals the toxicity of their hyper-rational rhetoric of manhood: it undermined not only justice, but also *sophrosyne* and shame, the primary social mechanism that prevented men from committing acts of violence. The Athenians argue that if the Melians were sensible (σωφρόνως βουλεύησθε), they would not be so concerned about cowardice: questions concerning manly virtue (ἀνδραγαθία) and shame (αἰσχύνη) are only relevant among equals (5.101.1). In times of peace, men competed for honour, but the fear of shame and humiliation ensured peace among citizens by discouraging acts of hubris, checking masculinity's penchant for escalation.[39] The superior power of the Athenians – the freest of all free states – meant that shame figured lightly in their risk assessment, while their superiority obviated all others' claims to manly virtue.[40] Athenian chauvinism ensured that the traditional, culturally constructed mechanisms – justice and shame – by which tension was de-escalated would be rendered impotent by the facts: their superior forces.[41]

Deliberating sensibly means understanding that shame and manly virtue are only relevant among equals.

The Athenians, as the superior power, not only reject the Melians' claims to manhood, they also redefine what constitutes shame given the power imbalance: the Melians should not turn to shame in the face of shameful and 'imminent dangers'; even when men know what is coming, they are still ruined by the 'sheer force' of shame. These men, because of their poor judgement (ἀνοίας), 'choose to suffer even more humiliation than fate otherwise had in store' (5.111).[42] Here shame is understood best in terms of masculinity: fear of the shame incurred by surrendering – the fear of being dominated and perceived as weak – ruins men, like the Melians, so much so that they succumb to hope, and in doing so are even more shamed and humiliated because they did not have the good sense to surrender. Like Cleon, who regards yielding to Mytilene as emasculating, the Melians' refusal to submit is framed in terms of their own identities as men. The Athenians' rational calculation allows them to redefine what constitutes being 'sensible' or 'self-controlled' and what constitutes shame in accordance with their interests. This masculine culture of calculating dominance erases the viability of any opposing viewpoint grounded in traditional morality or shared experiences as men through which empathy and compassion could be cultivated.

The Athenians, however, attribute their behaviour not to their own identities as men, but to nature: 'ἡγούμεθα γὰρ τό τε θεῖον δόξῃ τὸ ἀνθρώπειόν τε σαφῶς διὰ παντὸς ὑπὸ φύσεως ἀναγκαίας, οὗ ἂν κρατῇ, ἄρχειν', 'we believe that gods and know that people always seek to rule wherever they can. It is in their very nature' (5.105).[43] They did not establish this principle, and they assure the Melians that if they were in a similar position of strength, they would behave similarly. The Athenians' construction of nature – that the strong rule not because they fear slavery or being shamed, or because yielding would tarnish their claims to manhood, but because they can – is itself shaped by their position of power, and the perceived naturalness of men's right to rule, evidence for which could be found in their domination of women, children, social inferiors and slaves. Athenian 'nature' reflects a social world in which the Athenians occupied a privileged position. By equating their behaviour to 'nature', the Athenians absolve themselves of responsibility, hiding the real impetus for their actions: the precarity of their own identities. The language of masculinity, however, offers the Melians, the weaker party from the perspective of the Athenians, an ideological framework to justify their obstinacy, thus revealing the Athenians' own construction of nature to be cultural, stemming from a crisis of masculinity.

The dialectical tension between Cleon and Diodotus' respective masculinities altered the contours of restrained manhood, resulting in the hyperrational masculinity of the Melian Dialogue Athenians. This new masculinity replaced the earlier incarnation of Athenian hegemonic manhood, the foundation of which was restraint. This restraint ensured the proper functioning of the social mechanisms, such as shame, that preserved peace. Thucydides' Melian Dialogue, however, reveals the toxicity of hyperrational masculinity: it engenders a logic of domination masquerading as human nature that destroys language's potential to avert armed conflict.

THUCYDIDES AND POLITICAL REALISM

One of the central organising principles of political realism is the belief that men are by nature aggressive and will pursue their interests despite law or morality. But as Hooper points out, 'realism can be seen to embody hegemonic masculinity, in that it is the perspective of elite white men, in which the ideal of the glorified male warrior has been projected onto the behaviour of states'.[44] Although Thucydides is often regarded as the 'father' of political realism, realism only partly explains the decisions of city-states, since ideals shared between city-states seem to matter as much as the raw pursuit of interest demanded by human nature.[45] Crane suggests that Thucydides rejects ideological underpinnings, ideologies which, according to Habermas, 'are illusions outfitted with the power of common conviction', noting that the Athenian ideology of human nature never becomes common sense and, therefore, invisible, as many ideologies are.[46] Masculinity, however, is the invisible ideology in accordance with which human nature was constructed, and which informed the Melians' rejection of Athenian realism. The Athenians' rejection of justice is as motivated by identity as the Melians' own intransigence. Human nature does not exist independent of men, but is an expression of both men's prerogatives and their insecurities.

The masculinity of the Melian Dialogue Athenians, a violent, calculating exercise of domination that erased the social mechanisms moderating men's behaviour in times of peace, is the result of a crisis of identity exacerbated by war. The outcome of the Melian Dialogue – the execution of the Melian men and enslavement of women and children – suggests even a restrained masculinity's potential to exact violence informed by reason. The perspective of the powerful renders the weaker party's obstinacy through claims to masculinity irrational, even as the Athenians' own rational 'realist' agenda is, in fact, shaped by the protocols of manhood. War's zero-sum stakes produced a toxic form of restrained masculinity, one which erased the weaker party's claims to manhood and rendered invisible masculinity's incentivisation of war by masquerading as human nature.

A gendered reading of Thucydides reveals the extent to which the Athenians' construction of human nature was a product of a masculine culture shaped as much by dominance as by fragility. Masculinity not only informs Athenian realism, it also explains its shortcomings. Realism fails because states are comprised of men: identity, it turns out, really does matter. When Thucydides' Athenians claim that their own actions are guided by honour, fear and self-interest (1.76.2), we must also consider how these too are shaped by masculinity. Honour, fear, and self-interest only exist so long as there are winners and losers. If the Athenians' espousal of an inchoate realism was shaped by masculinity, then realism itself – the privileging of power over shared norms – was itself normative, shaped by the protocols of masculinity, exposing nature as a construction foregrounded in masculine culture.

As Neville Morley has documented, modern pundits and politicians routinely turn to Thucydides for authority, guidance and platitudes.[47] The most harmful beliefs are perhaps those most often quoted by conservative thinkers: that history is doomed to repeat itself; that Thucydides' history is useful, a possession for all time; that the strong rule and the weak concede. A gendered reading of Thucydides reveals how rooted in masculinities these conclusions are. We must ask ourselves why Thucydides' history and his observations about human nature continue to guide our own understanding of the world. If Thucydides' observation of human nature was shaped by slave-owning societies in which women were fundamentally inferior and their best virtue was silence, to what extent is Thucydides being deployed to justify social inequalities? Thucydidean masculinities are toxic precisely because men's dominance in war supported systems of inequality at home, but even more toxic is our belief that Thucydides understood anything about human nature, as if human nature were a knowable, definable essence. As J. J. Winkler warns, for nature, read culture.[48]

The conditions which led to a kind of power politics later theorised as realism were, in fact, shaped by identity politics – a crisis of masculinity. War incentivised bold action, creating opportunities for men to express their masculinity as citizens of an empire. An examination of gender as a process – not static but fragile – reveals how what is regarded as an 'anarchic' state of nature was in fact a construction shaped by masculinity: identity matters, perhaps no more so than when its operations seem invisible. Whereas some read Thucydides' history as a grim verdict on humanity, we might instead see hope in a caveat: the events of Corcyra, says Thucydides, will repeat themselves as long as the nature of people remains the same (3.82.3). David Brooks, in a 2017 op-ed entitled 'Before Manliness Lost Its Virtue', reinscribes masculinity as a solution to our current crisis without considering how the fragility of even a virtuous masculinity might be the source.[49] The classical world might offer insight, but it will not offer a cure. Thucydides' observations of human nature were based on events precipitated and determined by a particular demographic. Ours need not be.

NOTES

1. Hooper 2001 and Cohn and Enloe 2003.
2. Crane 1996, 77.
3. Nagel 1998.

4. Kimmel 2006; Wendt and Andersen 2015; and Kimmel 2017.
5. Connell 2005, 76.
6. Kupers 2005, 716.
7. Connell and Messerschmidt 2005, 838.
8. Connell and Messerschmidt 2005, 833.
9. Sculos (2017, 1) associates the following characteristics with toxic masculinity: 'hyper-competitiveness, individualistic self-sufficiency . . . tendency towards or glorification of violence . . . chauvinism . . . sexism . . . misogyny . . . rigid conceptions of sexual/gender identity and roles . . . heteronormativity . . . entitlement to (sexual) attention from women, (sexual) objectification of women, and the infantilization of women'.
10. Dover (1978), Halperin (1989) and Winkler (1990a) all note both the absence of sexual identities such as homosexual or heterosexual and the legal implications for a man accused of allowing his body to be penetrated, arguing that sexuality is socially constructed; sex was a zero-sum game in which the winners penetrated, and the losers were penetrated. Others, such as Davidson (1997, 2008), find the position of the constructivists too limiting, focusing instead on the lived experiences of individuals, whose sexual preferences seem less shaped by the power structures articulated by the constructivists. These two schools of thought need not be so mutually exclusive. As modern scholars of masculinity have noted, the power of hegemonic discourses of masculinity lies in the inability of men to achieve the hegemonic ideal. According to Connell and Messerschmidt (2005, 838), 'hegemonic masculinities can be constructed that do not correspond closely to the lives of any actual men. Yet these models do, in various ways, express widespread ideals, fantasies, and desires. They provide models of relations with women and solutions to problems of gender relations. Furthermore, they articulate loosely with the practical constitution of masculinities as ways of living in every-day local circumstances. To the extent they do this, they contribute to hegemony in the society-wide gender order as a whole.' For a survey of the debates concerning essentialist and constructivist arguments, see Robson 2013, 59–63.
11. 'ἕως ἂν ἡ αὐτὴ φύσις ἀνθρώπων ᾖ.'
12. For a more thorough treatment of the effects of *stasis* on culturally constructed language, see Price 2001, 39–67.
13. Bassi 2003, 25–58.
14. This sentence has been the subject of much debate. According to Allison (1997, 169), the meaning of the words do not change, but rather men's judgement as to whether these constituted manly or unmanly behaviour. See also most recently Bassi 2003, 28 and Loraux 2009, 261–92. Unless otherwise indicated, translations are my own.
15. For an analysis of how this dynamic plays out in the context of Periclean rhetoric and the Sicilian Debate, see Evans 2019. For a discussion of this passage in the context of *andreia* see also Bassi 2003 and Balot 2014, 119–20.
16. Ober 1989, 250–1 and Nortwick 2008, 27.
17. Winkler 1990a. For an analysis of masculinity's fragility today see Pascoe 2011.

18. Wohl 2002, 117–18.
19. Cartledge 1998, 62.
20. Cartledge 1998, 62–3. The 'political identity' of the lower-class citizens who 'lacked distinction and identity' was paramount (Raaflaub 1996, 159).
21. Wohl 2002, 171–214.
22. Cf. Thuc. 2.37.3. Here Pericles makes a similar argument: the Athenians conduct themselves in daily life without fear or suspicion, since they obey the magistrates and the laws. This becomes another piece of evidence that a democracy is unfit to rule an empire, as Cleon states at the beginning of this speech (3.37.1).
23. Hutchings 2008.
24. For a discussion of whether war is a cause of masculinity or an effect of it see Hutchings (2008) and her comprehensive review of scholarship on the topic. There is little agreement among scholars concerning this question.
25. Wohl 2002, 94–5.
26. Translation Hanink.
27. The only other explicit reference to the *phauloteroi* – Cleon's target audience – appears in the Corcyra episode. According to Thucydides, the *phauloteroi* were 'apprehensive of their own deficiencies' and distrusted the *suneton* of their adversaries. These men had bold (*tolmeros*) recourse to action because they feared that the clever would plot against them first, and so they fared better in war (3.83.3).
28. For a discussion of Cleon's 'manly anger' see Balot 2014, 120–3.
29. For a discussion of the ways Cleon set both the tone and agenda of Diodotus' speech see Orwin 1997, 142–62.
30. Ober 2001a, 94–104.
31. Translation Hanink.
32. For a discussion of Pericles' unorthodox war strategy see Balot 2014, 115–17.
33. Although identity politics has traditionally been associated with marginalised communities, scholars have increasingly noted the prevalence of identity politics among white, heterosexual, cisgendered men. See Walters 2017, 473–88.
34. Demetriou 2001.
35. Debnar 2000, 166.
36. These are, in fact, just a few of the central tenets of political realism. For a more thorough treatment of ancient and modern realism see Crane 1998, 61–71. For a discussion of some of the difficulties of reading Thucydides' history as a realist text see Crane 1998 and Ober 2001b.
37. Translation Hanink.
38. Translation Hanink.
39. According to Thucydides' Pericles (2.37.3), harmony was preserved through laws and shame which their subsequent violation stirs: 'Though we conduct our private lives without offense, we have fear to thank for the fact that we are law-abiding. Fear is what drives us to obey our leaders and our laws – fear especially of the laws that exist to protect victims and of those which, though unwritten, are known to bring disgrace if broken' (trans. Hanink). Fisher (1992, 394–5) notes that Thucydides praised Pericles in his eulogy (2.65) for checking 'the untimely

rush into aggressive or imperialist acts through overconfidence', but that this praise is limited to the perspective of the powerful; Athens' enemies might think otherwise.

40. For a discussion of Athens as the freest of all free states see Raaflaub 2004, 166–92.

41. Cairns (1993, 2) defines *aidōs* as 'an inhibitory emotion based on sensitivity to the protectiveness of one's image'. In other words, to feel *aidōs* is 'to picture oneself losing honour, while to show respect is to recognize the honour of another' (13). Thucydides' Spartans claim at 1.84.3, 'we are warlike because self-control contains honor (*aidōs*) as a chief constituent, and honor bravery (*aiskunē*)' (translation Strassler). Plato (*Charmides* 160e) notes that modesty or *sophrosyne* makes a man feel *aiskhunē* and that *sophrosyne* is *aidōs*.

42. Translation Hanink.

43. Translation Hanink.

44. Tickner 1992 and Hooper 2001, 96.

45. Lebow 2001, 547–60 and Zumbrunnen 2015, 297–8. While historically scholars have tended to see constructivism and realism at odds with one another, some, such as Zumbrunnen, drawing upon Nietzsche, view power relations not as 'determinative realism, but a kind of realist-constructivism' in which individuals both pursue interest and, in doing so, construct the character of the city.

46. Crane 1998, 8–9.

47. Morley 2018, 83–4 and 100–7, and Morley 2019.

48. Winkler 1990b, 17.

49. Brooks 2017. For a discussion of the ways Brooks' privilege shapes his mediocre analysis, to which academics must respond by virtue of his status as a 'public intellectual', see Cottom 2018, 199–223.

CHAPTER 4

Manliness as Motive for Action: A Discussion of (Toxic) Masculinity in the *Antigone* and the *Lysistrata*

Davide Morassi

In this chapter, I will discuss how masculinity was represented in two exam-ples of Attic theatre from the second half of the fifth century: Sophocles' *Antigone* and Aristophanes' *Lysistrata*.* I highlight how the ideal of masculin-ity shaped not only the self-representation of Athenian (and Greek) men, but was also recognised as a reason for behaviours which were excessive and thus frowned on – in other words, features of masculinity which today we would define as 'toxic'.[1]

First, a brief summary of how Athenians conceptualised manliness and ideal masculinity. As Bassi points out, the spread of elite cultural values and virtues to a greater diversity of people had a profound influence on Greek culture(s).[2] This is also true for masculinity. The traditional aristocratic *ethos* and values, as presented in Homer, could still be recognised in many aspects of the Classical Athenian ideal masculinity: independence, courage, honour.[3] However, the harshness of some behaviours associated with these values was in many cases toned down to a more urbane fashion.[4] There was less emphasis on physical prowess;[5] *sophrosyne* – temperance – and self-mastery became more prominent, and citizens were expected to comply with the rules and laws of the city.[6]

Men were expected to adhere to the social expectations of their role and char-acteristics. The notion of *aidōs*, the sense of shame which pushed men to act according to the paradigm so as not to lose their honour, well encapsulates the social pressures placed on Athenian men.[7] Being perceived as an *anēr agathos* – a 'good' man, but also a 'real' man – was high praise, used to exalt the war dead[8] but also to motivate men, especially before a fight.[9]

Not only was one's personal honour at stake, but also one's identity as a man.[10] Xenophon makes a distinction in the philosophical dialogue *Hiero* between *andres* and *anthropoi*.[11] While the former adhere to the ideal of mascu-linity, pursuing a public role and personal honour, the *anthropos* lives a simpler, unambitious and almost animal-like life.[12] *Anthropos* was a rather generic term, but it was often associated with barbarians, slaves or women, and thus human beings who were believed to lack the important characteristics that defined the Greek man.[13] In particular, the lack of self-control, the passivity and the servility that marked these categories are relevant. It is important to remember that, from a legal point of view, the Athenian woman was treated as a minor. The *kurios*, the oldest man and head of the household, had absolute power over women and slaves, while he himself had no master.[14]

To return to unmanly men, a similar distinction also emerges in other definitions of non-hegemonic males. A *malakos* – 'soft', also meaning effeminate – allegedly lacked the self-control necessary to exercise manly virtues, being overindulgent, weak and cowardly.[15] This stereotypical characterisation was even stronger for the *kinaidos*, a term which scholars have often interpreted as a man who takes a passive role in sex.[16] The lack of self-mastery, and thus independence, and the passive role were frequently associated with the feminine sphere.[17] The roasting of the poet Agathon in Aristophanes' *Thesmophoriazusae* is an excellent example, although likely exaggerated, of the negative characterisation of 'unmanly' men. Aristophanes sketches the poet Agathon as being dressed as a woman, and having feminine features: white skin, delicacy, no body hair, and a woman's voice.[18] The mockery of Agathon gives us a good idea of what it meant not to adhere to the ideal of manliness in fifth-century Athens.[19]

Agathon's characterisation is not surprising. As with the modern formulation, a link existed between the Athenian definition of masculinity and how women were perceived.[20] A polarity existed in which men and women and their respective characteristics were seen as opposites.[21] Thus, in affirming that men had to be courageous, involved in public life, and dominant,[22] the implication was that women were expected to be timid, stay at home and submit to male authority.[23] Much like with their male counterparts, certain characteristics were associated with these roles, the most notable of which were a lack of self-restraint[24] and a lack of courage.[25]

A man who did not comply with the standards of hegemonic masculinity risked being associated with the feminine and its corresponding characteristics, thus negating all his manly virtues. A passage from Herodotus exemplifies this way of thinking. Telines, the ancestor of the tyrant Gelon, displayed uncommon courage in bringing back the exiles to the Sicilian city of Gela. Fearless, he led the group of exiles without any other protection than a religious emblem.[26] Herodotus does not hide his surprise that an individual with a reputation for being effeminate (θηλυδρίης τε καὶ μαλακώτερος, literally 'effeminate and very soft') could perform such courageous deeds.[27] In short, there was the expectation that a 'feminine' man shared the alleged weaknesses of women.[28]

With this framework in mind, we can now start the analysis of toxic masculinity in the chosen texts. The plot of Sophocles' *Antigone* is well known. Creon – new ruler of Thebes – promulgated a law that forbade giving funerary rites to the prince Polyneices, who had attacked his own city. When Creon learned of Antigone's subsequent disobedience, his focus shifted towards the opposition of the sexes:[29]

This girl was already well versed in insolence when she transgressed the laws which had been laid down; and, when she had so acted, here was further insolence, to boast of these things and exult at having done them. Now I swear that she is the man and I am not, if she is to prevail in this and go unpunished. (Trans. Brown)

αὕτη δ᾽ ὑβρίζειν μὲν τότ᾽ ἐξηπίστατο,
νόμους ὑπερβαίνουσα τοὺς προκειμένους·
ὕβρις δ᾽, ἐπεὶ δέδρακεν, ἥδε δευτέρα,
τούτοις ἐπαυχεῖν καὶ δεδρακυῖαν γελᾶν.
ἦ νῦν ἐγὼ μὲν οὐκ ἀνήρ, αὕτη δ᾽ ἀνήρ,
εἰ ταῦτ᾽ ἀνατὶ τῇδε κείσεται κράτη.[30]

Certainly, Creon is presented as a tyrant who rules through fear,[31] and the attendant scholarship has noted his concern for maintaining power through the persecution of Antigone.[32] However, Sophocles depicts Creon as equally concerned with his manliness. If his actions aimed only at protecting his autocratic power, Antigone's gender would not be so central to his speech. Pomeroy suggests that gender roles were a secondary theme in many plays, and she is right;[33] however, Sophocles stresses this theme in his *Antigone*.[34] Indeed, while Creon justifies his condemnation of Antigone with rational arguments (that she is breaking the law), he reads Antigone's boldness as a challenge to his masculinity,[35] a theme that emerges time after time in his speeches.[36] Ronnet recognises the stress placed on Creon's masculinity as a sign of his authoritarian ruling.[37] Pomeroy frames Creon's stance within the patriarchal mindset, arguing that equal power could not be shared with women because of the fear of being repressed in return.[38] Similarly, Fox argues that bold and courageous women were regarded as disruptive in the face of social order.[39] Antigone's defiance threatens the patriarchal social order, and Creon reacts to keep the balance; he was Antigone's *kurios*, and her legitimate ruler.[40] Creon feels challenged in his role as a male, and thus in his masculinity more generally.[41]

As Butler remarks in her analysis of the *Antigone*, manliness was not shareable.[42] The same concept emerges in different contexts too. Aeschylus represents Clytemnestra in his plays through a related series of oxymoronic juxtapositions.[43] While she generally presents herself as a woman,[44] she also exhibits power and control that was considered 'manly' by the other characters.[45] As the co-conspirator and lover of such a manly woman, Aegisthus is presented as weak, unassertive and incapable of attaining his revenge like a man:[46] indeed,

Aegisthus is explicitly compared to a woman.[47] In short, when the women are men, the men have to be women, and thus become weak, impotent and incapable of imposing themselves on their female counterparts.[48]

To return to the *Antigone*, Creon's masculinity is threatened by Antigone's defiance, like any woman showing independence from men.[49] Undoubtedly he felt pressure to reassert his hegemonic position, but, interestingly, Creon's reaction to Antigone's defiance is rage and unreasonable cruelty, especially in his intention to persecute the innocent Ismene.

The influence of the ideal of masculinity on Creon's motivation emerges in his fight with his son Haemon, in the third episode of the play.

CREON: It seems he is fighting on the woman's side.
HAEMON: If you are a woman. It is you that I care for.
CREON: You utter villain, putting your father on trial!
HAEMON: Do I not see you at fault in what is right?
CREON: Am I at fault in upholding my authority?
HAEMON: You are not upholding it when you trample on the prerogatives of the gods.
CREON: You vile character, giving way to a woman!
HAEMON: Well, you will never find me giving way to what is shameful.
CREON: All your words, at least, are spoken for her sake.
HAEMON: And for your sake and mine and that of the gods below.
CREON: You woman's slave, do not cajole me!

(Trans. Brown)

Κρέων: ὅδ᾽, ὡς ἔοικε, τῇ γυναικὶ συμμαχεῖ.
Αἵμων: εἴπερ γυνὴ σύ. σοῦ γὰρ οὖν προκήδομαι.
Κρέων: ὦ παγκάκιστε, διὰ δίκης ἰὼν πατρί;
Αἵμων: οὐ γὰρ δίκαιά σ᾽ ἐξαμαρτάνονθ᾽ ὁρῶ.
Κρέων: ἁμαρτάνω γὰρ τὰς ἐμὰς ἀρχὰς σέβων;
Αἵμων: οὐ γὰρ σέβεις τιμάς γε τὰς θεῶν πατῶν.
Κρέων: ὦ μιαρὸν ἦθος καὶ γυναικὸς ὕστερον.
Αἵμων: οὔ τἂν ἕλοις ἥσσω γε τῶν αἰσχρῶν ἐμέ.
Κρέων; ὁ γοῦν λόγος σοι πᾶς ὑπὲρ κείνης ὅδε.
Αἵμων: καὶ σοῦ γε κἀμοῦ, καὶ θεῶν τῶν νερτέρων.
Κρέων: γυναικὸς ὢν δούλευμα μὴ κώτιλλέ με.[50]

Certainly, Creon demands absolute obedience from his son and the whole city and sees Haemon's objections as an open betrayal and challenge to his tyrannical power. However, it is significant that Creon lingers on Antigone's gender and Haemon's alleged, shameful subordinance to her: he mentions it three times in eleven verses. The idea that Creon's masculinity is somehow endangered is supported by Haemon's unconscious paralleling of Creon with a woman at verse 741, a statement that incenses Creon so much that he calls his son παγκάκιστε – utterly evil.

About thirty years after the *Antigone*, Aristophanes describes in the *Lysistrata* a similar relationship between men and the ideal of masculinity. After the Athenian women had taken over the Acropolis, the old Athenian men planned to burn the rebellious women alive, an action that Dorati recognises as irrational, if not foolish.[51] Their intention is similar to that of Creon: to reaffirm their power – and honour – through violence.

> WOMEN: Rest, ho! – What might this be? Wicked, wicked men, that's what! No man of any piety or decency would ever have been doing this [besieging the Acropolis].
> MEN: Here comes a thing we never expected to see: here's another swarm of women outside, coming to help the first lot!
> WOMEN: Why so deadly scared of us? You don't mean to say we seem a great multitude? And yet you haven't seen the ten-thousandth part of us so far!
> MEN: Phaedrias, are we going to let these women jabber so much? Shouldn't someone have broken our timber on their backs by now? (Trans. Sommerstein)

> Χορὸς Γυναικῶν: ἔασον ὦ. τουτὶ τί ἦν; ὦνδρες πόνῳ πόνηροι·
> οὐ γάρ ποτ' ἂν χρηστοί γ' ἔδρων οὐδ' εὐσεβεῖς τάδ' ἄνδρες.
> Χορὸς γερόντων: τουτὶ τὸ πρᾶγμ' ἡμῖν ἰδεῖν ἀπροσδόκητον ἥκει·
> ἑσμὸς γυναικῶν οὑτοσὶ θύρασιν αὖ βοηθεῖ.
> Χορὸς Γυναικῶν: τί βδύλλεθ' ἡμᾶς; οὔ τί που πολλαὶ δοκοῦμεν εἶναι;
> καὶ μὴν μέρος γ' ἡμῶν ὁρᾶτ' οὔπω τὸ μυριοστόν.
> Χορὸς γερόντων: ὦ Φαιδρία ταύτας λαλεῖν ἐάσομεν τοσαυτί;
> οὐ περικατᾶξαι τὸ ξύλον τύπτοντ' ἐχρῆν τιν' αὐταῖς;[52]

The women's mocking tone underlines the attention that Aristophanes gave to the battle of the sexes in this comedy. Women should be neither brave nor warlike, and thus should not be feared by 'real' men. The women shamed their male counterparts, who reacted with the threat of violence to shut the insolent woman up.[53] However, the women, acting 'manly', did not give up and humiliated the Old Men by soaking them.[54] Dorati recognised this humiliation and noted the detailed extinguishing of the fire as a metaphor for impotence and castration.[55]

Meanwhile, the Athenian *proboulos* exhibits a similar obnoxious, misogynistic attitude. When the Scythian archer – overwhelmed by the incoming, menacing women – backs off, the magistrate claims that it is not possible to endure such an offence from women.[56] The same theme emerges later on, when the Old Men undress and appeal to their physical manhood in the faces of the women who were taunting them:[57]

> Now are not these doings utterly outrageous? And I think they will grow to be even more so. This is something that must be resisted by every man with any balls!
> Let us take off our tunics; a man ought to smell like a man right from the start, he shouldn't be swathed up like a rissole.
> Now come on, you Whitefeet,
> We who went against Leipsydrium
> When we still were something,
> Now, now we must become you again and revitalise
> Our whole body and shake off this old skin of ours.
> If any of us lets these women get even the least purchase on us, there's no work to which they'll fail to set their assiduous hands. They'll even build warships, and try as well to attack us with them and ram us, like Artemisia. (Trans. Sommerstein)

> ταῦτ᾽ οὖν οὐχ ὕβρις τὰ πράγματ᾽ ἐστὶ
> πολλή; κἀπιδώσειν μοι δοκεῖ τὸ χρῆμα μᾶλλον.
> ἀλλ᾽ ἀμυντέον τὸ πρᾶγμ᾽ ὅστις γ᾽ ἐνόρχης ἔστ᾽ ἀνήρ.
> ἀλλὰ τὴν ἐξωμίδ᾽ ἐκδυώμεθ᾽, ὡς τὸν ἄνδρα δεῖ
> ἀνδρὸς ὄζειν εὐθύς, ἀλλ᾽ οὐκ ἐντεθριῶσθαι πρέπει.
> ἀλλ᾽ ἄγετε λευκόποδες, οἵπερ ἐπὶ Λειψύδριον ἤλθομεν ὅτ᾽ ἦμεν ἔτι,
> νῦν δεῖ νῦν ἀνηβῆσαι πάλιν κἀναπτερῶσαι
> πᾶν τὸ σῶμα κἀποσείσασθαι τὸ γῆρας τόδε.
> εἰ γὰρ ἐνδώσει τις ἡμῶν ταῖσδε κἂν σμικρὰν λαβήν,
> οὐδὲν ἐλλείψουσιν αὗται λιπαροῦς χειρουργίας,
> ἀλλὰ καὶ ναῦς τεκτανοῦνται, κἀπιχειρήσουσ᾽ ἔτι
> ναυμαχεῖν καὶ πλεῖν ἐφ᾽ ἡμᾶς ὥσπε, Ἀρτεμισία.[58]

Here, the Old Athenians underline their masculinity with a parody of macho attitude. Not only do they take their clothes off to mark themselves out as athletes or heroes,[59] but they also refer to their sexual prowess, a clear nod to their masculinity. This association was even more evident on the stage: as Sommerstein underlines, without clothing the Old Men exposed the fake phallus worn by all comic performers.[60] The memory of the glorious deeds of the past pushes them even further.[61] The ancestors' example, and their masculinity, is a standard to match. Reaffirming their belonging to this glorious and manly stock, the Old Men attempt to enhance their manliness by association. This ridiculous display could be interpreted as an attempt to regain lost masculinity and to reaffirm an old-fashioned paradigm, one based on physical prowess and military glory.[62] The stress on their hairiness – which they associate with Myron and Phormio, two successful Athenian military leaders – again emphasises their male attributes, using the glorious past of the city to strengthen their claim.[63]

The pattern that emerges from the men in the *Lysistrata* parallels that of the *Antigone*. Once a man felt threatened by the boldness of a woman, or her refusal to submit, he felt castrated. In order to re-establish his 'natural' superiority over the woman, the man would, on the one hand, threaten or resort to violence, while on the other, his efforts would often drive him to take rash and foolish actions. In other words, the ideal of hegemonic masculinity has what we would define as toxic aspects.

How representative these plays are of men and masculinity of the second half of the fifth century is difficult to assess. Drama and comedy present situations and behaviours that are both exaggerated and extraordinary.[64] However, the recurrence of similar behavioural patterns in very different contexts and genres suggests that Sophocles and Aristophanes were drawing on their experience as Athenian men. Furthermore, considering the differences in plot, context and tone, it would be difficult to explain the presence of the same pattern of behaviour without acknowledging a reference to something that the audience knew and could relate to.

Interestingly, a passage of Herodotus supports this assumption. Artemisia was a Carian queen who fought for Xerxes against the Greeks in the Second Persian War (480–479 BCE). Herodotus reported that the Athenians felt outraged that a woman had dared to fight against them:

> If he [Ameinias] had realised that Artemisia was on board, he would not have stopped until he had either captured her or been captured himself, not just because a reward of ten thousand drachmas had been offered for capturing her alive, since the Athenians were furious that a woman was attacking their city. (Trans. Waterfield)

> εἰ μέν νυν ἔμαθε ὅτι ἐν ταύτῃ πλέοι Ἀρτεμισίη, οὐκ ἂν ἐπαύσατο πρότερον ἢ εἷλέ μιν ἢ καὶ αὐτὸς ἥλω. τοῖσι γὰρ Ἀθηναίων τριηράρχοισι παρεκεκέλευστο, πρὸς δὲ καὶ ἄεθλον ἔκειτο μύριαι δραχμαί, ὃς ἄν μιν ζωὴν ἕλῃ· δεινὸν γάρ τι ἐποιεῦντο γυναῖκα ἐπὶ τὰς Ἀθήνας στρατεύεσθαι.[65]

Herodotus emphasises Artemisia's femaleness, and Harrel stresses how the prowess of the Carian queen underlined the alleged effeminacy and weakness of the Persians.[66] However, the contempt the Athenians felt towards her, which Herodotus justified on the grounds of her sex, appears emblematic. We thus see masculinity and its negation as motives also in historical contexts. Being challenged by a woman was both diminishing and insulting and was reason enough to spend a ridiculous sum of ten thousand drachmae to 'wash away' the offence.

However, could these examples be recognised as 'toxic masculinity'? Certainly, many of the scenarios given by Kupers as examples of toxic masculinity are recognisable in the passages analysed above. When the masculinity of the agents was jeopardised, the first reaction was to threaten or to resort to violence in order to reinstate a position of superiority and honour. We can recognise this as an all-out request for respect, for the recognition of the social role assigned to the male (controlling women) and as the recognition of being inherently male (in other words, not being emasculated); the same motivation individuated by Kupers. The consequences of these behaviours were negative for society as well as for the agents. The marginalisation of non-canonical masculinities and women is the most obvious, but it should be stressed how, by reaffirming their masculinity, Creon and the Old Athenians destabilise and damage their city in a more immediate sense.

To what extent does this reading superimpose anachronistic categories onto Athenian culture? According to our standards, Athenian masculinity could be recognised as toxic, and was often the cause of the toxic behaviour in both drama and historical writing. Sophocles and Aristophanes recognised the need to adhere to the standards of masculinity as a valid motive for action, yet one that caused overly violent behaviours, potentially endangering the *polis* itself. Creon – as with many of Sophocles' characters who push the individualistic aspects of traditional values too far[67] – destroys his own family and his fortune, while the men in the *Lysistrata* are blatantly ridiculed. However, a substantial and coherent critique of the toxic aspects of masculinity is absent.[68] Indeed, the authors appear to focus their criticism on the lack of measure – *sophrosyne* – of the characters. Interestingly, *sophrosyne* was a crucial element of the Athenian ideal of masculinity too.[69] Consequently, in their anxiety to adhere to the canon of masculinity, these fictional characters focus on the wrong – or as we would say, toxic – aspects of masculinity.

Perhaps more importantly, the core element of Kupers' definition does not appear in the ancient sources; that is, 'masculinity' *per se* was not recognised as 'disruptive of society'.[70] The anxiety about sticking to the standard of masculinity might have brought some men to behave recklessly, but there is no evidence that the idealisation of masculinity was open to discussion for this reason. Hegemonic masculinity was seen as the very basis of society; women who stood up for themselves were regarded as an anomaly, a world of opposites.[71]

In conclusion, the concept of toxic masculinity does not seem to completely fit the texts under examination and, more indirectly, Athens of the latter half of the fifth century BCE. While masculinity is represented as a valid motive for action, and the prejudices involved in its definition could have brought about behaviours that we would define as toxic, the ancient writers did not appear to find this behavioural pattern a problem of gender, but rather a personal one. It therefore does not appear possible to apply this viewpoint to Classical Athens, even if modern sensibility would read this pattern in such terms. Only the lost voices of women and marginalised men would have provided the necessary evidence for defining the 'toxic' efforts to defend the reputation of males with methodological soundness. But, alas, this perspective has seldom reached us.[72]

NOTES

* This paper would not have been possible without Dr Andrea De Marinis, whose feedback helped me to frame the modern and ancient concepts of masculinity. My thanks go to Jasmine Doris for her unfaltering support and to the editors, Drs McMaster and Racette-Campbell, for making this project a reality. Any mistakes are obviously my own.

1. See the definition in Kupers 2005 and its discussion in the Introduction.
2. Bassi 1999, 22.
3. Foley 1981, 146; Fisher 1998, 68–97; Roisman 2005, 110; Holmes 2012, 112. Berg (2011, esp. 109–10) stresses the importance of age in the definition of masculinity. There was indeed a stark difference between the approved behaviours and virtues of different age groups. Hubbard (2011, 189, 191) warns against the generalisation of 'Mediterranean masculinity', a set of stereotypical traits associated with ancient and modern cultures of the Mediterranean basin. However, it is undeniable that many of these traits (e.g. honour, revenge, shame) are well-attested in our sources.
4. Lawrence 2005, 18–33 and Roisman 2005, 52–63.
5. Bassi 2003, 33–6, 44–6.
6. Bassi 1999, 22; Rademaker 2003, 119; Berg 2011, 108–9; Foxhall 2013, 84. Roisman (2005, 72–5) suggests that two conflicting paradigms existed in Classical Athens. *Sophrosyne* was the mark of the elites, at least following Plato's biased statements (*Resp.* 8.560d–e), while the average Athenian appreciated the importance of violence and occasional excesses.
7. Cairns 1993, 1–4, 43–51, 180; Lawrence 2005, 28; Roisman 2005, 64; Berg 2011, 110. On social pressure, see Roisman 2003, 136–40.
8. E.g. Aeschin. 3.152; Hyp. 6.8.; Roisman 2003, 129; and Roisman 2005, 48, 67–71.
9. E.g. Thuc. 4.95, Xen. *Hell.* 1.1.27.
10. Bassi 2003, 40–9 and Holmes 2012, 120–1.
11. Xen. *Hier.* 7.3.
12. Newell 1983, 889–92; Rood 2004, 310–11; Roisman 2005, 64; Holmes 2012, 111.
13. Cf. Berg 2011, 103–4.
14. Ar. *Pol.* 1259b–1260a; *Eth. Eud.* 1238b, 1241b–1242a; Foley 1981, 129–30; Foxhall 2013, 29–30.

15. Roisman 2005, 16, 144, 153–4, 188–9, and Odgen 2014, 39–40.
16. Traditionally, scholarship acknowledges that the Athenians perceived a passive role in sex as unbecoming for a free man. Dover 1978, 74–6, 103–5; MacDowell 1995, 254–5; Rademaker 2003, 123. This reading, which was first introduced by Dover, has been criticised for being oversimplistic and paying little attention to important variables like age, class and gender. Fox 1998, 6–22; Murray 2000, 34–43, 99–111; Davidson 2001, 3–51; Hubbard 2011, 190–1, 202–3; Foxhall 2013, 83–5; Ogden 2014, 38.
17. Dover 1978, 17, 75, 149; Loraux 1993, 34; Cartledge 1998, 60–2; Fox 1998, 7–13; Roisman 2005, 116, 144; Penrose 2006, 38; Foxhall 2013, 83.
18. Aristoph. *Thesm.* 189–93. Cf. Aeschin. 2.26. See Loraux (1995, 98) on white skin, without scars, as a female characteristic; MacDowell (1995, 255) and Austin and Olson (2014, 119) for the other attributes.
19. Aristoph. *Thesm.* 190–201, 206–7.
20. Harrel 2003, 80 and Penrose 2006, 12. Holmes (2012, 111) warns about oversimplifying a complex phenomenon into two categories. She is right to emphasise that these categories could be blurry, and that *andreia* could be associated with women too, but the Greeks did recognise some biological differences between men and women. See Foxhall 2013, 68–89, esp. 68–73.
21. Pomeroy 1975, 78; Gould 1980, 56; Loraux 1995, 233–4; Stafford 1998, 53.
22. McClure 1999, 21; Rademaker 2003, 119.
23. Thuc. 2.45; Soph. *Ant.* 61–8, *Elec.* 997–8. Foley 1981, 132; McClure 1999, 21; Georgoudi 2015, 202.
24. E.g. Eur. *Med.* 315–23, 569–75; Aristoph. *Lys.* 124–42, 194–238, 707–61; Ar. *Pol.* 1.1252a. Walcot 1984, 40; Konstan 1993, 435; Loraux 1993, 154–5; Berg 2011, 103; Holmes 2012, 98–9.
25. Xen. *Oec.* 7.23–5; *Symp.* 2.9; Ar. *Pol.* 1260a. See Mattioli 1984, 15–17. Cf. Georgoudi (2015, 203) on the difference between male and female *andreia*.
26. Hdt. 7.153.2–3.
27. Hdt. 7.153.4. As Holmes (2012, 115–17) correctly points out, some physical characteristics were recognised as either masculine or feminine, despite being found in both men and women.
28. It is perhaps no surprise then that being called a woman was used as an insult in Homer (e.g. Hom. *Il.* 8.163–4) and by the Persians (Hdt. 8.88.4; 9.20).
29. Pomeroy 1975, 99 and Chrystal 2017, 34.
30. Soph. *Ant.* 480–5.
31. Ronnet 1969, 89; Bennet and Tyrrell 1990, 442, 456; Des Bouvrie 1990, 174, 177; Sommerstein 2017, 280, 285.
32. On Creon as a tyrant, see Sommerstein 2017, 280–3.
33. Pomeroy 1975, 97–8, 102.
34. Pomeroy (1975, 100) notes the unusual number of references to Antigone as a male. See also Holt 1999, 677.
35. Segal 1981, 169, 183. Kierstead (2017, 291, 294–8) argues that Creon represented the dark side of rationalism, a mechanical and logical way to exercise power that does not take into account the religious and ethical norms, nor the

will of people, thus becoming unreasonable. Nonetheless, the scholar completely undervalues the intrasexual dynamic, so evident and central in the text.

36. Soph. *Ant.* 524–5, 541–2, 593–4, 752–61.
37. Ronnet 1969, 89.
38. Pomeroy 1975, 99.
39. Fox 2001, 16–18.
40. Holland 2017, 6.
41. Segal 1981, 183; Griffith 1999, 480–3. Cairns (2016, 42–3) underlines how the authority of Creon both as ruler and as a male was challenged.
42. Butler 2000, 9–10. *Contra* Lefkowitz (1983, 51) argues that Creon uses the argument of Antigone's gender as a justification for his arbitrary decisions, unsupported by others. Nevertheless, Creon needs no justification: Antigone broke the law.
43. McClure 1999, 73, 75, 77–9.
44. E.g. Aesch. *Agam.* 1401. McClure (1999, 75) argues that Clytemnestra uses gender to strengthen her claims, thus appearing more masculine when she wants to appear reliable, and more feminine when asking for sympathy.
45. Aesch. *Agam.* 10–11. Foley 1981, 151; Mattioli 1984, 88–90; McClure 1999, 74, 97–8. Cf. Vernant (1965, 108), who comments about the representation of Clytemnestra in Sophocles' *Electra*, while the same statements also seem appropriate for Aeschylus' version.
46. Cairns 1993, 181; Pomeroy (1975, 94) remarks how the role of Aegisthus in the version of the myth in the *Odyssey* (3.255–76) is more proactive, underlining the shift in tragedy. Fisher (1998, 78–80, 82) stresses how revenge was still a fundamental aspect of masculinity, even in a society of law.
47. Aeschyl. *Ag.* 1625, *Choe.* 304; Eur. *Elec.* 947–85. Cf. Mattioli 1984, 13–14; and Zeitlin 1996, 92.
48. Loraux 1995, 233; Cartledge 1998, 57; Harrel 2003, 81–6; Chrystal 2017, 44.
49. On how powerful women were seen as castrating men, see most recently Penrose 2006, 36 and Butler 2009, 6, 8–9. Griffith (1999, 484–5) states that Creon's desire to regain power over Antigone was likely sympathised with by the Athenian audience.
50. Soph. *Ant.* 740–56. Please note that Brown's edition prints vv. 756–7 between 749 and 750.
51. Aristoph. *Lys.* 266–71. Dorati 1999, 82–3.
52. Aristoph. *Lys.* 351–8.
53. Dorati (1999, 83) suggests that, bearing a cleansing fire, the Old Men are trying to fulfil the role of males, protecting the city from disruptive forces. Konstan (1993, 436–7) instead recognises the anxiety of men over women's independence.
54. Aristoph. *Lys.* 381–6.
55. Dorati 1999, 84.
56. Aristoph. *Lys.* 449–52. Cf. vv. 437–8, 476–83. Sommerstein (1990) recognises a 'near-quotation' of Soph. *Ant.* 678.
57. Aristoph. *Lys.* 558–82. Chrystal 2017, 36.
58. Aristoph. *Lys.* 659–76.

59. Bassi (2003, 33–6, 44–6) underlines how the physical attributes of courage and masculinity were marked considerably more in the epics than in fifth-century literature, where *andreia* indicates more the absence of traditional manliness. If Bassi is right, the Old Men are putting on an outdated, traditional display of masculinity here.

60. Sommerstein 1990, 662.

61. Cf. Aristoph. *Lys.* 273–6. On the reference to past glory, see Perusino 1999, 71–2 and Bassi 2003, 48. MacDowell (1995, 234) reads in these references not only the memory of past glory, but also a joke, putting on the same plan the menace of the Spartans and the Persians with mere women.

62. Lysistrata is, indeed, defined as 'the manliest woman' (Aristoph. *Lys.* 1108). Cf. MacDowell 1995, 247. On the physicality of masculinity in the epics, and its normative function, see Bassi 2003, 33–4.

63. Aristoph. *Lys.* 801. See Somerstein, *Aristophanes. Lysistrata, ad. loc.*; Bassi 2003, 33–4, 36. The observations of McClure (1999, 219–20) on the *Thesmophoriazousae* could be applied to this passage of the *Lysistrata*.

64. E.g. Foley 1981, 135.

65. Hdt. 8.93.2.

66. Harrel (2003, 82–6) recognises the ambiguity of Artemisia's ethnicity as a crucial element of her *andreia*. She could be this way because Persians were not 'true men'. The same pattern is also visible in the myth of the Amazons. Bowie (2007, *ad* 8.88) remarks that Herodotus did not spend much energy in pushing the stereotype of the effeminacy of the Persians. This reading is quite controversial, considering the space given to Artemisia in book 8. As Xerxes epitomises (Hdt. 8.88.3), an ἀνδρεῖα woman made the men around her womanly.

67. Lawrence 2005, 22–7, 30; Roisman 2005, 45, 52–5, 58–60, 62–3, 72, 79.

68. Zeitlin 1996, 364. Fox (2001, 17) underlines the positive stereotypes associated with women that emerge in these plays. Cf. Foxhall 2013, 84–5, on how violence against women was substantially accepted.

69. Roisman 2003, 127; Berg 2011, 110; and Foxhall 2013, 85.

70. Kupers 2005, 716–17.

71. Graf 1984, 250–4. *Contra* Georgoudi 2015, 207–10. Cf. Konstan (1993, 434) on the temporal limits of Lysistrata's 'revolt'.

72. On bias in the ancient sources, see e.g. MacDowell 1995, 247; and Zeitlin 1996, 347.

CHAPTER 5

Toxic Masculinity as a Lens for Middle Byzantium: The Case of Nikephoros II Phokas

Mark Masterson

INTRODUCTION

I believe that when we do history, we write from where we currently sit whether we want to or not. Necessarily, then, we find ourselves executing a careful dance to show good enough faith with the past and to ask questions of it that may be anachronistic to a degree but which matter in the present moment. Questions asked about how people in the past lived and made sense of their milieux are framed by our present hopes and fears for the future.[1] And so, I have come to write on medieval Byzantium and this term 'toxic masculinity'. And I write with hope for the future and anxiety for it, for while the Byzantine evidence shows a partially favourable picture of male homosociality, there is also what we can with justice call toxic masculinity lodged in the durable structures of the medieval empire, structures which have current analogues. Toxic masculinity addresses two different but connected areas. It designates harm to men themselves when they try to live up to and embody the ideals of masculinity. It also speaks of how the behaviour of men harms others. In other words, it points to how a man harms himself in his pursuit of manhood and how his practices of masculinity harm others too.

The goal of this chapter is twofold. In the first place, I mean to serve the interests of history and elucidate the Byzantine past. I consider the manifold discourse around the tenth-century emperor Nikephoros II Phokas, who, from the moment of his assassination, inspired evaluations that ran at cross purposes.[2] In the second place, I am interested in how our notion of toxic masculinity sheds light on dynamics in both the life of Nikephoros and the Byzantine perspectives on him. In his life, a predatory masculinity in the arena of war coexisted with a strong impulse towards religious asceticism pursued in a single-sex setting, and toxicities obvious and not so obvious were present in both. Conflict between the modes of behaviour appropriate to these discrete arenas, one secular and the other religious, helped create the conditions that led to Nikephoros' assassination: hence a toxicity at the personal level for the man himself. Furthermore, analysis reveals the presence of homosociality in these two milieux, military and ascetic, that held men together and was emotionally fulfilling, while at the same time creating bonds that could be and were dangerous to others. In terms of evaluations of Nikephoros after his death, toxic masculinity led to apparently ineluctable misogynistic perspectives in the historical accounts, that is, the woman is always at fault. On the basis of little evidence and amid differing perspectives on Nikephoros as emperor, tenth- to twelfth-century historians and one poet were certain that Empress Theophano was mostly to blame for the assassination of Nikephoros. One more thing: it is certainly the case that an emperor is not a typical man, but the discourse around him addresses three areas – asceticism, the army and marriage – that engage Byzantine men and their masculinity. Considering what was said about Nikephoros in these matters therefore illuminates broader societal expectations. I should also add that not all the things I identify as toxic would have been seen as such by the Byzantines. Harming the body in asceticism was regarded as positive for the soul and indulging in misogyny or raping captives after a battle were, respectively, normal gender relations and an unremarkable aspect of warfare. We make judgements to understand dynamics in the past as clearly as possible and should not merely reproduce contemporary Byzantine moral judgements on phenomena when we do history.

A brief sketch of the life and career of Nikephoros is in order.[3] Nikephoros II Phokas was born probably in 912 into a notable Anatolian family, the Phokades. The Phokas family produced important military leaders, among whom was Nikephoros.[4] He was a wildly successful general and the author of a military handbook, the *Praecepta militaria*. He oversaw wars that led to the Byzantine reconquest of Crete, Cilicia and Cyprus. He became emperor in 963 when the previous emperor, Romanos II, died leaving two sons and a daughter, all under the age of six.[5] Relying on his considerable military success, Nikephoros had himself acclaimed emperor. He pledged to honour the positions of Romanos' sons, who had been made emperors at a very young age, and married Romanos' widow, Theophano.

At the same time, this military man, who possessed and acted on secular ambitions, was drawn to asceticism and wanted to withdraw from the world. He had a close friendship with Athanasios of Athos, who was one of the founding figures of the Mount Athos monastery complex; this monastery was founded on complete exclusion of nearly all that is female, down to the farm animals.[6] Two surviving *vitae* of Athanasios tell us that Nikephoros wanted to leave the world and practise monastic devotion alone, or almost alone with Athanasios. An important feature of his demeanour as emperor, therefore, was that he was an aspiring ascetic.

Nikephoros was emperor until December of 969. Towards the end of his reign, he lost favour with the people because of controversial ecclesiastical legislation and unpopular initiatives in monetary policy and taxation. His own nephew, the man who succeeded him on the imperial throne, John Tzimiskes, murdered him as he slept, semi-ascetic-style,[7] on the floor of his chambers in the palace. Nearly all accounts also implicate Empress Theophano in the assassination, saying that she was romantically involved with Tzmiskes and even helped the conspirators enter the palace. It is not clear, however, what exactly happened. But Theophano, in any case, has endured heavy damage to her reputation.[8] Nearly all the sources,[9] whether they are well disposed to Nikephoros or critical of him, see her and her marriage with Nikephoros in a negative light.

In sum, Nikephoros II Phokas was far from being an incompetent emperor and had considerable successes. The opening of his reign was remarkable for the general positive feelings of the populace.[10] But he was not a member of the Macedonian dynasty, which, in its fifth generation, had a great deal of clout and after him would continue for nearly another century. This meant that he was in substance a vulnerable caretaker whom others regarded with suspicion as to his ultimate ambitions: would he want to end the dynasty and take the throne for himself? Furthermore, he was a man of contrasts. Not only was he drawn to things of the world but also to ascetic withdrawal from it. His posthumous reputation shows contrary evaluations of him, with his press sometimes critical and sometimes good, or even very good, as there survives an *akolouthia*[11] for Nikephoros that shows that some anticipated he might be made a saint. In the context of an investigation into toxic masculinity in history, the contrasts both in aspects of his life and in tenth- to twelfth-century evaluations of him are illuminating material to work with.

First up, then, is Nikephoros' ambition to become an ascetic, which provides an opportunity to think about masculinity in asceticism. In ascetism, something important to the Byzantines, we can see toxicity in general and to Nikephoros himself, even if the Byzantines would not have recognised it.

AN ASCETIC

Nikephoros appears in two *vitae*, called *A* and *B*, that celebrate Athanasios of Athos.[12] *Vita A* appears to be from the first decade of the eleventh century, while *Vita B*, which mostly depends on *Vita A*, comes from later in the eleventh or early twelfth century.[13] The *vitae* together offer a portrait of Nikephoros' ascetic ambitions, the social milieu of the ascetics, and Nikephoros' interactions with this milieu.[14] My practice is to read them together as they mostly agree and because I am interested in the depiction of Nikephoros across a number of works and genres.

We learn from the *vitae* that Nikephoros was a religious man. He adored prayer and homilies in the company of Athanasios,[15] and was interested in withdrawing from the world. Nikephoros stated his wish to withdraw to Athanasios: 'I desire, Father, to find peace away from the storm of the world and I have decided to withdraw from all the things of the world and to serve God.'[16] His relationship with Athanasios was affectionate and they would spend time alone together.[17] At one point, Nikephoros speaks of his ambitions for the future that include an enduring closeness between Athanasios, various other brothers, and himself:

> The time has come, which I [Nikephoros] have desired for a long time, for fleeing the world, and there is nothing in the way of this for us except that we construct a place for us to live in. And I beg of your holiness first to construct cells of tranquillity for us, and establish a church and fit it out for monastic communal living, so that I and you, with three other brothers may be alone in these cells of tranquillity, and together on Sundays we can come together at the *laura*[18], and share in the holy sacraments, and eat together with the brothers and the leader, and then go back.[19]

This desire of Nikephoros for a life of prayer with homosocial togetherness was not one-sided. Athanasios shared Nikephoros' hopes for the future and he was actively preparing for it, setting aside money for the place that the two of them one day would share.[20]

But Nikephoros' ambition to withdraw from the world as an ascetic conflicted with his desire to be a great general and emperor. As far as Athanasios was concerned, Nikephoros' military commands were best regarded as prelude to his real life in ascetic withdrawal, and he should not have taken the throne.[21] Both he and Nikephoros felt that Nikephoros embarrassed himself by his over-investment in things of this world. Seeing Athanasios after he became emperor, Nikephoros was both overjoyed to see his friend and quite affectionate with him, but also abashed by his own lofty rank:

> Perceiving his [*sc.* Athanasios'] approach, the emperor is riven by shame and joy: by joy on account of his great desire and great affection for him; by shame on account of the [imperial] purple which he had embraced instead of the blessed quiet life [of asceticism].[22]

> The emperor, having learned that he [*sc.* Athanasios] was approaching, was rejoicing because he desired to see him, but he was feeling ashamed because he was about to be seen by him in imperial regalia. Therefore he went to meet him not as emperor, but as one of the many, having taken his hand, and having led him away with a kiss to his own bedchamber, and having sat down with him alone, he said . . .[23]

What conclusions come from these scenes that show Nikephoros' ascetic ambitions and the conflicts they occasioned? First of all, the place of ascetic vocation is a homosocial space. Nikephoros wishes to pursue these ambitions with the approval of God in a single-sex milieu. It is also clear that there are emotional satisfactions to be had. Wishing for close proximity and physical demonstrations of regard, he desires to be with precisely this man to realise his religious goals. Furthermore, control of bodily appetites of all kinds had long been coded as masculine and opposed to both femininity and effeminacy. Saying no to the body is exercising manly control over the bodily appetites that are gendered feminine in relation to this ambition for control.[24]

The present investigation into toxic masculinity can also tease out downsides to these activities. First, asceticism is frequently a hyperbolic activity. While there are moderate versions of asceticism, the extreme versions, objectively unbalanced, are frequently lionised, for the models for this activity are the deadly travails of Christ and the martyrs.[25] Food and sex are moralised and the body is asked to do arguably toxic things in service to God. We read of such things in the *vitae* of Athanasios. For example, among the monks who made their way to Athos to place themselves under the direction of Athanasios were monks who wore heavy chains.[26] And they frequently were miserable men who lacked even the most rudimentary comforts.[27] *Vita B* (section 44) shows the feat of Nicholas the Cook, who, in imitation of Eupraxia, a saint in the *Thebaid* in the fifth century,[28] stood for forty-five days.[29]

Asceticism also conjures the spectre of misogyny, as it is dependent on the very old 'association of men with the mind and women with the body', an association correlative with other 'similar dichotomizations: mind/rationality/activity describing the male and body/irrationality/passivity describing the female'.[30] Failure at this godly masculinised somatic regime is a surrender to feminised excess and lack of control. Even more specific in the present instance is the fact that Athanasios was a, if not the, founding figure of the Mount Athos complex, which, as noted above, is famous for its exclusion of women and the female. But to return to Nikephoros and his asceticism, the expectations he had of being a man of ascetic piety arguably sabotaged his life when he was emperor: he disappointed Theophano sexually, and some sources report that this may have contributed to his death.[31]

To sum up, then, ascetic manhood could be sustaining because of the masculine fellowship to be found in monastic contexts, but it was also destructive to the body and capable of mobilising misogyny through the fact that it was to be a masculine activity and was predicated on the exclusion of women from male-only spaces. Asceticism also, it appears, might have contributed to Nikephoros' death.

A GENERAL

In this section we consider both Nikephoros the brilliant general of his armies and Byzantine military culture more generally. A prolegomenon about the situation in the south and south-east of the empire in the middle of the tenth century is necessary first.

The late 950s and 960s saw increasing weakness in Byzantium's enemies that enabled imperial expansion. An expedition in 961, led by Nikephoros himself, recovered Crete, which had been lost to the empire in the 820s. The years leading up to Nikephoros' reign also saw successful expansion into the south-east. Military engagements savaged Cilicia, a region lost to the Arabs in the early 700s, in preparation for its reincorporation into the empire by 965. The Cilician campaigns were in essence the destruction of a fortified frontier zone, or *thughur*, that had been a thorn in Byzantium's side for about 200 years.[32] In 961, after recovering Crete, Nikephoros campaigned in Cilicia and even sacked Aleppo deep in Syrian territory in the following year. This incursion hobbled the support from the Hamdanid ruler, Sayf ad-Daula, that the fortified cities in the Cilician *thughur* needed to withstand the Byzantines. Cilicia was now open to progressive annexation by the Byzantines, an annexation that concluded with the taking of Mopsuestia in July 965 and the fall of the strongest city of them all, Tarsos, in the following month. Cyprus was also reintegrated into the empire at this time.

In his *Historia*, which he probably wrote in the last decade of the 900s, Leo the Deacon makes a comment that gives us a look at Nikephoros as paramount military leader.[33] Leo imagines what Nikephoros' enraged thoughts were when he was not able to take Tarsos at some point in the early 960s (he eventually did so in 965, as noted above):

> He considered the matter an insult, a straight-up violation, and an indelible rebuke, if he, Nikephoros, being a Phokas, lately excelling among the generals, and in turn proclaimed *Domestikos of the Scholai*, if he had once destroyed myriads of cities, had burst them open, laid waste to them with fire, and if he had once *andrapodised* prosperous lands, had overcome warlike peoples in pitched battle, peoples not strong enough to meet face-to-face his strength and his unconquerable onslaught in arms.[34]

In this description of Nikephoros' frustrated anger, fuelled by *amour propre* based in lineage, offices and prior savage campaigning, is a term that I have left untranslated: to *andrapodise*. We would do well to pay attention to recent advances in the understanding of what it meant to *andrapodise* a population, of what *andrapodismos* was.[35] This is something toxic indeed.

Writing an important article in 2010, Kathy Gaca teases out the meaning of *andrapodising*, which shows up in historical sources from antiquity and Byzantine times.[36] She discovers that this verb and related noun, and various compounded forms,[37] speak to what happens to women, children and the elderly of captured populations, that is, those who don't know how to fight after their warriors have been defeated. In essence *andrapodising* is this: a disorganised group of civilians, some of whom have value on the slave market (girls and women of child-bearing age particularly) and others who do not (e.g., babies and the old), are brought to heel through selective shows of violence. For example, babies or old people are killed so that the soon-to-be merchandise, properly cowed, will be pliable.[38] Gaca also notes that rape can be part of this.[39] To *andrapodise*, then, is euphemistic of predatory and objectifying practices of captive management,[40] practices which can with justice be called toxic. And, as seen above, Leo the Deacon attributes accomplished oversight of it to Nikephoros: '. . . if he had once *andrapodised* prosperous lands . . . '[41]

This dark side to masculinity in a military context is balanced by homosociality, a negative thing finding its counterpoint in masculine togetherness, as it did in the previous section of this chapter on the ascetic context. We see it in Nikephoros' own *Praecepta militaria*, where he addresses various issues related to leading armies.[42] An important component of best practices Nikephoros identifies is fostering relations between the men in the army. At 3.10 he speaks of housing the *kataphraktoi* (the heavy-armoured infantry):

> The *kontoubernia* of the *kataphraktoi* must be arranged according to friendship and kinship in battle array, in encampments, and on the march. Each line should have a commander, the bigger lines two apiece, who quarter, live, and march together with them. Not only those officers, but the whole unit should be under the command of one head officer, and the men should quarter and march together with him.[43]

A good commander takes advantage of kinship and previous or developing relations of friendship to foster unit cohesion. It is possible that the term *kinship* (συγγένεια) here could also refer to ritual or spiritual brotherhood (ἀδελφοποίησις), which has attracted scholarly attention in recent decades.[44] The closeness and connection already present between the men then spreads to relations between them and their leaders, and this creates a bonded force able to defeat the enemy and to *andrapodise* non-combatants so they can be sold and lose, alas for them, their bonds of kinship and friendship. One might also imagine that the group of soldiers feels more comfortable dehumanising these people because they draw human companionship and validation from one another. This is homosociality at its most destructive, and it poses questions about the practice of war and the dangers of bonded groups of men that remain urgent.

THE END OF AN EMPEROR

A third view of Nikephoros I wish to present is his death, which is seen in all the historical accounts as closely related to his marriage.[45] Again, homosociality emerges, this time along with misogyny.

On the night of 10–11 December in 969 – as Nikephoros slept ascetic-style on the floor of his bedchamber on a bear rug that was a gift from his uncle, the notable ascetic Michael Maleïnos[46] – the (soon-to-be) next emperor, John I Tzimiskes, along with a number of accomplices, was hauled up the palace walls in a basket. He made his way to Nikephoros' bedchamber and assassinated him. John benefited from this, becoming emperor and having a successful reign.

The story immediately sprang up that the empress and widow, Theophano, was responsible. Usually in the accounts she is accused of conspiring with John because she had taken him as a lover.[47] This makes her quite the villain, because Nikephoros is sometimes portrayed as bewitched by Theophano and so attracted to her that he gives her everything she wants.[48] These sources also generally report that she did not find him attractive and used her wiles to get what she wanted. There is, however, also another view. In his *Historia Syntomos*, composed in the eleventh century, Michael Psellos writes that Nikephoros abstained from sexual relations with women altogether from an early age and that his marriage with Theophano was sexless, a state of affairs that made her hate him:

> From its first maturity his [Nikephoros'] life had been chaste, and he had not ever approached women. And when he had taken on the cares of empire, he was holding himself aloof from intercourse with the empress. This became for her a kindling of hate . . .[49]

When we read the historical sources, then, we discover that whether Nikephoros was smitten by Theophano or disdainful of her, she is always blamed. If he desires her, she is a seductress who grows tired of her husband (if she ever really desired him) and who schemes to get handsome John Tzimiskes into her bed. On the other hand, if he avoids sexual congress, she's a sexually frustrated woman who schemes because she desires sex and has a good-looking man available.[50] A homosocial contract, say of 'bros before hoes', between the historical figure and his chroniclers seems to mediate all the historical accounts.

This dynamic is visible not only in the histories of the time, but in the poetry of the late tenth-century poet John Geometres.[51] This poet wrote a number of poems on Nikephoros that emphasise how it was a woman's guile that brought him down.[52] For example, *Poem 61*, in which Geometres presents Nikephoros speaking in the first person, exemplifies this impulse, which has a corollary in *all* the historical accounts:

> Having held the reins of the godly people for six years,
> and during as many years, I suppressed the Ares of Skythians.
> And I laid low all at once the cities of Assyrians and the Phoenicians,
> and I put stubborn Tarsos under the yoke.

I went against the barbarian spear and cleansed the islands,
great Crete and shining Cyprus.
East and West trembled at my threats,
the Nile, giver of wealth and rocky Libya.
But I fell in the middle of the palace and a woman's
hands I could not escape, ah me, wretched in my weakness.
There was a city. There was an army. There was a double wall within.
But it is true that nothing is weaker than mortals.[53]

This poem shows Geometres praising Nikephoros the conqueror and paying no mind to anything negative about his rule. In Geometres' view, the reign was a glorious succession of victories until Nikephoros, but mortal flesh, was done in by the machinations of his wife.

In summation, then, even though the Byzantines are divided on his legacy – e.g., Leo the Deacon and John Geometres are positive while John Skylitzes is negative – all agree in harmonious homosociality that Theophano is at fault no matter what. Manly concord here is arguably toxic to historical accounting itself.

THE *AKOLOUTHIA* AND CONCLUSION

I have written this chapter to explore ways in which the developing concept of toxic masculinity may connect with and illuminate both a different historical era – in this case, Byzantium of the 900s – and the life of emperor Nikephoros II Phokas. Toxic masculinity helps us understand the downsides to asceticism through highlighting extreme bodily practices and misogyny. In the military context, we see a bonded and predatory male homosocial group *andrapodise* civilians, underscoring a dark side to masculine homosociality. Finally, nearly all contemporary commentators on the death of Nikephoros II Phokas perform misogyny, sticking together on this point even as they may disagree in their ultimate assessments of his reign.

To conclude and tie these things together, I return to a work already mentioned: the *akolouthia* for Nikephoros. As noted above, an *akolouthia* is a collection of hymns and prayers for a service that would have commemorated Nikephoros as a new saint.[54] Composed most probably in the tenth century, the *akolouthia* is a document for a future that did not happen, as Nikephoros was not made a saint. In any case, this considerable work of just over 700 lines brings together many of the things already seen in this chapter – though not all of them, as misogyny is not present in this work, which features frequent praise for the Virgin Mary.[55]

The *akolouthia* proposes that Nikephoros is a martyr[56] whose blood brings benefit ('to work miracles and cure diseases') to the people, that he is 'a propitiatory offering'.[57] Nikephoros, the worthy and beneficent martyr, became a man whose murder would be a martyrdom through his literally life-denying, and hence toxic, ascetic practices:

> You interrupted perfectly, with the muzzle of asceticism, the temptations of demons and burning provocations of pleasures. You made your body a corpse, and you put the swellings of the passions to sleep, o you who have been inspired by God.[58]

And so this good man, who made his body a corpse, practising violence against it, reached the acme of goodness through ultimate violence against his person. The *akolouthia* also connects his deadly self-directed activities to his use of power as emperor. As he was master of himself and wanted to destroy his passions, so he did the same thing to the objects of his military might: '. . . overturning with his strength enemies unseen and seen with the allied battling of you [the Virgin Mary]'.[59] The 'unseen' enemies are the demons and desires he had to discipline as he pursued his ascetic goals, and the 'seen' were the others against whom he campaigned as emperor. The Arabs[60] and barbarian peoples[61] face annihilating power, as do his passions or *pathē*, and the thing all these have in common is that they are all rightly controlled and the implication of extermination is real.[62] And later, martyrdom is rolled into his characterisation such that one cannot see where martyrdom ends and asceticism begins, or how we are to perceive his secular office as separate in any meaningful way from his personal religious practices:

> The streams of your blood mixed with the spring of your tears contrived a double baptism, which you, baptised, put on as a robe of justice from tears and a gleaming crown from the blood of martyrdom, [and] you, oh glorious one, proceeded wearing the crown surrounded by choruses of angels and martyrs and applauded by the people. Nikephoros, to the ends of the earth your arms clearly declare you to be a soldier, your campaigns a general, your crown a most powerful emperor, your contests an ascetic, and your struggles a martyr! And so the city has gathered, honouring you and praising your contests and your victory and your blessed end [of life].[63]

In a related detail to be found in the *akolouthia* at another point, Nikephoros' everlasting life in heaven is envisioned: 'you inhabit victory's house as a tentmate of martyrs'.[64] The place of the afterlife is one of homosocial togetherness in the military camp of a successful army. In sum, then, the *akolouthia* blends ascetic martyr with military emperor, creating a composite figure that is terrifying in its apologetic power to license abuse at the personal and geopolitical levels.

A study such as this one entails a critical and sometimes unsympathetic approach to the sources, steeling itself to call out evasions and bad faith. This seems right to me. It is a dangerous and limiting thing to adopt the viewpoint of our sources, sources that may be invested at times in not telling the truth. But even as our current ideas about how people should live together – hence the term 'toxic masculinity' – cut through to realities back then, we may find ourselves learning things from this earlier time; as critique goes back in time, so it can come forward to speak to us now. If such is needed, the durability of serious problems with armies on campaign, especially when they have religious sanction, is highlighted for us yet again, as is the capacity for men to come together reflexively against women. On a more positive note, the sustaining and caring homosociality that we see in the story of Nikephoros' desire for ascetic withdrawal with his friend Athanasios can been be seen as a critique of cold, atomised modern Western masculinity. In sum, all is material to consider as we endeavour to make a future.

NOTES

1. It is a frequent refrain in discussions of the nature of historiography that what we relate about the past is concerned with the future. For instance, Scott (1996, 15) says that 'history's role has been to furnish resources by which futures can be imagined'. This is sensible. Present things of value that we hope to preserve for the future tell us what is worthwhile to investigate in the past.

2. For example, the historiographer John Skylitzes is critical, while Leo the Deacon (also a historiographer) and poet John Geometres are laudatory. These contradictions exist because Byzantine historiographers were closely associated with the imperial court and various reigns required that different attitudes towards imperial forebears be manifested in accounts. In other words, propaganda could and sometimes did win out over factuality. For more on this, see Treadgold 2013.

3. I draw on the following for this sketch of Nikephoros' life: Ostrogorsky 1968; Morris 1988; Garland 1999; Burke 2014; Kaldellis 2017; and the *Prosopographie der mittelbyzantinischen Zeit Online*.

4. For example, Bardas Phokas, Nikephoros' nephew and an able commander, led a serious revolt against Emperor Basil II in the 980s.

5. The eldest child, future emperor Basil II, had been born probably in 958.

6. The prohibition was against even female animals on Mount Athos: 'As one who has removed himself utterly from the female, you should not possess an animal of the female sex for any working need' ('Οὐ σχοίης ζῶον τῶν ἐκ τοῦ θήλεος γένους εἰς χρείαν ὑπουργικὴν ὁ τῷ θήλει παντάπασιν ἀποταξάμενος', text: Meyer 1894, 113). This is from section 31 of the *typikon* of Athanasios of Athos (Thomas et al. 2000, 259), which dates from 973–5 (Thomas et al. 2000, 245). This prohibition is copied from the *typikon* of Theodore the Studite, which dates from after 842 (Thomas et al. 2000, 84). NOTE: All translations in this chapter are my own, unless otherwise credited.

7. John Skylitzes, *Synopsis historion*: *Nikephoros II Phokas* 22/p. 280. The fact that he sleeps alone on a gift from his ascetic uncle on the floor marks him as ascetic. But one would have to say it is definitely the case that he is a semi-ascetic. He is in a palace, after all, and sleeps on scarlet-dyed felt and bearskin, a combination which would seem to offer at least some measure of luxurious comfort. This scene encapsulates how Nikephoros had one foot in the world and the other foot in withdrawal from it. The *akolouthia* also makes much of his sleeping on the floor of his bedchamber (Sullivan 2018, 206).

8. Kaldellis (2017, 64) remarks that 'gossip and imagination colored everything . . . and Tzimiskes, once on the throne, had every reason to blame it all on her. It is not even certain that Theophano did in fact facilitate his entry into the palace on that snowy winter night.' Also see Garland (1999) for more on Theophano.

9. The *akolouthia* does not mention Theophano at all.

10. John Skylitzes, who is critical of Nikephoros, tells us of the general rejoicing when Nikephoros entered Constantinople to be crowned (*Synopsis historion*: *Basil II and Constantine VIII* 7/pp. 258–9).

11. An *akolouthia* is a programme, a sequence of elements, for a church service, frequently dedicated to a saint. The *akolouthia* proposed for Nikephoros is discussed at the end of this chapter.

12. For text of the *vitae*, see Noret 1982.

13. See Noret 1982, cx; cxvi–cxxvi (dating for *Vita A*) and cxxvii–viii (dating for *Vita B*). Also see Morris' (1988) discussions. *Contra* these datings, however, is the suggestion of Krausmüller (2007), which has been accepted by Greenfield and Talbot (2016, xii), that *Vita B* is earlier and that both *vitae* follow an original that has been lost.

14. The *akolouthia* also speaks of his ascetic ambitions.

15. *Vita A*, 28.5–6.

16. *Vita B*, 11.42–4: 'Ποθῶ, πάτερ, ἡσυχάσαι ἀπὸ τῆς κοσμικῆς ζάλης καὶ ἐθέμην ἀποτάξασθαι πᾶσι τοῖς τοῦ κόσμου καὶ τῷ Θεῷ δουλεῦσαι . . . '

17. *Vita A*, 30.1–3; *Vita B*, 34.6–8.

18. A *laura* is, in general, a monastery set-up that involves a number of cells for individual monks, or pairs of monks, arranged around a chapel and perhaps a common building.

19. *Vita B*, 22.31–41: 'ἐπέστη δὲ καιρός, οὗ ἔκπαλαι ἐπεθύμουν, πρὸς τὸ φυγεῖν τὰ τοῦ κόσμου, καὶ οὐδέν ἐστιν ἡμῖν ἄρτι εἰς τοῦτο ἐμπόδιον, εἰ μὴ μόνον τὸ οἰκοδομηθῆναι ἡμῖν οἰκητήρια· καὶ δέομαί σου τῆς ὁσιότητος πρῶτον μὲν οἰκοδομῆσαι ἡμῖν κελλία ἡσυχαστικά, θεμελιῶσαι δὲ καὶ ναὸν καὶ ἀπαρτίσαι αὐτὸν εἰς κοινόβιον, ὡς ἂν ἐγὼ μὲν καὶ σὺ μετὰ καὶ ἑτέρων τριῶν ἀδελφῶν ἐν τοῖς ἡσυχαστικοῖς κελλίοις μονάζωμεν, τῇ δὲ κυρίᾳ ἡμέρᾳ κατερχώμεθα ἅμα εἰς τὴν λαύραν καὶ τῶν θείων ἁγιασμάτων μεταλαμβάνωμεν καὶ συνεσθίωμεν τοῖς ἀδελφοῖς καὶ τῷ ἡγουμένῳ, καὶ πάλιν ἀνερχώμεθα.'

20. *Vita A*, 70.7–8. At *Vita B*, 23.23–5, we read how Athanasios was getting things ready for Nikephoros when, in the coming years, he finally withdrew from the world.

21. *Vita A*, 90.2–5; *Vita B*, 30.1–9.

22. *Vita A*, 102.1–4: Ὁ δὲ βασιλεὺς τὴν ἄφιξιν αἰσθόμενος αὐτοῦ αἰδοῖ μερίζεται καὶ χαρᾷ, χαρᾷ μὲν διὰ τὸν πολὺν περὶ αὐτὸν πόθον καὶ τὸ μέγα φίλτρον, αἰδοῖ δὲ διὰ τὴν ἁλουργίδα, ἣν τῆς μακαρίας ἀντησπάσατο ἀπραγμοσύνης . . .ʼ

23. *Vita B*, 34.2–8: Ὁ βασιλεὺς δὲ μαθὼν τοῦτον ἐρχόμενον, ἔχαιρε μὲν ὅτι ἐπόθει τοῦτον θεάσασθαι, ᾐσχύνετο δὲ ὡς μέλλων ὀφθῆναι αὐτῷ ἐν βασιλικῇ τῇ στολῇ· διὸ καὶ ὑπήντησε τούτῳ οὐχ ὡς βασιλεὺς ἀλλ᾽ ὡς εἷς τῶν πολλῶν, καὶ τῆς χειρὸς αὐτοῦ λαβόμενος μετὰ τὸν ἀσπασμὸν καὶ πρὸς τὸν ἴδιον κοιτῶνα ἀπαγαγών, συγκαθεσθεὶς αὐτῷ καταμόνας ἔφη . . .ʼ

24. Self-control as a masculine activity of praiseworthy elites has been discussed in the secondary literature. Michel Foucault (1985 and 1986) made this topic central to his work. For much further scholarship, please see Masterson 2014, 94fn12.

25. As I wrote in *Man to Man* (2014, 108): 'The models [guiding ascetic practice and the at times unstated predicates of ascetic literature] are Christ and the martyrs. The literature from the *eremos* [desert: the place where Christian asceticism makes its start] is one of the ways the deadly ideals embodied by the saviour and those who died for their faith were domesticated for use in a life to be lived.'

26. *Vita B*, 43.24–7.

27. *Vita A*, 159.1–3.

28. Greenfield and Talbot 2016, 684.

29. In the *akolouthia* (discussed below), Nikephoros stands as part of his ascetic practice also: Sullivan 2018, 204–5 and 218–19.

30. Masterson 2014, 37–8; also see 38fn88 for further discussion of these dichotomies.

31. As Psellos reports; see discussion below.

32. Garrood (2008) provides a good narrative of the subduing of Cilicia over the course of the years of 955–65. See also Kaldellis' (2017, 38–40 and 46–51) discussions of these campaigns.

33. For a translation, which I consulted, of Leo the Deacon's *Historia*, see Dennis et al. 2005. The Greek text is Hase's (1828).

34. *Historia* 4.1/pp. 55–6: 'καὶ τὸ πρᾶγμα προπηλακισμὸν καὶ ὕβριν ἄντικρυς ἐλογίζετο, καὶ ὄνειδον ἀνεξάλειπτον, εἰ Νικηφόρος ὢν ὁ Φωκᾶς, καὶ πρώην ἐν στρατηγοῖς τελῶν, καὶ αὖθις ἀναρρηθεὶς Δομέστικος τῶν σχολῶν, τοτὲ μὲν μυριάδας πόλεις κατέσκαψε καὶ δηώσας ἠθάλωσε, τοτὲ δὲ εὐδαίμονας χώρας ἠνδραποδίσατο, καὶ μάχιμα ἔθνη τρεψάμενος ἐκ παρατάξεως ὑπήγετο, μηδὲ ἀντοφθαλμεῖν ἐξισχύσαντα πρὸς τὴν τούτου ἀλκὴν καὶ τὴν ἀκαταγώνιστον ἐν τοῖς ὅπλοις ὁρμήν.'

35. In the context of this study of toxic masculinity, it seems that *andrapodise* and the related words, given that they apparently contain the stem of the Greek word for man, *aner/andros*, would read immediately as referring to men and masculinity. This is incorrect, however, as these words in the first case refer to one of the Greek words for slave: *andrapodon*. All this said, the stem of the word for men is still visible at one remove, as it were, and as such, provokes musing about the relationship between 'man' and 'slave'.

36. See especially Gaca 2010, 132–5.

37. Here are some of the forms: ἀνδραποδίζειν, ἐξανδροποδίζειν; ἀνδραποδισμός, ἐξανδραποδισμός.

38. Gaca 2010, 142–3.
39. Gaca 2010, 134.
40. Gaca 2010, 153: 'Hence, to andrapodize a city, village, or countryside is a highly compressed way to signify the standard military steps by which armed fighters who prevail in their offensive carry out the andrapodizing of a locale in order to remove the desired youthful dependants.'
41. 'εἰ . . . τοτὲ δὲ εὐδαίμονας χώρας ἠνδραποδίσατο . . .'
42. See McGeer (1995) for text and translation of the *Praecepta militaria*.
43. Trans. McGeer 1995, 39 (3.10, lines 73–80): 'εἶναι δὲ αὐτῶν τῶν καταφράκτων τὰ κοντουβέρνια κατὰ φιλίαν καὶ συγγένειαν ἕν τε παρατάξει καὶ ἀπλήκτοις καὶ ὁδοιπορίαις. καὶ μία ἑκάστη ἀκία ἐχέτω ἀρχηγόν, αἱ δὲ μεγάλαι αὐτῶν ἀκίαι καὶ ἀνὰ δύο ἀρχηγοὺς ἐχέτωσαν συναπληκεύοντας καὶ συνδιαιτωμένους καὶ συνοδοιποροῦντας μετ' αὐτῶν. καὶ οὐ μόνως αὐτοί, ἀλλὰ καὶ τὸ ὅλον τάγμα ὑπὸ τοῦ ἐξάρχοντος ἀρχηγοῦ ὁμοῦ καὶ ἀπληκευέτωσαν καὶ συνοδοιπορείτωσαν αὐτῷ'), cf. *Praecepta militaria* 4.1, lines 1–5 (McGeer 1995, 39) for similar comments on the proper arrangement of men in the *bandon* (another military unit).
44. Boswell 1994 and Rapp 2016, 15–16; also see my recent discussion of brotherhood (*adelphopoiesis*) in the tenth century: Masterson 2022, 121–54. Relevant in the present moment is the report in *Vita B* of Athanasios of Athos (at number 44) that Nikephoros was a spiritual brother (πνευματικὸς ἀδελφός) of the governor of Thessalonike.
45. Garland's (1999) discussion of Theophano is essential reading for this episode from Nikephoros' life.
46. Kaldellis 2017, 64.
47. Leo the Deacon, *Historia* 5.6/p. 58; Psellos, *Historia syntomos* 105/p. 102; Skylitzes, *Synopsis historion: Nikephoros II Phokas* 22/p. 279.
48. Leo the Deacon, *Historia* 5.6/p. 58. The twelfth-century historian Zonaras notes that Nikephoros was interested in sexual relations with Theophano (*Epitome historiarum* 16.28, cf. Skylitzes, *Synopsis historion: Nikephoros II Phokas* 22/p. 279).
49. *Historia syntomos* 105 (Aerts 1990, 100, ll. 28–31): 'Σεμνὸς ἐκ πρώτης ἡλικίας ὁ βίος καὶ οὐ πάνυ τι ἐπλησίαζεν γυναιξίν. Ἐπεὶ δὲ καὶ τῶν τῆς βασιλείας φροντίδων ἐγένετο, τῆς πρὸς τὴν βασίλειαν ὁμιλίας ἀπείχετο.Τῇ δὲ μίσους τοῦτο ὑπέκκαυμα γίνεται.' The *akolouthia* also takes this position on his sexual interests: 'Having stood altogether aloof from the defilements of the flesh from extreme youth and having been called the (soldier's) tent of virtues . . .' (Sullivan 2018, 200: 'Ὅλος ἐκστὰς ἀπὸ βρέφους/τῶν τῆς σαρκὸς/μολυσμῶν καὶ σκήνωμα/χρηματίσας ἀρετῶν . . .'). Of interest here is the influx of military imagery: '(soldier's) tent of virtues' (σκήνωμα . . . ἀρετῶν). Nikephoros' ambitions to sanctity via ascetic means are never far from military things and indeed wind up leading to the envisioning of heaven in military terms (see discussion in the last section of this chapter).
50. History shows too, by the way, that even if it is true that she was scheming, she was not successful. She did not marry John and was instead sent to a convent.
51. For background on John Geometres, see Lauxtermann 1998 and 2003.

52. *Poems 61, 80* and *147* and the *Epitaph* (texts are to be found in Opstall 2008 [poems] and Mercati 1921 and Skylitzes, *Synopsis historion: Nikephoros II Phokas* 33/pp. 282–3 [epitaph]).

53. Ἑξάετες λαοῖο θεόφρονος ἡνία τείνας,
    τόσσ᾽ ἐπ᾽ ἔτη Σκυθῶν Ἄρεα δῆσα μέγαν,
    Ἀσσυρίων δ᾽ ἔκλινα πόλεις καὶ Φοίνικας ἄρδην,
    Ταρσὸν ἀμαιμακέτην εἷλον ὑπὸ ζύγιον·
    νήσους δ᾽ ἐξεκάθηρα καὶ ἤλασα βάρβαρον αἰχμήν,
    εὐμεγέθη Κρήτην, Κύπρον ἀριπρεπέα,
    ἀντολίη τε δύσις τε ἐμὰς ὑπέτρεσσαν ἀπειλάς,
    ὀλβοδότης Νεῖλος καὶ κραναὴ Λιβύη.
    πίπτω δ᾽ ἐν βασιλείοις μέσσοις, οὐδὲ γυναικὸς
    χεῖρας ὑπεξέφυγον, ἆ τάλας ἀδρανίης.
    ἦν πόλις, ἦν στρατός, ἦν καὶ διπλόον ἔνδοθι τεῖχος,
    ἀλλ᾽ ἐτεὸν μερόπων οὐδὲν ἀκιδνότερον. (Opstall 2008, 210)

54. His feast day would have been 11 December.

55. E.g., Sullivan 2018, 224.

56. It is relevant too that Nicholas the Cook, amid his standing vigil of forty-five days (discussed above), prays to Nikephoros Phokas and calls him a martyr in *Vita B* of Athanasios of Athos (44.41–7).

57. Sullivan 2018, 226: ʻθαυματουργεῖν καὶ θεραπεύειν τὰς νόσους᾽ and 210: ʻἐξίλασμα δοὺς αἷμα τὸ σόν᾽

58. Sullivan 2018, 222:

    Δαιμόνων τοὺς πειρασμοὺς
        καὶ ἡδονῶν ὑπεκκαύματα
    τῆς ἐγκρατείας κημῷ
        τελείως ἐξέκλινας
    καὶ σῶμα ἐνέκρωσας,
        τῶν παθῶν εὐνάσας
    τὰ οἰδήματα, θεόπνευστε.

59. Sullivan 2018, 216: ʻδυσμενεῖς κατὰ κράτος/τοὺς ἀοράτους τροπούμενος/καὶ τοὺς ὁρατοὺς συμμαχίᾳ σου᾽.

60. Sullivan 2018, 218.

61. Sullivan 2018, 196, 226 and 236.

62. Sullivan 2018, 196.

63. Sullivan 2018, 234:

    Αἱ ῥοαὶ τῶν αἱμάτων σου
        τῇ πηγῇ τῶν δακρύων σου
    συγκραθεῖσαι βάπτισμα
        ἀπειργάσαντο
    διπλοῦν, ὃ σὺ βαπτισάμενος,
        στολὴν δικαιώσεως

ἐκ δακρύων καὶ φαιδρὸν
   μαρτυρίου ἐξ αἵματος
στέφος, ἔνδοξε,
   περιθέμενος ἔβης
στεφηφόρος,
   τῶν ἀγγέλων καὶ μαρτύρων
χοροῖς καὶ δήμοις κροτούμενος.

Στρατιώτην τὰ ὅπλα σε,
   στρατηγὸν ἡ παράταξις,
βασιλέα κράτιστον
   τὸ διάδημα,
ἀλλ᾽ ἀσκητὴν οἱ ἀγῶνές σε,
   τὰ ἆθλα δὲ μάρτυρα
καταγγέλλουσι τρανῶς,
   Νικηφόρε, τοῖς πέρασιν·
ὅθεν ἤθροισται
   καὶ τιμῶσά σε πόλις,
εὐφημοῦσα
   τοὺς ἀγῶνας καὶ τὴν νίκην
καὶ τὸ μακάριον τέλος σου.

64. Sullivan 2018, 198: ʿοἰκεῖς νίκης ἐνδιαίτημα,/μαρτύρων σύσκηνοςʾ.

CHAPTER 6

Boy Toys: A Ciceronian Invective Trope

Joanna Kenty

γάμῳ προσέσχε, Φουλβίαν ἀγαγόμενος τὴν Κλωδίῳ τῷ δημαγωγῷ συνοικήσασαν, οὐ ταλασίαν οὐδὲ οἰκουρίαν φρονοῦν γύναιον, οὐδὲ ἀνδρὸς ἰδιώτου κρατεῖν ἀξιοῦν, ἀλλ᾽ ἄρχοντος ἄρχειν καὶ στρατηγοῦντος στρατηγεῖν βουλόμενον, ὥστε Κλεοπάτραν διδασκάλια Φουλβίᾳ τῆς Ἀντωνίου γυναικοκρατίας ὀφείλειν, πάνυ χειροήθη καὶ πεπαιδαγωγημένον ἀπ᾽ ἀρχῆς ἀκροᾶσθαι γυναικῶν παραλαβοῦσαν αὐτόν.

Antony married Fulvia, the widow of Clodius the demagogue, a female who did not think about weaving or domestic work, who did not think it was worthwhile to dominate a private citizen, but wanted to rule a ruler and command a commander. Thus, Cleopatra owed Fulvia a debt for Antony's education in gynocracy, having found him quite tamed and disciplined from the beginning to listen to women. (Plutarch, *Life of Antony*, 10.3)

Plutarch makes Fulvia sound like quite the villain, like an evil queen from a fairy tale. But does this tell us anything about the real Fulvia, a historical figure who lived and died in the first century BCE? The rejection of the quintessential woman's task, weaving, and the lust for power are not specific to Fulvia. Instead, they are clichés in ancient literature, used when an author wants to characterise a woman as deviant and harmful. Getting a sense of the real Fulvia from such a description is like trying to reconstruct a realistic portrait from a cartoon caricature.[1] Furthermore, ancient authors often included women like Fulvia in historical accounts less for their own sake, and more in order to help readers understand the men with whom they were associated. Fulvia's character is only described in order to reveal a flaw in Mark Antony's, because he voluntarily made himself a subject of several gynocratic regimes.

Plutarch was not the first to describe Fulvia and Antony in this way: he lived centuries after Fulvia and relied on earlier authors like Cicero, who was Antony's political enemy during his lifetime. Cicero used the same clichés of the power-hungry, unfeminine woman in his speeches to argue that Antony was weak-willed and a poor leader. Cicero often used women like Fulvia as weapons in his rhetorical arsenal, tools with which to shame and discredit his political opponents for being 'unmanly'. This trope, claiming that a politician is weak and despicable because he is a 'boy toy' subject to a woman's power, mirrors the way that the ideology of a certain toxic construction of masculinity today designates effeminacy as the ultimate insult. Also toxic then and now, I argue, is the underlying premise that political leadership is correlated with hegemonic masculinity and with sexual dominance as a defining characteristic of manliness in the first place.

Some men, both today and in ancient Rome, feel threatened by the notion of women who are not under male control, as we can see in common expressions ranging from old-fashioned taunts about who 'wears the pants' in a relationship to the modern slur 'cuck'.[2] Even if accusations of this type are untrue, they often succeed in changing the way an audience feels about the target. The similarities between Roman political invective and modern parallels point to a deeper shared assumption that political authority must be linked with sexual dominance, an assumption which has broader, toxic effects on political cultures today. Many leaders of the United States have identified Rome as a sort of cultural ancestor. In doing so, they have also taken on board some sexist assumptions and underlying principles from antiquity which are incompatible with modern democratic ideals. A closer look at Roman models can help today's readers to think more critically about the 'inheritance' we have taken from ancient Rome, and its implications for politics in the present day.

DEFINING KEY CONCEPTS

Like the ancient Romans, modern Americans live in a patriarchal society, a society where the people who hold power in families, groups and governments are customarily or exclusively men. When individuals in patriarchal societies think of powerful people, they usually picture men. For individuals who grow up in a patriarchal society, this seems normal, even natural. Kate Manne writes that patriarchal societies, in order to explain and justify why things are the way they are, promote sexist ideologies which attribute the greatest physical, emotional and cognitive strength to a few privileged men.[3] The supposed greater strength of these men is then cited to explain and legitimise their monopoly on financial and political decision-making, along with the power they have over women and others who do not embody this restrictive version of masculinity, who aren't 'real men'.[4] A patriarchal system gains acceptance when members of the society assume that the men who hold power are stronger and smarter than those who do not have power.

Not all men have power in a patriarchal society, and not all masculinities – all ways of being a man, or of being manly – are equally valued. The version of masculinity idealised by the society's sexist (and often racist and colonialist) ideology, the stereotype of the most powerful kind of man, is sometimes called hegemonic masculinity.[5] This ideal justifies and promotes the idea that the 'right' kind of men should have power over their social groups (hegemony). The version of masculinity which is 'hegemonic' or normative differs from one culture to another, and from one time period to another. Hegemonic masculinity is an idea, not a person or group of people. It is not necessarily a version of masculinity which is based on actual individual men, but the ideal does exert powerful pressure on real people nonetheless.[6] Men who come closer to embodying this model (or seem to) are admired, desired and valued more than those who do not. Individuals tend to internalise this value system, shaping their own behaviour to try to conform to it, usually without consciously intending to. They often police themselves, changing or hiding physical traits or behaviours that don't match the stereotype. They also police one another's behaviour in social groups by criticising or mocking those who fail to conform. Powerful individuals acquire and maintain power by showing that they have mastered masculinity, sometimes by shaming those who fail to embody it.[7]

Toxic masculinity as an ideology imposes the same restrictive norms and upholds the same patriarchal power structure as hegemonic masculinity does, but with an important difference. Toxic masculinity is defined, in my view, by an impulse to punish individuals who are seen as threatening to hegemonic masculinity. It also dictates that a 'real man' is defined not just by having power over others, but by controlling, manipulating and dominating others, even to the point of using force to do so.[8] According to the ideology of toxic masculinity, people who reject or challenge the paradigm of hegemonic masculinity are a threat to society, which is taken as justification for punishing them. This extreme ideology encourages the use of harmful speech – particularly misogynistic, homophobic or transphobic – and even the direct or indirect use of violence as a means of enforcing dominance.[9] People under the influence of toxic masculinity see themselves as being personally threatened by the freedom and equality of women and individuals who do not conform to patriarchal gender norms.[10]

In Roman society, hegemonic masculinity automatically included domination over others. For example, Roman ideology valorised militarism and imperialism, and the Roman *paterfamilias* at least notionally had the power of life and death over everyone in his household, including enslaved people. Women were not equal to men in the eyes of the law, nor could any women exercise the full rights of citizens.[11] Because of these fundamental differences between Roman and modern democratic societies, some interactions which would be categorised as misogynistic or toxic now were considered normal then, although they still did harm. The Roman habit of using harmful speech to insult opponents as not being 'real men' reflects the same repressive enforcement of gender norms and the same punitive attitude as modern toxic masculinity. Among Cicero's speeches, *Against Verres* 2.1 and *Philippic* 2 provide the most prominent examples. In each of these speeches, Cicero goes beyond attacking the leadership and political activity of his opponent and attacks his masculinity as well, by claiming that he is a 'boy toy' subjugated to a domineering woman. He does not merely criticise his opponent, but tries to shame him for his sexual practices, using the same viciously punitive stance that is associated with toxic masculinity in modern America.

THE PROSECUTION OF VERRES

It was common for Rome's leading men to launch nasty, abusive verbal attacks on one another, accusing each other of falling short of masculinity in various ways in what Richlin calls a sort of game.[12] Cicero's speeches contain many such attacks. In modern political rhetoric, it is frowned upon as a logical fallacy (but not uncommon) to make attacks *ad hominem*, targeting an individual opponent's character rather than arguing against their political ideas and arguments. In the elite social circles of Rome, however, no one's private life was off limits, including their sex lives. The Greek biographer Plutarch commented with curiosity on the Roman census, in which senators (and other citizens) were investigated for public and private immorality: 'they do not think that a man's marriage or procreation or lifestyle or behaviour at a drinking party should be free from judgement or scrutiny, with each man left to his own desires or choices. They think it is especially in these things, rather than in public or political activities, that a man's character can be observed' (Plutarch, *Life of Cato the Elder* 16.1–2).[13] Private conduct was thought to reveal a man's true nature, which directly affected his abilities as a leader in his community.

This scrutiny of private lives extended to the courts as well, where Roman lawyers relied on character as a type of evidence of guilt or innocence: they argued that their clients had lived virtuous, respectable lives and therefore would never have committed the crimes of which they were accused – or if they did, that they had had good reasons. Orators also engaged in *ad hominem* attacks against their opponents. At their most extreme, they argued that their opponents (i.e. the defendants they prosecuted, and/or any of the defendants' advocates or political supporters, depending on who was the easiest target) were malicious, immoral villains who had been evil ever since they were children or adolescents, always looking for ways to destroy the reputations of decent people. Sexual misconduct – having too much sex, having sex with the wrong person, or having the wrong kind of sex – often featured in a Roman orator's arsenal in character assassination, not just for its own sake (although lurid accusations must have helped to hold the attention of jurors and audiences) but as a part of a more general assault on the target's moral character, and even on their qualifications as a politician.[14] An audience or jury was less likely to listen to a man they perceived as weak or depraved. This is how patriarchy and the hegemony of a particular version of masculinity reinforce each other: those who are 'unmanly', or who perform a version of masculinity which is not idealised, are granted less credibility and authority.

The speeches against Verres (the *Verrines*) provide a good example of what I would call Cicero's toxic weaponisation of hegemonic masculinity. Gaius Verres had served as the governor (*propraetor*) of the Roman province of Sicily, and in 70 BCE he was prosecuted for corruption by Cicero, then a young advocate at the start of his career. Verres left before the conclusion of the trial to live in exile in Massilia (modern Marseilles, France), but Cicero published a version of the speech he had delivered in the trial (*Against Verres* 1) as well as five more speeches he would have delivered if the trial had continued (*Against Verres* 2.1–5).[15] Every aspect of Verres' life and career was dredged up in Cicero's attacks, including an unusual feature of his tenure in the office of praetor in 74 BCE: Cicero alleges that a large part of it was conducted not from Verres' own house, where he lived with his wife and children,[16] but in the house of an alleged sex worker named Chelidon, with whom Verres had been living before taking office.[17]

As praetor, Verres proved to be unreliable and fickle, reversing his decisions at will, but his petitioners found that if they approached Chelidon instead, she would tell Verres what to do and he always followed her instructions:

> When that man was praetor, she not only governed the Roman people in civil law and disputes of all private citizens, but was also mistress of these repairs and public buildings. (2.1.136)[18]

Thus the houses of legal consultants and jurists were empty, while Chelidon's house was filled, as Cicero describes with outrage (*Verr.* 2.1.120, 136), with men who never would have been seen in a prostitute's house otherwise (137). In Cicero's portrait, Verres' lack of discipline and integrity results in his failure to fulfil his responsibility to his community, and worse, results in his giving away his power to a low-status woman as if he is her dependant. Remarkably, Cicero pauses his argument to interject: 'I'm afraid that someone who was not present at the first part of the trial might think that I have made these things up, because they're so incredible, due to his extraordinary immorality. You, however, gentlemen of the jury, learned them before' (138).[19] To support his claims, he cites testimony given under oath by men who had petitioned Chelidon for help (139). Apparently, fabricating claims like this in a court of law was common enough that some readers might have suspected Cicero of lying.

Chelidon died after Verres had gone to Sicily, and she willed her property to Verres (2.2.115), who then decorated it for himself with art he stole from the Sicilians (2.4.7, 83, 123). Cicero claims that he filled her place with other women: one named Pippa (or Pipa), a Syracusan who used her husband's position as a tax farmer to squeeze money out of her fellow citizens, and one named Tertia, a mime actress (2.3.77–80), as well as a harem of other dissolute women (2.5.29–40).[20] 'And thus one city of our allies and friends was paying taxes to two worthless whores while Verres was praetor' (2.3.79),[21] Cicero rails. He insinuates that both women worked in the sex industry, which we may or may not choose to take literally.[22] Verres cannot or does not control his sexual appetites, nor can he control the women around him; with no one in control, these women seize illegitimate power and create a shadow government, in Cicero's colourful depiction.

It is particularly noteworthy that these shrewd, allegedly libidinous women are depicted by Cicero as exercising the power which should have been wielded by Verres; Chelidon takes over the functions of the praetor almost entirely, while Pippa and Tertia act as tax farmers. Bauman has proposed that Chelidon – a wealthy, authoritative and apparently politically savvy woman – was a sort of political fixer who was responsible for getting the rather inept Verres elected praetor in the first place and continued to exercise influence through him behind the scenes.[23] This is how Cicero wants his audience to see her role in 74 BCE: as undermining the entire patriarchal order.

A sex worker was apparently resolving legal disputes, assigning contracts to repair public buildings, making decrees and laws. What does this have to do with the legal charges against Verres? He behaved dishonourably as a praetor in going back on his word and dispensing unjust decisions; what did it matter that he was living with or taking advice from Chelidon? He was corrupt in appointing officials and collecting taxes in Sicily; was it relevant that he shared the profits with women in exchange for sex? What difference did it make that these women might have been sex workers or actresses as opposed to matrons? For the legal case, none; for Cicero's character assassination, however, these allegations are all crucial in establishing that Verres was a bad person who consorted with bad people,[24] which (in Roman eyes) made accusations of political impropriety more credible.

Cicero implores the jury to put things right by punishing Verres, depriving him of his political rank and citizenship, and thus to use shame to enforce the norms of hegemonic masculinity. It seems likely that Cicero exaggerated or even fabricated some of this material. He thought that a jury would respond strongly to assaults on Verres' masculinity, maybe even more than they would respond to accusations of unethical governance – and he may have been right. The hegemonic version of masculinity in ancient Rome dictated that Verres' relationship with Chelidon was unmanly, unacceptable, especially for an elite public official.

Cicero took it upon himself to punish Verres for deviating from that hegemonic masculinity, and engaged in a toxic *ad hominem* attack.

MARK ANTONY'S INDISCRETIONS

Twenty-six years later, near the end of his career in 44 BCE, Cicero used the same rhetorical strategy in his attacks on Mark Antony in the *Philippics*. As consul in 44 BCE, Antony had attacked Cicero in a speech in the Senate, and Cicero then wrote and circulated an attack of his own, the *Second Philippic*. At the outset of this chapter, I quoted Plutarch's characterisation of Antony's subjugation to his third wife Fulvia;[25] but Antony was also found in compromising positions with several other partners, at least according to Cicero. Soon after he assumed the *toga virilis* (adult man's toga) to mark his coming of age at fifteen or sixteen years old, Cicero mockingly claims, Antony turned it into a *toga muliebris* (a toga worn by a female sex worker) by acting as the passive partner in anal sex. He is said to have done so 'first as a common whore', then in 'a strong and stable marriage'[26] with Gaius Scribonius Curio the Younger, who was a few years older than Antony (*Phil.* 2.44).[27] Both Curio and Antony had since gone on to distinguished political careers, and both served with Julius Caesar in the civil war which broke out in 49 BCE.[28] Cicero used this rhetoric to try to shame Antony (decades after the fact) for acting in a way which Cicero labelled as effeminate, evidence of Antony's early moral degradation. This punitive attitude towards sex between men mirrors the modern American ideology of toxic masculinity, which demands that 'real men' be sexually dominant and have sex only with feminine cis women.[29]

In the interim, Antony had also had a relationship with a mime actress named Volumnia, also known by her stage name Cytheris.[30] In a letter to his friend Atticus, Cicero refers to Antony as *Cytherius*, 'Cytheris' man', as though he is a dependant who does not even have his own individual identity (*Att.* 15.22.1). Cicero expresses outrage in the *Second Philippic* that Antony, while serving as tribune of the plebs, rode from town to town accompanied by Volumnia:

> The tribune of the people was carried in a chariot; his lictors preceded him with their laurels, and a mime actress was carried in their midst in an open litter. Honourable citizens from the towns were forced to come and meet her, and they greeted her not by that notorious stage name, but as Volumnia. They were followed by a wagon for pimps, his worthless companions; his own mother was relegated to following her disgusting son's girlfriend as if she were a proper wife. O ruinous fertility of a wretched woman! That man left traces of his depravity on all the towns, prefectures, colonies, even the whole of Italy (*Phil.* 2.58, also described in *Att.* 10.10.5).[31]

Cicero sets up Volumnia as an enemy to the reputations of Antony's wife and mother and respectable woman everywhere, whom Cicero defends with all due chivalry.[32] While Antony subverts the social hierarchy by honouring Volumnia above his mother and even degrades himself, Cicero takes on authority as the embodiment and enforcer of traditional conventions. Like Verres, Antony is said to have dishonoured his magistracy by flaunting a relationship with a disreputable woman and allowing some of the trappings of his official power to pass to her.[33] He has also dishonoured good men, for whom greeting an actress respectfully was viewed as humiliating, just as Verres' petitioners were ashamed to be seen in Chelidon's house. Antony thus degrades himself, but also threatens to bring the patriarchal social order down with him. It would have been better, Cicero implies, for Antony to hide his relationship with Volumnia, to be ashamed of it. However, Fertik suggests that Antony's public embracing of his physical and sexual side may have made him more popular among less censorious Roman citizens.[34]

Like Verres, Antony could not or did not control himself around his partner, which is portrayed as effeminate, a surrender of his own power – not to Volumnia, however, whose agency and perspective are totally absent from Cicero's account. Just because a man loses power around a woman does not mean that the woman is empowered. Volumnia was a former slave, possibly a sex worker and a mime actress who did not have autonomy in her relationships, but was under the control of her patron Volumnius Eutrapelus.[35] Mime actresses in general suffered mistreatment enabled by their low social status: another client of Cicero's, Plancius, while on trial for electoral bribery, was accused of raping a mime actress 'with the old sort of liberty in the treatment of actors, especially in towns' (*Planc.* 30).[36] Volumnia's patron did take her to social gatherings among the elite, including a bashful Cicero (*Fam.* 9.26.2),[37] and Cicero's wife seems to have sought a political favour from her as a proxy for Antony (*Fam.* 14.16.1), but that does not mean that she had real freedom to live her life as she chose. In Cicero's rhetoric, she is a tool to be used against Antony. In fact, in comparison with Chelidon and Fulvia, Volumnia seems to have a marked lack of political influence.

Antony's relationship with Volumnia may have compromised his political authority: Cicero claims that when Antony appeared with Volumnia before his comrades in the military, they all regretted following Antony (2.61), regardless of his abilities as a soldier or commander. When Antony then rose through the political ranks, he broke up with Volumnia to become more respectable, which Cicero calls the most honourable thing Antony ever did (2.69). Elite Roman men were only supposed to have publicly acknowledged relationships with women of a certain status (although norms allowed them to have sex with prostitutes and slaves as they wished, as long as they played the active sex role and showed discretion). However, Antony then allegedly allowed his new wife Fulvia to wield the powers of his magistracy (the consulship in this case) in his stead, as Cicero comments in a speech he delivered against Antony in the

Senate: 'in the inner part of his house, there was a hot trade in selling off the whole Republic; his wife, whose good luck did not extend to her husbands,[38] auctioned off provinces and kingdoms' (*Phil.* 5.11).[39] In a speech delivered to the citizen assembly, Cicero sums up: 'Antony has always been dragged where his libido takes him, or whims or rage or drunkenness; two dissimilar groups have always controlled him, pimps and thieves; he enjoys sex crimes at home and murder in the forum, so much that he obeys an insatiable woman faster than the senate and Roman people' (*Phil.* 6.4).[40] Antony owes his service to the state, but chooses to serve a woman instead, and an immoral, unfeminine woman at that. Cicero smears both Antony and Fulvia, attempting to shame both of them, all in order to undermine Antony's political authority and make Antony pay for attacking Cicero.

The greedy, tyrannical Fulvia here fits another stereotype familiar from other orations of Cicero. In other examples, however, the women are defamed not in order to shame a man by association, but to exculpate him as an innocent casualty of a woman's power grab; 'Cicero, naturally, cuts his coat to fit his cloth', as Richlin observes.[41] In his oration *In Defence of Cluentius (Pro Cluentio)*, Cicero argues that his client Cluentius (on trial for murdering his stepfather) was set up by his conniving, evil mother, Sassia. At the emotional climax at the end of the oration, he exclaims: 'but what a mother she is! You see her blind with cruelty and carried away by wickedness; no infamy has ever slowed down her lust; with the vices of her mind she has turned all human laws to the most evil purposes. . . . She's so far gone now that she has no resemblance to a human except her body' (*Cluent.* 199).[42] Sassia is not the one on trial, but she makes an appealing scapegoat for all the woes of poor, innocent Cluentius, in Cicero's account. She is depicted as a monster like the mythical Medusa, who must be slain by the heroic defenders of masculinity, if only symbolically, through the vindication of Cluentius.

In Cicero's speech *In Defence of Caelius (Pro Caelio)*, he takes a similar approach in portraying his client Caelius as the innocent victim of another scheming widow, Clodia. Like Sassia, Clodia is accused of trumping up false murder charges against the guileless young male hero (*Cael.* 1, 55); in this case, because Caelius had broken up with her after a torrid affair.[43] Cicero pretends not to accuse Clodia of anything outright so that no one can criticise him for attacking a wealthy matron, but he insinuates plenty:

> I'm not saying anything about that woman now, but if there were a woman, unlike her, who whored herself out to everyone, who always had someone publicly designated as hers, in whose gardens, house, and place at Baiae everyone's appetites had free rein, who even supported young men financially and supplemented their fathers' stinginess with her own money – if a widow lives without restrictions, if a shameless woman lives without modesty, if a rich woman spends too much, if a lustful woman

lives like a prostitute – should I think a man is having an affair, if he greets a woman like that in a way that's a little too familiar? (*Cael.* 38; argument repeated at 49).[44]

Clodia, after her husband's death, is said to have turned his house from a private home into a public brothel,[45] and has even used her money to become a surrogate father or patron to the young men she wants to seduce.[46] Cicero's outrage here, however, is not really targeted at Clodia, but rather at an argument the prosecution had made: that Caelius had dishonoured Clodia and therefore had a bad character himself. To exculpate his client and shame the prosecutors for associating with Clodia, Cicero turns the tables and argues instead that Clodia had dishonoured herself and lured Caelius into her grasp. These examples show how Cicero used patriarchal norms to humiliate and degrade both men and women, depending on the case he was trying to make. If his opponents' sex lives involved anything outside the hegemonic norm of men exercising dominating power over their wives, or even if there was a rumour to that effect, Cicero exploited it in toxic attacks.

CONCLUSION

There are more examples of evil women subverting the fabric of society in Roman literature – Sempronia in Sallust's *Catilinarian Conspiracy*, Tullia Minor in Livy's account of the Roman monarchy, and members of the family of the Julio-Claudian emperors, including Livia, Julia the Elder and Agrippina the Younger. This stereotype, which Cicero uses to shame his male opponents, was prominent also in the writing of Roman history, and distorts our view of the real women behind the stereotype. These women do not seem to be mentioned by these authors because they shaped Rome's history; instead, they are described as a way of shaming the men who should have controlled them, according to the logic of elite Roman hegemonic masculinity. This logic dictates that any woman with autonomy or power has stolen it, and therefore must be a wicked and destructive woman like Clodia or Sassia, or a cruel gynocratic tyrant like Fulvia, all of them threats to all men everywhere.

It is difficult to know what kind of power these women really had, if any, and it is difficult to know if contemporary Roman audiences would have taken these descriptions as factual statements. What we can say with confidence is that these descriptions of women are used to tarnish the reputations of the men with whom they are associated. Power over households and power over political affairs both belong in the hands of men, according to patriarchal ideology, and in the hands of the right sort of men in particular. This parallel between private life and public life extends even further in Roman culture: to have authority and influence over others in public, a man must be seen to control and dominate his household in private, including enslaved people, children and women. That hierarchy and that degree of control were the norm in Roman society, but are no longer in modern America. Still, Cicero's invective tropes are similar to modern speech reflecting toxic masculinity, and they are toxic even in the context of Roman political culture, insofar as Cicero means to do harm both to Antony, by punishing him for having non-normative relationships, and to the reputations of women as collateral damage.

In both ancient and modern examples, this harmful speech reflects more basic sexist views beneath the surface, within the society's ideological foundations. First, it reflects an assumption that sexual preferences have a direct impact on political abilities, as Plutarch noted: non-normative sexual activities, because they are assigned a moral value and marked as deviant, are thought to be correlated with immoral or unjust political methods or policy views. Yet sexual norms are socially constructed and subject to change. The homophobic paranoia of the 'lavender scare' in 1950s American politics rested on such a view, but as norms have changed, openly gay and lesbian politicians have been elected to Congress, showing that a majority of their constituents do not believe they are morally compromised or unfit to serve. Hiding sexual preferences has led politicians to behave in corrupt or illegal ways, but their preferences only need to be covered up if they are perceived as socially unacceptable.[47] Secondly, a norm idealising men who are both sexually and politically dominant imposes restrictions on the kind of relationships men can have with their families and sexual partners, and even frames those families and sexual partners as potential rivals who can threaten a man's political standing.

The coupling of private and public under the ideology of hegemonic masculinity creates the impression that political influence consists of dominant authority and mastery over others. In fact, politics does not need to be a competitive, zero-sum game for dominance. Most if not all people, including most if not all men, are losers in that game.[48] Politics can be enacted instead through deliberation and collaboration by equal, free participants working towards a common good, regardless of their sexual preferences. This possibility has been recognised by radical feminists for decades. bell hooks quotes Cellestine Ware: 'radical feminism is working for the eradication of domination and elitism in all human relationships. This would make self-determination the ultimate good and require the downfall of society as we know it today.'[49]

NOTES

1. Hillard (1992) explores the relationship between rhetoric and reality in the treatment of powerful women. For Fulvia, see most recently Brennan 2012, 357–8. See also Skinner 1983 and 2011 on Clodia. Dixon (2001, 135–56) gives a history of how Clodia has been perceived in different ways.

2. In his treatise *On Obligations*, Cicero mentions a Roman equivalent, quoted from a lost tragedy: 'And so, in insults, we're quick to recite: "for you young men wear a feminine spirit, that maiden a man's"' (1.61). On the gender terminology he uses in Latin, see Santoro L'hoir 1992, 9–46.

3. Manne 2017, 79.

4. Kimmel and Wade 2018.

5. Connell 1987, 183–5 and Connell and Messerschmidt 2005, 882. Likewise, in ancient Rome, a *vir* was not just any biological man, but a free Roman man of good social standing, i.e. conforming to and embodying a hegemonic masculinity; see e.g. McDonnell 2006, 159–73.

6. Connell and Messerschmidt (2005, 846) stress in their return to the concept of hegemonic masculinity that hierarchies of masculinities exist, and that 'hegemony works in part through the production of exemplars of masculinity (e.g., professional sports stars), symbols that have authority despite the fact that most men and boys do not fully live up to them'.

7. Kimmel (2001, 281) describes homophobia as rooted in a desire to prove one's masculinity: 'being seen as unmanly is a fear that propels American men to deny manhood to others, as a way of *proving the unprovable* – that one is fully manly. Masculinity becomes a defence against the perceived threat of humiliation in the eyes of other men' (italics added for emphasis). Cf. Kupers 2005, 716. This experience of fear more or less corresponds to what Pleck called 'gender role strain' in his 1981 work.

8. Kupers 2005, 714: 'Toxic masculinity is the constellation of socially regressive male traits that serve to foster domination, the devaluation of women, homophobia, and wanton violence.'

9. Manne (2017, 63) describes misogyny as 'the "law enforcement" branch of a patriarchal order, which has the overall function of *policing* and *enforcing* its governing ideology'.

10. Kimmel 2001, 284–5: 'This is the manhood of racism, of sexism, of homophobia. It is the manhood that is so chronically insecure that it trembles at the idea of lifting the ban on gays in the military, that is so threatened by women in the workplace that women become the targets of sexual harassment, that is so deeply frightened of equality that it must ensure that the playing field of male competition remains stacked against all the newcomers to the game. Exclusion and escape have been the dominant methods American men have used to keep their fears of humiliation at bay. The fear of emasculation by other men, of being humiliated, of being seen as a sissy, is the leitmotif in my reading of the history of American manhood.'

11. On the legal status of Roman women see Gardner 1993, 85–109.

12. Richlin 1983, 97 and more broadly 96–104; Corbeill 1996, 128–73. This was true of Greek oratory as well: Glazebrook 2014.

13. 'οὔτε γὰρ γάμον οὔτε παιδοποιίαν τινὸς οὔτε δίαιταν οὔτε συμπόσιον ᾤοντο δεῖν ἄκριτον καὶ ἀνεξέταστον, ὡς ἕκαστος ἐπιθυμίας ἔχοι καὶ προαιρέσεως, ἀφεῖσθαι. πολὺ δὲ μᾶλλον ἐν τούτοις νομίζοντες ἢ ταῖς ὑπαίθροις καὶ πολιτικαῖς πράξεσι τρόπον ἀνδρὸς ἐνορᾶσθαι . . .'

14. On character (*ethos*) in Cicero's court speeches, see Kenty 2020.

15. Cicero wrote (or dictated to an enslaved scribe) his orations after he delivered them from memory and it is not clear how closely the written versions correspond to what he said.
16. Roman politicians often conducted business, met with clients and did other work at home, especially in the morning; senate meetings, public rallies or speeches, and trials usually took place in the forum.
17. On Chelidon, see Strong 2016, 77–80.
18. 'quae isto praetore non modo in iure civili privatorumque omnium controversiis populo Romano praefuit, verum etiam in his sartis tectisque dominata est'.
19. 'vereor ne quis forte de populo, qui priore actione non adfuit, haec, quia propter insignem turpitudinem sunt incredibilia, fingi a me arbitretur. ea vos antea, iudices, cognovistis'.
20. Langlands 2006, 293: 'This coincidence of behaviours has seemed strange to modern scholars, since it does not fit standard modern sexual categories, where "effeminate homosexual" and "womaniser" are mutually exclusive stereotypes.' On Cicero's treatment of Verres as effeminate, see Frazel 2009, 140–9.
21. 'ita civitas una sociorum atque amicorum duabus deterrimis mulierculis Verre praetore vectigalis fuit'. He calls them *mulierculae*, a diminutive of a disrespectful word for women; see Santoro L'hoir 1992, 39–40.
22. He refers to 'the profits [Pippa] made at night' (78), and indirectly calls Tertia a *meretrix* (83).
23. Bauman 1992, 66–7; he characterises Clodia in the same way, 69–73. On wealthy women patrons as independent economic actors, including Clodia, Fulvia and Cicero's wife Terentia, see Bielman 2012.
24. Actors and actresses, especially those who acted in mimes or pantomimes, were regarded as low-class and morally corrupt – Roman antiquity's porn stars. See Edwards 1997.
25. He first (probably) married a woman named Fadia, the daughter of a freedman (*Att.* 16.11; *Phil.* 2.3, 13.23); second, the daughter of Cicero's co-consul of 63 BCE, Antonius Hybrida (*Phil.* 2.99); then Fulvia; then Octavia, the sister of Octavian, his colleague in the second triumvirate. He had children with each of them, and with Cleopatra.
26. 'sumpsisti virilem, quam statim muliebrem togam reddidisti. primo volgare scortum; certa flagiti merces nec ea parva; sed cito Curio intervenit qui te a meretricio quaestu abduxit et, tamquam stolam dedisset, in matrimonio stabili et certo conlocavit'. I translate *scortum* as 'whore' because the Latin word is pejorative slang; the more technical term for prostitute is *meretrix*, literally 'a woman who earns money'.
27. Cf. Sussman 1998.
28. Fulvia was married to Curio until his death in 49 BCE, and married Antony a few years later. Her first husband was Publius Clodius Pulcher (d. 52 BCE), the enemy of Cicero and brother of Clodia, discussed below. Fulvia had two children with Clodius, one with Curio and two with Antony.
29. On views of active and passive sex partners, see especially Levin-Richardson and Kamen 2015.

30. On Volumnia's life, see Keith 2011.
31. 'vehebatur in essedo tribunus plebis; lictores laureati antecedebant, inter quos aperta lectica mima portabatur, quam ex oppidis municipales homines honesti, obviam necessario prodeuntes, non noto illo et mimico nomine, sed Volumniam consalutabant. sequebatur raeda cum lenonibus, comites nequissimi; reiecta mater amicam impuri fili tamquam nurum sequebatur. O miserae mulieris fecunditatem calamitosam! Horum flagitiorum iste vestigiis omnia municipia, praefecturas, colonias, totam denique Italiam impressit.'
32. Myers 2003, 342–4.
33. It is worth noting that the men who went out to greet Volumnia, like the men who went to Chelidon's house, are verifiable witnesses to these spectacles who can fact-check Cicero, so that Cicero is limited in how much he can fabricate about these scenes, and the audience might be more inclined to believe him.
34. Fertik 2017.
35. Traina 2001 and Strong 2016, 69–77. Pomeroy argues that Volumnia had the freedom to choose her lovers (1976, 198), but Traina (2001) and Strong (2016, 72) disagree.
36. 'raptam esse mimulam, quod dicitur Atinae factum a iuventute vetere quodam in scaenicos iure maximeque oppidano'.
37. James (2006) discusses the depictions of courtesans at banquets in Plautus and Ovid.
38. Myers (2003, 345) describes Cicero as 'mythologizing [Fulvia], first as one who, like a black widow spider, is fatal for her mate, then as an androgyne who can mesmerize as well as manipulate'.
39. 'calebant in interiore aedium parte totius rei publicae nundinae; mulier sibi felicior quam viris auctionem provinciarum regnorumque faciebat . . .'
40. 'semper eo tractus est quo libido rapuit, quo levitas, quo furor, quo vinolentia; semper eum duo dissimilia genera tenuerunt, lenonum et latronum; ita domesticis stupris, forensibus parricidiis delectatur ut mulieri citius avarissimae paruerit quam senatui populoque Romano'.
41. Richlin 1983, 101.
42. 'at quae mater! quam caecam crudelitate et scelere ferri videtis, cuius cupiditatem nulla umquam turpitudo retardavit, quae vitiis animi in deterrimas partis iura hominum convertit omnia . . . eo iam denique adducta est uti sibi praeter formam nihil ad similitudinem hominis reservarit'.
43. Dixon (2001, 84) points out that this strategy was opportunistic, since 'Cicero sneered at Clodia and Sassia for hovering in the background of prosecutions, but deferred respectfully to Caecilia Metella, who virtually engaged him to defend her dependant [sic], Roscius of Ameria (*Pro Roscio Amerino* 27).'
44. 'nihil iam in istam mulierem dico; sed, si esset aliqua dissimilis istius quae se omnibus pervolgaret, quae haberet palam decretum semper aliquem, cuius in hortos, domum, Baias iure suo libidines omnium commearent, quae etiam aleret adulescentis et parsimoniam patrum suis sumptibus sustineret; si vidua libere, proterva petulanter, dives effuse, libidinosa meretricio more viveret, adulterum ego putarem si quis hanc paulo liberius salutasset?'

45. Leen (2000) writes about the symbolism of Clodia's house as a den of sin in this speech, compared to other intact houses. On insinuating that Clodia is a *meretrix*, see McCoy 2006.
46. That was not actually extraordinary: Dixon 2001, 100–12.
47. This is not in any way to defend harmful, non-consensual or criminal sexual behaviour.
48. bell hooks (1984, 19) asks of mainstream white feminists: 'since men are not equals in white supremacist, capitalist, patriarchal class structure, which men do women want to be equal to?'
49. Ware 1970, 3.

CHAPTER 7

There's No Crying in Government: Romulus, Brutus and the Toxic Suppression of Grief

Jaclyn Neel

M y paper takes its title from the 1992 film *A League of their Own*, which is about women in professional sports during the mid-twentieth century.[1] After Tom Hanks' coach snarls at one of the players, she begins to cry; he is shocked, as 'there's no crying in baseball!'. The quote was included on the American Film Institute's top 100 quotes of all time.[2] A similar attitude towards tears is also visible in ancient Roman material: they are the province of women, rather than men. Amy Richlin has argued that male displays of grief were avoided as 'woman*ish*', although men clearly felt emotion;[3] Darja Šterbenc Erker has demonstrated that even at funerals, when grief was expected, the expected female (emotional, crying) role was differentiated from the expected male (rational, speaking/processing) role.[4] These norms, which are grounded in gender, already demonstrate hegemonic masculinity: male rationality supports men's superiority as heads of household and heads of state.[5] But behaviours that exceed the bounds of hegemonic masculinity may be toxic. In Rome, the hegemonic male was not expected to mourn excessively; was male suppression of grief then a toxic behaviour?

In this chapter, I examine the role played by visible grief in the early Roman *exempla* of Romulus and Brutus and its relation to hegemonic and toxic masculinity in the Roman world. The governing assumption of my analysis is that the actions I discuss are 'toxic' from the perspective of modern Western society; the murder of family members in particular is not normal. The question I address is whether the protagonists' responses to these actions were toxic from the perspective of the Romans: in particular, whether the protagonists' suppression of tears functioned as an authorial judgement that this behaviour is toxic.

Modern studies of masculinity suggest that the primary distinction between standard male behaviours and 'toxic' male behaviour(s) lies in the social consequences of any given act.[6] Thus behaviours in themselves are not toxic or normative; this judgement is culturally determined, in that it is the expectedness

of a given behaviour on the part of outside observers who share the same cultural and social background that makes that behaviour toxic or not.[7] In the case
of emotional suppression, as we see with unspoken restrictions on crying, the
consequences are primarily self-destructive.[8] Although this internally oriented
outcome may lead to other displays of toxic behaviour that affect others, such as
verbal or physical abuse, it need not.

Such internal effects are more difficult to measure in literary characters, who
cannot be subjected to research surveys; similarly, modern research findings
cannot be uncritically applied outside of their original context.[9] Societal expectations of male behaviour are not static. Ancient authors, however, did express
their own opinions of ancient behaviours via the reactions of an internal audience. Reference to linguistic cues and explanations can also help overcome the
culture gap between us and the original intended audiences.

A MODEL FOR MALE GRIEF

In order to further contextualise the behaviour of the characters from Roman
legend that I discuss, I will describe the limits of acceptable male grief based on
a historical case: Cicero's reaction to the death of his daughter Tullia. His experience offers a realistic parallel to what would have been 'standard' behaviour at
the time that accounts of these legendary figures were written. We know about
his grief not only from his five-book treatise on dying[10] but also from personal
letters. The latter seem to have been largely unedited and many provide an unfiltered view of his grief. Moreover, Cicero's fame even in his own lifetime suggests
that his works would have been familiar to at least Latin-speaking authors.

While Cicero, Livy and Dionysius were not social equals, they lived within
the same half-century span and commented on the behaviours of the same
classes.[11] Cicero's apparently extreme reaction to his daughter's death, and his
friends' response to that grief, shows us the limits of acceptable male mourning.
Based on Cicero's model, the reactions of Romulus and Brutus to the deaths of
their family members could be depicted as manifestations of toxic masculinity,
but could also be depicted in non-toxic ways.

ROMAN MEN AND GRIEF IN THE REPUBLIC

Modern researchers have emphasised that the suppression of grief is a common
male behaviour cross-culturally and transhistorically.[12] In the ancient world,
mourning was associated with women[13] and men were discouraged from actively
and openly grieving.[14] Male tears were expected and permissible on specific occasions, but limitations on male grief seem to have been policed, at least among
the high-status Romans who supply most of our literary evidence. It is rare to
hear from or about men of low social status in Roman literature; we cannot

assume that the standards for their behaviour were the same as those set for the *nobiles*. Indeed, Šterbenc Erker has argued that public grief was associated with lower social status.[15] Although brief appearances of sadness were acceptable and sometimes encouraged,[16] Cicero's first-hand account of grief offers evidence that Romans felt constrained by the expectations of male behaviour in Republican Rome.

The reactions of Cicero's friends to his overwhelming despair after the death of his daughter Tullia help us identify the boundaries of acceptable behaviour for high-status Roman men.[17] These responses suggest that a certain degree of emotional repression was normative:[18] when Cicero exhibits signs of depression, such as social withdrawal and rumination, his friends urge him to remember his social station and the greater importance of his civic duties.[19] Cicero's replies show that this encouragement to put his grief aside is ineffective and perhaps unwelcome;[20] however, it is clear from his letters that he is expected to return to normal activities as soon as possible.[21] Cicero's friends cannot not understand his inability to set aside his grief, as custom suggested that he should. This discrepancy between expected and actual experiences of grief suggests that the suppression of grief may have been a toxic aspect of masculinity in Rome, much as it is a toxic aspect of masculinity in the modern West.

Scholarship on male grief in antiquity suggests that tears were acceptable under certain circumstances, but grief ceased to be acceptable when it hindered active participation in civic life. This lesson is made clear from the outset of Roman history: according to Livy, when Lucretia died and Brutus founded the Republic, he urged the Romans to stop crying and act instead 'quod viros, quod Romanos deceret' ('as was right for men, for Romans').[22] This dichotomy of (female) grief and (male) action offers insight into normative male behaviour in Rome. Grief was acceptable, briefly; Lucretia's husband and father mourn immediately after her suicide.[23] Action, however, is more urgent, particularly action that benefits the state.

ROMANS AND THE *EXEMPLA* TRADITION

Exempla were traditional tales about exceptional Romans of the past. They were used as teaching tools and in literature as a means of conveying both Roman values and an author's own perspective on such values.[24] *Exempla* did not necessarily have a fixed meaning or significance – rather, they invited authorial moralising and were supposed to inspire critical thinking – but they generally did have a fixed virtue around which the *exemplum* was constructed. For example, the *exemplum* of Horatius Cocles centred on valour, while that of Lucretia emphasised chastity.[25] When thinking about gender behaviour, *exempla* of masculinity are similar to the ideal of hegemonic masculinity as it is described in modern research.[26] Like hegemonic masculinity, exemplary behaviours are not real.

Instead, they inform us about cultural ideals and provided ancient audiences with an authoritative picture of the socially correct way to respond to particular circumstances. These models could change over time, as different 'ideals, fantasies, and desires' about male behaviour came into being.[27]

The two characters I analyse, Romulus and Brutus, were founders of the Roman state.[28] As such, their actions held exemplary value to all Romans, but particularly to the wealthy Romans of the governing classes who were the most likely to read and write literary texts. Since the stories of both Romulus and Brutus involve civic strife, they were particularly resonant during and after the civil wars of the first century BCE. In surviving authors, civil war is often assimilated to familial conflict; Romulus' and Brutus' failures to grieve thus offer commentary on both public and private behaviours.

There is some debate about the historicity of both Romulus and Brutus, but I will analyse them from the perspective of useful and moralising fictions. That is, I am not concerned with the putative historical reality upon which their deeds are based;[29] rather, I start from the presumption that Romulus and Brutus are models for Roman civic behaviour. Their characters were malleable; their emotions, motivations and aims[30] could be depicted differently in different authors. Such flexibility has significance for the question of toxic behaviour. Moreover, as *exempla* the behaviour modelled by Romulus and Brutus was, ideally, iterative.[31] Because their behaviours could be held up as ideals, Romulus and Brutus also shaped later generations of Romans.

There is a certain degree of circularity in examining figures who are both shaped by contemporary thought and who also shape subsequent thought. The fact that both characters were the subject of a long tradition of historical thinking helps, but only a little; the dynamism of this tradition is a recurrent theme in scholarship.[32] As Langlands observes, however, exemplary figures are 'both exceptional and representative' of the Roman community.[33] As such, they are good test cases for the extremes of male behaviour. As exceptional successes, their emotional responses may differ from those of the elite men whose values were informed by such *exempla*. In particular, since grief makes a man act like a woman (from a Roman perspective), these founding figures of Rome avoid displaying open grief. Authors differ, however, in their evaluations of this grief avoidance.

ROMULUS' AND BRUTUS' GRIEF

The need to hide grief is a key feature of the legends of both Romulus and Brutus. Unlike Cicero, who could not have prevented the death of his daughter Tullia, some versions of Romulus' story portrayed him as responsible for the death of his brother, and Brutus ordered the deaths of his sons. Close-kin murder in itself was not necessarily a toxic behaviour in Roman society.[34] Brutus' role in his sons' deaths in particular is not due to toxic masculinity in the modern sense of the term; rather, as many scholars have shown, his decision to put the safety of the state before the wellbeing of his family is an admirable quality from the Roman perspective.[35] But it is less clear that his lack of grief was not toxic. The Greek immigrant author Dionysius of Halicarnassus says that Brutus' lack of grief was remarkable, which suggests that this Roman behaviour may have been viewed as toxic by contemporary Greeks, including Dionysius himself. Indeed, the evidence from Livy and Dionysius is interesting from the perspective of toxic behaviour, since Livy portrays Romulus as a murderer and Brutus as a justified executioner; Dionysius, in contrast, depicts Romulus grieving his brother's death and Brutus as unfeeling.

ROMULUS

Both Livy and Dionysius provide two options regarding the death of Remus. In one version of the story, Remus dies in an anonymous brawl before the foundation of the city, and in another Remus is killed while the city's walls are being built.[36] Livy's language makes it clear that both versions occur in an atmosphere of intense competition. Romulus and Remus are seized with the desire (*cupido*) to found their own city.[37] The word *cupido* generally has negative connotations, which are enhanced when Livy reiterates that the desire for the city is accompanied by an ancestral curse of wishing to be king ('avitum malum, regni cupido'). This language prepares the reader for the coming struggle between Romulus and Remus' partisans, which Livy describes with a succession of terms relating to conflict: 'cum <u>altercatione</u> congressi <u>certamine irarum</u> ad <u>caedem</u> vertuntur' ('having gathered for <u>debate</u>, they went from a <u>contest of insults</u> to <u>slaughter</u>').[38] Remus dies, either at this point or later, when as a joke (*ludibrio*), he jumps across the walls that Romulus is building; furious (*irato, increpitans*), Romulus kills him.[39]

Livy offers little commentary on Remus' death or Romulus' reaction. Rex Stem has argued that Livy's silence is meant to make the reader consider the force of the *exemplum*: is Romulus behaving irrationally, or does Remus deserve it for joking about a serious matter like the foundation?[40] Some scholars have taken the latter view, arguing that Romulus is protecting the city wall and therefore demonstrating a key Roman virtue: that is, putting the safety of the state before personal or family gain.[41] Others, however, point to Romulus' later characterisation as a tyrant and suggest that the death of Remus is the first manifestation of this negative characteristic.[42] From the perspective of this chapter, it is more important that Romulus does not grieve when his brother dies; instead, he utters a *sententia* about the walls. Livy thus reinforces the idea that men should not mourn even when faced with the death of their closest relatives.

Livy does not avoid depicting grief elsewhere: Loredana de Libero has catalogued many examples of tears in Livy.[43] Although many of these tears come from people of lower status, supporting Šterbenc Erker's argument about the class-based element of crying, historical examples of bereaved Romans suggest that it was culturally acceptable to briefly mourn an unexpected death, even in a situation of conflict.[44] While other examples in Livy's history depict the absence of grief in the service of the state,[45] Remus' death is motivated by Romulus' anger ('ab irato Romulo').[46] There is no indication in Livy's narrative that Romulus' anger disappears after Remus has died, that he regrets the death of his brother, or even that he buries Remus.[47] The text shifts away from these uncomfortable questions to tell the story of Hercules and Cacus,[48] and when we next see Romulus (in 1.8) he is determining the laws of the new city.

Dionysius relates the same options for Remus' death as Livy: Remus dies in a brawl (1.87.3) or is killed when he jumps over the walls (1.87.4). The emphasis of Dionysius' account, however, is on Romulus' grief. Immediately after relating the brawl, Dionysius characterises Romulus' accession to the kingship as a 'bitter victory' (νίκην οἰκτίστην), because it had cost him the life of his brother and many citizens. Dionysius goes on to specify that Romulus buried his brother and was initially so depressed that he considered suicide.[49] This reaction parallels historical accounts of accidental murder in both Greek and Roman texts.[50] As we saw above in the case of Cicero's grief, Romulus was encouraged to end his mourning and continue with the business of state; unlike Cicero, the exemplary Romulus follows this advice.

In Dionysius' view, the civil strife of the foundation mirrors the intense degree of competition between Romulus and Remus. Dionysius is even more explicit than Livy about the tyrannical end of Romulus' reign: he prefers the story that Romulus was murdered because of his regal behaviour.[51] Yet Remus, who has been tricked out of the kingship, is also angry.[52] It is curious, then, that Dionysius' account of Romulus, which depicts a brother grief-stricken over the accidental death of his twin, has more commonly been seen as 'idealising'.[53] Instead, Dionysius seems to follow Roman norms of male grieving behaviour more closely than Livy does.

In Dionysius' account, Romulus mourns briefly, but is recalled to his public duties, much as Cicero's friends advised him to do. Although Dionysius was writing at the end of a period of intense civic strife in Rome, it is unlikely that his account of Romulus was wholly driven by that conflict. Dionysius' primary audience seems to have been Greek, and he takes pains to explain Roman customs.[54] It is likely that Romulus' behaviour here provides an accurate depiction of masculine norms at the time.

Livy's account of Romulus, in contrast, is more ideologically oriented: Romulus shows a degree of control over his emotions that is not paralleled in surviving accounts of historically attested grief.[55] Livy's emphasis on Romulus' anger, together with his later descent into tyranny, suggests that Romulus' lack of grief over Remus is abnormal. This suppression of emotion, perhaps connected to his evil (*malus*) ambition to be king, may be seen as a toxic restriction of normal male grief. Yet Livy's language suggests that Romulus' reaction to Remus' death is a symptom, rather than the cause, of his toxic masculinity. The truly toxic behaviour lies in both twins' unbridled ambition to rule, which Livy describes in the tragic terms of ancestral inheritance.

BRUTUS

As a consul after the expulsion of the ruling dynasty, Brutus was tasked with negotiating the permanent departure of Rome's kings. Some citizens chafed under the republican regime and conspired to bring the kings back. Two of these conspirators were Brutus' only sons, and when their treason was uncovered, Brutus had to execute them.

As in the case of Remus' death, Livy and Dionysius tell the same basic story with a different emotional twist.[56] It is important to emphasise, however, that in both authors Brutus is acting both as *paterfamilias* (head of the family) and as a magistrate with *imperium* (the power of life and death). These two offices represented the highest levels of power available to a Roman of the Republic: the *paterfamilias* had the most power in a private setting, while the magistrate with *imperium* bore the full power of the state. The combination of these two powers was so striking that there was a series of *exempla* on the theme 'fathers who killed their sons for not following the laws'.[57] These stories were only partially prescriptive: in most of them, the father killed his only son, thus putting an end to the family line. This behaviour was thus a form of self-sacrifice that also removed the responsibility of later repetition. But the overall message of state over self and community over personal gain was important to the promulgation of these *exempla*.

As Andrew Feldherr has emphasised, Livy's account centres not on Brutus, but on the observations of the Roman citizens around him.[58] The importance of Brutus being watched is emphasised by Livy's use of words relating to sight (*conspectius, spectator, oculos*). The episode is written to draw the reader's sympathy to Brutus. Livy notes two ironies of the affair, in inverse order: first, that Brutus should not have had to see his sons' execution, but was forced to oversee that execution as the chief magistrate;[59] and second, that the sons should not have conspired against the state at all, since their father had freed it.[60] In Livy's version of the story, Brutus' grief is within acceptable bounds: he is visibly, but silently and tearlessly, moved by the death of his sons ('pater voltusque et os eius spectaculo esset','they watched the father's face and mouth'). The use of both *vultus* and *os* here is likely a hendiadys for 'face', yet it is significant that Livy does not draw attention to Brutus' eyes, which would be the most significant part of his anatomy if Brutus were close to tears.[61] The specific reference to his mouth (*os*) as well as his general expression (*voltus*) suggests a clenched jaw or compressed lips as a way of controlling emotion. Instead of focusing on Brutus' internal response, Livy focalises his external reaction through the spectators. This emphasis again deflects the possibility of Brutus' grief and instead focuses on his duty to punish his sons' treason. Brutus' mental state ('eminente animo patrio', 'with his *patrius* spirit clearly visible') is similarly impassive; while *patrio* may here have the same significance as *paterno* and refer to his 'fatherly emotion',[62] the context of Brutus as an *exemplum* makes it equally likely that he is displaying his 'familial' or 'hereditary' sense of duty to his country (*patria*).

If this interpretation is correct, then Brutus' lack of emotion at his sons' death is marked in Livy's narrative. Livy emphasises that Brutus is the object of everyone's gaze, but also carefully notes his self-control. Brutus keeps his duty to the country in mind, and becomes an *exemplum* because he does not show his emotion. Moreover, Livy does not directly comment on Brutus' actions, but presents them as normative. This reticence is in contrast to Dionysius, who opens his account of the episode with a caveat to his readers: 'Τὰ δὲ μετὰ ταῦτα ἔργα θατέρου τῶν ὑπάτων Βρούτου μεγάλα καὶ θαυμαστὰ λέγειν ἔχων, ἐφ᾽οἷς μέγιστα φρονοῦσι Ῥωμαῖοι, δέδοικα μὴ σκληρὰ καὶ ἄπιστα τοῖς Ἕλλησι δόξω λέγειν' ('I am about to relate the impressive and awe-inspiring actions of Brutus, one of the consuls, which followed. Romans think most highly of them, but I am afraid that they will seem harsh and incredible to Greeks').[63] Dionysius draws attention to the impressive nature of Brutus' actions, and while the rest of his sentence takes up the theme of the θαυμαστὰ (that is, why Greeks might not believe in Brutus' behaviour), the rest of the story centres on the μεγάλα (that is, why the behaviour is impressive). The description of Brutus' actions as σκληρὰ gains additional power when we remember that Dionysius was writing primarily for Greeks. This word implies a hardness that can be both admirable (in the sense of strong-willed) and repellent (in the sense of cruel). It is noteworthy because Dionysius' opinion of most Roman leaders is positive; at the outset of the work, he notes that Rome was able to conquer Greece due to its 'μυρίας . . . ἀνδρῶν ἀρετὰς' ('thousands of varieties of male excellence').[64] Thus Dionysius more typically approves of Roman actions. Although he does not explicitly state that Brutus' behaviour is toxic or wrong, Dionysius leaves the possibility open; a contemporary observer would be aware that Brutus is awe-inspiring, but not necessarily a positive role model for Dionysius' own culture (as opposed to the Roman culture that Dionysius describes).

Unlike Livy, who describes Brutus' sons only in terms of what happens to them, Dionysius gives the young men a voice and emotions. Their reaction is set in contrast with Brutus' lack of emotional response – a contrast which emphasises Brutus' ability to control himself and focus on the task at hand. After his sons' role in the conspiracy is discovered and Brutus condemns them to death, the sons weep and attempt to rouse his paternal affection for them.[65] The language emphasises that the sons are, in fact, weeping: ὀλοφυρομένους in particular is used of lamentation over the dead, allowing the reader to understand that the sons are mourning their coming fate. The boys' relative youth and lack of power may make it more acceptable for them to show public displays of emotion. But it is also a call for public sympathy, which Dionysius notes was effective: the crowd in his retelling is aghast at Brutus' decision, although they know that the sons are criminals.

Dionysius notes that Brutus' even-handedness in carrying out the penalty was amazing (θαυμαστὸν again): a consul had the ability to lessen the severity of the penalty, but Brutus holds to the letter of the law and does not grieve at his sons' public humiliation and execution. This behaviour is more noteworthy in contrast to the actions of his fellow consul Collatinus, whose nephews were implicated in the same conspiracy. Collatinus pleads with Brutus to spare his nephews' lives, even at the cost of being exiled himself.[66] Dionysius has juxtaposed the very different behaviour of Brutus and Collatinus to drive home the lesson of Brutus' *exemplum*. By showing his Greek readers the behaviour that they might expect to see (Collatinus'), he makes the unexpected behaviour of Brutus both more credible and more awe-inspiring.

Dionysius describes Brutus' self-control as the most amazing aspect of the entire story. It requires several sentences for him to adequately explain the power of Brutus' utter lack of emotional response to his sons' death, in contrast to the weeping of the other spectators:

> ὑπὲρ ἅπαντα δὲ τὰ παράδοξα καὶ θαυμαστὰ τοῦ ἀνδρὸς <u>τὸ ἀτενὲς</u> <u>τῆς ὄψεως</u> καὶ <u>ἄτεγκτον</u> ἦν· ὅς γε τῶν ἄλλων ἁπάντων ὅσοι τῷ πάθει παρεγένοντο κλαιόντων μόνος <u>οὔτ᾽ ἀνακλαυσάμενος</u> ὤφθη τὸν μόρον τῶν τέκνων <u>οὔτ᾽ ἀποιμώξας</u> ἑαυτὸν τῆς καθεξούσης τὸν οἶκον ἐρημίας <u>οὔτ᾽ ἄλλο μαλακὸν οὐθὲν ἐνδούς</u>, ἀλλ᾽ <u>ἀδακρύς</u> τε καὶ <u>ἀστένακτος</u> καὶ <u>ἀτενὴς</u> διαμένων εὐκαρδίως ἤνεγκε τὴν συμφοράν. οὕτως ἰσχυρὸς ἦν τὴν γνώμην καὶ βέβαιος τὰ κριθέντα διατηρεῖν καὶ τῶν ἐπιταραττόντων τοὺς λογισμοὺς <u>παθῶν καρτερός</u>.[67]

> The <u>directness of his gaze</u> and <u>his relentless lack of tears</u> was the most incredible and awe-inspiring part. All the others who were there lamented, but he alone was seen <u>not crying</u> over the death of his children, <u>not bewailing</u> the desolation about to settle on his house, <u>not</u> showing any <u>softness or give</u>; rather, <u>his eyes were dry, he did not groan, and he held his gaze continually firm</u> as he endured his misfortune with resolution. In this way he was firm in his decision, sure of the judgement, and <u>in control of the emotions</u> that trouble rational thought.

Dionysius emphasises Brutus' lack of tears by reiterating this self-control multiple times per sentence. The opening sentence returns to the awe-inspiring quality (θαυμαστὰ) of Brutus' behaviour, and the closing sentence revisits the impression that a Greek audience might have. At the beginning of this story, Dionysius expresses his concern that a Greek reader might find Brutus' behaviour too severe (σκληρὰ), which implies that it is beyond the norm in a negative way – in other words, it is toxic.[68] Dionysius tries to redefine this behaviour in Roman terms at the end: rather than σκληρὰ, Brutus' behaviour is the behaviour of a strong (ἰσχυρὸς, καρτερός) hegemonic male. Although we do not know how Dionysius' audience would have responded to this redefinition, the fact that he needed to introduce the idea of overly harsh behaviour only to redefine it suggests that he expected a negative reaction.

The story of Brutus' sons provides a good example of how behaviour is judged differently by different cultures; as Dionysius noted, the Romans are proud of Brutus' resolve. Livy's account provides an example of this pride. It does not centre on Brutus' lack of grief, as Dionysius' does; rather, it takes Brutus' resolve as understood and emphasises his attachment to civic duty. Dionysius, in contrast, must explain Brutus' behaviour to a different culture; in doing so, he is careful to point out the ways in which Brutus maintains Roman norms of male behaviour. Therefore, although Dionysius seems aware that his audience would perceive Brutus' behaviour as beyond the bounds of typical male action, he tries to normalise it in its cultural context. Rather than centring on the civic duty of killing one's treasonous children, Dionysius' account focuses on the masculine behaviour of controlling one's emotion. In doing so, he makes Brutus' non-standard behaviour more palatable to a Greek audience. As a result, even Dionysius' account does not suggest that Brutus' execution of his sons is a manifestation of toxic masculinity.

CONCLUSION

This chapter has approached two exemplary stories in two different authors. Much more could be said: both Romulus and Brutus are discussed by numerous other authors (including Cicero, Vergil, Ovid and Plutarch) and from a variety of different generic perspectives. Although Livy and Dionysius are both writing about the legendary past from a historical perspective, their accounts indicate that they had different approaches to the topic of appropriate masculine behaviour.

In regard to the two case studies I examine, the death of Remus at the hands of Romulus and Brutus' execution of his treasonous sons, the evidence for toxic masculinity is inconclusive. The killing of relatives is, in itself, not an inherently toxic behaviour to either author. The reactions of Romulus and Brutus to these deaths, however, are depicted differently. In Livy, neither Romulus nor Brutus grieves; Brutus is praised for this dedication to Rome, but Romulus' reaction is suspicious due to his desire for personal gain (*regni cupido*). In Dionysius, by contrast, only Romulus grieves. In Dionysius' view, this grief is natural and does not receive comment. Brutus, on the other hand, does not grieve over his sons' death, and Dionysius takes pains to explain why that absence of grief is laudable. This effort suggests that Dionysius expected his audience to find that behaviour toxic; however, his emphasis on the amazing quality of Brutus' self-control does not require that he himself found Brutus' behaviour toxic.

Based on the evidence in this chapter, toxic masculinity in antiquity cannot be located in individual behaviours. Rather, the commentary and judgement of ancient authors can support a modern claim for toxic male behaviours. Authorial discussions provide the necessary context with which to read an episode from Roman eyes. Thus, while a modern view may see the endemic violence of antiquity as toxic in itself, Romans differentiated between violence that was beneficial and violence that was harmful. Similarly, a man's effort to hide public displays of grief was not toxic when he did so with the explicit aim of continuing to govern; but a total lack of grief, as with Livy's Romulus, or an inadequate display of grief, as Dionysius fears his Greek readers will read into Brutus, were abnormal. This unexpectedly absent grief, which is marked in ancient narratives, may be viewed as toxic in our terms, but this judgement requires additional support from the text(s).

NOTES

1. The plot summary of the film can be found on the American Film Institute's website (https://catalog.afi.com/Catalog/moviedetails/59298), which also notes that the line 'was inspired by a story conference meeting on another film . . . [in which] a male producer lost his patience with a female director who cried. The producer reportedly said under his breath, "What is this crying? Did Howard Hawks ever cry at a meeting?"' (AFI, n.d.).
2. See https://www.afi.com/100years/quotes.aspx; the scene is on YouTube: https://youtu.be/6M8szlSa-8o.
3. Richlin 2001, 234.
4. Šterbenc Erker 2011.
5. See Messerschmidt 2019, 86–7, 90: hegemonic masculinity always serves to subjugate women, but may also serve to differentiate men of different status.
6. Kupers 2005, 717, with earlier references; see also Rosenwein 2010, 19–21, for the social construction of emotion. 'Standard' behaviour is not a term of scholarship, and I use it here to differentiate the observed roles and behaviours that are neither 'toxic' (that is, causing harm to the self or others) nor 'hegemonic' (reinforcing dominance; for the debate about this term and reaffirmation of its transhistorical and cross-cultural relevance, see e.g. Connell and Messerschmidt 2005, esp. 845–53, and Messerschmidt 2019).
7. See this volume's Introduction (2–4) for an overview of the modern literature on the topic of toxic and hegemonic masculinity.

8. See e.g. Creighton and Oliffe 2010, esp. 409–10; Parent, Gobble, and Rochlen 2018.

9. See Connell and Messerschmidt 2005, 846–7.

10. The *Tusculan Disputations*.

11. The precise dates of composition and circulation of Livy's and Dionysius' works are debated, but a general consensus would place Livy in approximately 30 BCE and Dionysius two decades later (in contrast, Tullia's death in 45 BCE is secure).

12. Creighton et al. 2013, esp. 36: 'gender restraints can constrain men's expressions and perhaps experiences of death related grief'; Veissière 2018, esp. 277: 'across cultures and throughout histories, these [gender] archetypes have been proven to be highly similar'. Han Baltussen has studied Cicero's grief over Tullia in particular: see Baltussen 2009, 2013. He argues that there are several aspects of Cicero's experience that can be analysed using approaches developed in studies of modern grief (e.g., Baltussen 2009, 356–8); however, he also offers the salutary warning that scholars must differentiate between 'the expression of how he *felt* . . . and how he chose to channel his feelings into actions' (Baltussen 2009, 363, original emphasis). Unfortunately, the latter aspect is rarely available in ancient evidence.

13. See e.g. Šterbenc Erker 2011.

14. E.g., Cic. *Fam.* 4.5.2, *Att.* 12.13–28. Kappas (2009, 420–1) suggests that globally, masculine norms discourage extended grief; Kampen (2012, 168–70) argues that these norms come from a desire for public composure, rather than a denial of emotion in men. See also Wilcox 2005, esp. 244–50, for a discussion of the competitive aspect of consolatory rhetoric.

15. See e.g. Šterbenc Erker 2011.

16. For example, men on trial often wore mourning to indicate their innocence: see e.g. Livy 6.20.1–2.

17. See e.g. Gleason 1995 *passim* (explicitly stated at e.g. 159); Williams 1999, esp. 151–6; McDonnell 2006, esp. 166–72 (but see 205 for Brutus' sons); Balmaceda 2017, 17–19.

18. Seider (2016) comes to a similar conclusion about Catullus, arguing that the poet found available male models of grief inadequate, and turned to female mythological characters to work through the pain of his brother's death. The problematic nature of male grief holds true in later authors as well: Schorn (2009, 354–6) doubts whether Plutarch's ascription of grief to Cato the Younger is complimentary; Fögen (2009, 195) states that 'in Ovid, male tears are never mentioned without a certain comic aspect'; Lateiner (2009, 129) argues that male tears in Plutarch arise from 'a generous pity for others, never a self-centered grief or anxiety for self'. Konstan (2010) provides an overview of grief in antiquity.

19. See esp. *Fam.* 4.5.2, 4.5.5; 4.6.2 for Cicero's response.

20. E.g., *Att.* 12.14; 12.15; 12.20.1. According to Treggiari (1998, 14–22), even Cicero's grief about Tullia's death (for which he was criticised) was defensible and correct in Cicero's view; Hope (2017, 60–2) argues that Cicero's openness about his grief prefigured the broader acceptance of familial emotion under the Principate. Wilcox (2005) observes that Cicero is in some ways hypocritical, as he uses the same rhetoric to address his friends' grief; see esp. 251–2.

21. As Hope (2017, 61) notes: 'Cicero was criticized, not because of his genuine grief for his daughter, but because for a short while he neglected his public persona'; however, she also admits that socially acceptable practices of the bereaved in the Roman world were 'only related to public image' and probably did little to 'alleviat[e] . . . real pain' (p. 64).
22. Livy 1.59.4.
23. See Livy 1.58.12–59.4; the description of Brutus as *castigator lacrimarum* in 1.59.3 is reminiscent of the role played by Cicero's friends.
24. As such, Romulus and Brutus can contribute to an 'emotional community' (Rosenwein 2010) that elucidates and embodies communal norms.
25. For Cocles, see e.g. Roller 2004 and 2018, 32–65. For Lucretia, see e.g. Joshel 1992 and Seita 2000, 503–12.
26. See Connell and Messerschmidt 2005, 832, 838 and 846: the hegemonic male is an ideal rather than reality, and is not found in any living men.
27. Connell and Messerschmidt 2005, 838.
28. I have discussed the historical development of these stories previously (see Neel 2014, 142–206, esp. 146–8 and 199–200); only the most important works and additions to the literature since 2014 are provided in the notes.
29. The faith of modern scholars in the historicity of Romulus and Brutus varies. Smith 2007 e.g. makes Brutus an 'improved' Romulus. For Romulus, see e.g. De Sanctis 2009 for his historicity; Mastrocinque 1993 for cross-cultural comparanda; Wiseman (1995) argues that the story is a relatively late invention. For Brutus, see e.g. Poucet 2000, 261–70 and Welwei 2001. Wiseman (1998b (=2008, 307–12) argues that the accounts that have reached us are attempts to reconcile mutually inconsistent versions. Wiseman (1998a), Seita (2000) and Koptev (2012) argue that drama may have transmitted some historical facts to Roman audiences before the advent of written history; Wiseman (2008, 293–305) also adds the role of family history, and expresses doubts about the historicity of early Republican history in an important afterword (312–19).
30. See Shay 2000 for the examination of a similar trio of qualities ('attachments, ideals, and ambitions', e.g. p. 33) as a means of measuring emotion in Homeric characters.
31. See Roller 2004, 23–4, on the importance of 'structural imitation' for the creation of an *exemplum*.
32. See Neel 2014, 142–206, with references, for examples of these arguments.
33. Langlands 2018, 38.
34. Although this chapter is not concerned with the legality or correctness of either Romulus' or Brutus' actions, this legality has been the focus of much scholarship and may be surprising to non-specialist readers. It is helpful to consider the non-toxic nature of Romulus' and Brutus' early careers, both of which involve murder that is sanctioned by the community and hence is clearly not toxic. Although the familial strife that marks the early lives of both Romulus and Brutus would be considered toxic in the modern West, Romulus and Brutus are depicted as heroic. Romulus, in fact, is hegemonically masculine: young and strong, he rescues his kidnapped brother and imprisoned grandfather. Brutus, on the other

hand, responds to the violence in his own household by withdrawing into an outwardly effeminate role. In this feminised form, Brutus is disregarded and hence permitted to survive.

Romulus and his twin brother Remus were exposed by their great-uncle Amulius, a usurper who had possibly killed their mother (e.g., Livy 1.3; Dion. Hal. 1.76–9; Plut. *Rom.* 3–4). Rescued as infants, they were raised in ignorance of their true identity. As adolescents, they learned of their exposure and returned to the palace to kill Amulius, a deed that is viewed positively by all ancient sources. This murder is justified on several grounds: Amulius is a tyrant; he holds the throne illegitimately; he had tried to kill the boys; and he had committed multiple murders. Because Romulus and Remus did not seek the throne for themselves but returned it to the rightful king Numitor, the act of killing Amulius is depicted by ancient authors as deliverance from tyranny. Similarly, Brutus begins his career by killing his uncle, the seventh king of Rome Tarquinius Superbus. Like Amulius, Tarquin is a tyrant (e.g., Livy 1.49; Dion. Hal. 4.41, 4.68) who holds the throne illegitimately, having gained it through multiple murders (of the previous king, his own brother and wife, and Brutus' father and brother). Ancient accounts make clear that he had also attempted to kill Brutus, but Brutus' feigned mental disability had made the murder seem unnecessary. As with the murder of Amulius, our authors imply that the overthrow of Tarquin is justified because of his violent behaviour. The violence of tyrants can only be remedied with force.

35. See e.g. Saller 1994, 102–32; Shaw 2001, 56–68; and Haimson Lushkov 2015, 30–60. The ancient evidence is summarised and cited in O'Hara 1998, 212. A number of scholars have addressed the question of the *ius vitae necisque* and its relation to *patria potestas*: see e.g. Thomas 1984; Capogrossi Colognesi 1990; Gardner 1993; Lentano 2005. esp. 558–60 and 581–6; Gaughan 2010, 21–45 (esp. 28–9 on Brutus); and Sanna 2014.

36. Livy 1.6–7, Dion. Hal. 1.87.2–3. This episode is much discussed; for the history of the question, see Neel 2014, chapters 3 and 5.

37. Livy 1.6.3, 'Romulum Remumque cupido cepit . . . urbis condendae'. See Miles (1995, 146–8) on Romulus' abandonment of kinship in this episode.

38. Livy 1.7.2.

39. Livy 1.7.3.

40. Stem 2007, 444–8.

41. E.g., Bremmer 1987; De Sanctis 2009.

42. See Livy 1.15.8 (esp.) –16.5 for Romulus' tyrannical characteristics, including a bodyguard and popular appeal. The connection with Remus' death was made by Krämer 1965; other negative views include Classen 1962 and Strasburger 1968. This negative interpretation has found little favour in modern scholarship (see e.g. Cornell 1977 and Ampolo 1988), but has the benefit of being attested in antiquity: see e.g. Horace, *Ep.* 7 and Cic., *Off.* 3.41 (discussed in Neel 2014, 79–87). Greek authors also discuss the tyrannical end of Romulus' life; see below, p. 109 n. 47.

43. See de Libero 2009, 218–21.

44. See e.g. Bannon 1997, 149, citing Livy *Epit.* 79 and Val. Max. 5.5.4; Richlin 2001, 232–4.

45. In addition to Brutus, discussed below, see the story of Horatius Pulvillus in Livy 2.8.

46. See e.g. ver Eecke (2008, 207–22) on the relationship between the death of Remus and Rome's civil wars in the first century BCE. Most of the scholarship on anger in antiquity analyses evidence from the Greek world: e.g. Konstan 2005, 2008 and 2015, 403–4. According to Konstan (2005, 243), ancient definitions of anger require insulting behaviour from a person of lower status. Although Livy emphasises the equality of the twins Romulus and Remus in 1.6, Remus' death comes after an initial contest which each twin believes he had won. It is therefore possible that, focalised from Romulus' point of view, Remus is lesser and has committed a grave insult by jumping over the wall. Bannon (1997, 165) notes that the use of passives is curious, given Livy's emphasis on Romulus' anger.

47. As Kaster (2005, 66–83) notes, the Roman 'emotional script' of regret differs from ours, but regret was a recognised and recognisable emotion. The discussion of regret, *utilitas* and *honestas* is relevant to Cicero's characterisation of Romulus in *Off.* 3.41, which Livy had presumably read, but this language is absent from Livy's own narrative.

48. Bannon (1997, 166) points out the parallelism between the civilisers Romulus and Hercules, which suggests that Remus is parallel to the brigand Cacus; see also Stem 2007, 449. Although Livy is again silent about Hercules' burial of Cacus, context makes such a burial unlikely.

49. Dion. Hal. 1.87.3.

50. See e.g. Adrastos in Herodotus 1.35–45; Huskinson 2011, 117. Magdelain (1984, 560–1) discusses the importance of intent in Roman law.

51. Dion. Hal. 2.56 for the death of Romulus; §3 for Romulus' tyranny.

52. Dion. Hal. 1.87.4, 'ἀχθόμενον δὲ καὶ δι' ὀργῆς ἔχοντα'; there is a parallel story in Diod. Sic. 8.5–6.

53. Fox 1993, 34–5; note, however, that Fox thinks Dionysius' account is more likely to be typical of the tradition before Livy. Contrast Delcourt (2005, 245–58), who emphasises the originality of Dionysius' presentation; in particular, Dionysius is the only author to omit a version in which Romulus kills Remus (258).

54. See e.g. Dion. Hal. 2.6 on the importance of auspices.

55. See Richlin 2001, 233, 'moralizing stories about men who do not grieve suggest that this represented unusual self-control'; Seider (2016, 282–3) agrees, with further references; see also above, p. 106, nn. 14–15.

56. See Livy 2.3–5; Dion. Hal. 5.8–10.

57. As Shaw (2001) notes, this behaviour is exemplary but atypical: the only examples of fathers killing their adult sons without penalty are when those sons have committed a crime against the state.

58. Feldherr 1998, 197–203, esp. 201–2.

59. Livy 2.5.5, 'poenae capiendae ministerium patri de liberis consulatus imposuit, et qui spectator erat amovendus, eum ipsum fortuna exactorem supplicii dedit'.

See also Haimson Lushkov 2015, 31, 'were Brutus not a father, the execution would have been a routine trial . . . without the moral dilemma . . . Filicide, in this context, is problematic not only for its own moral quandaries, but also because it replicates to some degree the perversion of family bonds under the monarchy to which Brutus himself had drawn particular attention.'

60. Livy 2.5.7.

61. Compare, for example, Cic. *De Or.* 3.221: 'imago animi voltus est, indices oculi'.

62. As Ogilvie (1965, 246) notes (*ad* Livy 2.5.8), Brutus' show of paternal emotion is otherwise unattested. Ogilvie himself thinks that Brutus' emotion is a Livian innovation to increase the tragedy of the scene, as '*emineo* is only used where an emotion or the like is conspicuous'. Brutus' *virtus* and *pietas* are also conspicuous in this episode, and Brutus' exemplary civic virtue is notable here.

63. Dion. Hal. 5.8.1. This type of extradiegetic comment has been analysed by Fromentin (2010) and Sautel (2015, 14–29), neither of whom includes this passage; it seems likely that it falls under Fromentin's category of 'apologetic' and Sautel's category of 'personal commentary'. See also Poletti 2015, 243: Dionysius thus 'makes clear that Brutus' action must be judged in a Roman perspective and according to Roman moral values', not Greek; compare Polyb. 6.54.5 on the 'unnatural' (κατὰ φύσιν) nature of this episode.

64. Dion. Hal. 1.5.3; he goes on to explain that these are primarily found in the city's leadership.

65. Dion. Hal. 5.8.3.

66. See Dion. Hal. 5.9.1–11.1. This aspect of the story is absent from Livy.

67. Dion. Hal. 5.8.6. I have underlined the words that emphasise Brutus' lack of visible grief.

68. As Dionysius was trying to demonstrate that Rome was a Greek *polis* – see e.g. 1.89–90; the consequences of this argument are discussed by e.g. Fromentin 2010, 269–71; Schultze 2011, 80–2 (with specific attention to Brutus); and Wiater 2011, esp. 70–87 – he is understandably concerned about explaining away customs that may seem un-Greek.

PART II

Ancient Critique

CHAPTER 8

Toxic Masculinity in Petronius' *Satyrica*

Jordan D. G. Mitchell

Although toxic masculinity as a concept is relatively new, the acts and ide-ology that define toxic masculinity have been present in different forms in various cultures and times; there have always been acts of manhood that foster socially regressive practices.[1] Toxic masculinity refers to specific socially destructive aspects of hegemonic masculinity, a concept developed and defined by Raewyn Connell in the 1980s as the dominant notion of masculinity in a particular historical setting.[2] Hegemonic masculinity, 'as the configuration of gender practice . . . which guarantees (or is taken to guarantee) the dominant position of men and the subordination of women', is a product of interconnected and mutually reinforcing power relations.[3] Other masculinities exist along with hegemonic masculinity, including subordinate, complicit and marginalised, in which there are intersecting factors that prevent some men from equal access to the qualities that define hegemony.[4] Thus when analysing masculinities, both modern and ancient, we must discuss access, power, inequality and the institu-tions that reproduce toxic gender relations.[5] Along with hegemonic masculinity, Connell developed the concept of emphasised femininity, defined as women's compliance with subordination and orientation to accommodating the interests and desires of men.[6] Hegemonic masculinity is dependent upon emphasised femininity's existence, which it sustains through various controlling methods.

In this chapter, then, utilising the theoretical framework of hegemonic mas-culinity, I argue that in Petronius' *Satyrica*, a Roman novel most likely written in the latter half of the first century CE, subordinate and marginalised individ-uals and groups of men engage in compensatory manhood acts, which are acts that include displays of exaggerated masculinity in order to emulate the most dominant form of masculinity in society.[7] The effect of these compensatory acts is the continual re-establishment of gender stereotypes as policing mechanisms and the subordination of women. Because of their own subordinate status in society, certain groups of men in the *Satyrica* are prohibited from positions of institutionalised power and the cultural masculine ideal, which leads them to compensate for their marginalised status. It is through these acts, moreover, that we can see an example comparable to the modern concept of toxic masculinity. For example, the freedmen, former slaves, in the *Satyrica* imitate the actions and ideals of the social membership with which they desire to associate. By taking on these ideals as their own, the freedmen become responsible for the rages, insta-bilities, ambivalences and failures of the social membership they imitate.[8] They perform the toxic behaviours associated with our modern notion of hegemonic masculinity and by doing so exemplify acts such as misogyny, both verbal and physical aggression, and domination of others, which define the most exalted form of masculinity within Roman society. We will begin with a comparative analysis of compensatory masculinity in both a modern and ancient context and then switch to a textual analysis of specific scenes emphasising the role of litera-ture in reifying behaviour similar to modern definitions of toxic masculinity for the purpose of controlling female behaviour.

Matthew B. Ezzell, in his study of groups of men undergoing treatment for substance abuse, showed how men whose lives were stripped of all control, when given the chance to assert control through 'group-accountability sessions', did so by 'reinforcing dominant ideologies of misogyny'.[9] The men undergoing mandatory treatment for two years were disproportionately poor and Black. The goal of the group-accountability sessions was to do identity work with a primary focus on 'being a man'. They engaged in exaggerated 'acts of manhood' during the sessions, which were the only allocated time these men had in which to signify some form of self-agency during their treatment. These acts arose, argues Ezzell, as part of an inability to enact the hegemonic masculine ideal, which was undermined by the men's subordinate status within the institution and reinforced by their subordinate status in society at large.[10] With the men's access to semiotic resources for self-making constrained, they compensated for their subordinated identities within the programme by performing an approxi-mation of dominant and dominating masculinity.[11] The specific 'manhood acts' performed by the men in treatment coincide with the behaviour of the freed-men in the *cena Trimalchionis*, or Trimalchio's dinner.

As was said before, most men present at the *cena Trimalchionis* were once enslaved. The fact that they are former slaves who in turn are surrounded by current slaves is never far from the reader's attention. As former slaves they are marked with a stigma that can never be removed, which alludes to a time in their lives when they lacked any form of control or self-agency, and therefore rep-resents a liability for their current efforts to signify a masculine self.[12] Trimalchio, the host of the dinner, alludes to this stigma when he speaks about being used sexually by his former master, saying that what a master orders is not shameful.[13] In fact, Trimalchio comments on how he tried to avoid becoming his master's sexual favourite by rubbing lamp oil around his mouth in order to grow facial hair faster and thus appear less desirable.[14] When these men were slaves their bodies were open and available to the master for coercion, abuse, sexual assault, starvation and elimination free of moral or legal consequence.[15] Like the men in treatment, the freedmen are a subordinate group and compensating for this fact means performing toxic aspects of hegemonic masculinity. This includes multiple acts where the men strive to prove dominance over others, both male and female. Let us then turn to the specific 'acts of manhood' in question.

Hegemonic masculinity's primary focus as defined by Raewyn Connell is the dominant position of men in relation to the subordination of women. In its toxic form this is achieved through the suppression and denigration of women through misogyny.[16] Whenever they were speaking about women, the men undergoing treatment referred to them most often as 'bitches' and framed women as 'out to get them'.[17] In the *cena Trimalchionis*, we see the same usage of degrading language whenever women are mentioned. Repeatedly, women are called 'kites' in reference to a rapacious kind of bird, implying that the women are predators, or a 'magpie' alluding to the chattering nature of that bird.[18] Fortunata, the wife of Trimalchio, is called a viper and a common whore.[19] It is implied, moreover, that both wives at the dinner are only out to get their husbands' money. The wives compare jewellery, noting affectionately that they were gifts from their husbands. In response, their husbands coldly demean the women for their jewellery. This is quickly followed by Trimalchio having a scale brought out so that the guests at the dinner can see how much his own jewellery weighs.[20] Examples such as these demonstrate how those further down the hierarchy of masculinities, such as Roman freedmen, will use whatever they have as a claim to superiority, in this case their gender.[21]

The verbal abuse against women at the dinner transforms into physical abuse. Habbinas, a friend of Trimalchio, sneaks up, seizes Fortunata by her legs, and flips them up over her head, exposing what is underneath her dress. In reaction, Fortunata hides her face, burning with shame.[22] Trimalchio does not react to the physical abuse of his wife, thus showing that Fortunata remains at risk for sexual abuse as if she is still a slave.[23] Later in the dinner, when Trimalchio kisses a slave boy, Fortunata calls him a *canis*, a 'dog', or it could be argued a 'bitch', the only insult a woman hurls at a free man during the dinner. Trimalchio responds by throwing a cup at her face, hitting her in the eye. The atmosphere between men and women at the dinner, then, is one revolving around control, with the men crafting performances that deliver a single, critical message: that women are subordinate and made subordinate through collective acts of manhood that involve the denigration of women.[24] There is an understanding, moreover, that the subordination of women is to the benefit of the group of freedmen, that perhaps they see themselves as 'in on the deal', as Øystein Gullvåg Holter puts it, meaning that if you imitate what is believed to be the acts of more privileged groups of men in society, then you too will join their ranks.[25]

Ezzell also observed that the men at the treatment facility used verbal aggression and confrontation to compensate for their lack of control.[26] Anger and aggression were encouraged during group sessions because they were seen as 'masculine' acts. We saw that already in how men spoke about women, but it is most often present when speaking to men who are perceived as 'other'. Ezzell records a particular incident when a man named Simon, who saw himself as better than the other men in treatment because he only had issues with alcohol and not drugs, was screamed at by other residents saying that he was no different from them, and they continued to scream at Simon, growing louder and more personal in their attacks.[27] The men screaming at Simon were compensating for their perceived subordination to him through anger and aggression. Once again, we see a similar event occur during the *cena Trimalchionis*.

Hermeros, one of the freedmen at the dinner, sees Ascyltos, the friend of Encolpius, the protagonist of the *Satyrica*, laughing at and making fun of Trimalchio's dinner festivities. Hermeros' response to this is a long and angry verbal attack against Ascyltos. Hermeros begins by effeminising Ascyltos, calling him a *vervex*, a castrated ram.[28] This tactic of placing another man into the symbolic role of an effeminate man, and therefore as inferior, frequently occurred during the group sessions at the treatment centre.[29] This is perhaps why Fortunata called Trimalchio a *canis*, utilising the feminising language with which men were accustomed to prove their masculinity over another. Hermeros interprets Ascyltos' laughter as demeaning him and all the other freedmen at the dinner because they were once slaves. Unprompted, Hermeros assumes that Ascyltos is wondering how Hermeros ended up enslaved. 'Why then were you a slave?' asks Hermeros rhetorically out loud, and then goes on to defend the fact that he was a slave by describing how he chose to enter slavery, but that now he is a 'human among humans'.[30] That Hermeros does this without Ascyltos even mentioning his past shows how much the former lives of these freedmen are present as a stigma for which they must compensate.[31]

As this comparative example shows, the behaviours that now mark toxic masculinity existed in an ancient context and were performed for a similar reason in order to achieve a similar outcome, that is, the formulation of a masculine identity that fits with what society deems to be the most exalted form of masculinity. There is another aspect of toxic masculinity, however, that is present within the *Satyrica*: literature as an upholder of an ideology that justifies and naturalises male domination.[32] Toxic masculinity is compelled to repeat illusory idealisations, which have the effect of policing and enforcing governing norms and expectations.[33] In the *Satyrica*, several of these idealisations are citational, meaning that through the frequency of citing literary norms that govern masculinity they gain their power as norms. Literature becomes the imitable authority from which men pull their repetitious performance. The spectre of an illusory threat of women is a constant theme in literature and one of the norms of hegemonic masculinity, as we have seen. Trimalchio's indecent treatment of his wife, like every other aspect of his lifestyle, is derivative of toxic norms that exist as a result of constant derogatory literary depictions of women.

Women are seen as a direct threat to the physical manifestations of this culture of toxic masculinity. A scene between Encolpius, our protagonist, and a woman called Circe revolves around Encolpius' inability to get an erection. Circe's name alone conjures an allusion to her dangerous and powerful namesake in Homer's *Odyssey*.[34] Moreover, Encolpius compares Circe's voice with the singing of the sirens.[35] These two images of dangerous literary women pose a threat to Encolpius' masculinity and he is unable to perform sexually. Encolpius equates his inadequacy with a loss of masculine identity: 'non intellego me virum esse, non sentio. funerata est illa pars corporis, qua quondam Achilles eram', 'I do not know myself to be a man, I do not feel it. That part of my body, which once was an Achilles, it has been buried.'[36] The argument, that Circe is perceived as a threat because of Encolpius associating her with toxic conceptions of female literary figures, is based on what follows their first unsuccessful attempt at sexual intercourse.

Encolpius visits an old woman to cure his impotency and she does so almost immediately. When he returns to Circe, however, again he is unable to achieve an erection. Encolpius' impotence, therefore, is directly related to whose presence he is in and whether that person possesses any sort of power or autonomy that can be interpreted as threatening to Roman conceptions of masculinity. This is further proven by the fact that Encolpius was unable to get an erection in the presence of Quartilla, the priestess of Priapus, as well. In fact, the only two occasions when Encolpius is not impotent within the extant *Satyrica* are with Giton, his young boyfriend, and in the hands of the old woman, two figures whose exclusion from the category of threatening women keeps them from threatening the illusory constructions of masculinity.

In Encolpius' interaction with the priestess of Priapus, Quartilla, she has an extended monologue that shows how easily men in the *Satyrica* can be manipulated through an appeal to traditionally masculine signifiers of literature. When Quartilla enters the scene she immediately takes centre stage. Her entrance is marked by an explicit display of sorrow, a downpour of tears, which Encolpius, although alarmed, seems to recognise as a disingenuous display.[37] In response to this, Quartilla 'uncovered her proud head and bound her hands until the joints cracked'.[38] Her first display of emotion was not convincing enough, therefore she prepares to begin her monologue like an athlete preparing for a match: she removes her hood, projecting her proud head, and cracks her knuckles. This will be a speech of both epic and tragic proportions and it is signalled by her actions before delivery. Quartilla begins by saying, 'Where did you learn outrages surpassing even those in fictions?'[39] She projects Encolpius and his friends' actions into the context of a *fabula*. She begins building them up, appealing to their 'learned' sensibilities by alluding to them as epic figures in a story. It is no surprise, therefore, when Quartilla continues to describe herself and Encolpius as living in a world where 'it is easier to find a god than a man'.[40] There is a sense here that Quartilla is referring to how men fabricate illusions for themselves in a culture saturated by mythology and epic, where men routinely mythologise themselves and their surroundings. Whenever a woman uses allusions to myth and epic tropes in the *Satyrica*, men become easy to convince through their willingness to step into the familiarity of such literary tropes. Encolpius, once sceptical of Quartilla's intentions, is seduced by the 'damsel in distress', but what exactly is her distress?

Quartilla describes a sickness, her 'tertian fever', caused by an unspeakable – and unspecified – crime committed by Encolpius and his friends. 'Having been disturbed during the night, I shivered with such a dangerous chill.'[41] What Quartilla describes as her 'disease' is either a description of the act of masturbation or the experience of orgasm, something that Encolpius is unable to discern. Moreover, Quartilla even states what she desires but it also seems to fly over Encolpius' head: 'aetate magis vestra commoveor quam iniuria mea', 'I am more disturbed by your age than my injury.'[42] The Latin word *commoveo* usually implies worry, to thoroughly move something or someone, but it can also mean sexual arousal. Quartilla tells Encolpius that his young age arouses her. She follows this by calling Encolpius and his friends *imprudentes*, 'ignorant'.[43] Quartilla likes her men both young and dumb, a point that is further proven by Encolpius' inability to catch the double meaning of any of Quartilla's wordplay. Quartilla, then, alludes to the sexual nature of what is to come, but Encolpius only understands her words as a cry for help. Encolpius' inability to learn that words and intentions can include multiple meanings further shows how shallow his understanding is. His actions become predictable as he sees himself step into the role of the hero – ready to cure Quartilla's 'disease' – completely unaware of any ulterior motive, which becomes obvious once Quartilla begins her sexual ritual.[44] Later, Quartilla's sarcasm peaks when she calls Encolpius a 'sharp fellow and fount of natural wit', after he fails to understand that the word *embasicoetas* – a phallus-shaped drinking-cup or an effeminate person – has two different meanings.[45]

With Quartilla, then, we see a woman skilled with words run rhetorical circles around a young Roman man who is easy to manipulate because his identity is formed based on a specific literary set of signifiers pulled from a very select collection of recognisable signs. Encolpius the *scholasticus* lacks an education based in reality, which forces him into uncomfortable situations, especially with powerful women. As Encolpius tries to create a traditional gender arrangement as it pertains to hegemonic masculinity – the dominant position of men and the subordination of women – he fails because he lacks the power of language that Quartilla holds.[46] In the end it is not Encolpius' desire that must be satisfied, but Quartilla's, and she pulls the strings in this episode because she knows how to manipulate a man who bases his masculinity on literature that has justified and naturalised male dominance.[47]

The reinforcement of toxic masculinity's image of women is continued in the Widow of Ephesus, a story that the poet Eumolpus tells in the *Satyrica*. This story is an example of how men reinforce hegemonic masculinity through literature by attempting to police the behaviour of women and reinforce emphasised femininity. As James W. Messerschmidt writes, it is only 'when both masculine and feminine qualities legitimate a complementary and hierarchical relationship between them, we have hegemonic masculinity'.[48] The Widow of Ephesus 'had been known for such chastity that she drew women even of neighbouring communities to her display'.[49] However, Eumolpus turns the meaning of his tale towards a more negative purpose. '[Eumolpus] began to throw many things against the fickleness of women, how easily they fall in love, how quickly they forget even their own sons, and that no woman is so chaste that she cannot be diverted even to eager desire by lust for a foreigner.'[50] Eumolpus' story about the widow of Ephesus is intended to be an example of a singular male discourse that heaps insults upon woman and her 'nature'. However, the story that we receive is far more complex than Eumolpus' simple summary.

The Widow of Ephesus, overwhelmed by grief, followed her dead husband down into his tomb and 'she began to watch over the body and weep for entire days and nights'.[51] The Widow's mourning for her husband is tremendous; she refuses to leave the tomb even when her family and magistrates plead with her to come out. At the same time, however, her self-sacrificing sorrow earns the respect of all within the city. Why would the whole city regard highly a woman who has decided to take her own life because her husband has died? Because by acting as a sacrificial object on behalf of her husband, as a grave good for her husband, she assumes the proper place of the feminine within this masculine idealisation.[52] The Widow, therefore, by enacting an emphasised femininity, reinforces normativity by fulfilling her social obligation to go to her death seen by all as an exemplary woman. Thus, we can see some form of societal benefit for women who comply with their own subordination: they receive near-universal admiration.[53] The Widow's loyalty provides emotional satisfaction to the men in the audience; through suicide, the Widow demonstrates that she is utterly dependent on her husband to give her life meaning. For what is femininity in this society if not a form of indulgence towards real or supposed male expectations?[54]

After five days of no food, the Widow's continued sounds of mourning attract the attention of a soldier who is stationed nearby guarding the location where three criminals have been crucified. The sight of the Widow alarms the soldier and he attempts to persuade her not to take her own life, but to eat some food that he has brought into the cave. At first, the Widow resists more ardently than before, because her performance is still bound up in her compliance with what is expected of her as a proper woman who has lost the thing that gave her life meaning. However, her maid, an enslaved woman who has accompanied her down into the cave, by quoting the words of Anna, Dido's sister in Vergil's *Aeneid*, convinces her mistress to eat and continue living.[55] But food is not all that tempts her; the soldier then begins to attempt to seduce the Widow.[56] Once again, it is the Widow's maid who convinces her to indulge, saying, 'will you fight against even an agreeable love? Does it not come into your mind in whose fields you are sitting?'[57] The maid's second question – 'nec venit in mentem, quorum consederis arvis' – is another direct quote from the *Aeneid* and provides an important context for why the Widow should allow herself to be seduced.[58] These words, again spoken by Anna, function to remind Dido that she is a woman without a man in a land surrounded by enemies.[59] These words make explicit recognition that the Widow's continued survival in this society requires that she attach herself to a man. In the *Aeneid*, Anna's words 'kindled [Dido's] heart with love, gave hope to a doubting mind, and scattered shame'.[60] So too the maid's words for the Widow who gives herself to the soldier, the *victor miles* (conquering soldier).

The Widow's transgression, however, sleeping with the soldier and abandoning her *pudicitia*, her famed chastity, does not condemn her to death but restores her life.[61] We should now see the contradiction that exists for the Widow and for all women within this particular society, at least as defined by the poet Eumolpus. On the one hand, the death of the Widow's husband meant her own death, an act of *pudicitia* admired by all; on the other, sleeping with the soldier, and thus attaching herself to another man (by necessity?), allows her to renew her purpose within the domain of hegemonic masculinity, bringing her back to life but forfeiting her defining attribute, *pudicitia*. The Widow, then, simultaneously unsettles and reifies emphasised femininity.

The story becomes further complicated when the soldier realises that one of the bodies of the three crucified criminals is missing. He neglected his duty by continuously visiting the Widow, and now decides to avoid punishment by taking his own life. The Widow, however, says no: 'I prefer to expend a dead man than kill a living one.'[62] She instructs the soldier to put her dead husband on the empty cross, and by doing so save his own life. This last act steps outside of the literary authority that has thus far controlled the Widow narrative; the Widow effectively rewrites the *Aeneid* and, instead of perishing on a pyre like Dido, she puts her husband's body on the cross, saving the soldier, her Aeneas.[63] No one dies in this story. The Widow gets her man, the people get their *exemplum ad imitandum* without another woman dying (like a Dido, a Lucretia or a Virginia), and the patriarchal body ends up crucified; Petronius disrupts the citational authority of a foundational text that venerates unequal gender relations.

When Eumolpus finishes telling the story of the Widow, there is a varied response from his listening audience. First, 'the sailors received the story with laughter'.[64] Why do they laugh? Is it because of the behaviour of the Widow? A woman with agency over her actions enacting disobedience against societal expectations is a comedic episode for the sailors, received with ridicule. Next, the captain of the sailors, Lichas, does not laugh, but with anger he says, 'if the magistrate had been just, he ought to have returned the body of the husband to the tomb, and put the woman on the cross'.[65] The thought of the Widow finding new life apart from her husband, outside of her social duty, is met with anger on account of its impropriety. Lichas cannot imagine a woman escaping death in this scenario. Finally, the only response of a woman that is recorded is that of Tryphaena, who receives the story 'with a great deal of blushing'.[66] *Erubesco* also means to grow red with shame, just as Fortunata did when Habbinas laid his hands on her at the dinner of Trimalchio. Does the shame Tryphaena shows on her face come from the internalised policing mechanisms of toxic masculinity that make her see the Widow as an embarrassment to her own sex? Or perhaps Tryphaena is ashamed because of her all-male company, who provide negative reactions to a story that was presented negatively. The repetitious effects of a toxic literary culture that privileges the heroics of men and vilifies the actions of women are clearly seen here within the reactions of these characters and throughout the *Satyrica*.

By using Petronius' *Satyrica* as a sociohistorical text I have shown that particular behaviours within it correspond with our modern understanding of toxic masculinity and I have argued for why they are associated with particular characters in the text: Trimalchio and the freedmen in their attempt to imitate a hegemonic masculinity as compensation for their past and current position within society, and the poet Eumolpus because of his association with literature and the citational authority it lends to toxic masculinity. Between these two main examples, the scenes with Circe and Quartilla show the impact of a literary culture consumed by an obsession with a particular kind of masculinity that depicts women as predators and witches and men as heroes in a *fabula*. The establishment of such a correspondence between an ancient text and a modern concept should lead to fruitful enquiry in the future. Several questions remain as to the awareness of such behaviours as toxic among the Romans themselves, and whether a writer like Petronius could be using his text as an epistemological testing ground for a rapidly changing society that saw growing uncertainty about class and the autonomy of women. There is also some hint that Petronius is engaging in a form of dissimulation, focusing on the 'other' in society as a way of critiquing the behaviour of those at the top while maintaining plausible deniability.[67] The most potent examples of this are at Trimalchio's dinner, which is stuffed full of allusions to the Julio-Claudian *principes*. Speculation aside, the tension present in the *Satyrica* surrounding the negotiations of masculinity will be recognisable to a modern reader fully aware of the present discourse concerning toxic masculinity.

NOTES

1. Kupers 2005, 714.
2. Kupers 2005, 716. Hegemonic masculinity does not always equal toxic masculinity, which materialises through physical violence and other noxious practices, cf. Messerschmidt 2018, 39. Thus hegemonic masculinity often legitimates unequal gender relations through consent and compliance. However, by legitimating a hierarchy that always positions the masculine above the feminine, I do not see how hegemonic masculinity can escape the charge of toxicity.
3. Pascoe and Bridges 2015, 14–15.
4. Messerschmidt 2018, 28.
5. Pascoe and Bridges 2015, 38.
6. Pascoe and Bridges 2015, 20.
7. Ezzell 2012, 191.
8. Berlant and Warner 1998, 553.
9. Pascoe and Bridges 2015, 188.
10. Ezzell 2012, 191.
11. Pascoe and Bridges 2015, 192.
12. Pascoe and Bridges 2015, 192.
13. 75.11: 'nec turpe est quod dominus iubet'. All Latin translations are my own unless otherwise stated.
14. 75.10.4–11. We assume that Trimalchio's master was attracted to boys who lacked facial hair and thus were quite young. Trimalchio mentions being his master's favourite at fourteen years old, or for fourteen years; the exact meaning of 'annos quattuordecim fui' is debated but the former seems more likely, cf. Roth 2021, 216–18.
15. Lenski 2016b, 285.
16. Ezzell 2012, 200.
17. Ezzell 2012, 200.
18. 42.7.2–4 and 37.7.3.
19. 37.7, *lupatria*, and 77.2.
20. 67.7–12.
21. Holter 2004, 20.
22. 67.13.
23. Gloyn 2012, 265.
24. Ezzell 2012, 197.
25. Holter 2004, 23.
26. Ezzell 2012, 198.
27. Ezzell 2012, 205.
28. 57.2.
29. Ezzell 2012, 201.
30. 57.4–5 'homo inter homines sum'.
31. '[B]ecause he does not have the privilege of power society has taught him "real men" should possess. Alienated, frustrated, pissed off, he may attack, abuse, and oppress . . .' hooks 1984, 74.

32. Pascoe and Bridges 2015, 40.
33. Manne 2017, 78.
34. For one interpretation on the danger of Circe's name, cf. Rimell 2002, 147–50.
35. 127.5.
36. 129.1.
37. 17.2.
38. 17.3 'retexit superbum pallio caput et manibus inter se usque ad articulorum strepitum constrictis'.
39. 17.8–9 'ubi fabulas etiam antecessura latrocinia didicistis?'
40. 17.6 'ut facilius possis deum quam hominem invenire'.
41. 17.7.1–2 'ipsa quidem illa nocte vexata tam periculoso inhorrui frigore'.
42. 17.6.2–3.
43. 17.6.3.
44. 19.3.2–3.
45. 24.2–3 'o inquit hominem acutum atque urbanitatis vernaculae fontem'.
46. Pascoe and Bridges 2015, 15.
47. Pascoe and Bridges 2015, 40.
48. Messerschmidt 2018, 121.
49. 111.1–2 'tam notae erat pudicitiae, ut vicinarum quoque gentium feminas ad spectaculum sui evocaret'.
50. 110.7–8 'multa in muliebrem levitatem coepit iactare: quam facile adamarent, quam cito etiam filiorum obliviscerentur, nullamque esse feminam tam pudicam, quae non peregrina libidine usque ad furorem averteretur'. *Levitatem* is important here because it is a synonym of the two words used by Mercury to describe women in Vergil's *Aeneid* 4.569–70: 'varium et mutabile semper femina', 'a woman is always a changeable and fickle thing'. Eumolpus channels Mercury's misogyny, and the reason will become obvious below when we see how this story revolves around allusions to Vergil's Dido.
51. 111.2–3 'corpus custodire ac flere totis noctibus diebusque coepit'. My interpretation of the Widow of Ephesus is heavily indebted to Oliver 2016.
52. 'The [Widow's] futurity, in conventional terms, is ruptured by the death of her husband, and dying over his body is the most "virtuous" thing she can do: her timeline ends with his, and she thus becomes the perfect *univira*, her virtue solidified by death and frozen for all time,' Oliver 2016, 95.
53. Pascoe and Bridges 2015, 20.
54. Bourdieu 2001, 66.
55. Verg. *Aen.* 4.34. What is fascinating about this scene and the following one is that the Widow's maid uses the authority of literature to convince her mistress to act contrary to the expectations for which an entire society admires her. That admiration, however, was leading her to her own death. 'Citation of cultural institutions . . . animates the world of the *Satyrica* with the energy of novelty,' Oliver 2016, 97.
56. 112.1–2.
57. 112.2.3–4 'placitone etiam pugnabis amori? nec venit in mentem, quorum consederis arvis?'

58. Verg. *Aen.* 4.39.
59. Verg. *Aen.* 4.40–4.
60. Verg. *Aen.* 4.54–5 'his dictis impenso animum flammavit amore spemque dedit dubiae menti solvitque pudorem'.
61. For an opposing view, cf. Rimell 2002, 138.
62. 112.7–8 'malo mortuum impendere quam vivum occidere'.
63. Oliver 2016, 94.
64. 113.1 'risu excepere fabulam nautae'.
65. 113.2 'Si iustus imperator fuisset, debuit patris familiae corpus in monumentum referre, mulierem affigere cruci.'
66. 113.1 'erubescente non mediocriter'.
67. Cf. Bartsch 1994.

CHAPTER 9

Real Roman Men and the Greeks Who Hate Them: *Disciplina*, Cato the Elder and Plutarch

Elizabeth A. Manwell

I suspect that I am unlikely to shock anyone by suggesting that Cato the Elder, that stodgy and Stoic censor, held traditional Roman values in high regard. Consider, as an example, this fragment from a speech quoted by Festus:

> Still from the beginning I held my entire youth apart in frugality and in hardness and in industriousness by working the fields, the Sabine rocks, and by digging up and sowing its flinty soil.

> ego iam a principio in parsimonia atque in duritia atque industria omnem adulescentiam meam abstinui agro colendo, saxis Sabinis, silicibus repast-inandis atque conserendis. (Festus p. 350 L. = ORF (4) no. 8, 128)

These few lines capture not only what we think we know about Cato, but more specifically the image of himself that Cato has chosen to project: that of a man who from his earliest years chose a life of self-discipline and self-denial, a path of labour, ennobled by his efforts in the most traditional of Roman pursuits, working the land.

Emma Dench has used this passage as an illustration of Cato's self-fashioning as a *novus homo*, or 'new man'.[1] It is, perhaps, not surprising that Cato the Elder as an outsider felt the need to embody an overt and excessive *Romanitas* (Roman-ness), especially in terms of how he exercised personal self-control (*disciplina*) as a feature of his masculinity, enabling his commanding performance in all these various male-coded pursuits.[2] Yet, even as this represented a meaningful form of self-fashioning for Cato himself and a compelling persona in political wrangling, this portrait of *disciplina* does not earn universal acclaim. Anyone even slightly familiar with Cato's biography recalls that ancient perceptions of his behaviour – his harshness, his plain clothing and food, his cold self-containment – veer between admiration and disdain.[3]

One way that we, viewing Cato from a distance, might characterise his hyper-Stoic formulation of masculinity is as what is often termed 'toxic masculinity' in today's parlance. While there is no set or completely agreed upon definition of toxic masculinity, the term calls to mind stereotypically male-coded behaviours and attitudes that cause harm – to other individuals, to society and to the men themselves as well. Such behaviours and attitudes are typically perceived as promoting violence or are associated with biases that can lead to violence, such as misogyny and homophobia. The tolerance or promotion of violence in boys and men flourishes along with a concomitant repression of emotion.[4] Moreover, these behaviours and attitudes, when cast as part of a dominant societal ideology, can prove hard to argue against, let alone to eradicate. Michael Kimmel formulates the difference between an idealised masculinity and a toxic performance by distinguishing between being a 'good man' and a 'real man'. When questioning cadets at West Point, Kimmel pressed the men to define these terms. In response the cadets associated the 'good man' with 'honor, duty, integrity, sacrifice, do[ing] the right thing, stand[ing] up for the little guy, be[ing] a provider, be[ing] a protector'.[5] They attested that they identify these qualities as a cultural patrimony, bequeathed to them through literature, religion and cultural heritage. Kimmel continues:

> I said, 'That's fine, okay. So, that's what it means to you to be a good man. Now tell me if all of those traits – integrity and honor and responsibility and sacrifice – tell me if those show up for you when I say this: "Man the F up, be a real man".'
> And they said, 'Oh no, that's completely different.'
> I said, 'Well, what is that?'
> And they said 'Tough, strong, never show weakness, win at all costs, suck it up, play through pain, be competitive, get rich, get laid.'
> I said, 'Okay, that's what it means to be a real man? Where did you learn that?'
> And they said, in order, 'My father, my coach, my guy friends, my older brother.'
> So here's what I think they were telling me. First of all they were telling me that the real man is the performative part. The real man is the part that has to perform for others, to validate their masculinities. The real man is homosocial. The good man is abstract. It's not necessarily interactive.[6]

I quote this rather lengthy passage because I think it gets at an important distinction: the 'good' man who upholds and endorses societal values in ways that benefit the entirety of the community (and that one could argue are societal, non-gendered values) and the 'real' man, who embodies many (perhaps all) of these same qualities, but in ways that have to be performed, and thus open themselves up to possible instantiations of masculinity for other men that could fall into toxic behaviour. While it is certainly anachronistic to cite a Roman of the second century BCE as an exemplar of American toxic masculinity, Kimmel's distinction between the 'good' and the 'real' offers a provocative model for thinking about Cato's performance of masculinity as recounted and critiqued by Plutarch. That is, by Kimmel's definition we can read Cato's performance of his 'real' self as a kind of toxic masculinity. The features that Kimmel highlights – toughness, competition, hardness, virility – almost seamlessly map onto that place where Cato's Stoic ideology intersects with his valorisation of *disciplina*, which was exercised by men to enhance their *duritia* (hardness) and *virtus* (manliness). These guiding values, while they can be viewed as positive cultural formations that promote social cohesion and devotion to the work of the Republic (that is, the qualities of 'good' men), nevertheless can also be used to justify extreme behaviour that causes harm to individuals and to the state.

Moreover, although *disciplina* and its constituent values are notable for their durability over centuries as guiding principles for Roman self-conceptualisation, we also hear ancient voices pushing back against them. Thus, the value of *disciplina* is evident across time, whether in Cato's encouragement of industry in an estate's overseer (*Agr.* 5.1), Caesar's attribution of the temporary success of Spartacus' revolt to the discipline learned at the hands of their Roman masters (*Gal.* 1.40), Cicero's lament of Caelius' lack of self-control (*Cael.* 39) or Seneca's exhorting the application of reason and discipline in the same breath (*Dial.* 3.11.5). In these contexts – and countless others – we witness *disciplina* as a critical quality of a 'good man', whose self-control regulates his behaviour so that he acts in ways that are honourable and promotes sacrifice for others. Yet one can conceive how *disciplina* and its constellation of similar values, especially with their ties to a militaristic hardness and self-sacrifice, might also be appropriated in performances of 'real' masculinity, where it might appear as callousness, disregard for human frailty, endurance, excessive competitiveness and aggressiveness. An episode from Livy provides an illustration: when Cato vociferously opposes repeal of the Lex Oppia, the tribunes counter that Cato, a man of strictest conduct, nevertheless performs a kind of hardness in his speech that is absent from his true nature (*AUC* 34.5).

In this chapter, I look at one example of resistance to *disciplina* – Plutarch's *Cato Maior*. In particular, Plutarch's assessment of Cato's exercise of *disciplina* (in Greek, ἐγκράτεια or σωφροσύνη) offers a stern critique of that most Roman of virtues (and the constellation of virtues that we may say are aligned with it, such as *industria, parsimonia, duritia* and the like).[7] Indeed, the way that Plutarch interrupts his biography to critique Cato highlights the latter's adherence to a Roman masculinity that Plutarch finds not only unseemly in its callous disregard for other humans, but even immoral. That is, in Plutarch we observe a proto-critic of what we might recognise as a form of toxic masculinity, as he exposes the fault lines in Roman *disciplina*, reveals how Cato's adherence to it has consequences for his private household, and infers that a masculinity of this sort uncovers what is rotten in Roman society and possibly in the Roman imperial project more broadly.

PLUTARCH'S HOT TAKE ON THE 'REAL' CATO

Most scholars seem to agree that Plutarch had an explicit moral goal in writing the *Parallel Lives*: the biographies ought to provide exempla of both virtue and vice, some *Lives* in their entirety, others only in discrete episodes.[8] While numerous *Lives* show positive and negative qualities of both Greeks and Romans, several scholars have argued that Plutarch positions himself as a critic of Roman power, which the biographies' conceit, pairing a Greek with a Roman leader, no doubt facilitates.[9] In addition, Plutarch asserts that his attention to smaller or overlooked aspects of his subjects' lives may reveal crucial character traits, and in *Cato Maior* he focuses his severest disapproval on Cato's personal rather than political behaviour, which reveals his 'toxic' actions in two episodes involving his slaves.[10]

The first episode occurs in an early passage, in which Plutarch highlights Cato's extreme frugality: his food and drink were barely adequate, he refused to hold on to luxury goods that made their way to him, his house was unadorned. And this same parsimony extended to the slaves he purchased:[11]

> He never bought any slave for more than 1500 drachmas, since he did not want dainty and handsome, but rather hard-working and stout slaves, like horse grooms and cattle drivers; and he thought that it was necessary for him to sell them when they became rather old and not to feed useless men.
>
> οὐδένα δὲ πώποτε πρίασθαι δοῦλον ὑπὲρ τὰς χιλίας δραχμὰς καὶ πεντακοσίας, ὡς ἂν οὐ τρυφερῶν οὐδ' ὡραίων, ἀλλ' ἐργατικῶν καὶ στερεῶν, οἷον ἱπποκόμων καὶ βοηλατῶν, δεόμενος· καὶ τούτους δὲ πρεσβυτέρους γενομένους ᾤετο δεῖν ἀποδίδοσθαι καὶ μὴ βόσκειν ἀχρήστους. (Cat. Mai. 4)

Plutarch reflects on Cato's behaviour, offering two possible explanations for it: either these actions merely reflect his natural stinginess (μικρολογίαν, *Cat. Mai.* 5), or his behaviour was a deliberate model for emulation and a corrective for those around him (ἐπὶ διορθώσει καὶ σωφρονισμῷ τῶν ἄλλων, *Cat. Mai.* 5). That is, Plutarch attributes to Cato a sense of his own moral superiority and a performance of a kind of Roman-ness and maleness that could instruct others – if not to be like him, to at least be more like him.[12]

If at this point one anticipates an elaboration of one or both of these perspectives on Cato, the skinflint or the pedagogue, the reader is immediately brought up short, since Plutarch instead intervenes with his own opinion, which is exclusively about Cato's treatment of his slaves, and not about any of the other miserly behaviour that he has detailed in chapter 4.[13] Indeed, the entirety of chapter 5 is devoted to Greek attitudes towards living creatures. In it, Plutarch outlines a rationale for his antipathy towards Cato's practice. The argument proceeds thus: (a) Plutarch likens Cato's treatment of slaves to the treatment of draught animals (ὑποζυγίοις, 5.1), which Plutarch considers characteristic of a very unbending nature (ἀτενοῦς ἄγαν ἤθους ἔγωγε τίθεμαι, 5.1); (b) although humans only exercise law and justice towards other humans, we frequently exhibit good works and favour (εὐεργεσίας δὲ καὶ χάριτας, 5.2) towards other living creatures; (c) Plutarch details three specific examples of Greeks who demonstrated kindness to animals who played pivotal roles in Greek cultural success,[14] with the result that; (d) we should not treat creatures that have a *psyche* as we treat material objects when they wear out. His conclusion is poignant and pointed:

> I certainly would not sell even an ox that had worked for me, just because he was old, much less an elderly man, removing him from his habitual place and customary life, as it were from his native land, for a paltry price, useless as he is to those who sell him and as he will be to those who buy him. But Cato, exulting as it were in such things, says that he left in Spain even the horse which had carried him through his consular campaign, that he might not tax the city with the cost of its transportation. Whether, now, these things should be set down to greatness of spirit or littleness of mind, is an open question.
> But in other matters, his self-restraint was beyond measure admirable.

> ἐγὼ μὲν οὖν οὐδὲ βοῦν ἂν ἐργάτην διὰ γῆρας ἀποδοίμην, μή τί γε πρεσβύτερον ἄνθρωπον, ἐκ χώρας συντρόφου καὶ διαίτης συνήθους ὥσπερ ἐκ πατρίδος μεθιστάμενον ἀντὶ κερμάτων μικρῶν, ἄχρηστόν γε τοῖς ὠνουμένοις ὥσπερ τοῖς πιπράσκουσι γενησόμενον. ὁ δὲ Κάτων ὥσπερ νεανιευόμενος ἐπὶ τούτοις καὶ τὸν ἵππον, ᾧ παρὰ τὰς στρατείας ὑπατεύων ἐχρῆτο, φησὶν ἐν Ἰβηρίᾳ καταλιπεῖν, ἵνα μὴ τῇ πόλει τὸ ναῦλον αὐτοῦ λογίσηται. ταῦτα μὲν οὖν εἴτε μεγαλοψυχίας εἴτε μικρολογίας θετέον, ἔξεστι τῷ πείθοντι χρῆσθαι λογισμῷ.
> Τῆς δ᾽ ἄλλης ἐγκρατείας ὑπερφυῶς θαυμαστὸς ὁ ἀνήρ. (Cat. Mai. 5.5–6.1)

Plutarch's critique has an explicit ethnic dimension. Greeks engaged in the most glorious activities of their cultural heritage – the Periclean building project, Olympic victories, the defeat of the Persian invasion – not only acknowledge the value of animals, but honour them in perpetuity. He, therefore, connects Greek society to a sympathy with all living creatures, a notion we might question when we consider, say, Aristotle's taxonomic hierarchy of living beings.[15] But Plutarch seems to tend towards a cultural rather than a biological explanation: Greeks value kindness to all living beings; the line between human and animal is fuzzier for Greeks, since animals desire to support Greek cultural efforts and are rewarded as part of the project. Moreover, the Greeks are supported by animals in male-coded activities: warfare, games and literal state-building, so that the kindnesses shown to them appear not weak and effeminate but the natural result of a male stance which rewards loyalty and service to the greater good. Plutarch's reluctance to sell a long-working ox since it would seem as though he is tearing it from its fatherland (ἐκ πατρίδος, 5.5) may appear a particularly odd formulation, but it also makes explicit the inherent sympathy of the Greeks and their superior (in their minds) moral framework in contrast with the practice of Cato, a model and teacher of idealised Roman male behaviour.[16] Plutarch's commentary could be read as a rejoinder to Cato's well-established antipathy to all things Greek, but this is not merely a repudiation of Cato's assessment of Greek culture. Instead, Plutarch takes aim at that most essential quality of Cato – his self-discipline, and all that results from it – and links it to a kind of performance of Roman masculinity that stands in direct opposition to Greek societal norms.

If Plutarch does not offer a fair and balanced view of the Romans, it is also the case that he is not wholly unmoved by the Roman exercise of *disciplina*.[17] His transitional observation that ἐγκράτεια is not only efficacious but admirable (θαυμαστός, 6.1) details Cato's restraint when on campaign and his refusal to pillage. Though in such cases self-restraint acts as a check on unnecessary cruelty towards other humans, this exacting and rigorous attitude can also result in severity in his exercise of law and fulfilment of edicts, as Plutarch details later on.

If Plutarch's critique in chapters 4 and 5 centres on Cato's cruelty as an example of Roman moral lapses, then chapter 24 is a companion critique, focused on Cato's lack of self-restraint. Here Cato, widowed and living with his son and daughter-in-law, is caught sleeping with a slave girl (παιδίσκη, 24):

> After the death of his wife, he married his son to the daughter of Aemilius Paulus, the sister of Scipio, but he himself, in his widowerhood, took solace with a slave girl who secretly visited his bed. Of course, in a small house with a young married woman in it, the matter was discovered, and once, when the girl seemed to flaunt her way rather too boldly to his chamber, the old man could not help noticing that his son, although he said nothing, looked very sour, and turned away.

> ἀποβαλὼν τὴν γυναῖκα τῷ μὲν υἱῷ Παύλου θυγατέρα, Σκηπίωνος δὲ ἀδελφὴν ἠγάγετο πρὸς γάμον, αὐτὸς δὲ χηρεύων ἐχρῆτο παιδίσκῃ κρύφα φοιτώσῃ πρὸς αὐτόν. ἦν οὖν ἐν οἰκίᾳ μικρᾷ νύμφην ἐχούσῃ τοῦ πράγματος αἴσθησις· καί ποτε τοῦ γυναίου θρασύτερον παρασοβῆσαι

παρὰ τὸ δωμάτιον δόξαντος ὁ νεανίας εἶπε μὲν οὐδέν, ἐμβλέψας δέ πως πικρότερον καὶ διατραπεὶς οὐκ ἔλαθε τὸν πρεσβύτην. (Cat. Mai. 24.1–2)

Rather than cause discomfort in his home, Cato chooses to remarry, but selects for his bride the daughter of a former undersecretary, in all likelihood a freedman. Plutarch avoids any commentary about Cato's behaviour in this episode until the end of his comparison of the pair of lives, in which he condemns Cato's deficiency in *sophrosyne* compared to Aristides, because he contracted a marriage contrary to his status and time of life:

> Once more, that temperance which Cato always decked out with the fairest praises, Aristides maintained and practised in unsullied purity; whereas Cato, by marrying unworthily and unseasonably, fell under no slight or insignificant censure in this regard.

> Ἦν τοίνυν πλείστοις ὁ Κάτων κεκόσμηκε καὶ καλλίστοις ἐπαίνοις ἀεὶ σωφροσύνην Ἀριστείδης μὲν ἄθικτον ὡς ἀληθῶς καὶ καθαρὰν ἐτήρησεν, αὐτοῦ δὲ τοῦ Κάτωνος ὁ παρ' ἀξίαν ἅμα καὶ παρ' ὥραν γάμος οὐ μικρὰν οὐδὲ φαύλην εἰς τοῦτο διαβολὴν κατεσκέδασε. (Comp. Arist. et Cato Mai. 6.1)

Plutarch assesses this decision as 'in no way fine' (οὐδαμοῦ καλόν), no matter Cato's motivation, whether he was prompted by pleasure (ἡδονὴν) or anger at his son's disapproval (ὀργῇ), summing the whole affair up as disgraceful (αἰσχύνην).

One should note that it is not Cato's use of a slave as a sex partner that Plutarch finds horrific, but the cascade of events that it unleashes. The behaviour of the bride and the slave are obliquely criticised, since by implication the former is nosy and interfering, the latter brazen and stroppy. Yet Cato's choice of new wife provides the object of Plutarch's disdain. Cato has chosen a mate of lowly status to birth more male offspring, which would be sufficient cause for rebuke, even if that was his goal all along. In addition, the elderly man spent an excessive amount of time content with a concubine and kept it secret as long as he could. That is, again, Cato's behaviour is morally suspect: as a man of status he should behave as such. This behaviour reveals a lack of *sophrosyne*, in comparison with Aristides, whose *sophrosyne* was without blemish.

Moreover, the lack of self-control in rendering a slave a quasi-concubine explicitly has an impact on Cato's performance of his Roman masculinity. Although one might simply view this act as a personal failing, in fact Plutarch couches it as a moral failure that has an implication for the citizen body. Cato's choice to have a secret liaison with a slave who struts the halls of his house with abandon causes discord within his household. Yet when he elects to marry a young woman of lower status for the purpose of siring sons in status-conscious Rome, he amplifies the friction within his home (since even Plutarch suggests the marriage was in part a punishment for his son and daughter-in-law's meddling in his sex life, *Comp. Arist. et Cato Mai.* 6.2). Moreover, Plutarch continues, Cato could have chosen a bride whose status would have granted him further honour and thus offspring of noble blood. His choice of a freedman's daughter, as Plutarch implies, means that Cato fails not only as a 'real' man, but also as a 'good' one, foisting a low-class step-mother upon his adult son, thumbing his nose at social convention and providing the state with future citizens from an ignoble mother.

GOOD AND REAL ROMAN MEN

The *Cato Maior* is a shorter biography than many of the others, and this may be due in part to a sense of Cato as a quasi-mythic figure of the distant past. It is easy to see Cato being co-opted into narratives that feel fictive: Hartmut Wulfrum gleefully details, for example, the way that the tale of Cato's affair with the slave and his lack of sexual self-control fits into a model of the *senex* of New Comedy, or of Hermesianax's poetry, or even the mythic Heracles and Omphale.[18] Moreover, it is clear that Plutarch finds much to admire in Cato: as Wulfrum asserts, Plutarch has no desire to completely dismantle Cato ('Plutarch lag es jedoch fern . . . Cato völlig zu demontieren').[19] Thus, Plutarch's narrative is complicated, and I do not want to deny the tension in this work. Rather, I suggest that this tension is rooted in *disciplina* itself, and its usefulness for Plutarch as a key quality in a good man, as well as its possible misappropriation as a marker of 'real' manhood.

One way to think about how Catonic *disciplina* is performed in Plutarch's biography is to turn to another concept that seems to intrigue Plutarch, that of rivalry or ambition (φιλονικία).[20] Cato, as a *novus homo*, constantly strives in his public performance of his Roman-ness to burnish his reputation as a 'good' man, since as an outsider his Roman identity has to be better, more traditional and more convincing than others whose ancestors have been magistrates for generations. Such a performance makes concrete abstract cultural ideals, and so Cato – in Plutarch's telling an old, abstract ideal himself – shows *disciplina* in his frugality, courage and temperance. Yet this same self-control bumps up against the 'real' Cato that Plutarch takes pains to unmask. When Cato hides behind ἐγκράτεια in his attempt to save money by behaving cruelly, Plutarch calls him out. When Cato seems to believe in his old age that σωφροσύνη is optional for him, Plutarch excoriates him for his inconstancy.[21] For Plutarch, Cato's *disciplina* reads either as an excuse for immoral behaviour as part of some ancient 'bro code' or baggage that can be dropped when it becomes inconvenient.

It may be a stretch to suggest that in these moments Plutarch sets himself as Cato's next best rival in a contest over *disciplina*, yet the suggestion arises because Plutarch ever so carefully builds towards such a conclusion, pitting Cato's vocal anti-Hellenism against Plutarch's Hellenism.[22] Cato's model Roman masculinity, which treats humans worse than animals and opposes Greek culture at every turn, is revealed to be not that of a 'good' Roman but rather a barbarian, due in no small part to his refusal to embrace the lessons of Greek society.[23] The Cato who embodies a model of agricultural know-how, who is the reference for generations who desire to make their lands productive, errs when it comes to 'ploughing furrows' in his own home.[24] Read in this way, Cato's excess or lack of *disciplina* means that he misidentifies human categories and humans' places in the world, a problem only to be remedied by an appropriate corrective from a temperate and knowledgeable Greek.

In both cases we observe Plutarch framing a Greek resistance to a Roman model of masculinity through the bodies of the enslaved. In both instances, Plutarch first articulates an explicit Greek position in contrast to a Roman performance of *disciplina* which he finds morally suspect or wanting. Second, he enhances the ethnic or cultural differentiation by choosing examples where Cato's behaviour towards a slave is the catalyst for the critique. The objects of Plutarch's criticism – both of which take aim at Cato's explicitly Roman masculine performance – show the possibility of judging Roman imperial rule by analysing the most extreme results of Roman values and demarcating a contrast between the exercise of 'good' values and the performance of 'real' masculinity. Thus, in both examples the bodies of slaves are the impetus for the critique, in the first case because Cato fails to recognise their humanity, in the second because he prefers the humiliation of an inferior marriage to the continuation of a liaison with a slave. Bernat Montoya Rubio has argued that in the Second Sophistic we witness an increased interest in the suffering of slaves, a concern that he identifies in numerous places throughout Plutarch's works. Plutarch's rhetorical move here, then, may be visible not only at a microscopic level, in the moral failings of a particular man in relation to an oppressed other – it may also function at a macroscopic level, where Plutarch underscores the failures of *disciplina* as a Roman guiding principle vis-à-vis an oppressed Greek other. This identification of Cato's misuse of *disciplina* makes explicit the ways that the values of Roman *imperium* and its most powerful adherents are implicated in its exercise. Plutarch's interrogation of the uses to which *disciplina* is put compel us to do more than take Cato's persona at face value. His behaviour might serve as an ideal for a 'good' Roman man, but its consequences show us the 'real' Cato.

NOTES

1. Dench 2002, 85. *Novus homo* designated any man who was the first in his family to become a member of the Roman senate, as well as the first man of a senatorial family to achieve the consulship. As such, it implies both the extraordinary effort and nobility of the 'new man', but also has a whiff of the upstart. See Wiseman 1971.

2. Dench (2002, 85–94) argues for Cato's alignment with a Sabine identity as a way to validate his status as new man and outsider and promote himself as morally virtuous. On Cato's moral self-fashioning in opposition to Hellenism, see Gruen 1992, 52–83. The *locus classicus* for explication of the concept of gender performance is found in Butler (1990 and 1993). Jiménez (2002, 253–70) takes note of Plutarch's presentation of Cato's moralising rhetoric as a performance.

3. In addition to Plutarch's biography, ancient sources for Cato's life include laudatory accounts by Cornelius Nepos (*Life of Cato*) and Cicero (*de Re Publica* and *Cato Maior de Senectute*), and more critical assessments by Livy (books 29, 32, 34, 36, 38–9, 43 and 45). Some near contemporaries of Plutarch, Fronto and Aulus Gellius, revive Cato as a model of thought and behaviour.

4. Toxic masculinity, as a comparatively new notion and contested in academic circles, has no set definition, but has been interrogated in both academic circles and the popular press. See, for example, Addis and Cohane 2005, 633–47, as an example of the impact of toxic masculinity on men's health, and Banet-Weiser and Miltner 2015, 171–4, on popular reception of male fragility. On the American context, see Kimmel 2013.

5. Kimmel and Wade 2018, 238.

6. Kimmel and Wade 2018, 238–9.

7. The literature on Roman virtues is lengthy, but on *disciplina* and other male-coded behaviours one might begin with Earl 1967; Hellegouarc'h 1972; Barton 2001; and McDonnell 2006. See Hall (2009, 11–12) on such values as constituent of *Romanitas*. Cato, especially as censor, championed moral values as a public good in service of the state; see Astin 1978, 182–210.

8. Sansone 1989, 5, 8; Duff 1999, 52; and Stadter 2015, 215–45. Indeed, Duff (1999, 9) describes Plutarch's project as a complex one, of presenting readers with questions of morality and virtue that are not easily resolved.

9. Stadter (2015, 45) observes that the *Lives* were written for both Greeks and Romans, where 'the Romans represented an especially important segment of that audience, in as much as they were more powerful and therefore more in need of the kind of moral education [Plutarch] could offer'. Swain (1996, 161) argues that Plutarch opposed 'political integration with Rome' and otherwise attributed Roman failings to a lack of Greek *paideia*. Plutarch makes similar claims in the *Moralia* (813E).

10. Plutarch most clearly articulates his project at *Alex.* 1.1–3, suggesting that character is likely to be revealed in small, everyday matters. Plutarch's attention to slavery in the *Cato Maior* has been detailed in Astin (1978, 261–6). I choose to examine the episodes in chapters 4 and 24 regarding treatment of the enslaved, since Plutarch explicitly critiques them, and set aside chapter 21, on which he offers no commentary.

11. This is virtually a direct quotation from Cato (*de Agr.* 2.7).

12. See Sansone (1989, 12–13) on Plutarch's emphasis on his subjects as teachers. Gruen (1992, 77–81) catalogues Cato's didacticism, including the anti-Greek sentiments in *ad filium*, and its political as well as didactic postures, in particular as a part of Cato's innate rivalry and desire for φιλοτιμία.

13. Astin (1978, 261–6) offers a detailed account of Cato's treatment of slaves, noting both ingenuity in creating incentives for obedience and in devising and enforcing harsh penalties.

14. Plutarch's examples elevate the status of animals: the Athenians building the Parthenon always allowed mules to rest, but gave special care to an exceptionally hardworking mule, even in its old age, after it was put to pasture; Cimon buried the horses which helped him win at the Olympics near his family burial plot; and Xanthippus buried the dog that swam alongside his ship to Salamis in a place of honour (*Cat. Mai.* 5.3–4).

15. Aristotle's taxonomy places plants in servitude to animals, and animals to humans (*Pol.* 1.5, 1.8–9 and *HA* 8.1). It is clear that Greek appreciation of animals is not a static cultural value, though it has been argued that the Greeks had greater reverence for animal life than we in the twenty-first-century West may show. On the complexity and variety of attitudes towards animal life, see Bodson 1983, 312–20 and Calder 2011. On Plutarch's belief in animals' ability to reason and the justice due to them as moral coequals, see Newmyer 2005.

16. Montoya Rubio (2014, 160) observes that Plutarch in a later passage (21) takes care to excoriate Cato, by connecting Cato's harsh treatment of slaves, the acquisition of wealth and *hybris*.

17. As Pelling (2002, 369) notes, 'it is characteristic of Plutarch, in his best work, to bring out how the same qualities contribute both to a man's greatness and to his flaws: for instance, the elder Cato's antihellenism, his attitude toward wealth, his austerity, his lack of compromise . . .'

18. Wulfrum 2009, 73.

19. Wulfrum 2009, 74: 'Plutarch, however, was far from . . . completely dismantling Cato.'

20. See especially Stadter 2015, 270–85.

21. Astin (1978, 105) proposes that Cato as an old man perhaps believed his reputation to be secure and able to endure an intemperate choice of wife.

22. Cato created his persona through the disparagement of the Greek, setting himself in opposition to it as a way to 'elevate the stature of Roman culture' (Gruen 1992, 78).

23. Montoya Rubio (2014, 173–4) argues that Plutarch views slavery as a source of *hybris*, in that an enslaver's exercise of hubristic power can lead him (as in Cato's case) to see himself as out of reach of even divine wrath.

24. Aristotle *Gen. An.* 716a5–23 is the *locus classicus* for this agricultural metaphor.

CHAPTER 10

(Toxic) Masculinity between Hegemony and Precariousness: Alternatives to Heteronormativity in Briseis' Portrait of Achilles (Ov. *Her.* 3)

Simona Martorana

S taged as a letter written by Briseis to Achilles, Ovid's *Heroides* 3 features an ambiguous version of the Homeric hero, who is suspended between epic and elegy, the performance of manhood and more stereotypically feminine attitudes. This chapter demonstrates how Briseis' portrait of Achilles helps us to reassess the contemporary sociological concept of toxic masculinity in relation to Ovid's *Heroides* according to a more fluid, and less binary, view of gender relationships. While Achilles' epic attitudes can be seen as an example of hegemonic masculinity, which has been defined as an affirmation of men's dominant position and the subordination of others (see Donaldson 1993 and Connell 2005), the description of his behaviour in *Her.* 3 places him more within the contemporary category of toxic masculinity (Kupers 2005), in that it harms Achilles himself and the community to which he belongs.

This toxicity is evident in certain passages of the Ovidian epistle, where Achilles' greed and violence are depicted as being dangerous and harmful, whereas other activities (linked to the elegiac sphere) are presented as preferable (cf., for instance, line 116; see below). Achilles' hegemonic attitudes thus coexist with his more toxic behaviour. Being problematised within Briseis' fictional narrative in *Her.* 3, the notion of toxic masculinity that Achilles appears to embody will be reinterpreted vis-à-vis the recent sociological and theoretical development around the concept of 'masculinities', which has become more fluid and unstable.[1] This fluidity and instability represent a challenge to what we would define as heteronormativity and gender binarism.

Binarism and heteronormativity[2] are recent concepts, so these terms cannot be imposed wholesale upon the ancient world but need to be reassessed in the context of the Greco-Roman world. 'Heteronormative' and 'non-binary' are hereafter used to indicate the divide between the actions which (those who were identified as) men were expected to perform and the actions which (those who were identified as) women were expected to perform.[3] This translated also into the sexual sphere, where heteronormativity led to the enforced normativity of heterosexuality as an erotic configuration. While it is important indeed to keep in mind that there are differences between the contemporary and the ancient world, it is likewise crucial to note that certain aspects of the Greco-Roman world may be profitably compared to, and help us understand, some criticalities (such as heterogeneity, fluidity in the subject–object relationship, blurring of gender, as well as social, categories) of the contemporary social, cultural and gender debate.[4] Concerning gender fluidity in particular, the notion that gender roles in antiquity were perpetually redefined and went beyond the biological mirrors certain contemporary theorisations on gender identities,[5] from Butler's gender performativity to the conceptions of gender as a flux which stand as the theoretical foundations of my argument.

Before focusing on the portrayal of Achilles within *Heroides* 3, I provide some background on Achilles as a mythological figure.[6] A complex, multidimensional and polysemous character in the *Iliad*, which is the Ur-text for Ovid's Achilles in *Her.* 3, Achilles fluctuates between the embodiment of heroic and epic values and a cruel and self-centred warrior led by violence and *hybris*. These latter attitudes emerge from his refusal to fight (and all the damages that refusal causes to the Greeks) and from his brutal treatment of Hector's body.[7] This brutality coexists with his affective relationship with Patroclus, which has been interpreted as homoerotic, both by ancient sources and modern scholarship.[8] The potential homoeroticism, along with his greed and excessive violence, did not compromise the depiction of Achilles as the quintessential epic hero, at least within the narrative of the *Iliad*. Nonetheless, the Homeric poems do present certain ambiguous features for Achilles, as well as controversial elements of his mythological background. These elements may have informed the later more problematic accounts or narratives related to this character and thus challenged his depiction as an embodiment of quintessentially competitive and aggressive – that is, hegemonic – masculinity.[9]

In this respect, the episode of Achilles' retirement from battle due to Agamemnon's decision to take Briseis away from him to be his own concubine (cf. *Il.* 1.1–303) could be seen as a reaction to the offence against his honour (*time*), as well as an attempt to (re)establish his hegemonic role, and therefore his masculinity, among the Greeks.[10] At the same time, Achilles' abstention from battle also represents a suspension of a highly masculine activity. Moreover, his proclivity towards music (cf. *Il.* 9.182–98), which distracts him from more epic activities related to warfare, as well as his excessively grief-stricken reaction to Patroclus' death (cf. *Il.* 18.1–126), may also be interpreted as a performance of femininity, particularly if one takes into account later receptions of the Homeric poem.[11] What is missing from Homeric poetry is an account of the pre-Iliadic episode of Achilles' cross-dressing on Skyros, which, by contrast, is well attested in visual arts from the fifth century BCE onwards, as well as in later sources like Statius' *Achilleid*.[12]

Having seen the contradictions within the Homeric portrayal of Achilles, we can now move closer to the elegiac Achilles, who coexists with his epic *Doppelgänger* within *Her.* 3. The Homeric hero is a well-known character within the elegiac genre, where he is not so Homeric, nor much of a hero either. Among the passages from elegiac poetry featuring Achilles, for the sake of this chapter Prop. 2.8.29–40 and 2.9.9–16, as well as Ov. *Am.* 1.9.33–4, *Ars* 1.691–6 and *Ars* 2.709–32 are worth noting.[13] In the first passage, Propertius chooses the example of Achilles to express his own desperation, along with his anger at Cynthia's infidelity. The poet portrays Achilles' reaction after his *coninux* ('partner'), Briseis, was *abrepta* ('stolen') as excessive (29), since he stopped fighting and, therefore, was not able to prevent Patroclus' death (30; 33–4). Moreover, Propertius reinterprets Achilles' myth by stating that he underwent *omnia* ('all sorts of things') due to his love for Briseis (35), and accordingly that he returned to battle only after Briseis had been given back to him (37–8).[14] Conversely, in Prop. 2.9.9–16, Briseis mourns Achilles' death, expressing her severe distress by beating her face with her hands (9–10) and tearing at her own hair (13–14).[15] In *Am.* 1.9.33–4, Ovid presents Achilles as a quintessentially elegiac lover: 'ardet in abducta Briseide magnus Achilles' ('the great Achilles burns because of his stolen Briseis').[16] In *Ars* 1.691–6, which refers to Achilles' cross-dressing on Skyros, the hero is depicted performing feminine tasks, such as weaving (691), instead of fighting (693–4).

In *Her.* 3, Ovid incorporates both the epic and the elegiac features of Achilles, thus creating an unconventional character whose liminality and ambiguity appear particularly enhanced. That the depiction of Achilles in *Heroides* 3 articulates the coexistence of two voices, the voice of the fictional female persona (Briseis) and the voice of the male author (Ovid), further contributes to blurring the boundaries between literary genres and genders. On the one hand, elegy is perfectly suitable to vocalise the feelings of abandoned women, as the *Heroides* do; on the other hand, elegy is characterised by a reversal of roles, insofar as the male poet expresses his complaint through (what has been defined as) a feminine attitude.[17] Ovid, in particular, seems to re-employ in his exile poetry the patterns of the abandoned and complaining lover that we can remark in the *Heroides*: he has been said to take inspiration from his own writing, thereby creating a link between the fictional persona of the *Heroides* and his autobiographical persona in the exile works.[18] This tension between female and male sides is never reconciled within the *Heroides* but emerges from the constant reversal of roles between the two main actors of the epistles, the female fictional author and the male addressee (in this case, Briseis and Achilles respectively), as well as the coexistence of various literary genres. Polyphony, multifariousness and variety of gender and genre enhance the ambiguity and irony of the heroines' discourse, which sanctions their departure from expected social roles and political norms. Like the other heroines of the collection, Ovid has Briseis play with this coexistence of genders and genres, as well as engaging with the previous literary tradition.

In Briseis' letter, Achilles encapsulates many of the features from previous literary accounts and at the same time anticipates the subsequent reworkings of his own narrative (such as Statius' *Achilleid*).[19] The epistle features Achilles as both an epic hero and an elegiac lover; moreover, he performs actions and behaviours which cannot be attributed simply to binary gender categories (in the way that these are conceptualised in relation to the ancient world).[20] To show this fluidity of identities, I analyse three macro-motifs of *Heroides* 3: the affirmation and consequent denial of Achilles' toxic masculinity, which finds multiple expressions in Briseis' portrayal of an epic Achilles; the gender role reversal; and the emphatic description of Achilles' (un)masculine attitudes (which are both markers of the elegiac genre). This survey encourages us to reassess Achilles' masculinity as fluid, polymorphic and heterogeneous, as well as resituating it in the contemporary discussion about 'masculinities'.

ACHILLES AS AN EPIC (AND TOXIC) HERO

Concerning the epic Achilles, Briseis repeatedly overstates what we can define as Achilles' hegemonic role in her epistle. In the very first line of the poem, for instance, she calls herself *rapta* ('stolen'), which is an epic and military word, while holding at the same time a highly elegiac connotation (cf. Prop. 2.8.29; 2.20.1, *abducta*; Ov. *Am.* 2.9.29; 2.12.17; *Ars* 3.190, *cum rapta est*). Through this expression, she emphasises Achilles' superiority, as well as his control over her.[21] At line 5, the heroine then addresses Achilles as *dominoque viroque* ('master and husband'), while at 27–38 she emphatically lists the *dona* ('gifts', 30) offered to Achilles through Ulysses, Ajax and Phoenix in order to persuade him to go back into battle. The richness and opulence of these *dona* highlight Achilles' quasi-alpha male position among the Greeks. This position appears further emphasised in Briseis' description of Achilles' heroic deeds when he defeated her city and killed her family (45–50):

> diruta Marte tuo Lyrnesia moenia vidi –
>   et fueram patriae pars ego magna meae;
> vidi consortes pariter generisque necisque
>   tres cecidisse, quibus, quae mihi, mater erat;
> vidi, quantus erat, fusum tellure cruenta
>   pectora iactantem sanguinolenta virum.
>
>   (Ov. *Her.* 3.45–50)

I saw the walls of my city (where I had been a person of rank) levelled by your army; I saw my three brothers fall, comrades in birth and death as well; I saw my husband stretched out at full length on the gory ground, his bloody chest heaving.[22]

The violence of Achilles' acts is denoted by various lexical and stylistic choices: the hyperbaton of 'diruta . . . Lyrnesia moenia' (45) amplifies the idea of Achilles' destructive capability;[23] the slaughter of Briseis' siblings (47–8) is then recounted in dramatised form, which is conveyed, for instance, by the rapid rhythm of the couplet from the caesura of line 47 onwards;[24] the description of her husband's death (49–50) is also very emphatic ('tellure cruenta; pectora . . . sanguinolenta'), while the extremely long hyperbaton of 'fusum . . . virum' provides a sense of the dreadfulness and cruelty of Achilles' actions.[25] As a consequence of this massacre, Briseis not only acknowledges her captor Achilles as her master but, rather paradoxically, also continues to profess her love for him: 'tu dominus, tu vir, tu mihi frater eras' ('you were my master, my husband, and my brother', 52).[26] Moreover, Briseis claims that she is willing to follow the hero as a prisoner or a slave (69);[27] accordingly, she imagines herself performing feminine, but also servile and humiliating, tasks: 'nos humiles famulaeque tuae data pensa trahemus,/et minuent plenas stamina nostra colos' ('As for me, I shall be a lowly slave of yours and spin off the given task, and the full distaff shall grow slender at the drawing of my threads'; 75–6).[28]

From these passages, Achilles emerges as the perfect realisation of male, epic heroism: inflexible, incapable of affection, concerned only with honour and in continuous competition with other men in order to demonstrate his superiority. The world in which Achilles acts is itself male-dominated and violent.[29] This world reflects the Homeric epos, where Achilles' violence is not simply justified but is an essential part of epic ethics. Within some passages of the epistle, Achilles is thus an embodiment of toxic masculinity, as defined by psychologist and sociologist Terry Kupers: 'male proclivities associated with toxic masculinity include extreme competition and greed, insensitivity to or lack of consideration of the experiences and feelings of others, a strong need to dominate and control others . . .'.[30] Achilles' toxic masculinity is determined by his brutal treatment of his enemies, as well as control over women, like Briseis. Moreover, Achilles' hegemonic masculinity is specifically toxic in that his refusal to return to battle (cf. *Her.* 3.113–24; see below) jeopardises the survival of his social group, that is, the Greek army.

GENDER ROLE REVERSAL

However, Briseis' letter is not only about Achilles' toxic masculinity. In fact, this toxic masculinity is questioned to such an extent that Achilles' behaviour appears, in some cases, actually unmasculine. This presumed lack of masculinity that the epistle reveals may be read as an alternative – or as many alternatives – to toxicity, namely strictly epic masculinity, as it is depicted in the passages from *Heroides* 3 examined above. The masculinity that is presented as hegemonic, and therefore permitted and encouraged in epic, is by contrast seen as toxic in elegy. Accordingly, the emphasis on the 'feminising' aspects of Achilles' character in elegy serves to mitigate that toxicity. In other words, by presenting Achilles as a multidimensional character, the epistle proposes the existence of other, alternative forms of masculinity. The emergence of these alternative masculinities is marked by the presence of elegiac patterns, which cooperate in the deconstruction of the traditional concept of masculinity.

At line 14, for instance, Briseis regrets not having been able to give kisses (*oscula*) to Achilles while she was forcefully separated from him: this reference to the *oscula* (a hallmark of erotic poetry) lends a very elegiac colour to the entire picture.[31] Moreover, she defines Achilles' *ira* as *lenta* ('slow', 22), a markedly elegiac adjective, which is often used for elegiac partners who are 'slow' in requiting their love.[32] Similarly, while line 69 ('victorem captiva sequar, non nupta maritum'; 'As a prisoner let me follow my captor, not as a wife my husband') superficially hints at Briseis' servile condition, the conceptual and linguistic references to slavery (cf. *captiva*) also recall another kind of slavery, the elegiac *servitium amoris*.[33] Briseis is thus underlining her status as a slave, while simultaneously pointing out that she takes part in a more refined kind of *servitium*, the servitude of love. Achilles' presumed hegemony becomes, within the elegiac universe of *Her.* 3, a mere rhetorical and literary topos, thereby losing its epic significance.

Briseis also depicts an erotic scene that recalls *Ars* 2.709–32, where Ovid shows that Achilles is not only *utilis* (like Hector at line 710) in war but also very competent in sex.[34] However, the erotic content, as well as the description of sexual relations, is much more explicit in the passage from the *Ars Amatoria* than at *Her.* 3.131–2, where there are only allusions to actual sexual intercourse: 'est aliquid collum solitis tetigisse lacertis,/praesentisque oculos admonuisse sui' ('It is something to have touched a lover's neck with the accustomed arms, and to have reminded your eyes of one's existence in person').[35] In the following couplet, Briseis states that, in spite of Achilles' hard manner and fierceness (133), she would nonetheless be able to overcome his resistance: 'ut taceam, lacrimis conminuere meis' ('even if I stay silent, you will be broken by my tears'; 134).[36] By stating that the tears of a woman may be able to persuade Achilles to change his decision, Briseis demonstrates that the laws of elegy can make Achilles' masculinity more precarious than it appears in the epic world.

This precarious manhood is further problematised in other passages of the epistle, where Briseis literally overcomes the gender hierarchy between herself and Achilles, as well as performing a reversal of their gender roles. At lines 83–98, the heroine exhorts Achilles to return to the fight.[37] The situation appears somewhat paradoxical: while Achilles, the supposedly epic hero, refuses to fight (the epic activity par excellence), Briseis, his female lover, wishes him to return to battle. This gender role reversal shows Achilles' rejection of the sort of masculinity that is appropriate in an epic context, but which can be seen as toxic from the perspective of Ovid's elegiac poetry.[38]

THE HEROIDEAN ACHILLES AS A MODEL OF NON-BINARISM

From the words of Briseis hitherto analysed, Achilles' masculinity emerges as problematic and complex.[39] Achilles' attitudes, and the gender role reversals, draw the picture of a non-binary, and more fluid, conception of gender. In *Her.* 3, the set of attitudes and/or performative actions that have contributed to a particular definition of masculinity, epic and toxic masculinity (verbal and physical violence; a desire to dominate; exhibiting behaviours which are harmful to other members of the community), are merged with, and cannot easily be distinguished from, those which are considered to be opposing tendencies, and thus stereotypical markers of femininity.

These aspects of Achilles' character, contrary as they are to the idea of toxic masculinity, should in fact be considered as not merely non-masculine, but as alternative examples of masculinity. By playing with the previous epic/heroic context, in which hegemonic, violent and toxic masculinity is the only possible form of masculinity, Ovid's Briseis moves within the elegiac world to challenge constructed gender categories as well as proposing a different idea of masculinity for Achilles. Recent scholarship in social sciences and gender studies posits the existence of many forms of 'masculinities' as well as viewing 'masculine' as a multilayered and malleable concept.[40] Drawing on these views, one can say that Achilles' masculinity is in a continuous process of becoming: it is fluid, evolving and cannot be defined unequivocally, but is a flexible category. According to gender theorist Todd Reeser, this kind of masculinity should be placed in a gender continuum and does not oppose femininity but integrates with it to the formation of the subject:

> Masculinity would then be constituted by a myriad of masculinities, by an endless series of different masculinities that never recur. And the other gender here would not be a problem or something to be feared or defined as other, but a possibility for movement and change, a possible springboard for pleasure in change.[41]

This multidimensionality of Achilles' masculinity finds expression at lines 113–24, where Briseis lists the activities which please the hero more than war.

> at Danai maerere putant – tibi plectra moventur,
>   te tenet in tepido mollis amica sinu!

et quisquam quaerit, quare pugnare recuses?
  pugna nocet, citharae noxque Venusque iuvant.
tutius est iacuisse toro, tenuisse puellam,
  Threiciam digitis increpuisse lyram,
quam manibus clipeos et acutae cuspidis hastam,
  et galeam pressa sustinuisse coma.
sed tibi pro tutis insignia facta placebant,
  partaque bellando gloria dulcis erat.
an tantum dum me caperes, fera bella probabas,
  cumque mea patria laus tua victa iacet?

                                                    (Ov. Her. 3.113–24)

The Greeks think you are moping – you are strumming a lyre, in the
warm embrace of a willing girlfriend. If anyone asks, why don't you fight?
Fighting hurts, while night, lyres and love delight. It's safer to lie on your
couch with a girl in your arms and play a tune on the Threcian lyre than
to hold a shield with your hands and a sharp-pointed spear, and support
a heavy helmet on your locks. You used to prefer illustrious exploits to
safety and get pleasure from the glory won in warfare. Did you only
approve fierce war so you could capture me? Is the victory over my country also the end of your prowess?

The heroine states that while the Greeks (*Danai*) think that Achilles is groaning,
he is actually spending his time playing the cithara (113) and having sex with
his concubine (114).[42] When someone asks him why he refuses to fight (115),
he replies that it is because 'fighting hurts, while night, lyres and love delight'
(116).[43] Indeed, it is safer to lie in bed, hold a *puella* and play the Thracian lyre
with fingers (117–18)[44] than to embrace shield and spear (*clipeos*; *hastam*; 119)
and support the weight of a helmet upon his locks (120).

The lexical (cf., for instance, the word *puella* at 117) and thematic choices
within these lines evoke a highly elegiac context. The elegiac reversal of traditional norms and social rules, as well as interfamilial relationships, is the antithesis to epic canons.[45] In this passage, Briseis exploits once more the potential of
the *Heroides* to make Achilles' behaviour appear simultaneously inappropriate,
from an epic point of view, and appropriate, from an elegiac perspective. In
doing so, the heroine is also playing with the intrinsic ambiguity of Achilles as
a mythological figure.

While Achilles is in fact portrayed playing the lyre also in the *Iliad* (cf. *Il.*
9.182–98), within the Homeric epos this may be considered as a legitimate
activity and categorised as a normal reaction to Agamemnon's offence, as well
as being linked to Achilles' *menis* ('anger').[46] In *Her.* 3, by contrast, this epic
pattern acquires a different meaning and contributes to the portrayal of Achilles

as an elegiac lover rather than as an epic hero. The permeability of elegy as a literary genre, as well as the peculiarity of the *Heroides*, allows us to rethink, and redefine, Achilles' (multiple) 'masculinities'. Achilles' alternative masculinity, which can be defined as elegiac, is antithetical to his heroic and hegemonic masculinity, which characterises his literary, epic, past.

This idea is developed at lines 121–4, where Briseis states that Achilles used to prefer the *insignia facta* to safe things (121), and that the glory from military victories pleased him (122).[47] The heroine then provocatively asks whether Achilles enjoyed fighting only until he had conquered Briseis' city and captured her (123–4). By mentioning the hero's previous proclivity towards war alongside his aggressive actions, Briseis further stresses the variety of Achilles' attitudes, which result in many forms of masculinities. These different types of masculinity do not deny the existence of his toxic masculinity, but rather propose certain alternatives: masculinity as a flexible, changeable and adaptable concept, which can be defined as a process as well as a set of relationships, and not as 'what-men-empirically-are', to put it in contemporary terms.[48]

If one thinks of masculinity as a set of performative acts and frees this concept from the bounds of binarism and heteronormativity, then 'masculinity' no longer exists in its traditional form but covers a wide spectrum of attitudes, behaviours and patterns.[49] The subversive content of elegy is not only the most suitable ground for the depiction of Achilles' fluid 'masculinities', but it also contributes to the construction of Achilles as an alternative to the patriarchal model and to heteronormativity.[50] Moreover, the genre and gender polyphony of *Her.* 3, and the *Heroides* as a whole, further develops the ambiguity, multifariousness and fluidity of Achilles' masculinity, thereby transforming the binary opposition between toxic masculinity and unmasculine behaviour into a different kind, and conception, of masculinity; that is, into multiple masculinities.

On the one hand, Achilles, alongside his epic narrative, may appear to affect Briseis' writing; as a woman and a prisoner, Briseis seems objectified, her subjectivity annihilated; her writing becomes a tool in the hands of the author (Ovid) and the dominant male character (Achilles). On the other hand, the heroine, as the fictional writer of her epistle, is not merely the bearer of a patriarchy-based discourse, as a ventriloquised puppet in the hand of her master, but also demonstrates her self-awareness and ability to express her own, quasi-subjective, voice. The coexistence of these voices and perspectives challenges the traditional idea of hegemonic masculinity, which is redefined as a process of becoming and includes its antithetic manifestations.[51] Achilles in *Her.* 3 is thus an example of how 'masculinity' has now become a multifaceted concept, which both discursively and ontologically eludes a univocal categorisation. This multidimensionality of masculinity, and its evolution into 'masculinities', has already been theorised and is commonly accepted by the scientific community. However, the concept of masculinity itself (and masculinities) is still in evolution, and needs (and indeed undergoes) continual redefinition and reassessment:

> The strain paradigm asserts that there is no single standard for masculinity nor is there an unvarying masculinity ideology. Rather, because masculinity is a social construction, ideals of manhood may differ for men of different social classes, races, ethnic groups, sexual orientations, life stages, and historical eras.[52]

This analysis of Achilles' toxic masculinity has helped us to delineate and legitimise the existence of its opposite, namely non-toxic masculinity. This non-toxic masculinity is the expression of a wider spectrum of options for potential masculinities, as well as a possible alternative to the traditional, heteronormative notion of masculinity. *Her.* 3 thus reveals unexplored (and unexpected) angles of masculinity in the ancient world, encouraging us to think of masculinity as a plurality of non-gendered, non-binary manifestations, that is, as multiple 'Masculinities'.[53] Exploring Achilles in *Her.* 3 has thus allowed us to look beyond binary gender categories and challenge the stability of the concept of masculinity, both in the ancient and the contemporary world.

NOTES

1. See Levant 1996; Connell 2005; Connell and Messerschmidt 2005; Reeser 2010; Walsh 2010. The concept of masculinity in Rome also had multiple layers and is difficult to define; accordingly, by examining the multiple aspects of Achilles' masculinity, I position myself within a tradition of scholarly works which seek to define the possible meanings of masculinity in ancient Rome; cf. Williams 1999, 4, '*Masculinity* refers to a complex of values and ideals that can more profitably be understood as a cultural tradition than as a biological given: the concept refers to what it is to be fully gendered as "a man" as opposed to merely having the physical features held to signify "a male".'
2. For a definition of heteronormativity, as well as the related concepts of binarism and phallogocentrism, see Warner 1991, 3–17.
3. James 2003, 213: 'By the time elegy begins to flourish, Rome is [. . .] a male culture that creates female subjection by handing child-brides (from age twelve or so) over to adult males.'
4. For a discussion about the problematic application of modern labels (heterosexual, heteronormative, homosexual) to the ancient world, see Williams 1999, 4–8. More recently, in an edited volume about transgender dynamics in antiquity, Carlà-Uhink (2017, 3), while acknowledging that 'transgender' is a contemporary concept, states that 'nonetheless, in Classical Antiquity, it is possible to identify forms of behaviour and action which might fall into our modern category of transgender'. Carlà-Uhink also adds (4) that an analysis of

the behaviours which may be classified according to the contemporary category of transgender 'highlights . . . aspects of ancient sexuality which would otherwise be only partially visible'.

5. For gender identity in Rome as a social construct 'perpetually in the making', see Gleason 1995, esp. XXVI.
6. Cf. *RE* I 221–45, *s.v.* 'Achilleus' [Escher].
7. See e.g. Zanker 1994 and Clarke 2004, 74–90.
8. See, for instance, Aesch. *Myrm. TGrF* 135–7, 139; Athenaeus 13.601A; 602E; Plut. *Amat.* 751C, 761D; Plat. *Symp.* 179E–180B; Aeschin. *In Tim.* 142–50; Theoc. *Id.* 29.31–4; *Ant. Pal.* 12.217. In ancient Greece, however, male 'homosexuality' was a very complex concept (see Davidson 2007): this should not necessarily be seen as an effeminate trait, particularly when it is linked to educational practices or initiatory rites (see Dover 1978, 202–3 and Sergent 1986, 40–54). For homosexuality in Rome, see Williams 1999.
9. Some passages from the *Iliad* seem to allude to Achilles' homoerotic relationship with Patroclus: see e.g. *Il.* 9.209, 216–17, 620–62, with Clarke 1978, 390. For the comparison between the relationship of Achilles and Patroclus and a husband and a wife, see *Il.* 23.136–7, 19.321–7, with Warwick 2019, 115–39. Moreover, at *Il.* 9.182–98, Ulysses, Ajax and Phoenix find Achilles (together with Patroclus) playing the lyre. Although this is not necessarily a marker of effeminacy, at least as far as concerns Homeric epos, later authors (like Ovid) would nonetheless draw from this detail to emphasise Achilles' effeminacy.
10. As stated by Kupers (2005, 716), 'hegemonic masculinity is built on two legs, domination of women and a hierarchy of intermale dominance'. Achilles' wrath, then, may be read as a strategy to (re)establish his 'intermale dominance', which is indeed challenged by Agamemnon on both fronts.
11. In *Aen.* 9.614–20, Numanus Remulus mocks the Trojans by describing them as effeminate dancers and singers, equating singing with effeminacy: see Williams 1999, 146; Curtis 2017, 51–5. Particularly in the Augustan era, music became an aspect of 'luxury and pleasure' (Griffin 1976, 95). In later sources, however, Achilles' music is interpreted in a more ambiguous way and linked to an elegiac context (cf. *Tr.* 4.1.15–16; *Am.* 2.1.29–32; *Octavia* 814–15).
12. Cf. *RE* I 242–5, *s.v.* 'Achilleus'; *LIMC* I 1.55–69, *s.v.* 'Achilleus'. For an overview of the ambiguous construction of Achilles in Statius, see Heslin 2005; McAuley 2010, 37–60.
13. Cf. also Hor. *Carm.* 2.4.2–4; on references to Achilles in elegy, see McKeown 1989 *ad Am.* 1.9.33–4; Fedeli 2004, 157–71; Fantuzzi 2012, 157–73.
14. In this respect, Fedeli (2005, 268) rightly speaks of 'inserimento dell'eroe greco in uno schema elegiaco' ('an insertion of the Greek hero into an elegiac situation').
15. On this sort of emotional reaction as expression of 'unmanly' behaviour, see Goyette in this volume.
16. Cf. Prop. 2.22.29–32.
17. The poet (*amator*), who as a male would normally dominate, submits to the *puella*, who is often described as *dura* (while, as a female, she would be expected to be *mollis*) and indicated as *domina*. Furthermore, the poet is often

characterised by features that pertain rather more to the feminine sphere (emotionality, a lack of constraints, oscillation between opposing feelings); see Holzberg 2000, 28–9 and James 2003, 12 and 129: 'Elegy thus presents the lover-poet as violating all standards of upper-class Roman masculinity, through both servile behavior and inertia of character. So fundamental is this characterization of the lover-poet to elegy that some form of it appears in the beginning of each elegist's oeuvre.'

18. Cf. Rosenmeyer 1997, 29: 'I interpret his [*scil.* Ovid's] choice of the letter form for the exile poems as not only an allusion to, but also as an authorial statement of identification – on some level – with his earlier epistolary work, the *Heroides*.'

19. For background and sources on *Her.* 3, see Jacobson (1971, 331–56 and 1974, 12–42), who shows the links between Ovid's epistle and the Homeric narrative as well as other sources closer to Ovid – namely Latin elegy.

20. For an idea of heteronormativity in Rome as a system where (those who were identified as) men were expected to perform certain roles, see Gleason 1995, 159–65; Gunderson 2000, 7.

21. See also *Rem. Am.* 777, *in abducta Briseide*; *Her.* 8.86, *abducta . . . coniuge*.

22. For the Latin text, see Goold 1977; the English translation is adapted from Murgatroyd, Reeves and Parker 2017, with changes.

23. Cf. *Il.* 2.690–1; Ov. *Met.* 13.175–6; 12.108–9.

24. Note also the anaphoric repetition of *vidi* (45, 47, 49); cf. *Aen.* 2.499–501; 2.5–6.

25. The model for these lines is *Il.* 19.291–4, where Briseis mourns Patroclus' dramatic fate. However, Ovid's description is much more brutal than the Homeric one and may have been drawn from Roman archaic theatre: see Barchiesi 1992, 217–18.

26. This line strengthens the similarities between Briseis and Andromache, and may foreshadow Achilles' death: cf. *Il.* 6.429–30.

27. Cf. Cat. 64.161 (Ariadne); Hor. *Carm.* 3.27.63–6.

28. On Briseis' awareness of her condition as a barbarian and a slave, see Fantuzzi 2012, 140–3.

29. Jacobson 1971, 341–4.

30. Kupers 2005, 717.

31. Cf. *TLL* IX 2.1108.30–1115.52, *s.v.* 'osculum'.

32. Cf. *Her.* 1.1; 2.23; Prop. 1.6.12; 3.8.20; Ov. *Am.* 2.19.51; see Knox 1995, 88 *ad Her.* 1.1.

33. For Briseis' letter as an elegiac, and irreverent, rewriting of previous sources, see most recently Fulkerson 2005, 90–7 and Fantuzzi 2012, 133–43.

34. Janka 1997, 489–90, interprets this passage from *Ars* 2 as a patent parody of epic patterns. On the misogynistic content of the *Ars Amatoria*, see Marturano in this volume.

35. For text, translation and variant readings, see Goold 1977.

36. Cf. Prop. 1.14.17; Ov. *Tr.* 2.411–12.

37. Fulkerson 2005, 96: 'One of the notable features of *Heroides* 3 is that Briseis, deliberately and contrary to mythic precedent, portrays Achilles as an elegiac

lover, insinuating that he is a coward for not demanding her return and especially for refraining from battle.' See also Fantuzzi 2012, 138: 'These exhortations to war – so atypical of women in love poetry! – will have easily reminded the readers of Helen's scornful command to Paris to return to battle at *Il.* 3.428–33a.'

38. See Fantuzzi 2012, 137–40. These words from Briseis are linked to the idea that, according to the traditional conception of hegemonic and/or toxic masculinity, men always have to prove their manhood. On the modern concept of precarious manhood as well as unstable masculinity, see Bosson et al. 2008, 1326: 'Our main thesis is that manhood is widely viewed as both elusive, in that manhood status is not a developmental certainty, and tenuous, in that even once achieved, it is not guaranteed and can be lost. Because of the precarious nature of manhood, anything that makes salient its precariousness, or calls one's manhood status into question, should be especially anxiety provoking.'

39. Connell and Messerschmidt (2005, 836) summarise some critical and problematic views of masculinity: 'the concept of masculinity is blurred, is uncertain in its meaning, and tends to deemphasize issues of power and domination . . . the concept of masculinity is flawed because it essentializes the character of men or imposes a false unity on a fluid and contradictory reality . . . The concept of masculinity is criticized for being framed within a heteronormative conception of gender that essentializes male-female difference and ignores difference and exclusion within the gender categories.'

40. For a discussion on problematic masculinities, see Walsh 2010, 1–35.

41. Reeser 2010, 47.

42. Cf. *Her.* 3.114: 'te tenet in tepido mollis amica sinu' ('a tender mistress holds you in her warm embrace'); for the adjective *mollis* as opposite to the frame of war and epic, cf. Hor. *Carm.* 2.12.3; Ov. *Ars* 2.236; *Tr.* 2.411, *mollem . . . Achillem.*

43. In this line, I chose the reading *noxque* instead of *voxque*, which is the alternative preferred in Goold 1977.

44. Cf. Ov. *Am.* 2.11.31–2.

45. See Wyke 2002.

46. Moreover, in Homer Achilles sings about epic deeds, so that his music also seems appropriate by epic standards. For this conception of music as relaxing and suitable for educational purposes in the ancient world, cf. *Schol. ad Il.* 9.186; Hor. *Epod.* 13.17–18; Ov. *Fast.* 5.385–6; Val. Max. 8.8 *ext.* 2; see Barchiesi 1992, 234–5.

47. Cf. Achilles' reference to his choice between a peaceful life without glory and a glorious, though premature, death in battle (*Il.* 9.410–16).

48. Connell 2005, 69: 'The terms "masculine" and "feminine" point beyond categorical sex difference to the ways men differ among themselves and women differ among themselves in matters of gender.'

49. Connell 2005, 69: 'to define masculinity as what-men-empirically-are is to rule out the usage in which we call some women "masculine" and some men "feminine", or some actions or attitudes "masculine" or "feminine" regardless of who displays them'. On the fluidity of the concept of 'masculinities' in Rome, see Williams 1999, 153–9.

50. 'Crisis is [. . .] a condition of masculinity itself. Masculine gender identity is never stable; its terms are continually being redefined and re-negotiated, the gender performance continually being re-staged. Certain themes and tropes inevitably reappear with regularity, but each era experiences itself in different ways'; quoted from an unpublished paper by Michael Mangan in Walsh 2010, 9.

51. Building on Deleuze and Guattari's theory of the rhizome, Reeser (2010, 47–9) states that: 'masculinity would be defined as a series of possibilities, a series of constant becomings . . . Masculine subjectivity would thus not be a stable, unified event, nor would it be considered as something simply destabilized as one element of some binary opposition, or as one element of a series of binary oppositions. Rather, masculinity would be conceived of as something that is fully outside a binary system, in a constantly changing process of movement, always mutating. So masculinity may become like woman at some point, but that becoming would be only one of its stages, one way in which it moves on to something else that may or may not have to do with the category of woman. In this sense, then, there is no masculine being, but only a series of becomings.'

52. Levant 1996, 260. For more recent similar remarks on the fluidity in the definitions of masculinity, see Pascoe and Bridges 2015, 4.

53. Connell 2005.

CHAPTER 11

'Angry, reckless, savage': Problematising the Hypermasculine Germani

Rhiannon Evans

The modern stereotype of the ancient Roman man, particularly the Roman military man, is of a powerful but controlled figure, capable of exacting both violence and restraint. *Virtus*, literally 'manliness', implies courage, control over others such as slaves or provincials, and also self-control.[1] Roman historiography is replete with anxieties surrounding a decline in *virtus* via mechanisms such as foreign, particularly Eastern, luxuries.[2] In such scenarios, surrounded by exotic foods, clothes and jewels, moralists see manliness as compromised by a lack of self-restraint: masculinity is here not so much toxic, as merged into unmanliness or femininity. But is it possible to experience the opposite problem: to have *too much* manliness? This chapter considers Roman narratives of wild northern barbarians, the Germani, who live frugally, indulge in no luxuries and are extremely courageous; and it explores their potential as both role models and cautionary tales of masculinity gone too far.

MASCULINITY AND ETHNOGRAPHY

Roman representations of Germanic peoples tend towards the extreme. The Germani are huge, extraordinarily strong and 'fiercer than wild beasts', with preternatural toughness that involves wearing scanty animal skins and bathing in the cold water of rivers.[3] They lack discipline: *libido* ('desire', 'wilfulness') is a word frequently applied to them, but not in a sexual sense, implying instead that they are ungovernable in civic and military scenarios.[4] Their attitude towards war makes no sense to the Roman observer: Julius Caesar claims that they wage it for practice or for fun and to create desolation, rather than to build empire.[5] In the only exclusively ethnographic work of ancient Rome, Tacitus gives us Germani who are both squalid barbarians and admirably unconquerable. They confuse the Roman reader (and author) by mixing civic and military spheres – bearing arms in the assembly and allowing women and children to stand at the edge of the battlefield.[6] The presence of the Germani allows Roman writers to investigate the limits of acceptable masculinity: their model of masculinity is both attractively tough and shockingly brutish. In moralising Roman texts they are both a guide and a warning to Romans, who were often conceived as having deviated from the exemplary behaviour of their ancestors:[7] the Germani could help Romans to reorient their gender priorities.

The Germani's potential for self-destructiveness, as described in Roman texts, is the territory in which they might be said to meet contemporary definitions of toxic masculinity.[8] Self-harm lies at the heart of most discussions of the phenomenon, as toxic masculinity presupposes that men's pursuit of physical, social and cultural domination is ultimately destructive to both non-dominant groups and (crucially) to men themselves.[9] In a wider sense, the study of both hegemonic and toxic masculinities chimes with the recent theoretical trend of scrutinising non-marginalised categories (whiteness, heterosexuality). It is a development of the work done by feminist, postcolonial and LGBTQI historians which initially strove to uncover the perspectives of silenced and marginalised people, that is to broaden historical study out from the view of one dominant group. Studies of masculinity interrogate that dominant category, and the concept of toxic masculinity problematises this dominance, exposing its dynamic role in creating a hierarchy which both elevates and imprisons its supposed masters. This trend has a particular resonance for Classics, a discipline long associated with elitism, which has also frequently been espoused by those declaring the superiority of a particular ethnicity, gender and class, typically white and male.[10]

Here I aim to show one way in which representations of hypermasculine northern 'barbarians' help to illuminate the limits of acceptable masculinity for elite Roman writers and the point at which it might turn toxic. These texts, by Caesar, Tacitus and others, are overtly ethnographic, but often barely conceal the truism that ethnography can be at least as much about the self as it is about the other, employing the 'Us/Not Us' motif either to distance the reader from their own culture[11] or to reassure them of its normality. Peoples of northern Europe were a source of fascination, anxiety and othering for Greek and Roman authors: Herodotus writes of the Scythians as the 'youngest nation' on earth, in contrast to the 'oldest' Egyptians (or perhaps Phrygians) and 'middle-ground' Greeks.[12] Thracians are warlike and savage archetypes in Athenian tragedy and beyond.[13] And the Celts or Gauls had long been a threatening and terrifying enemy.[14] In these and many other cases, the belligerent, nomadic and/or primitive northern barbarian delineates the outer edges of the civilised world for Greek and Roman writers.[15]

ADMIRING THE SAVAGE

Although the Germani had appeared as a subgroup of the Gauls/Celts in Polybius' second-century BCE *Histories*, they are first put on the map as a large-scale ethnographic group by Julius Caesar in his commentaries on his wars in Gaul between 58 and 50 BCE. Here Caesar defines the Germani as distinct from the Gauls genetically, ethnographically and culturally, and specifies the Rhine as the dividing line between the two groups – a division that is not supported by archaeology, but which suits Caesar's propagandist and imperialist purposes well.[16] Caesar's taxonomy of northern barbarians draws the Gauls as disunited, in military decline, and thus ripe for conquest, while the Germani are hardened warriors, primitive, and intent on dominating Gaul themselves.[17] Caesar's designations were adopted by later ethnographers, geographers and historians,[18] so that his definition of Germani and their borders had been normalised by the time that Tacitus published the *Germania* in 98 CE.

Tacitus' Germani in particular have attracted a great deal of attention as archetypal 'noble savages'.[19] Strict adherence to gender roles and moral codes in particular are depicted as ideal from a Roman point of view,[20] as Tacitus asserts: 'plusque ibi boni mores valent quam alibi bonae leges' ('there good morals are worth more than good laws elsewhere').[21] Nowhere is Tacitus more clearly using ethnography to critique Rome. In all Roman accounts the Germani are primarily identified as a warrior people, and war contaminates their civic spaces in the way they dress and behave; they prize war above agriculture or even colonialism. Military behaviour defines both men and women in their culture. Even the oddness of Germanic women's presence on the sidelines of battle is presented as a positive, as they urge and shame flagging warriors to return to the fight.[22] From a modern point of view, the masculinity of the Germani in Tacitus might seem refreshingly egalitarian and uncomplicated – the antithesis of toxic masculinity. Militaristic societies, including Rome, are typically dominated by male warriors. Germanic women, however, have a significant and authoritative place on the battlefield,[23] are more valuable as hostages, and have sacred and prophetic roles.[24]

For Roman writers and their audiences, the formidable presence of Germanic men defines them as figures whose masculinity is to be respected and admired, at least in the field of warfare. In the earliest Roman account of the 50s BCE, Caesar uses comparative ethnography to mark them out as men who are now what the Gauls used to be. The Germani are rising in power, while the Gauls are an enervated group whose depleted *virtus* and liberty falls short of Roman ideals.[25] Ariovistus and other Germanic commanders lead formidable and united forces, while Orgetorix and Vercingetorix, the Gallic leaders at the beginning and end of Caesar's account, suffer conspiracies and betrayals, and struggle to maintain control over fractious alliances of unruly Gauls.[26] Valorised masculinity is often tied to military strength and success in the ancient world,[27] and the Germani compare favourably with Gauls in Caesar, and even with Romans in Tacitus.[28]

GERMANI: 'ANGRY, RECKLESS, SAVAGE'

War is one significant space in which hegemonic masculinity is frequently explored by Roman writers. The Germani's battle-hardiness is admirable. However, their behaviour is also rash, violent and hypermasculine, embodying an extreme and toxic variety of masculinity that subverts their ascendance to *humanitas*.[29] In this they are unlike the Gauls, who show potential for imbibing Roman values in Caesar,[30] and by Tacitus' time were long-established, though initially controversial,[31] members of the Senate. But Caesar's Germani are frozen in their insularity,[32] without knowledge of others' institutions, and with no means to develop civilisation or to regulate their brutality. The ethnography about them is dominated by what they lack: they have no property, no magistrates, no Druids, no anthropomorphic gods; and hardly any sacrifice or agriculture.[33] From Ariovistus, the king described as *barbarum, iracundum, temerarium* ('angry, reckless and savage') to the major Germanic subgroup, the Suebi, who are fierce in war but have no sense of duty and discipline, the Germani's lack of self-reflection is ultimately self-defeating.[34]

Ariovistus is the first Germanic individual to appear in the *Bellum Gallicum*, and is thus an important index of his people's character. Like many of the barbarian characters in Caesar and other ancient writers, he demonstrates strong rhetorical powers: an important skill for elite men at Rome. However, it is arguable that the plaudits should actually go to the writer himself, and, as if to emphasise this, Ariovistus' words are reported entirely in indirect speech.[35] And, importantly, although his speech is well-formulated, Ariovistus misconstrues the purpose of holding a colloquium with Caesar. First of all he subverts the idea of mediation, implying that the desire for common speech is a weakness: the Germanic king states that if he wants anything, he will come to Caesar, while, if Caesar wants anything, he himself should come to Ariovistus.[36] Caesar here displays several of Ariovistus' traits: his arrogance, his solipsism and his preference for avoidable confrontation and violence.

The latter trait, that of unconstrained belligerence, reflects Caesar and other writers' view of the Germani as over-determined by warfare and unable to limit their aggression. Because Germanic men are unable to achieve a balance of military and civic life, they are stuck in an inflexible mode of hypermasculinity; they cannot modify their behaviour when context demands it. Later in the book, under military pressure, Ariovistus does agree to a colloquium. However, while Caesar attempts mediation by reminding him of ancient ties between their peoples, Ariovistus uses the meeting to tactlessly warn that there are enemies back in Rome waiting for Caesar, and to make his own extraordinary claim to Gallic territory – 'provinciam suam hanc esse Galliam, sicut illam nostram' ('this was his own province of Gaul, just as that [Provincia] was ours').[37] This sense of entitlement, the idea that he is 'owed' an empire in Gaul and that Caesar has usurped his inalienable rights, resembles the kind of toxic masculinity whereby non-marginalised (in the modern case, white) men, 'arguably the most privileged people on the planet [nevertheless feel] pissed off'.[38] From Caesar's Romanocentric perspective, the Germani self-harm by crossing to Gaul, rather than living with the privilege they have in their 'proper' zone, east of the Rhine. Yet Caesar's characterisation of Ariovistus as needlessly aggressive is useful in the *Bellum Gallicum* to mollify perception of Caesar's own transgression, since the Senate had recognised Ariovistus as a *rex et amicus populi Romani* ('king and friend of the Roman people').[39] Dio asserts that Caesar himself incites the violence as an excuse to confront a German army, implying that he believes Ariovistus' pleas that Caesar is engaging in an unjust war.[40] Caesar, in his account, transfers any suggestion of Roman aggression to his barbarian foe.

Over a century later, however, Tacitus uses the Germani as exemplary figures in the domestic and sexual spheres – that is, those areas for which he saves his strongest critique of Roman morality. For this first-century CE writer, Roman inability to inculcate strong moral values seems far more toxic than Germanic primitivism. The readiness of Tacitus' Germanic women to support their men on the battlefield is, however, intimately connected to Germanic men's hyper-masculinity and uber-bellicosity. It is as though the Germani as a people occupy the toughest, sternest and most rigorous edge of humanity, with all the strengths and dangers inherent in such a position. Sometimes the paradox of positive and negative even appears within the same sentence. So the Germani are physically large and strong, but implicitly lacking in stamina: 'magna corpora et tantum ad impetum valida' ('bodies which are large and only strong for violent exertion').[41] The *tantum* ('only') undermines their strength, and Tacitus confirms this with a further paradox in the next sentence, as he claims that they have no tolerance (*patientia*) for hard work or heat, but that they can withstand cold and hunger through habit ('frigora atque inediam caelo solove adsueverunt'). This simple statement of their extreme physical prowess and extreme incapacity encapsulates the two sides of their peculiar masculinity in the *Germania*. Throughout the work the hardiness of Germanic men is paired with a corresponding rigidity, which cannot bear any changed conditions.

Theirs is a toughness which restricts itself to warfare and warfare alone. Thus, any farming or other manual labour is carried out by women and old men. The men laze around when not fighting, because they 'ament inertiam et oderint quietem' ('love inactivity and hate peace'),[42] a situation which Tacitus himself describes as 'mira diversitate naturae' ('an amazing inconsistency of nature'). The apparent contradiction is explained by their 'peacetime' activities: when not officially at war, the Germani continue to enact violence rather than engage in normative civilian practices. Even the rewards of war encourage further violence: unlike Roman practice, war horses, armour and banquets, rather than land, are given as the reward for military service, and brigandage is more highly prized than farming:

> materia munificentiae per bella et raptus. nec arare terram aut exspectare annum tam facile persuaseris quam vocare hostem et vulnera mereri; pigrum quin immo et iners videtur sudore adquirere quod possis sanguine parare.

> The means for [the chieftains'] generosity comes from war and robbery. You would not as easily persuade them to plough the land or to wait for the annual harvest, as to challenge an enemy and earn their wounds; indeed it is seen as lazy and unmanly to acquire by sweat what one can win by blood.[43]

This idea of acceptable pillage recalls and develops Caesar's statement that 'latrociniam nullam habent infamiam' ('there is no shame in robbery with violence') and is echoed elsewhere in Tacitus' picture of a Suebic king who had lived for three decades on the fruits of plunder.[44]

Germania's is an economy of labour in which masculinity, youth, strength and violence become sloth in any scenario outside of warfare, and, bizarrely, farm labour is seen as idleness. Working the land tended to be romanticised in the idealised 'soldier-farmer' fantasy of the Roman past, as in the story of the heroicised figure of Cincinnatus.[45] Germanic men are unable to measure up to this dual role; instead they associate agriculture with femininity and feebleness. Yet Tacitus, unlike Caesar, has the advantage of hindsight after two centuries of Romans battling Germani with little success; in addition, he looks back on, and resents, 125 years of the Principate.[46] While reflecting on imperial deceit and senatorial emasculation, he cannot deny the efficacy of the Germani's dedication to war: despite many attempts, Rome has failed to conquer Germania. Tacitus offers only aphorism: 'proximis temporibus triumphati magis quam victi sunt' ('in recent times they have been more triumphed over than actually conquered').[47] Although the Germanic version of masculinity veers far from Roman ideals, there is no doubt that, as a blunt, military instrument, it works.

The contradictions of Tacitus' work thus present us with Germanic men who are tough and intimidating, yet frequently unproductive and enervated; morally upright, yet lazy. The paradoxes of the *Germania* go even deeper. For in the second half of the work, Tacitus fragments the Germani into subgroups of relative functionality,[48] cataloguing Germanic peoples on a scale which runs from near-civilised to entirely savage. The absolutism of chapters 1–27 is effectively blown up, as it becomes clear that some Germani exceed Tacitus' generalised categories. One group, the Chatti, stands out as representing the very best that men can be among barbarians. They demonstrate considerable bravery, judgement and self-discipline, and in this they are measured against the norms of Germani and Romans:

> duriora genti corpora, stricti artus, minax vultus et maior animi vigor. multum, ut inter Germanos, rationis ac sollertiae: praeponere electos, audire praepositos, nosse ordines, intellegere occasiones, differre impetus, disponere diem, vallare noctem, fortunam inter dubia, virtutem inter certa numerare, quodque rarissimum nec nisi Romanae disciplinae concessum, plus reponere in duce quam in exercitu. omne robur in pedite, quem super arma ferramentis quoque et copiis onerant: alios ad proelium ire videas, Chattos ad bellum.

> This people has tougher bodies, sinewy limbs, a threatening expression. For Germani, they have considerable judgement and skill: they appoint their commanders and obey those they have appointed, they know how to keep rank, they seize opportunities, delay attacks, schedule their days, entrench their camps at night; they reckon good luck as something uncertain, but bravery as certain, and, an extremely rare trait, usually granted only to Roman discipline, they put more faith in their general than in the army. All their strength is in their infantry, whom, apart from their weapons, they also load down with tools and provisions: you might see others go off to battle, but the Chatti go to war.[49]

The Chatti are obsessed with and defined by their status as warriors, but they stand apart as one of the few groups to whom *virtus* is attributed. Their sense of discipline and control moves them closer to Roman standards of masculinity and civilisation, and away from the random, unruly nature of most Germani.

Tacitus also sets up a spectrum of gender norms and morality in the second part of the work. Germanic women are faithful and respected supporters of their warrior men,[50] but they lack direct political power, as was the case at Rome. However, Tacitus is disgusted by the inverted gender dynamics of the far northern Sitones, who are ruled by a woman, and he editorialises, 'in tantum non modo a libertate sed etiam a servitute degenerant' ('so far do they sink not only below freedom, but even below slavery').[51] This is the only fact that Tacitus notes about the Sitones, and it is clear that, in the remoter regions of Germania, any positive aspects of hegemonic masculinity are thoroughly undermined. As the itinerary moves further north and east, Tacitus himself seems to lose control of his subject matter, and is initially uncertain about whether these peoples are even Germani, eventually making the distinction on the basis of nomadism, which defines them as instead Sarmatian.[52] The final sentences of the work function as a touchstone for Tacitean discussions of both masculinity and humanity:

> Fennis mira feritas, foeda paupertas: non arma, non equi, non penates; victui herba, vestitui pelles, cubile humus: solae in sagittis spes, quas inopia ferri ossibus asperant. idemque venatus viros pariter ac feminas alit; passim enim comitantur partemque praedae petunt. nec aliud infantibus ferarum imbriumque suffugium quam ut in aliquo ramorum nexu contegantur: huc redeunt iuvenes, hoc senum receptaculum. sed beatius arbitrantur quam ingemere agris, inlaborare domibus, suas alienasque fortunas spe metuque versare; securi adversus homines, securi adversus deos rem difficillimam adsecuti sunt, ut illis ne voto quidem opus esset. cetera iam fabulosa: Hellusios et Oxionas ora hominum vultusque, corpora atque artus ferarum gerere: quod ego ut incompertum in medio relinquam.

> The Fenni are astonishingly savage and disgusting in their poverty: they have no weapons, no horses, no household; herbs for food, skins for clothes, the ground as a bed; their only hope is in their arrows, which they tip with bone, due to a lack of iron. The same hunting feeds the men and women alike, for women accompany men everywhere and seek their share of the kill. And for the children there is no protection from wild animals and rain, except that they are covered by some intertwined branches. This is where the young men return, and this is their refuge when they are old. But they think themselves more blessed than those who groan over fields and labour in the home, turning over their own and others' fortunes in hope and fear; secure from men and secure from gods, they have attained that most difficult thing: that they have no need even for prayer. The rest is the stuff of legend: that the Hellusii and Oxiones have the faces and features of humans, but the bodies and limbs of wild beasts. All this I shall leave open, as something unknown.[53]

The Fenni live in abject squalor – just one step away from fabled hybrid human-beasts. As such, they represent the apex of toxic masculinity in this work. Other Germani allow women into the sphere of war and their presence reminds warriors of what they must fight to protect,[54] but the Fenni drag women out to hunt and provide no protection for their families. They are perhaps Tacitus' answer to Caesar's representation of all Germani: both are represented entirely by what they lack. Agriculture is again an index of male investment in fostering civilisation, and here, rather than simply stealing what they could farm, the Fenni have stripped all such needs and desires out of their lives. We might see elements of their lack of materialism as commendable, but Tacitus is revolted by the lack of direction and regulation in their society. His spectrum of behaviour also acts as a roadmap for Roman masculinity, as the Fenni show that the logical conclusion of endurance is a loss of all self-respect, a state which is barely human.

CONCLUSION

The famously tough Germani give Tacitus and others space to explore the question of hypermasculinity, and to ask what would be the outcome if men were stripped of almost all impulses towards domesticity and cultivation. As an expansionist empire with a formidable army, Rome might well wonder whether a culture built entirely around militarism would bolster its imperialist aims, particularly as Romans often bemoaned the loss of a republican past, which had supposedly been grounded in *virtus*.[55] Caesar and Tacitus show that extreme belligerence damages society, impedes the chances of empire and ultimately harms men themselves, by freezing them in an undeveloped, formless state. They cannot organise or communicate well, nor can they sufficiently control themselves or others. Their inflexibility means that their only response to conflict is unrestrained violence, rather than speech or mediation. As such they function as a warning against embracing all aspects of Germanic militarism. Finally, we should note that these particular 'written Germani' appear during times of tectonic political change at Rome – the breakdown of the Republic and the aftermath of a hated dictator's murder. In each case the Germani allow the author to comment on how outrageous or toxic masculinity breaches the limits of *libertas* and damages society irreparably.

NOTES

1. Cic. *Tusc.* 2.43, 4.16; Williams 2010, 145–6.
2. E.g. Polybios 31.25.2–7, Diod. Sic. 31.26.6–7, Sallust *Cat.* 9–10, *Iug.* 41, *Hist.* fr. 1.11, Livy 39.6–7, Vell. Pat. 2.1.1, Pliny *NH* 17.244, 33.150.
3. Mela 3.26: *immanes* ('enormous'); Tac *Ger.* 4.1 'truces . . . magna corpora et tantum ad impetum valida' ('wild . . . large bodies, only powerful in attack'), and 20.1 'nudi et sordidi . . . in haec corpora quae miramur excrescunt' ('naked and dirty . . . they grow into those bodies which we admire'); Josephus *BJ* 2.16.4: τοὺς δὲ θυμοὺς τῶν ἀγριωτάτων θηρίων σφοδροτέρους ('their rage is fiercer than that of the most savage of beasts'). Caes. *BG* 4.1.10: 'magna est corporis pars aperta et lavantur in fluminibus' ('most of the body is uncovered and they bathe in rivers').
4. Mela 3.27: 'bella cum finitimis gerunt, causas eorum ex libidine arcessunt' ('sheer wilfulness causes them to wage war on their neighbours'); Tac. *Hist.* 4.76.9: 'nam Germanos . . . non iuberi, non regi, sed cuncta ex libidine agere' ('For the Germans cannot be ordered, they cannot be ruled, but always act out of wilfulness').
5. Caes. *BG* 4.3.1, 6.23.

6. Tac. *Ger.* 7.2, 8.1, 13.1.
7. E.g. Cic. *Rep.* 5.1–2, Sall. *Cat.* 10.1–6, Hor. *Carm.* 3.6, Livy 1. *pr.* 11.
8. Connell 2014, 8–9.
9. Connell and Messerschmidt 2005; Lidman 2018; Ford 2018.
10. Krebs 2011; Sears 2017; Zuckerberg 2018.
11. Geertz 1988, 120–2 and Thomas 1982, 125, 130.
12. Hdt. 4.5.1, 2.2–3, Hartog 1988, 16–18.
13. Hdt. 5.3, Soph. *Ter.* frag. 587, Eur. *Hec.* 24–9, 1055, 1197–8, Plato *Laws* 637d, Livy 36.7.4, Ovid *Met.* 6.401–674, Socrates *HE* 4.28.
14. Polybios 2.17–23.
15. Romm 1994.
16. Riggsby 2006, 60, 64–5; Cunliffe 1997, 237–8. The Rhine as an ethnic divider is convenient for Caesar, but he actually presents a much more complex situation, with Germanic and Gallic tribes found on both sides of the river. Similarly Powell (1980, 191) also suggests that the name Germani was originally the name of a Celtic tribe.
17. Caes. *BG* 1.31.11, 1.44.8.
18. E.g. Mela 2.74, Pliny 4.105.
19. The historical context is discussed in Krebs 2011, 42, 91. O'Gorman (2003, 146–8) discusses the application in the *Germania* with some nuance.
20. Tac. *Ger.* 18–20.
21. Tac. *Ger.* 19.5; compare Caesar's comments on Germanic chastity *BG* 6.21.4–5.
22. Tac. *Ger.* 18.4.
23. Tac. *Ger.* 7.2, 8.1, 18.4.
24. Tac. *Ger.* 8.1, 20.3, 8.2.
25. *BG* 6.24; also implied of non-Belgic Gauls at 1.1.3–4. See most recently Johnston 2018.
26. Ariovistus: Caes. *BG* 1.31–53; Suebi: Caes. *BG* 4.12–15; Orgetorix: Caes. *BG* 1.2–4; Vercingetorix: Caes. *BG* 7.4–5, 7.20.1–2, 7.28.6, 7.75.1.
27. Alston 1998, 219.
28. Tac. *Ger.* 37.
29. Roman suspicion and fear of hypermasculinity, particularly amongst the Germani, was longstanding, e.g. Velleius Paterculus writes of *feritas Germana* ('Germanic wildness') and describes them as ungovernable (2.106); see also Vell. Pat. 2.117.3; Strabo 7.1.3; Manilius 4.794. Alston (1998, 209–11) suggests a tension between control and freedom (*libertas*) is inherent in manliness (*virtus*), for both Romans and non-Roman military figures.
30. Caes. *BG* 6.24.5–6.
31. Tac. *Ann.* 11.23–34; *CIL* 13.1668.
32. Caes. *BG* 4.3.1, 6.21.1–2.
33. Caes. *BG* 6.21–3.
34. Caes. *BG* 1.31.13, 4.1.9–10.
35. Caes. *BG* 1.34, 1.36, 1.44; Grillo 2018, 134–8 and Murphy 1949, 122–3.
36. Caes. *BG* 1.34.2
37. Caes. *BG* 1.44.8.

38. Kimmel and Wade 2018, 236.
39. Caes. *BG* 1.40.2; App. *Celt.* fr. 16; Plut. *Caes.* 19.1.
40. Dio 38.34.3; Riggsby 2006, 184–8.
41. Tac. *Ger.* 4.1.
42. Tac. *Ger.* 15.1.
43. Tac. *Ger.* 14.3.
44. Caes. *BG* 6.23.6, Tac. *Ann.* 12.29.
45. Livy 3.26–9; cf. Evans 2008, 176–85.
46. Tac. *Ger.* 37.1, 37.5, *Agr.* 1–2, *Ann.* 1.1.1.
47. Tac. *Ger.* 37.5.
48. Tac. *Ger.* 28–46.
49. Tac. *Ger.* 30.2–3.
50. Tac. *Ger.* 18–19, discussed above.
51. Tac. *Ger.* 45.6.
52. Tac. *Ger.* 46.1–2.
53. Tac. *Ger.* 46.3–4.
54. Tac. *Ger.* 7.2.
55. Sallust *Cat.* 8–9; Edwards 1993, 42–7, 91–3 and Evans 2008, 5–6, 177–8.

CHAPTER 12

Toxic Masculinity in Xenophon's Account of the Trial of Sphodrias

Kendell Heydon

A t *Hellenica* 5.4.20–33 Xenophon writes that, in order to turn Athens against Sparta, the Thebans manipulated the Spartan harmost Sphodrias into invading Attica during peacetime. Sphodrias' subsequent failed attempt to capture the Piraeus left the Athenians calling for his blood and Spartan envoys in Athens promising that Sparta would provide it. However, Xenophon goes on to narrate how events transpired which resulted in Sparta exonerating Sphodrias at trial – despite his obvious guilt. Xenophon recounts that Sphodrias appealed to his son Cleonymus to advocate on his behalf to the boy's *erastes*,[1] Archidamus. Archidamus, in turn, agreed to beseech his father, King Agesilaus, to endorse Sphodrias' acquittal. While Xenophon asserts that Agesilaus was initially unreceptive to his son's efforts, Archidamus' persistent efforts initiated a thought process by which Agesilaus eventually came to support Sphodrias' acquittal (5.4. 24–33). Once so disposed, Agesilaus employed discourse centred on Sphodrias' personal excellence and achievement as justification of his endorsement and, due largely to Agesilaus' support, Sphodrias was pardoned. Cleonymus expressed his gratitude to Archidamus by vowing to never give him cause for shame in their friendship – a vow which Xenophon proclaims that Cleonymus kept, dying heroically at Leuctra in defence of the king. In the following analysis, it is not my intention to impose modern definitions of toxic masculinity onto this text. Rather, my aim is to explore it as an episode where an ancient author appears to identify and problematise certain Spartan masculine ideals.

The Sphodrias episode illuminates several ways in which Spartan masculine values, and the practices and institutions which promote them, prove detrimental to both individual Spartan men and Spartan society as a whole. First, Xenophon's treatment of the pederastic relationship shows the educational function of quasi-institutionalised Spartan pederasty, associated with the transmission of masculine values, being superseded by valorisation of male homosocial bonds (also associated with masculine excellence), which are manipulated for the circumvention of justice. Second, in this episode Xenophon represents Agesilaus as deploying discourse rooted in the ideology of individual masculine excellence to secure an unjust aim. This suggests the importance of masculine ideals in Sparta's societal hierarchy of values, but also problematises this prominence. Finally, undercutting both elements of the episode is the ethos of competitive masculine achievement, which is portrayed as forming the basis of both Cleonymus' and Sphodrias' characterisation, and as providing justification to excuse their personal failings. Therefore, the negative implications of this masculine ideology will feature in my analysis of both aspects of the episode. In what follows, I will examine each aspect individually. In so doing, I will explore what messages Xenophon may have intended to convey about Spartan masculinity, as well as how Xenophon depicts the targeted employment of masculine ideology within the context of the episode.

THE PEDERASTIC RELATIONSHIP

In this episode, Xenophon touches on ideals associated with Spartan pederasty, and interactions between these ideals and competing values and duties. In the *Respublica Lacedaemoniorum* (*Lac.*), Spartan pederastic relationships are associated with the ideals of manhood, inasmuch as they are represented as fulfilling an educative function for boys. Xenophon recounts that Lycurgus deemed ideal Spartan pederasty as the 'highest form of education' (καλλίστην παιδείαν) for boys.[2] In his description (*Lac.* 2.12–14), Xenophon emphasises the relationship itself, rather than specific qualities it imparts, as the main educative principle. The *erastes* would provide a positive example of an adult male to the younger partner, who would be nurtured via their close association.[3] Beyond providing a passive example for emulation, the text suggests that *erastai* could be expected to take an active role in ensuring the adherence of *eromenoi* to societally promoted standards of behaviour (3.3).[4] The relationship between Cleonymus and Archidamus is the most prominent example of a pederastic relationship in the *Hellenica* and Xenophon's most detailed example of official Spartan pederasty.[5] Xenophon's portrayal of this relationship is complex, as the narrative appears to enshrine the positive qualities and outcomes of Spartan pederasty, even as it represents the specific pederastic relationship in question as responsible for a decision that was unjust and had significant negative political ramifications for Sparta. How then should one interpret a relationship presented with such ambivalence? I suggest that Xenophon presents the reader with a twofold understanding, wherein he illustrates the masculine ideals enshrined by the relationship, but also represents the value that Spartan society placed on these ideals as problematic.

Despite accentuating the disgust many (likely including Xenophon himself)[6] felt at Sphodrias' acquittal (5.4.24), and emphasising the role of the pederastic relationship in securing this outcome, Xenophon opens the episode by portraying this relationship as honourable. Xenophon introduces Cleonymus as 'both the fairest (κάλλιστός) and the most esteemed (εὐδοκιμώτατος) of his generation (ἡλίκων)' (5.4.25). He frames Archidamus' love for Cleonymus within the context of those qualities, suggesting that Archidamus chose Cleonymus for noble reasons and, perhaps, that the relationship also cultivated these qualities.[7] Their association was open, conducted in public locations such as Archidamus' *syssition* (mess-hall) (5.4.28). This, combined with Xenophon's comment that Sphodrias' supporters were concerned when Archidamus stopped visiting Cleonymus (5.4.29), indicates public approval of the union. Xenophon's account of Archidamus' grief over Cleonymus' death (5.4.33) attests to the longevity of their intimacy. These factors suggest that this relationship is representative of the ideologically approved Spartan pederasty Xenophon outlines in the *Lac*.[8] Throughout the episode Xenophon provides indications that the values he associates with ideal Spartan pederasty are transmitted through Archidamus and Cleonymus' association. We are told that Cleonymus approached Archidamus to plead for his father at Archidamus' *syssition* (5.4.28), and that Archidamus was accustomed to visiting Cleonymus often (5.4.29). This suggests that interaction between pederastic partners was expected to be frequent and took place in a variety of settings. Additionally, the specific setting of the *syssition* possibly supports the suggestion that a boy's *erastes* played a role in providing him access to the world of adult men.[9] We are shown scenes where the relationship plays a role in providing emotional support and connectedness between the two men, in the depiction of Archidamus weeping with Cleonymus upon hearing of his father's plight (5.4.27), as well as in the gratitude and devotion towards his *erastes* expressed by Cleonymus upon hearing of his father's acquittal (25.4.33). We are told that Cleonymus' response to Archidamus' efforts on his behalf is expressed in a vow to prove his friendship worthy of honour, dutifully fulfilled, suggesting that the relationship inspired Cleonymus to conduct himself honourably not only in battle, but in all things.

Elements of the narrative's framing also support a positive interpretation of the relationship.[10] After the initial association of the relationship with 'the most unjust judgement ever determined at Sparta', the episode is framed to stress ideological considerations over those of politics or justice. The narrative downplays the injustice of Cleonymus' inappropriate manipulation of his pederastic connection by valorising *philia* (love/friendship)[11] between men in depictions of Cleonymus' relationships with both his father and *erastes*.[12] Likewise, Archidamus' efforts are made out of concern for his pederastic connection, a connection that Xenophon asserts was highly valued in Sparta and integral to the formation of Spartiate men (*Lac*. 2.13).[13] The episode closes by emphasising masculine excellence inspired by the pederastic bond as expressed in Cleonymus' heroic death, fighting to the utmost so that Archidamus would never have cause to feel shame over their friendship (5.4.25–7, 33).[14]

Despite its apparent respectability, however, the episode also envelops the relationship with an air of infamy. Xenophon does not permit the reader to forget the reason for which the relationship is discussed: its role in securing an unjust pardon. Admittedly, Archidamus' intercession was not the sole factor in Agesilaus' endorsement of acquittal.[15] Even within the narrative, Agesilaus avows that this was not the cause of his decision (5.4.28–32).[16] However, Xenophon constructs the narrative so that the episode is dominated by the influence of the pederastic connection. Archidamus' first entreaty to his father is flatly rejected (5.4.30), and Agesilaus' assurance that he did not blame Archidamus for making an appeal on Cleonymus' behalf does – in fact – carry a note of implied disapproval, since Agesilaus asserts that he could not grant this request without incurring censure. With his second approach (5.4.31), Xenophon has Archidamus change his tactic to echo those employed by Sphodrias and Cleonymus, asking his father to pardon Sphodrias – despite his wrongdoing – 'for our sakes' (ἡμῶν ἕνεκεν). Filial feeling does not sway Agesilaus,[17] but Archidamus' appeal nonetheless provides a watershed moment. Before Archidamus interceded, Agesilaus saw no grounds on which he could justifiably endorse pardon (5.4.30), but Agesilaus' response to his son's second entreaty indicates a shifting opinion: that he would be open to endorsing pardon if it could be framed as honourable. By presenting Archidamus as the sole outside contributor to the process whereby Agesilaus found justification to endorse the pardon, Xenophon portrays the pederastic relationship, which motivated Archidamus' involvement, as instrumental also.

There are also elements of the narrative, beyond the outcome of the trial, which cast the pederastic relationship and its members in an ambivalent light. Gray has aptly illustrated the tragic dilemma Archidamus faced. Depicted as torn between competing value systems, he is compelled to choose between the mandates of justice and loyalty to his *eromenos*.[18] The internal struggle Archidamus faced in approaching his father, and his persistence in the face of censure, garner sympathy.[19] This focus gives the impression of a respectable relationship between noble young men, tragically used by others for ignoble ends. However, to see the complete picture, one must subject Cleonymus to similar scrutiny.

Cleonymus is introduced, as Gray puts it, 'in a burst of light',[20] and this brilliance could blind readers to the incongruence between Cleonymus' reputation and behaviour. Moreover, descriptions of Cleonymus' excellence contain significant parallels to arguments for Sphodrias' merit. Xenophon states that Cleonymus was 'the age just out of the *paides* (boyhood)' (5.4.25), suggesting that, at the time of the episode, his personal excellence was established via performance in the first stage of Spartan education. The assertion that he was the most preeminent specimen of his current age group attests his ongoing excellence as a *paidiskos* (adolescent). The depiction of his death (5.4.33, 6.4.14) attests to his distinction as a *hebon* (young man). Later in the narrative, we learn that Sphodrias also gained an excellent reputation based on performance throughout his upbringing (5.4.32), indicating that Cleonymus' merit was akin to his father's. The description at 6.4.14, in particular, invites the reader to compare Sphodrias and Cleonymus' excellences, as it narrates their deaths in tandem. However, such similarity leads one to speculate whether father and son were also alike in their shortcomings. It is significant that Cleonymus' characterisation focuses on how he *appears* to others: he is fair and of good repute (5.4.25). Xenophon's focus on perceived excellence suggests that, as with his father, an excellent reputation did not guarantee excellent character or judgement. The episode's events seem to confirm such speculation, as Cleonymus' behaviour does not bear his reputation out – especially when his conduct is analysed in comparison to that of Archidamus. If one accepts Gray's interpretation of Archidamus in this episode, it follows that one should view Cleonymus through the same lens.

Cleonymus' dilemma was akin to that of Archidamus, but his conduct was strikingly different. If we can have sympathy for Archidamus choosing wrongly, because we can see him struggle to do right, we are not compelled to similar feeling for Cleonymus. Far from struggling between mutually exclusive ideals, Xenophon depicts Cleonymus as complying with his father's request, seemingly without a second thought, and with only enough delay to work up his nerve (5.4.26) – the expression of which appears ephemeral when compared to the prolonged agonising involved in Archidamus' approach to Agesilaus. Gray asserts that Archidamus' ingrained reticence paints him as the shining paradigm of a Spartan youth, who finally overcomes his innate deference with great difficulty.[21] If this is the case, should not the same standard (if not greater) of behaviour be expected of Cleonymus? At the time of the episode, Archidamus is not a *paidiskos* (adolescent), but an established young man.[22] It is Cleonymus whom Xenophon describes as being adolescent. Therefore, it is from Cleonymus that the standard of reticence, exhibited by Archidamus, should be expected.[23] Yet there is no suggestion of any reticence in Xenophon's depiction. The setting and manner of Cleonymus' plea to Archidamus are easy to overlook, as they are eclipsed by Cleonymus' emotional distress and Archidamus' noble concern. However, as Hodkinson rightly points out, these factors have significant implications for the portrayal of Cleonymus, inasmuch as they place him in violation of the code of acceptable behaviour for Spartan *paidiskoi*.[24] To take advantage of his connection with Archidamus, Cleonymus acted more brazenly than Xenophon elsewhere claims would have ever been acceptable for a youth of his age. The public spectacle created by Cleonymus' petition flies in the face of Xenophon's account in the *Lac.* (3.4–5) of the extreme public diffidence demanded of *paidiskoi*.[25]

However, Cleonymus' impropriety cannot be seen to reflect on himself alone. It reflects also on Archidamus, as well as on the relationship they share, by virtue of the quasi-institutional nature of Spartan pederasty.[26] Xenophon attests that Spartans considered pederasty to be the 'highest form of education'

(*Lac.* 2.13). Thus, Cleonymus' failure to emulate the ideals embodied by his *erastes* must be – on some level – a failure in educative efficacy in this most emblematic of Spartan pederastic relationships. However much Archidamus is shown to embody Spartan ideals, the episode indicates that he apparently failed to inspire the same standard of behaviour in his *eromenos*. Furthermore, Archidamus' response to Cleonymus can be viewed as an even more active failure in his role as *erastes*. Archidamus, observing the impropriety of the request – both in nature and manner – might have responded in a corrective manner, as Agesilaus did upon Archidamus' first approach. However, rather than immediately correcting Cleonymus' failings, and halting the perversion of justice in the process, Archidamus instead becomes complicit in Cleonymus' aims. Therefore, if decorous behaviour and concern for justice were ideals meant to be transmitted through pederastic relationships between men, this relationship is portrayed as failing. And, however shocking Cleonymus' behaviour may have been, he was merely an adolescent in need of instruction.[27] Therefore, it is likely that Xenophon did not intend the true censure to fall on Cleonymus, but on a system of values which not only failed to remediate his unthinking preference for personal connections over other considerations,[28] but is even depicted as reinforcing these incorrect priorities.

Xenophon can be seen to problematise the Spartan masculine ideals associated with pederasty – along with the institution of Spartan pederasty itself – in a number of respects. Archidamus' regard for Cleonymus is intrinsically connected to the latter's supreme reputation – indicating the high value placed on ideals of Spartan male achievement within the rearing process. Their *philia* is shown to further nurture Cleonymus' excellence, culminating in his noble death. Thus, both the educative quality of the pederastic relationship and the masculine ideals promoted by pederasty (evident in this episode) lie within the realm of competitive masculine achievement – a sphere which is presented with considerable ambivalence.[29] The role of the pederastic relationship in this episode calls into question the prominent place given to the ideal of masculine achievement within the Spartan hierarchy of values. Moreover, the episode also suggests that the private dimension of Spartan pederasty, characterised by concern for *philia* between men, eclipsed the publicly endorsed elements which were concerned with education and societal wellbeing. In so doing, Xenophon problematises homosocial bonds between Spartan males – and the ideological value placed on them – by depicting the manipulation of both familial and pederastic bonds in order to subvert the course of justice.[30]

AGESILAUS' TACTICS

In addition to mitigating any perception of wrongdoing in the case of Cleonymus, competitive masculine achievement is also depicted as a justification for excusing

Sphodrias' unjust conduct. When Archidamus first entreats his father to pardon Sphodrias, Agesilaus responds, 'I do not see how I could, myself, obtain pardon from the *polis* if I do not judge as unjust, a man who harmed the *polis* for the sake of money' (5.4.30). This response references two sets of ideological criteria by which Sphodrias' actions could be evaluated. Firstly, if Sphodrias were to be judged by the mandates of justice, he would be found guilty – this is clear from the text. Sphodrias' behaviour is shown to be motivated predominantly by selfish concerns of material wealth and personal reputation. Both factors are evident at 5.4.20 in insinuations that bribery may have factored into Sphodrias' decision to invade Attica and in Sphodrias' ill-conceived boast that, marching out from Thespiae after dinner, he would arrive at the Piraeus before daybreak. Moreover, in recounting not only that Sphodrias' attack appeared egregious to Spartans and Athenians alike (5.4.22–3), but also the wide-ranging outrage in response to his acquittal (5.4.24, 5.4.34), Xenophon indicates Sphodrias' infamy in the opinions of the Greeks at large.

The other ideological standard by which Sphodrias could be judged is the usefulness of his actions. Dillery has discussed 'the dichotomy between Sparta's internal *arete* and her external brutality'[31] and Xenophon does indicate, with his treatment of the case of Phoebidas (5.2.32), that what Sparta values is honourable conduct at home and effective conduct away – with the justice of the latter being subordinated to its efficacy. However, Sphodrias would still be found at fault even if Agesilaus used these criteria, as he did in the case of Phoebidas (5.2.32), whose character and action – an unauthorised seizure of the Theban Cadmea (5.2.25–8, 5.2.32) – bear many similarities to those of Sphodrias.[32] Whereas Phoebidas' actions benefited Sparta, at least in the short term,[33] Sphodrias' spectacularly unsuccessful attempt on the Piraeus did not.[34] Thus, if Sphodrias was to be pardoned, it could not be on the basis of either just conduct or benefit to Sparta.

Despite initially asserting the impossibility of Sphodrias' acquittal, Xenophon has Agesilaus experience a turning point at Archidamus' second appeal. This time, Agesilaus responds: 'if it can be possible for this to be honourable for us, it will be so' (5.2.30–1). This cues the reader that there is a possible justification for pardon, as yet unexplored. While Sphodrias' actions were impossible to vindicate, a case could be made to overlook those actions – if a justification could be found that would not reflect poorly on Agesilaus for proposing it. To this end, an alternative ideological argument would be required, which Agesilaus found by appealing to the ideology of competitive masculine achievement.

The official line Agesilaus gives to endorse Sphodrias' exoneration was that because: 'as a boy, a youth and a young man he did and accomplished every honourable thing, it is difficult to execute such a man, because Sparta has need for such soldiers' (5.4.32). The terms used for the ages at which Sphodrias demonstrated his excellence are the terms Xenophon employs in the *Lac.* when discussing institutionalised Spartan upbringing.[35] Additionally, the 'τὰ καλὰ' used by Agesilaus, here, does not merely suggest a general sense of honour. Rather, by employing this term within the context of Sparta's official rearing system, Xenophon evokes those benefits and requirements of Spartan men's way of life which are associated with citizenship.[36] Xenophon's use of such terminology here reveals the discursive approach he has Agesilaus employ. Xenophon portrays Agesilaus as seeking to evade reprisal for dishonourable conduct according to one ideological standard, by presenting another ideological standard – one in which Sphodrias excelled – as holding greater significance. The basis of Agesilaus' disinclination to execute Sphodrias is his superior performance throughout his formative education. Xenophon represents Spartan education as an institution that served to imbue Spartiate males with ideologically grounded patterns of behaviour, so much so that scholars have commented that Spartan education in the *Lac.* resembles not so much a traditional education as a process of indoctrination and socialisation, wherein boys internalised ideologies of Spartan manhood.[37] Through Agesilaus' emphasis on upbringing, the narrative suggests that performance during rearing was of considerable significance to men's later reputation and influence.[38] The line of reasoning given by Agesilaus here is the inverse of his reasoning in the case of Phoebidas. Employing the internal/external dichotomy in his evaluation of Sphodrias, Agesilaus asserts that greater significance should be placed on internal concerns. He advocates that Sphodrias' demonstrated internalisation of and commitment to ideals of masculine excellence within Spartan society should be sufficient to mitigate externally detrimental actions. The outcome of the episode suggests that such exclusive focus on ideal masculine comportment throughout upbringing allowed Agesilaus to use his influence to secure Sphodrias' pardon while avoiding accusations of injustice for this endorsement.

Sphodrias' personal excellence likely had little to do with Agesilaus' actual motivation for endorsing acquittal. Scholars have proposed several considerations and political motivations that informed Agesilaus' decision, and discussed how this narrative provides insight into Spartan political workings and patronage.[39] Mention of Agesilaus' many daily petitioners, combined with Archidamus' reference to individuals who could accomplish things for him in the *polis* (5.4.27–8), are intended to emphasise Sparta's patronage system, as well as Agesilaus' personal political agenda. Xenophon recounts that Sphodrias was a partisan of Agesilaus' rival king Cleombrotus (5.4.25), and the possibility of indebting members of a rival bloc may well have provided Agesilaus' true underlying motivation for endorsing the pardon.[40] This suggests that Agesilaus' emphasis on ideological concerns in his defence of Sphodrias is something of a smokescreen. By placing exclusive focus on the masculine ideals embodied in Sphodrias' personal accomplishments, Xenophon does not merely depict Agesilaus finding ideological justification for endorsing acquittal. He also portrays him as obscuring the political motivations that likely had greater bearing on the outcome of the trial than his professed ideological considerations.

This discrepancy between Agesilaus' explicit and implicit motivations highlights the utility of masculine ideology as a dressing for political manoeuvring. It conveys the prevailing sentiment that Xenophon's Agesilaus intended the recipients of his discourse to take away – a sentiment that the episode suggests was effective. Agesilaus could not advocate Sphodrias' acquittal based on the outcome of his actions – but neither could he justify his endorsement of a pardon on the basis that it would further his personal political goals, especially when the alienation of Athens (which would inevitably result from pardoning Sphodrias) would prove detrimental to Sparta.[41] Thus enters the discursive appeal to the ideology of masculine achievement. Even if Agesilaus' discourse was nothing more than empty rhetoric, rhetoric is useful to cover true motives only if it has a considerable level of mass appeal. That Xenophon depicts this ideological defence as successful in securing acquittal, in a situation where there was no legitimate justification to acquit, suggests that Xenophon intended to represent the ideals associated with masculine excellence as resonating with the Spartan mindset.[42] By depicting the rhetoric of excellent masculinity as so useful an ideological tool that it could be employed to influence real-world politics within the Spartan system – even to Sparta's injury – Xenophon illuminates not only the high place of individual masculine excellence within the Spartan hierarchy of values, but also the inherent detriment to Spartan society that resulted from granting masculine excellence such an inordinate level of esteem.

CONCLUSION

The Sphodrias episode highlights the value placed by Spartan society on ideals of competitive masculine achievement and homosocial bonds. In the *Lac.*, this ethos is shown to provide an essential foundation of a Spartan man's education and reputation throughout the formative years and in adult life. The ideal of competitive masculine achievement is also represented as having enough ideological clout within the Spartan hierarchy of values to provide effective cover for serious improprieties committed by those who embody it. Xenophon's valuation of Spartan homosocial bonds is largely ambivalent; in the episode he portrays admirable qualities inspired by such bonds while depicting the corruption by which educative relationships could be manipulated to serve individual desires. However, while Xenophon appears to maintain a level of sympathy towards the ideals inspired by Spartan homosocial bonds, his treatment of the value placed on competitive masculine achievement by Spartan society suggests that he views it as deeply problematic. The hyper-competitive nature of Spartan men, combined with their willingness to place individual achievement and glory above all other concerns – even the mandates of justice itself – is depicted as having disastrous results for Sparta as a whole. I therefore suggest that the emphasis Xenophon places on the role of this ideology, in episodes like the trial of Sphodrias, showcases the incompatibility of Spartan competitive masculine values with the necessities of both societal wellbeing and effective inter-*polis* relations; and depicts this ideology, and the societal value placed upon it at Sparta, as irreconcilably toxic in nature.

NOTES

1. *Erastes* and *eromenos* are terms used to refer to the senior and junior partners in pederastic relationships, respectively.
2. The main difficulty in examining Xenophon's depiction of pederasty's contribution to the education and formation of Spartan manhood is that, while Xenophon portrays ideal Spartan pederasty as educative, he does not recount what information or qualities – necessary for adult male life – it imparted. Xenophon's adamant emphasis on valuing boys' souls over bodies has been seen to reflect a concern with the cultivation of self-control (see Lipka 2002, 135, on *Lac.* 2.14[4]), but the text's stress here is more reflective of concern for the *erastes'* motivation and behaviour, rather than the qualities he should aim to impart to his beloved.
3. Cartledge 2001, 87 and Ludwig 2002, 326.
4. Xenophon relates: 'Establishing that the penalty if someone should flee from these duties was that he would no longer retain honours, he [Lycurgus] made it so that not only public officials, but also those who cared for each of them would take care, so that they would not, by shirking their responsibilities, become entirely without repute in the city.' One would expect that the *erastes* would be counted amongst those who 'cared for' a *paidiskos* (τοὺς κηδομένους), and thus would be engaged with monitoring his performance of required duties.
5. Interestingly, the relationship between Lysander and Agesilaus, labelled as pederastic by Plutarch (*Ages.* 2, *Lys.* 22.3), is not presented in this light by Xenophon. Indeed, Xenophon's account of Agesilaus' succession (3.3.1–4) tends to minimise Lysander's role in events, compared to Plutarch's treatment (*Ages.* 3, *Lys.* 22.3–6).
6. Tuplin 1993, 126; Humble 1997, 147–8; Parker 2007, 23.
7. For example, Xenophon's comments at *Sym.* 4.10–18 associate Spartan pederasty with good conduct in battle.
8. Hindley 1999, 80; Hodkinson 2007, 58; Gray 2007, 156 on [Xen. *Lac.*] 2.12–14.
9. Kennell 1995, 125–6 and Ducat 2006, 164–6, 169.
10. See Dillery (1995, 233–4) for discussion of the Herodotean, story-telling quality of the episode, and Gray (1989, 61–3) for discussion of features of Xenophon's account that mark the episode out as belonging to the tradition of *paidikos logos*.
11. The concept of *philia* does not translate simply to English. The term is evocative of love or enduring friendship, characterised by deep mutual regard. In the context of ideal Spartan pederasty, Xenophon attests that the Lycurgan ideal was that the pederastic connection should not be inspired by carnal attraction,

but that the *erastes* should be attracted to the excellence of a boy's soul and, out of such regard, seek to cultivate an enduring and mutually beneficial friendship (*Lac.* 2.13).

12. Dillery 1995, 233–4 and Hodkinson 2007, 57–9.
13. Powell 2018, 736.
14. Dover 1978, 202–3; Gray 1989, 61–2; Hodkinson 2007, 58, 61–2.
15. Tuplin 1993, 127. See p. 274 for further discussion.
16. See also Cartledge 1987, 136 and Cartledge 2003, 224.
17. Hodkinson (2007, 59–60) has noted that the apparent closeness between Cleonymus and his father emphasises the lack of similar feeling in the depiction of the relationship between Archidamus and Agesilaus. *Contra* Marincola, 2017, 114.
18. Gray 1989, 59–62.
19. Gray 1989, 61.
20. Gray 1989, 59.
21. Gray 1989, 61.
22. Indeed, if we are to judge by Xenophon's depiction of the *hebontes* at *Lac.* 4, whose defining characteristic is their contentiousness, we might have expected more boldness to be displayed by Archidamus.
23. At *Lac.* 3.1–5. Xenophon recounts the strict and arduous programme proscribed for *paidiskoi*, which results in their display of extreme modesty and reticence – considered to be the Lycurgan ideal standard behaviour for males at that stage of life.
24. Hodkinson 2007, 57.
25. Indeed, such behaviour at the *syssition* of one's *erastes* could have compromised Cleonymus' future prospects and acceptance into the world of adult males (see, e.g. Kennell 1995, 125–6; Ducat 2006, 93–4, 164; Link 2009, 98; and Davies 2018, 487).
26. For discussion regarding the degree to which Spartan pederasty was institutionalised, see e.g. Ducat 2006, 164–8 and Link 2009, 93–101.
27. Plutarch (*Lyc.* 18.4) attests that *erastai* were considered culpable for failings in their beloved's conduct.
28. See Cartledge (1987, 151–2; 2001, 86–105) and Link (2009, 93–101) for discussion of the ways in which pederastic relationships may have been involved in the creation and maintenance of the political elite through a system of nepotism.
29. Xenophon depicts extreme competitiveness as a characteristic feature of Spartan men, which often has a negative impact on the men who exhibit this trait, and on Sparta as a whole, as discussed later in this chapter.
30. Dillery (1995, 234) argues that the juxtaposition of Cleonymus at Leuctra with the acquittal of his father emphasises the point that ideological bonds of friendship prevail while the city is ruined.
31. Dillery 1995, 218, 233–4.
32. Tuplin 1993, 126 and Flower 2017, 308–9.
33. Although the harm done to Sparta took longer to materialise in the case of Phoebidas, Xenophon nevertheless portrays Phoebidas' actions as detrimental to Sparta.

Xenophon viewed the occupation as impious, and portrayed the retaking of the Cadmea – and, to a certain extent, Thebes' role in Sparta's loss of supremacy – as an act of divine retribution (5.4.1–12).

34. Dillery 1995, 218, 233–4, notes that Xenophon's Agesilaus was able to equate expedience with justice in his appeal on behalf of Phoebidas due to the latter's success.

35. Hodkinson 2007, 54–5, 113–15 and Davies 2018, 52–3.

36. MacDowell 1986, 42–3. The usage here seems similar to Xenophon's employment of τὰ καλὰ to describe the standard of behaviour expected of the Spartan *hippeis* at *Lac.* 4.5 (see pp. 107). For extensive discussion of Spartan καλὰ in the Sphodrias episode, see Davies 2018.

37. Humble 1997, 194; Cartledge 2001, 44; Ducat 2006, 144–5. The *Lac.* also depicts Spartan upbringing as a process involving intense competition. The general atmosphere of competition that pervades Spartan life in the *Lac.* is especially pervasive in portrayals of the upbringing. Xenophon records instances of formalised male competition including the following instances: for *paides*, ritualised competitive theft at the ritual of Artemis Orthia (2.9); for *paidiskoi*, the selection of particular *eirens* to act as leaders of boys (2.11); and for *hebontes*, the selection of the *hippeis* (4.3). The cumulative effect of such contests suggests a system of unending competition, necessitating men's demonstration of continual commitment to *polis* ideals.

38. Hodkinson 2007, 54–5; Davies 2018, 482–3; Richer 2018, 527.

39. Gray 1989, 62; Hodkinson 2000, 35–6; Cartledge 2001, 105; Ste Croix 2002, 75–6; Hodkinson 2007, 47–53; Hodkinson 2017, 47; Millender 2018, 465–6.

40. For discussions of possible political motivations behind Agesilaus' desire to acquit, see e.g. Cartledge 2003, 224; Hodkinson, 2017, 47; and Millender 2018, 466.

41. For discussion, see Ruzé 2018, 341–7 and Stewart 2018, 382.

42. Xenophon depicts Agesilaus as employing masculine ideology for effect in other instances as well, such as at *Ages.* 9.6, where he seeks to diminish the honour associated with chariot-race victories by showing that they demonstrate merely wealth and not ἀνδραγαθίας.

CHAPTER 13

Criticism of Roman Men and the Conspicuously Moral Masculinity of Scipio Aemilianus

Charles Goldberg

The closing scene of Plautus' *Miles Gloriosus* makes for an exhilarating finale: the pompous General Pyrgopolinices gets his comeuppance. Throughout the play, he has boasted of unearned military exploits, sneered at the *plebs* and pursued a married woman. The play's climax has the woman's husband and slave tie him down and beat him with a cudgel in mockery of the *fustuarium*, the traditional military punishment for those who receive anal sex on campaign, thus violating his bodily integrity and 'unmanning' him.[1] Finally, threatened with castration, the general is released only after promising 'to hurt no one' (5.19: *me nociturum nemini*) evermore. Pyrgopolinices is the onstage embodiment of the most destructive male values ancient Rome had to offer: hypersexual aggression, martial brutalisation and the pursuit of individual distinction at the expense of the common good. It is because of these traits that he is punished.[2]

When the *Miles* and other Plautine works were first staged around the turn of the second century BCE, Roman political elites, the real life Pyrgopolinices, were becoming masters of the Mediterranean.[3] Roman wealth and power grew apace, but theatrical scenes like the one above reveal that the same characteristics that fuelled the flame of Rome's growing Mediterranean *imperium* could have an ambiguous glow, even in the eyes of the *populus* who benefited from them. In this chapter, I examine criticism of the conduct of Roman elite men in the political and military spheres during this period, both in prose historical works as well as on the stage. I then investigate how one politician, Publius Cornelius Scipio Aemilianus, navigated this challenging political and social environment as a young man beginning in the 160s. Publicly disavowing the typical manly traits of aggression and competition, Scipio embodied a masculine ethos marked by Greek Stoic philosophy and general moral excellence. His conduct acknowledged the validity of critiques of Roman manly conduct while distinguishing him as singularly worthy of political power. But, despite appearances, Scipio Aemilianus remained well acquainted with the characteristic masculinity of Roman elites, to judge by his stellar military career. I end the chapter by situating these contrasting ethics within his Roman aristocratic worldview.

THE ELITE MALE ETHOS IN THE MIDDLE REPUBLIC

Both on military campaign and back home, Roman men in the Middle Republic had ample opportunity for sexual escapades. As long as they adhered to what Craig Williams has called the 'penetrative paradigm', playing the penetrative role in the sex act, and avoided *stuprum*, unauthorised sex with respectable persons like another senator's wife or children, there were few consequences for sexually exploitative behaviour.[4] On the other hand, putting sexual desires of any kind before one's duty as a citizen was ill advised. The prime example is that of L. Quinctius Flamininus, cos. 192, who brought along a boy prostitute named Philippus from Carthage as his sex toy on campaign. Philippus became depressed because Flamininus had made him leave the city right before the gladiator games. One night, the two of them were drinking when a noble Boian man arrived as a deserter seeking safe passage. Wishing to cheer up Philippus, Lucius (Liv. 39.43.5), 'mad with drink and desire', asked him, 'Do you still wish, since you have missed the gladiator shows, to see a dying Gaul?' Philippus gave a disinterested nod, and the general seized a sword and struck the man down.[5] Flamininus' actions demonstrate the close nexus in elite male life between sexual opportunism and power writ large: on campaign, Roman *viri* could satisfy their own sexual urges and abuse others. Sometimes, as here, at the same time.[6]

The defining achievements of any political career were election to consul, command of an army and a celebratory triumphal parade upon returning home. Generals needed impressive accomplishments to earn the parade and stopped at little to achieve them, which encouraged bellicose behaviour and created a deeply ingrained ethos of militarism.[7] Commanders sometimes forced unnecessary battles and pursued the enemy after the fighting had ceased in order to push the numbers of dead higher and deliver an impressive report to the Senate.[8] In 188, Q. Fabius Labeo went looking for trouble as naval commander on Crete 'lest he have a year of idleness in office' (Liv. 37.60.2). The next year, M. Fulvius Nobilior attacked the Ambracians 'even though they had obeyed the commands of the previous consuls' (Liv. 38.43.2). 'Every form of war had been waged against them – slaughter, fires, destruction, [and] plunder of the city . . .'. Wives and children were sold into slavery, and temples pillaged. The defence offered by an ally of Nobilior, Gaius Flaminius, to the Senate is key: no attention should be paid to the Ambracians' pleadings; they merely repeated the same wails and moans sent up by the Macedonians (in 197), the Gauls (in 189), the Aetolians (also 189) and the Syrians (in 188). In Flaminius' words, 'Things were done which are usually done when cities are captured' (Liv. 38.43.9), and the Senate should pay this latest occasion no mind. Fulvius received his triumph.[9]

Roman actions in battle could be especially brutal, even by the already bloody standards of the ancient Mediterranean. Polybius, a first-hand witness for some of the events he describes, writes that after the Romans conquered a city, it was 'impossible for them to relax the fury of their wrath' (6.52.7). Elsewhere, he describes in vivid detail the orgy of bloodlust that accompanied Roman victories: 'The object of this is, I suppose, to strike terror. Accordingly, one may often see in towns captured by the Romans, not only human beings who have been put to the sword, but even dogs cloven down the middle, and the limbs of other animals hewn off' (10.15.4–6). If actual barbarism failed to impress, embellishing the savagery of one's actions was also an option: several generals embellished military victories or invented them wholesale, even fabricating the surrender of entire towns.[10] Victory in battle also brought rampant looting, and after returning home, the spoils of war were often diverted from the public good to the general's own benefit.[11] M.' Acilius Glabrio was accused of misappropriating 'a large part of the royal treasury' after his campaigns, as was Cn. Manlius Vulso in 187.[12] Even Rome's greatest hero, P. Scipio Africanus, was impugned. He and his brother were accused of seizing a portion of the spoils of war following the war with Antiochus in the 170s.[13]

THE VIEW FROM THE STAGE

How did contemporary society interpret these actions? On the one hand, the Roman *populus* benefited directly from its empire, and we should not expect drastic differences in how elites and non-elites perceived Roman power.[14] But the nobility did not have a stranglehold on public discourse, and the stage was a prime site where non-elite discourse could flourish.[15] At times, this discourse differed little from the one we just explored.[16] However, dramatists did not thoughtlessly reproduce the aristocratic worldview. While criticism of specific powerful people was rare, playwrights did criticise aspects of elite culture.[17] The cudgelling and threatened castration of Pyrgopolinices in the *Miles* tapped into fantasies of revenge against soldiers specifically, and elite male values generally. It was not the only passage to do so.

Some passages critique the practice of triumph-hunting. Here, scheming slaves often serve as stand-ins for commanders. One, Chrysalus in the *Bacchides*, claims to be 'weighed down with loot' after capturing a 'city [that] has been taken through a trick' ('*urbe capta per dolum*'). He surprises the audience by claiming no interest in a triumph, but that is only, in his words, because they've become 'too common'.[18] Another slave, Libanus in the *Asinaria*, has no issue 'plundering the public treasury'. If it returns to haunt him later, he'll just 'deny it . . . and even give a false oath about it' and accept whatever consequences come his way.[19] 'There you go,' replies another slave, 'that's acting manly' (*istaec virtus est*). Another, Sosia in the *Amphytryon*, considers how to report his actions abroad, finally deciding to 'invent some of it, as is [his] wont'.[20]

Other passages zero in on the soldier's single-minded pursuit of glory. In the *Curculio*, Therapontigonus is credited with victories over 'half the nations of the earth' in a passage that mocks commemoration of victories.[21] After discovering that the parasite Curculio has stolen his ring, Therapontigonus embodies the distinctively Roman rage Polybius would later detail, announcing (533–5), 'I am walking along now, enraged not with some trivial rage now, but with that very rage with which I've learned to level entire cities.' After further mistreatment by the banker, Lyco, Therapontigonus laments (555–6), 'What's the point of having forced kings to obey me if this pencil-pusher has a laugh at me today?' The final insult turns the screw as the pimp, Cappodox, lampoons the soldier for losing his ring: 'You lost your ring (*anulus*)? This soldier fits in perfectly in a unit of discharged troops.' The joke here is the same as the conceptual unmanning of Pyrgopolonices in the *Miles*. Having lost his 'little anus' (the ring), he has unmanned himself, and has earned a dishonourable discharge.

One Plautine soldier, Stratophanes in the *Truculentus*, strikes a more earnest note lamenting how generals brag about their victories. 'Spectators,' he announces,

> don't wait for me to tell you of my battles. It's my custom to tell of my fights with my hands, not my speeches. I know that many soldiers have lied . . . and have been convicted and condemned for false battles. A man who is believed more by the one who hears him than by the one who sees him does not deserve praise. I don't like a man who is praised more by those who hear him than by those who see him.[22]

A sustained critique of the elite male ethos comes from the *Trinummus*, in an exchange between the wealthy old man Charmides and his slave, Stasimus, who starts the conversation bemoaning, 'I wish people's old customs and their old thriftiness were in greater honour here than bad customs!' Charmides, warning the audience, says, 'Immortal gods, he's beginning to talk about matters of state! He's looking for the old ways; you can see that he loves the old ways according to our forefathers' customs.' Stasimus continues:

> Customs nowadays don't care for what's allowed, only for what's pleasurable: bribery is now sanctioned by custom and free from the laws. . . . Through custom, public office is sought as a reward for criminal behaviour. . . . Through custom, they pass over more vigilant men at the elections. . . . Nothing is laid down as binding by law for them. The laws

are slaves to custom, while customs hurry to carry off everything both sacred and profane. . . . People of this sort are opposed to each and all and harm the entire populace. By keeping faith badly they take away faith even from those who haven't done anything wrong.[23]

Here, the sacking and looting of an enemy city has become the sacking and looting of contemporary Roman *mores*. Through the repeated references to custom (*mos*) and faith (*fides*), Plautus brings the actions of commanders, indeed the entire imperial project, under closer scrutiny.

SCIPIO AEMILIANUS AND CONSPICUOUS MORALITY

These passages demonstrate that certain aspects of the aristocratic ethos that appear toxic to many modern observers – unrestrained anger, single-minded pursuit of distinction and riches, the subversion of public interests for one's own benefit – were also problematised by contemporary Roman society. Passages like these helped to create a conceptual *vir malus*, a 'bad man', against which a politician might distinguish himself through conspicuous moral goodness. The best examples of Roman politicians doing just that are Cato the Elder, whose lifelong posturing as the embodiment of *mos maiorum* (the ways of the ancestors) has been explored by others, and P. Cornelius Scipio Aemilianus.[24] Scipio enjoyed a dazzling career: consul in 147 and 134, censor in 142, he oversaw the destruction of Carthage in 146, and later saw military service in Spain. In this section, I explore some aspects of Scipio's self-fashioning which directly engaged with many of the criticisms discussed above.

As a youth, Scipio worried about matching the reputations of his famous ancestors. An eighteen-year-old in 167, Scipio befriended the historian Polybius during the latter's years as a hostage in Rome.[25] Confiding in Polybius, Aemilianus was concerned that, 'I am believed by everybody to be a quiet and lazy man, with none of the energetic character of a Roman' (Polyb. 31.23.11–12) because he did not trade accusations in the law courts, like others did.[26] Polybius describes how Scipio could promote his own virtuous conduct in contrast to other youths'.[27] Polybius prescribed a virtuous regimen for Scipio, who first obtained a reputation for sexual temperance (*sophrosyne*), which Polybius says is usually difficult to acquire, but not so at Rome 'owing to the vicious tendencies of most of the youths' (31.25.2–5), many of whom engaged in love affairs with boys or prostitutes. Scipio emphasised his own behaviour against the voracious sexual appetites of other young Roman men.

Next, he 'distinguished himself from others in magnanimity (*megalopsychia*) and moral purity (*katharotēs*) in money matters' (Polyb. 31.25.9–10), again flipping the elite stereotype of amassing wealth through questionable means. Polybius tells us he did this in two ways. First (31.26), upon receiving a large inheritance from his aunt, he gave it to his mother, who had fallen on hard times. 'Such conduct would naturally be admired anywhere,' Polybius writes, 'but in Rome it was a marvel; for absolutely no one there ever gives away anything to anyone if he can help it' (31.26.9). Next, he paid a large sum on his aunts' dowry more quickly than required by law. This again draws Polybius' notice: 'no one would pay one talent before the appointed day; so universal and so extreme is their exactitude about money as well as their desire to profit by every moment of time' (31.27.10–11). Then, after his natural father died, Scipio gave his share of the inheritance to his brother (31.28).

It remained for Scipio to acquire a reputation for bravery, which Polybius notes is 'nearly the most essential virtue in all states and especially so in Rome' (31.29.1). Rather than publicise a reputation for battlefield aggression, Scipio demonstrated bravery by proxy. On campaign with his father, he took up hunting, having the right 'physique for such an exercise, like a well-bred dog' (31.29.7). Arriving back in Rome, his reputation as a hunter was distinctive in comparison to others, who

> could not win praise except by injuring some of their fellow citizens, this being the usual consequence of prosecutions in the law courts; but Scipio, without ever vexing a soul, gained this universal reputation for courage, matching his deeds against their words. So that in a short space of time he had outstripped his contemporaries more than is recorded of any other Roman, although the path he pursued to gain glory was quite the opposite of that followed by all others in accordance with Roman usage and custom.[28]

Aemilianus explicitly rejected several hallmarks of Roman toxic masculinity, both as moderns might define it, but also as they appeared to ancient observers. Mediated through Polybius, Scipio's strategy was informed by a complex Greco-Roman intellectual matrix that evolved in the early decades of the second century. As Rome expanded into the Greek world, Greek culture took hold in the Roman metropole, especially for elite families, like Scipio's, who could afford access to new forms of education, or *paideia*.[29]

Polybius' training had special value for someone like Scipio. Blue-blooded aristocratic families like his faced increasing pressure after the Hannibalic War from newer clans without prestigious backgrounds.[30] In the drive for consulships and prestige that dominated aristocratic life, the components of Greek *paideia* – oratorical mastery, philosophical sophistication, artistic connoisseurship – combined with traditional Roman *dignitas* and provided another venue in which men like Scipio could earn distinction.[31] As M. Sommer shows, inter-elite competition is central to Scipio's thinking: his initial conversation with Polybius centres on his reputation.[32] While most *viri* continued to parlay military *virtus* into electoral success, Scipio put to use Greek *paideia*, and, more broadly, *aretē*, towards his own benefit.[33]

Scipio succeeded in his aims. In a pithy line of Cato, when asked to compare him to other youths, he replied, 'He, and he alone, has wisdom; the rest are but fluttering shadows.'[34] Scipio maintained this policy of distinction through morality later in life through friendship with the philosopher Panaetius.[35] On a trip to Egypt, Scipio impressed Ptolemy VIII Physcon with his frugal lifestyle.[36] While on military campaign, he also instituted strict discipline among his troops, and he personally refused to allow his slaves and freedmen to loot after battles.[37]

From Panaetius, Scipio would have learned that *andreia*, traditionally focused on physical bravery, ought to be subsumed beneath *megalopsuchia* ('greatness of spirit') for the wise man.[38] Despite this downgrading of military masculinity, however, Scipio proved himself more than adept at the same kind of brutally aggressive actions we have defined as toxic. In the 150s, Scipio volunteered for military service in Spain specifically because his reputation for bravery lagged behind his reputation for 'noble character and temperance' (Polyb. 35.4.8). After serving with distinction, he later oversaw the utter destruction of Carthage in 146, which some have dubbed history's first genocide.[39] Later, at the siege of Numantia in 134, Scipio declined to treat the enemy with mercy, instead starving them out and destroying the city. Appian surmises that Scipio did this 'either because he thought that it would be for the advantage of the Romans, or because he was in a violent rage against the captives', or instead, merely for glory's sake.[40]

From a modern perspective, the butchery he inflicted on these cities and his immense success as a Roman general and politician appear diametrically opposed to the altruistic traits he fostered as a young man. His philosophical self-fashioning could appear as empty virtue signalling, a cheap façade papering over a more authentic, vicious interior.[41] In fact, Scipio's contrasting military and philosophical sides were complementary aspects of his life ethos, and entirely within the framework of Stoic thought in which he was steeped. According to Panaetius and his successor Posidonius, only the wise could align their soul with rational thought and action. All others followed baser appetitive impulses, and were thus considered beasts or slaves.[42] In such thinking, as Barlow notes, 'It was morally right to use force to master those who were subject to unreasoning impulses, since violence and war occurred among them if they were left alone'.[43] Or, in the words of Posidonius, 'It is natural for the worse to submit to the better.'[44] The true wise man needed discernment to determine necessary action. Therefore, to Scipio, uncompromising violence and altruistic generosity were merely different manifestations of justice, complementary traits for the statesman. As Velleius Paterculus remarks about Scipio, no one was 'more constant in his devotion to the arts either of war or peace'.[45]

CONCLUSION

Scipio's career illuminates how elites could respond to contemporary perceptions that their worldview was selfish and destructive. Through a regimen of conspicuous morality informed by Greek philosophical sensibilities, Scipio demonstrated his suitability for political leadership and social prominence. While remaining familiar with the traditional panoply of Roman militarism and aggression, Scipio's moral comportment and ethical sensibilities became additional markers of distinction, helping to demonstrate that he deserved his position at the apex of Roman society.

Scipio Aemilianus is a case study in the contestability of hegemonic masculinity, which, in R. W. Connell's formulation, 'is not a fixed character type, always and everywhere the same. It is, rather, the masculinity that occupies the hegemonic position in a given pattern of gender relations, a position always contestable.'[46] To Connell, hegemonic masculinity is a 'historically mobile relation' that is by definition open to challenge, but which, having been challenged, has still tended only to help 'guarantee the dominant position of men'. Scipio's career demonstrates this historical process in action in the Roman Middle Republic.

NOTES

1. On the *fustuarium*, see Polyb. 6.37; on its impact on Roman conceptions of manhood, see Walters 1997, 29–46.
2. Pyrgopolinices' possession of the *cognomen* 'Pulcher' (1037), his anxiety about others associating him too closely with the vulgar crowd (1035), his concern that a woman purportedly interested in him be freeborn (961) and that he is announced 'per epistulam aut per nuntium' (1225) all encourage identification with Roman nobility.
3. My analysis in this chapter is limited to c. 200–150 BCE, a segment of the period that historians call the Middle Republic (c. 264–133 BCE). All subsequent dates are BCE unless otherwise noted.
4. Williams [1999] 2010, *passim*, esp. 17–18. In Williams' words, 'A Roman man is ideally ready, willing, and able to express his dominion over others, male or female, by means of sexual penetration. Power in this sense meant the ability to experience sexual pleasure on one's own terms through the domination of others' bodies.'
5. Liv. 39.42.12. In another story (Liv. 39.43), Livy tells us that Flamininus boasted to a female courtesan about how many prisoners he had under chains awaiting a sentence of death. This may be merely another version of the story at 39.42.
6. On this theme in the Roman imperial context, see Mattingly 2013.
7. Harris [1979] 1985, 10–41.
8. Ser. Sulpicius Galba had a large number of Lusitanians executed in 150 after convincing them to disarm (App. *Iber.* 60); L. Licinius Lucullus resorted to

similar barbarism earlier in the same war (*Iber.* 51–5). On debates regarding the triumph in these years, see Pittenger 2008.

9. Livy reports other similar stories from these years: Cn. Manlius Fulvius 'had striven with all his might to break the peace' with Antiochus in 187, then attacked the Galatians without pretext in what some Roman observers described as a 'private piratical expedition' (Liv. 38.45.1–50.3; quotes at Liv. 45.2 and 45.7).

10. Val. Max. 2.8.1; additionally, a law of unknown date was passed stipulating a minimum death toll of 5,000 enemies to earn a triumph: Oros. 5.4.7. Fabricated surrender of a town: Liv. 33.22.7.

11. Booty and loot from war (*manubia*) was generally thought to be public property. See Churchill 1999, 85–116.

12. Glabrio: Liv. 38.57.4; Vulso: Liv. 38.54.7.

13. Liv. 38.40–50; Polyb. 23.14.

14. On the economic benefits of empire for the Roman *populus*, see Harris [1979] 1985, 41–53.

15. Many Middle Republican playwrights were of low status: tradition states that Plautus was a manual labourer before becoming a playwright (Jer. *Ab. Abr.* 1817, 200 BCE [p. 135h Helm]); Publius Syrus (Macrob. *Sat.* 2.7.6), Terence (Suet. *Vita Ter.* 1) and Caecilius (Suet. *Vita Caec.*) were all likely of servile background. On the make-up of republican theatre audiences, see Manuwald 2011, 98–108 and Richlin 2017, 12.

16. See, for example, Palinurus on the availability of sex in Plaut. *Curc.* 32–7: 'No one says "no", or stops you from buying what is openly for sale, if you have the money. No one prohibits anyone from going along the public road. Fuck whoever you want – just be sure you don't wander off it onto private tracks – I mean, stay away from married women, widows, virgins, young men, and boys of good family.' On sexual violence in comedy, see James 1998, 31–47 and Leisner-Jensen 2002, 173–96.

17. According to Gruen (1990, 129), 'The plays could serve as vehicles to address, promote, mock, or satirize items that held public attention or provoked public debate.' The discussion of several passages here is indebted to this work and to that of Richlin 2017.

18. *Bacch.* 1072: *peruolgatum est.*

19. *Asin.* 321–2.

20. *Amph.* 197.

21. *Cur.* 439–46. As the parasite Curculio puts it, 'within twenty days he singlehandedly subjected the Persians, the Paphlagonians, the inhabitants of Sinope, the Arabs, the Carians, the Cretans, the Syrians, Rhodes and Lycia, Gobbleonia and Booziania, Centaurobattaglia and Classia, Onenippleania, Libya, and the entire coast of Wineknockoutia, in short, half of all nations on earth' (trans. de Melo). Half of these locations are invented. The description mimics how aristocratic achievements were commemorated on funerary inscriptions (see, for example, *CIL* VI 1285, from the tomb of the Scipios), and in funeral speeches (Plin. *NH* 7.45).

22. *Truc.* 483–94.

23. *Trin.* 1032–49. On this passage, see Anderson 1979, 333–45; Gruen 1990, 142 n. 88; and Slater 2013.
24. On Cato's moralistic posturing, see Astin 1978; Reay 2005, 331–61; and Sciarrino 2011.
25. Since Polybius relied on the Scipios as his patrons during his stay in Rome, it is important to recognise his bias towards the family in his *Histories*, which colours his descriptions of Aemilianus' character. On this, see Sommer 2013, 313–17.
26. This may refer to a flurry of legal cases against Roman magistrates at the end of the 170s, most of them brought by young tribunes of the plebs: Liv. 42.21.1–8; 43.8.9; *Per.* 43.
27. On this passage in Polybius see most recently Barlow 2018, 112–27.
28. Polyb. 31.29.10–12; cf. Cic. *Tusc.* 2.62.
29. McDonnell 2006, 105–41.
30. For example, see Livy's description of electoral battles in the years 192 (35.101), 191 (35.24.4) and 189 (37.47.6), for which see also Feig-Vishnia 1996. Goldberg (2015, 347–8) illustrates diminished electoral fortunes and several family embarrassments for the Cornelii Scipiones beginning in the 170s.
31. Hölkeskamp [2004] 2010, 107–24.
32. Sommer 2013, 312.
33. McDonnell (2006, 105–41) describes how influence from Greek *aretē* expanded the linguistic range of Latin *virtus* during this period; cf. Balmaceda 2017, 19–25.
34. Plut. *Mor.* 200A.
35. Plut. *Mor.* 201A; 777A; 814C–D.
36. Cic. *Acad.* 2.2.5; Diod. Sic. 33.28b; cf. Cic. *Off.* 1.108.
37. Plut. *Mor.* 201C; 200B.
38. Cic. *Off.* 1.61–92; Dyck 1996, 183–5; Barlow 2018, 118.
39. Diod. Sic. 32.4.5, 14.1, 26.2; App. *Pun.* 128–35; First genocide: Kiernan 2004, 27–39. One thing might be said in Scipio's defence: the notion that the Romans salted the earth to ensure that nothing would ever grow in Carthage again is a nineteenth-century fantasy: Ridley 1986, 140–6.
40. App. *Hisp.* 98.
41. As far back as 1965, Strasburger found these contrasting aspects of Scipio's character a 'gigantic paradox'. See Strasburger 1965, 40–53.
42. Cic. *Off.* 1.101, 132; 2.18 (= Pan. frs. 87–9); *Rep.* 3.33–41, with Erskine 2011, 192–204.
43. Barlow 2018, 125.
44. Sen. *Ep.* 90.4–13 = Posid. fr. 284 (Edelstein and Kidd no. 58).
45. Vell. Pat. 1.13.3.
46. Connell 1995, 76.

PART III

Ancient Meets Modern

CHAPTER 14

Scipio Africanus and the Construction of Fascist Italian Masculinities

Samuel Agbamu

In recent years, scholarship has highlighted the ways in which classical antiquity has been used to support and construct racist, misogynistic, homophobic and transphobic ideologies, including toxic masculinities.[1] For example, in 2017, classicist Matthew Sears wrote an article in *The Conversation* on toxic masculinities' 'misreading' of classical antiquity. In this, he wrote that he is 'haunted by this co-optation of [his] discipline by the so-called "alt-right" and other self-styled "defenders of Western civilization"'. However, the very discipline of Classics is rooted in white supremacy, colonialism and patriarchy. These intersecting structures of oppression underpinning the discipline have been explored in a wealth of scholarship, published both in the wake of Martin Bernal's controversial *Black Athena*, and as a result of Classics' accelerating uptake of feminist theoretical frameworks in the last decades of the twentieth century.[2] Such scholarship shows that contemporary alt-right and misogynistic appeals to Greco-Roman antiquity can best be addressed by acknowledging the unattractive past, and indeed present, of the discipline. Indeed, a growing field of research has examined the use of the ancient Greek and Roman worlds within ideologies of Fascism and Nazism.[3] In laying bare the mechanisms behind previous uses of classical antiquity to promote oppressive structures, the harmful contemporary ideologies which appropriate antiquity are historicised and can more effectively be dismantled.

Through a discussion of the constructions of masculinities in Carmine Gallone's 1937 film *Scipione l'Africano*, this chapter shows that grounding racist and misogynistic politics in classical antiquity is no twenty-first-century innovation: it has a long history, with its most obvious and devastating implications borne out under 1930s and 40s European fascisms. Therefore, I take the Italian Fascist appropriation of Roman antiquity as a limit case for historical examples of the use of the Classics to support oppressive structures. By emphasising the structural roots of manifestations of toxic masculinities and understanding toxic masculinities in terms of hegemonies, this chapter asks whether hegemonic masculinities, in being defined against an 'Other', whether against the gendered, sexualised or racialised other, are themselves toxic, since they legitimise structures of oppression. Such ideologies of white male supremacy coalesce in the Fascist image of Scipio Africanus, vanquisher of the African Hannibal at the Battle of Zama, 202 BCE, the subject of Gallone's film.

I begin by outlining how this chapter understands the 'toxic masculinity' of this volume's title, before moving on to sketch out how Scipio has been used to promote hegemonic masculinities in his post-classical Italian reincarnations. Next, I turn to Scipio's reconfiguration into an idealised embodiment of Fascist Italian masculinity during the *ventennio fascista*, the most significant expression of which was featured in Carmine Gallone's film. I focus on the film's construction of hegemonic femininity and its use in supporting the hierarchical supremacy of Fascist hegemonic masculinity. Concurrent to this was the elevation of Italian imperialist masculinity represented by Scipio over the subordinated, colonised masculinity represented by the Carthaginians and Numidians. I end by considering the value of looking at articulations of toxic masculinities in receptions of classical antiquity for wider struggles against structures of oppression.

The conceptual tool of toxic masculinity, first rising to prominence in psychology scholarship in the 1990s, and indebted to feminist theorists, seeks to identify aspects of constructions of masculinities deemed destructive or harmful, such as violence, misogyny, homophobia and domineering behaviour.[4] The concept builds on Raewyn Connell's notion of hegemonic masculinities: constructions of masculinity that are the social norm in a specific society at a specific time, deviation from which risks ridicule or social stigma for men.[5] These constructions, Connell argues, are articulated in relation to subordinated masculinities and in relation to women. In other words, theories of masculinity necessarily relate to those of femininity.

Thus, more recently, scholars have pointed to the under-theorised role of articulations of hegemonic femininity in the context of hegemonic masculinities. Mimi Schippers (2007) argues that hegemonic femininities are those which are intertwined in a complementary relationship with hegemonic masculinity, subordinate to masculinity, but positionally superior to other femininities. Schippers stresses the implication of hegemonic femininities and masculinities with other systems of inequality. This intersectional analysis is reinforced in recent articles by Connell which emphasise the need for a postcolonial approach to hegemonic masculinities which is lacking in much discussion of toxic masculinities.[6] The coloniality of gender and sexuality has long been underlined by Black and post/decolonial feminist scholars.[7] Hegemonic masculinities and femininities, therefore, are racialised and are inextricably bound to the legacies of colonialism. This chapter thus foregrounds the racist and colonial underpinnings of hegemonic masculinities, as well as emphasising the centrality of constructions of hegemonic femininity to hegemonic masculinities. If, therefore, hegemonic ideologies of gender rest on colonial and patriarchal foundations, should they be considered toxic in themselves? And how has Scipio been used to promote these gendered and racialised hierarchies?

Scipio has a long history of being appropriated to embody idealised constructions of masculinity in art and literature from the Italian peninsula, such that Scipio has been seen to represent what classicist Raymond Marks describes as Italy's 'synecdochic hero'.[8] Influenced by an episode related by Livy (26.49–50), in which Scipio releases a Celtiberian princess, captured during Rome's campaign in Spain against Carthage, to her betrothed, Scipio came to embody chasteness, sexual continence and reverence for marital love in his post-classical receptions, especially in early modern Italy: this story was cited by Machiavelli in his sixteenth-century *Discourses on Livy* as exemplary of Scipio's good governance and was also a popular subject for art in domestic contexts of elite Italian Renaissance homes.[9] Florentine humanism conceived of the family as a microcosm of the state, thus Scipio's presence in the private sphere of the Renaissance home resonates with his later co-optation by Fascist ideologies of the family and the state.

As a result of his famed sexual continence and financial generosity, Scipio featured on numerous fifteenth-century Italian *cassone* or marriage chests.[10] Art historian Cristelle Baskins (2012) examines such uses of Scipio in Italian domestic imagery of the Renaissance to gauge performances of elite masculinity in this period. There was, however, a much more sinister image of Scipio's sexuality explored in early modern Italian literature. In Petrarch's early Renaissance work of fictional dialogues, the *Secretum*, Hannibal, in crossing the Alps, is represented as the rapist of Italy; later, when Scipio invades Africa, he is represented as opening up the continent with his sword, leaving Hannibal likened to a raped matron.[11] Thus, in these Renaissance representations of Scipio, we see the double-edged nature of hegemonic masculinities. Scipio's self-possession is enabled by his positional superiority over the racialised and feminised Other, over which he is able to exercise his dominion. This idealised masculinity underpinned by aggressive exercises of power would come to constitute important ingredients for the Fascist reincarnation of the Roman general.

The Fascist use of ancient Rome has, in recent decades, been the subject of a sub-field of Classical Reception scholarship.[12] From its symbols and ceremonial, its idealisation of militarism to its imperialist agenda, Fascism modelled itself assiduously on what it saw as its national and spiritual forebear: Rome. Mussolini worked hard to cultivate associations between himself and Roman emperors, most prominently Augustus, an ideological endeavour which reached fever pitch during the celebrations of the first Roman emperor's bimillenary in 1937–8.[13] However, during Italy's 1935–6 invasion of Ethiopia and its aftermath, during which the national consensus for colonialism in Africa was consolidated, another famous Roman was elevated to prominence in order to celebrate Fascist Italy's African conquest: the Roman Republican general, vanquisher of the African menace Hannibal, immortalised in the opening lines of the Italian national anthem – Scipio Africanus. Scipio was used to promote an idealised form of Fascist, imperialist masculinity, such that in Italy's imperial imaginary, he became a proto-Fascist, and the Fascist, male imperialist, a modern-day Scipio.[14]

Mussolini's regime had been encouraging the production of a film based on Scipio Africanus as early as 1933, contemporaneous with the beginning of preliminary planning for the invasion of Ethiopia.[15] In 1937, Luigi Freddi wrote an article in the newspaper *Il Popolo d'Italia* on 'the great films of Italian production'. In this, he writes that '*Scipio* was conceived of in the footsteps of the African endeavour and begun immediately after victory . . . in order to frame, in the august tradition of the race, the African endeavour of today, as a logical corollary of a glorious past and the indisputable justification of a present life no less glorious'. The film thus officially linked Roman antiquity to contemporary Italian imperialism in Africa, leaving little open to independent interpretation. A central component of this parallelism was the identification of Mussolini with Scipio Africanus. The links forged by the film between Mussolini and Scipio go much further than the Zama-Ethiopia equation; as Scipio avenged the defeat at Cannae with victory at Zama, Mussolini avenged the Italian defeats in Ethiopia, at Dogali in 1887 and Adwa in 1896, with victory in 1936. *Scipione l'Africano* is a strongly anti-democratic film, ideologically aligned with Fascist dictatorship. Moreover, it is a film deeply invested in promoting idealised figures of the New Man and Woman of Fascist imperialism.

HEGEMONIC AND SUBORDINATE FEMININITIES IN *SCIPIONE L'AFRICANO*

Italian Fascism had, from its very inception, a violent virility at its core. The ideology's deeply conservative attitudes towards gender aimed to return Italian women to the hearth and home, restore patriarchal authority and restrict the role of women to social reproduction. As Victoria De Grazia shows, the creation of the 'Nuova Italiana' – the new Italian woman – was as important to Fascist ideology as the creation of the 'Nuovo Italiano', the new Italian man.[16] This was, in Mussolini's mind, a mission firmly rooted in Roman antiquity. In a 1934 article published in *Il Popolo d'Italia* on the incompatibility of 'Machine and Woman', he exhorted Italian women to be 'illustrious, prolific mothers', 'great, like the women of Ancient Rome' and 'faithful vestal virgins'.[17]

Such attitudes towards the role of women hardened by the time of the film's production. During the war in Ethiopia, the context in which the film was produced, Italy was subject to sanctions imposed by the League of Nations.

This led to an increased drive for autarky, with women being placed at the forefront of this campaign for self-sufficiency. This drive was a core theme of Fascist propaganda, with sanctions becoming a mobilising propagandistic tool for Italy's imperial mission, in which women played a prominent role. The war against the sanctions on the home front was conceptualised as the women's counterpart to the war being carried on overseas by men.[18]

This facet of the role of women in Fascist imperialism coincided with an increased preoccupation with the threat of miscegenation, which saw increased prominence in the Italian imperialist imaginary after the conquest of Ethiopia, and the later institution of racist and antisemitic laws.[19] If colonial authority relies on the positional superiority of the coloniser over the colonised, then this is a boundary that needs policing against the confusion of miscegenation. So, on the one hand, we see the positive side of women in the Fascist imaginary, as Italian soldiers on the home front, waging war against the League of Nations sanctions; on the other hand, we see the negative foil of the foreign woman, temptress and corrupter of the purity of the Italian race. These interrelations, between masculinity and femininity, Italian self and foreign other, illustrate the hierarchical nature of constructions of hegemonic masculinity; Fascist imperialist supremacy was buttressed by hegemonic femininity, which in turn was elevated above the subordinate femininity of the colonised female other.

Manifestations of hegemonic femininity as promoted by Mussolini resonate with representations of Roman womanhood in *Scipione*, exemplified by Scipio's wife, Aemilia Tertia, and the fictional Roman noblewoman Velia, played by Isa Miranda, one of Fascist Italy's few internationally famous film stars. Against these women stands their antithesis, the sinister, Orientalised seductress Sophonisba, constructed as a subordinate femininity to the hegemonic 'Nuova Italiana' of Fascism. I suggest that the film's portrayals of these three women act not only as exempla or negative mirror images of idealised Fascist femininities, but also as tools for the construction of the model for Fascist imperialist masculinity, since the hegemonic masculinity of Fascism was defined by its positional superiority over Fascism's hegemonic femininity.

Of the three main female characters of the film, Aemilia Tertia occupies the least space and remains silent throughout the film. If Scipio represents the perfect Italian imperialist, then Aemilia Tertia represents the idealised Romano-Fascist wife. We first see her placing her jewellery into a box, which is subsequently carried away by an attendant legionnaire, having just heard Cato, whose presence in the Senate is anachronistic, state that the Senate would not pay a single sesterce to fund Scipio's war in Africa.[20] Similar contributions of jewellery to fund Scipio's campaign were made by Roman matrons during the Second Punic War.[21] The Italian audience of the film is likely to have made a connection between Aemilia Tertia's action and the *Giornata della Fede*, 18 December 1935. On this day across Italy, men and women donated their jewellery, especially

wedding rings, to be melted down to fund Italy's war in Ethiopia, also signifying their metaphorical marriage to the state. The most publicised of these
rituals occurred at the *Altare della Patria* in Rome, at which Queen Elena of
Italy and Mussolini's wife donated their wedding rings. The ceremonies were
symbolic, devoid of any practical use: little of the jewellery collected on that day
was melted down, and only then for the cameras.[22] Aemilia Tertia's symbolic
marriage to the state with the donation of her jewellery also identifies Scipio
with the state, his masculinity standing in as metonymic of the Fascist state's
promotion of its masculine ethics of speed, aggression and imperial expansion.[23]

Aemilia Tertia is always seen with her son, presumably Scipio's eldest
child, who shared his father's name. Marcia Landy sees her as an allusion to
the Madonna and child, but Rachel Feig Vishnia instead considers this to be
an emphasis on paternal leadership, locating Scipio firmly at the head of the
patriarchal family. The film thus gestures towards the inextricability of the
political and paternal roles of Scipio and aligns the strength of the family with
the strength of the nation.[24] This interpretation corroborates the controversial
German Marxist psychoanalyst Wilhelm Reich's 1933 argument, made in the
context of the rise of National Socialism in Germany, for the patriarchal family
as the fundamental social unit of the authoritarian state. The fact that Aemilia
is never seen without little Scipio alludes to the role of the Fascist woman as
mother, and Mussolini's pro-natalist drive, announced at his Ascension Day
speech in 1927, which reinforced the role of the Nuova Italiana as limited to
social reproduction.

The end of the film shows Scipio in retirement at his country estate, following his victory at Zama. The last line of the film is spoken by the victorious
general. Picking up a handful of grain, he announces, 'the grain is good, and
tomorrow, with the help of the gods, we will plant it'. Federico Caprotti argues
that this is in reference to the Battle of the Grain, a Fascist initiative to increase
national agricultural production, including the exploitation of Italy's African
colonies, as part of the regime's drive for self-sufficiency.[25] Rhiannon Welch similarly links this line to the idea of the geographical reclamation of the Pontine
Marshes, which she reads in terms of avenging the bodily and territorial loss and
dismemberment of Italy, in the aftermath not only of Italy's nineteenth-century
defeats in Ethiopia but also of the First World War, in which Italy saw itself
as the recipient of a 'mutilated victory'.[26] The grain was also identified as a
metaphor for a Fascist future initiated by the foundation of empire. In a 1939
special issue of the film magazine *Bianco e Nero* on *Scipione l'Africano*, a child
who had seen the film was cited as saying, 'at the end of the film, one sees Scipio
taking a handful of grain and saying, "Oh what nice grain, tomorrow we'll plant
it." I say that each grain represents a *balilla* [Fascist youth] of today and each
ear of grain a brave soldier of tomorrow.'[27] This analysis is rendered especially
pertinent since, after Scipio speaks this line, he ruffles his son's hair, linking the

grain and the idea of a tomorrow with youth. His wife, Aemilia Tertia, is also present, though silent, evoking ideas of family and motherhood in this theme of a Fascist future. Thus, the submissive figure of Aemilia Tertia is deployed in Gallone's film to reinforce the authoritarian family with Scipio in the position of the patriarch.

The Roman noblewoman Velia represents another form of the idealised construction of Italian femininity. It should be noted that Velia's name is etymologically linked to the Latin *velare*, to cover, signifying her modesty. Indeed, when we first see Velia, she is praying with her husband Arunte to a statue of Venus in her garden, veiled and chaste in marriage. Arunte is about to set off for Africa as part of Scipio's invading army, and each spouse prays for the other's safety while they are separated. Once Arunte departs, the marital harmony represented by the patriarchal unit of the nuclear family is disrupted when a band of raiding Carthaginians irrupt into the domestic idyll of Velia's villa. The Carthaginians are depicted as violent, dark-skinned, bearded drunkards. They corral the women in the atrium of the villa, before herding them off into captivity. The final shot of this scene shows a young child left alone, crying in the ransacked atrium of the villa, metonymic of the disturbed social equilibrium of the patriarchal family. This scene, the first to show Carthaginian interactions with Romans, reveals the film's construction of various hierarchies: of the hegemonic femininity of Velia, which, when left without the protection of Arunte's hegemonic masculinity, is prey to the subordinate, denigrated (literally) masculinities of the barbarous Carthaginian Other.

In the Carthaginian camp, the captured Roman women are leered at by the bug-eyed Carthaginian brutes. The women defiantly draw their veils (again, we are reminded of Velia's name) across their faces, to shield themselves from the libidinous gaze of their captors. A Carthaginian soldier stops and stares at Velia, who menacingly grasps her brooch pin. Presumably incensed by her courage, he drags her off to Hannibal's tent. It is through her encounters with Hannibal that Velia's role as the feminine complement to Fascism's hegemonic masculinity becomes most clear. Velia, dazzlingly white, compared with Hannibal, represents the light which is only called into being in contrast to the darkness of the African. As Italian postcolonial scholars have argued, it was in contrast with the dark-skinned African that the Italian became Italian.[28] The film's representation of the Carthaginian leader echoes Livy's characterisation of him as a man 'more Punic than Punic holding nothing sacred, with no fear for the gods, faithless in oaths, and of no religion' (Livy 21.4). In comparison to this, Velia tells Hannibal that 'the Romans only fear their gods', elevating Roman piety over Carthaginian impiety. Furthermore, to contrast Hannibal's mistreatment of prisoners, Velia recounts the generosity and reverence for love, and by implication, the institution of marriage and the family, shown by Scipio when he released a captured Celtiberian noblewoman to her betrothed, during his Spanish campaign (Livy 26.50).

This, as we have seen, was a popular theme in Renaissance representations of Scipio, and further serves to contrast Roman (Italian) masculine sexual continence with the hypersexual, racialised male Other.

Finally, the representation of the Carthaginian femme fatale Sophonisba in *Scipione l'Africano* owes much to Petrarch's *Africa*, itself expanded from Livy's narrative.[29] Sophonisba's role in the film is to allow Scipione to demonstrate his exemplary chasteness and good counsel as well as to offer the negative image of the subordinated foreign femininity against which the hegemonic femininity of Fascist imperialism could be constructed. Sophonisba, the daughter of Hasdrubal, was married to the Numidian king Syphax, who was an ally of Rome against Carthage but who, following his marriage, switched allegiances to Carthage. Massinissa, a Numidian prince allied to Rome, defeats Syphax and hands him over to the Romans. However, to complicate matters, Massinissa falls in love with Sophonisba, and refuses to hand her over to be paraded in triumph by the Romans. Scipio prevails upon him to surrender his lover, but, rather than allow herself to be humiliated, Sophonisba, like Cleopatra, commits suicide by drinking poison.

Sophonisba's first appearance in the film establishes her as a sexualised figure of temptation, dressed in tight-fitting, revealing clothes, in contrast with the chaste modesty of the veiled Velia and Aemilia Tertia. She is shown first lying on a luxurious couch, through diaphanous curtains which bear a pattern of symbols resembling a uterus or stylised ears of corn, signifying fertility and sexuality. From the outset, she is represented as sexually desirable to the male viewer. She is surrounded by handmaidens, evoking Orientalist, erotic tropes of the harem, 'a monument to the male scopic desire, a phallocentric fantasy'.[30] At the same time the image of the harem constitutes a microcosm of the despotic Oriental state, embodying oppression of women, as displayed by the Carthaginian treatment of Roman women, and Hannibal's treatment of Velia. Such representations of the harem provided European colonialism with legitimacy, establishing the conditions for what Spivak observes as 'white men . . . saving brown women from brown men'.[31]

The camera moves through the curtain, as if transgressing the boundaries of her purdah and introducing the male gaze, to reveal Sophonisba more clearly. She has pale skin and dark hair, resembling the version of that other Oriental seductress of antiquity, Cleopatra, in DeMille's 1934 film. In this way she stands in contrast to the representations of the other North African characters, roles for which the actors had been darkened with make-up. Her white skin also places her in a liminal space of being both exotic but familiar, desirable yet feared, loved but hated, instantiating the threatening temptation of miscegenation. Her representation invites the viewer to enjoy this ambivalent attraction to her as a lesson in colonial desire. The film summons up the threat of this desire in the viewer, manipulating it, in order for it to be defeated by the patriarchal figure of Scipio.

Wilhelm Reich speaks of the link between the libidinous mechanism of Fascism, whereby the internalised father-figure of the psyche's repression of sexuality – here embodied by Scipio – contributes to the inherent authoritarianism of the individual, and imperial militarism. He points to the use of sexualisation of colonies in promoting wars of imperialism, citing examples of posters of the Royal Navy, representing foreign lands as an exotic woman to be conquered.[32] In such a way, Sophonisba represents an object of desire to be figuratively conquered by the male coloniser, but who, because of the threat that she poses, must be destroyed.

After the viewer meets Sophonisba, Syphax enters her chamber. He presents an emerald to his wife, who reminds him of his allegiance to Carthage. Syphax appears totally in her thrall, ineffectual and physically unimpressive, reinforcing the trope of the effeminate Oriental man. The articulation of colonial hegemonic masculinities against the effeminate and subordinated masculinities of the colonised, especially in Orientalising discourse, has been well discussed in scholarship.[33] I will turn to the representation of masculinities subordinate to the hegemonic masculinity of Fascist imperialism in more detail later in this chapter, but for now I want to draw attention to the relationship between Syphax's masculinity and the 'Other' femininity of Sophonisba, and how this relates to the articulation of imperial hegemonic masculinities and femininities.

Later in the film, an embassy from Scipio arrives at Syphax's palace to negotiate with the Numidian ruler. In characteristic 'noble generosity', Scipio gives Syphax a chance to honour their old friendship by acting as a mediator between Carthage and Rome. Before Syphax can speak his piece, Sophonisba enters, initially appearing only as a silhouette behind a curtain before emerging, implicitly transgressing from the feminine realm of the harem to the masculine sphere of diplomacy. Nevertheless, she commands more authority than Syphax, and speaks against the Roman embassy's proposal. In close-up shots of Sophonisba, her face is cast in shadows, with only her eyes illuminated, giving her a threatening, mysterious air. Sophonisba's demonstration of hegemonically masculine traits of leadership and judiciousness do nothing to improve her standing in the audience's eyes – on the contrary, this reinforces her alterity. At the same time, Syphax is further feminised by her actions, which serves to further denigrate his masculinity and, at the same time, elevate the colonial masculinity of the Romans and their modern Fascist counterparts.

The threat of miscegenation which confuses the boundary between the coloniser and the colonised is implicit in the attractiveness of Sophonisba. This threat that she poses is defeated through Scipio's good counsel to Massinissa and ended by her suicide. Massinissa, with Scipio's help, thus wins his greatest victory, according to Scipio, corroborating Ruth Ben-Ghiat's interpretation of Fascist films being all about the male body 'trying to break free of temptation and render themselves to the service of Fascist goals'.[34] Sophonisba's death is her defining moment, embodying the defeat of the sexual temptation of the Orient and the triumph of the Italian *stirpe* – bloodline – in maintaining its purity. Feig Vishnia wrote that Sophonisba is 'doomed, like all the femme fatales of the silent era . . . there is only one fate for this decadent, scheming, transgressive woman'.[35] That fate is her death, which guarantees the triumph of the Fascist New Man in defeating the threat of miscegenation and ensuring the positional superiority of the patriarchal authoritarianism of Italian imperialism.[36]

HEGEMONIC AND SUBORDINATE MASCULINITIES

My discussion of the representation of women in *Scipione l'Africano* aimed to show that the construction of Fascist, imperialist hegemonic femininity, positioned above the 'Other woman', stands as a complement to the hegemonic masculinity of Italian imperialism. The enforcement of such gendered hierarchies through constructions of hegemonic femininity as subordinate to hegemonic masculinity must, I argue, be considered a manifestation of toxic masculinity, since it necessitates male supremacy. Assertions of such forms of hegemonic masculinity therefore manifest themselves as exercises of power over women on the level of the individual – whether in thought, speech or acts – or structurally and culturally. It is in defence of such positional superiority of masculinity over femininity that the toxic 'angry white men' of contemporary 'men's rights activists' circles and other groups of the alt-right/alt-light mobilise themselves.[37] Yet the relationship between masculinity and femininity is but one, albeit highly significant, facet of the entrenchment of nationalist-imperialist hegemonic masculinities promoted by Gallone's film. Earlier, we saw how racialisation played a role in articulations of hegemonic femininity in *Scipione*. Likewise, the racialised aspect of masculinities is an important angle which is often neglected in discussions of hegemonic masculinities that do not explicitly employ an intersectional or postcolonial approach.[38] *Scipione l'Africano* illustrates vividly the racialisation of hegemonic masculinities, with the white male coloniser's supremacy dependent on the subordination of the non-white, colonised male.[39]

We have already seen that the threatening femininity of Sophonisba is defeated by Scipio's good counsel to Massinissa, the quasi-colonial subject. The representation of Scipio as the judicious, objective dispenser of wisdom situates Gallone's Scipio within wider colonial discourses of the impartial benevolence of colonial masculinity. For example, Jonathan Saha confronts the myth of the impartial British judge in the colonial archive of South Asia to show that the purported objectivity of the colonial justice system was based on the embodiment of justice as white and male.[40] Non-whiteness and non-hegemonic masculinity therefore becomes an aberration. Massinissa's indiscreet affair with Sophonisba plays into narratives of the hypersexual African or Oriental male

Other, a stereotype which stretches back to Greco-Roman antiquity.[41] Massinissa therefore needs the guidance of the wise male coloniser – the sexually continent Scipio.

In contrast to Scipio, Hannibal appears in Gallone's film as a sex-crazed brute. The film implies that he rapes Velia, fulfilling the trope of the Oriental man as a rapist.[42] This stereotype betrays colonial anxieties of miscegenation, at the same time as justifying colonial and racist violence: if brown and Black men are all potential rapists, then they must be pre-emptively disciplined. This trope is pertinent to Hannibal's representation as an Islamo-Semitic despot, since the image of Christendom being represented as a vulnerable woman to Islam's male rapist goes back at least to fifteenth-century propaganda deployed to mobilise support for a crusade against the Ottomans who had recently taken Constantinople.[43] Representations of non-white men as rapists in racialising rhetoric have a long and bloody history. In the UK context, from which this chapter is written, the exploitation of the fear of Muslim men as rapists has seen the far right make huge strides into mainstream politics.[44] Thus, *Scipione* stands as a moment in the development of this xenophobic trope, which calls the (male) defenders of whiteness to arms in defence of white women against the, here, Orientalised rapist. However, the racialisation of this male Other is flexible, with this racist discursive weapon having historically been levelled at Black Americans, Jewish Europeans, Latin Americans and any other group whose scapegoating is called for by the hegemonic narrative. *Scipione l'Africano* is able to reinforce the hegemony of Fascist imperial masculinity by representing the male Other as deficient in some way: Syphax, the spineless, effeminate 'Oriental'; Massinissa, an indiscreet subject requiring education; and Hannibal, the rapist.

It is not coincidental that this increasing emphasis on race as biological rather than cultural coemerged with the foundation of the Italian empire. Colonial power depends on the policing of the boundary between coloniser and colonised, a boundary which is confused by mixing between the two groups.[45] *Scipione l'Africano* emerged at a point when Italy was edging towards its 'totalitarian turn', concurrent to an increasingly close relationship with Nazi Germany, and legislated antisemitic racism from 1938, characterised as '"modernist" witch hunts'.[46] The racist discourses which were articulated in Fascist imperial culture, exported and put into action in Italy's African colonies, return to the Italian peninsula in the shape of the devastating consequences of institutional antisemitism. The racist masculinity elaborated and promoted by *Scipione* played a part in this radicalisation of Italian racism.

Additionally, Scipio's use as a conceptual tool in the construction of Fascist masculinities contributed to the promotion of Fascism's deeply patriarchal attitudes, which reduced women to instruments of social reproduction and the guarantor of the perpetuation of the Italian race.[47] In line with Schipper's argument, this chapter suggested that hegemonic femininity served to complement hegemonic masculinity, albeit as an inferior partner. This hegemonic femininity relies, for its hegemonic status, on the subordination of the 'Other' femininities, in the case of *Scipione*, on the basis of race. Yet the only real winner of these processes of hierarchisation is the hegemonic masculinity of Fascist imperialism.

CONCLUSION

My discussion of the use of Roman antiquity to promote the hegemonic masculinity of Fascist Italian imperialism has centred constructions of femininity and dynamics of racialisation in theorisations of hegemonic masculinity. In this way I hope to have drawn on recent critiques which seek to address the place of femininity and coloniality in discourses of gender. Because such forms of hegemonic masculinity as produced in *Scipione* rely on the oppression of non-hegemonic forms of masculinity, as well as all articulations of femininity, we are forced to conclude that they are necessarily toxic, since they necessitate the oppression of subordinated gendered and racialised identities. If 'toxic masculinity' designates those aspects of masculinity that are harmful to the male self and others, then clearly, masculinity that promotes racism and misogyny must be considered toxic.

This is not to say that masculinity writ large is necessarily harmful. Returning to the Gramscian roots of Connell's hegemonic masculinity, which underpins the concept of toxic masculinity, reminds us that hegemonies are contestable. The task then must be to articulate a counter-hegemonic masculinity which is not built on oppressive hierarchies structured along lines of race, gender, class and sexuality. Thus, while the 'toxic' designation is useful in considering what is most harmful about constructions of masculinity, it risks the occlusion of the structures which promote the view that men are worth more than women, with white skin endowing its wearer with even greater worth. Not paying the necessary attention to the structural causes of manifestations of egregiously toxic masculinity has serious consequences. Thus, we find toxic masculinity extending its hegemony.

NOTES

1. Zuckerberg 2018.
2. See also, for example, Rabinowitz and Richlin 1993; Goff 2005; McCoskey 2012; and Holmes 2012.
3. For a summary, see Roche and Demetriou 2018.
4. Kupers 2005, 714.
5. Connell 1987.

6. Connell 2014; Connell 2014b.
7. Hill Collins 1990; Lugones 2010.
8. Marks 2005, 80.
9. Machiavelli 1996, 289.
10. Cf. Gell. *NA.* 7.8; Val. Max. 6.7.1; Petrarch *Canzone* 360 for depictions of Scipio's less-than-chaste behaviour.
11. Petrarch *Secretum* passages taken from *Petrarch's Secret*, trans. Draper 1911, 114–15; *Trionfi, Triumphus Pudicitie* 169–71; *Africa* 8.265–8.
12. For significant Anglophone studies, see, for example, Visser 1992; Stone 1999; Nelis 2011; Arthurs 2012; Lamers and Reitz-Joosse 2016; and Roche and Demetriou 2018.
13. Wilkins 2005; Marcello 2011.
14. Most notably, see Festa's (1926) essay on Petrarch's *Africa*.
15. Feig-Vishnia 2008, 253.
16. De Grazia 1992, 1–2.
17. Quoted in Macciocchi 1976, 72.
18. Willson 2007, 489.
19. Ben-Ghiat 1996.
20. For possible sexual undertones, see Doniger (2017, 1–24) for a cultural history of associations of jewellery and rings with sex and possession.
21. Feig-Vishnia 2008, 258.
22. Willson 2007, 489.
23. See, for example, Mosse (1985) on the link between nationalism and masculinity.
24. Landy 2000, 58–9; Feig-Vishnia 2008, 257.
25. Caprotti 2007, 243; Stewart-Steinberg 2016.
26. Welch 2016, 192.
27. Quoted in Carabba 1974, 53.
28. Re 2010.
29. On Livy's Sophonisba in the context of Augustan imperialism, see Haley 1989.
30. Lowe 1991, 48.
31. Spivak 1988, 93.
32. Reich 1933, 31–2.
33. See, for example, Sinha (1995) for this discourse in British India.
34. Ben-Ghiat 2012, 21.
35. Feig-Vishnia 2008, 259.
36. Cf. the self-immolation and absences of unassimilable, whether through extreme alterity or unbearable likeness, female Others in imperial literature written by women, Spivak 1985.
37. Kimmel 2013; Nagle 2017, 86–100.
38. See Connell and Messerschmidt (2005, 831, 839–42) for discussions of the problems of reifying masculinities as, by default, white and middle class.
39. However, Pomeroy (2018, 280) suggests that the film does not participate in racist ideology, citing a lack of a tradition of racism in Italian cinema at that time, and discusses race no further.
40. Saha 2017.

41. See, for example, Clarke (1996) for hypersexual black men in Augustan art, Brakke (2001) for patristic literature and Schick (1999, 140–7) for later colonial discourses.
42. Schick 1999, 140–7.
43. Schick 1999, 107.
44. Tufail 2015.
45. Re 2010; Welch 2016, 191–230.
46. Cagnetta 1979, 97–105; Ben-Ghiat 1996; Ben-Ghiat 2000, 209; Aguirre 2015, 372.
47. See, however, Macciocchi (1979), who warns us against seeing Italian women solely as passive victims of Fascism, as this exonerates Fascist women.

CHAPTER 15

Insult to Injury: Senecan Stoicism, Misogyny and the Semantics of 'Special Snowflake'

Michael Goyette

The English adjective 'stoic' suggests an ability to endure pain, injury and/or adversity without the display of physical or emotional suffering.[1] It traces its origin to the disimpassioned Stoic philosophers of ancient Greece and Rome,[2] whose approach to moral philosophy often called for the suppression of bodily and emotional vulnerability. This outlook looms large in the vast and diverse literary corpus of Seneca the Younger, a first-century CE Roman philosopher, dramatist and political adviser and a major source for modern conceptions of Stoic thought. While Seneca's works acknowledge the frailties of the human body and vicissitudes of the human condition, they nevertheless valorise a way of life that subjugates the experience of distress and the expression of emotions, regarding them as manifestations of personal weakness. Evaluated not only in terms of their conceptualisation, but also their uses of rhetoric and their modern analogues, Seneca's works inscribe a viewpoint and a lifestyle that are as machoistic as they are masochistic.

In this chapter, I examine the machismo and the misogyny that are bound up in the rhetoric with which Seneca presents his approach to bodily and emotional vulnerability. Focusing on selections from Seneca's philosophical prose where this sort of rhetoric is especially prevalent, the *Moral Letters to Lucilius* and *On the Firmness of the Wise Man*,[3] I show that Seneca repeatedly correlates physical and emotional stability with both moral virtue and masculinity, including hypermasculine figures from ancient history and literature; these works conversely disparage physical and mental illness, injury and supposed moral lapses as feminine or emasculating. Despite Stoicism's reputation for being one of the most feminist of ancient philosophical systems,[4] I contend that Seneca's rhetoric exposes an attitude towards both the emotions and the body that was and is toxic in its sexist tropes, its misogyny and its repression and shaming of the emotions. Like other chapters in this volume, my analysis illustrates how toxic masculinity can manifest itself as a hegemonic system that morally justifies ideologies and practices which are, in fact, harmful to both the individual and society, while stigmatising mindsets and ways of being that are healthier and more constructive. The label 'toxic' is also particularly apt in this context because it can imply a potential to spread and contaminate, like an infection. Given the profound influence of Stoic philosophy in the ancient world[5] and Seneca's prominent position in the Roman imperial court and the literary canon, his chauvinistic rhetoric and tropes accrue a virulent[6] degree of toxicity. Indeed, vestiges of this toxic Stoic mindset reverberate in the twenty-first century, and in the second part of this chapter I identify parallels in discourse concerning vulnerability and sensitivity from contemporary media, politics and popular culture, particularly the recent rise in derisive uses of the phrase 'special snowflake'. Considering contemporary news media and cultural phenomena alongside scholarship in the area of reception studies, I show how the gendered, regressive rhetoric of Senecan Stoicism still circulates with disturbing familiarity.

TOXIC MASCULINITY IN SENECA'S STOIC PROSE

The metaphysical and ontological tenets of Stoic philosophy offer little assurance to those who seek to achieve the Stoic lifestyle its proponents so insistently advocate. As I have shown elsewhere in my analysis of language, imagery and metaphors of fluidity in Seneca's writings, Seneca and earlier Stoics emphasise the feebleness and inconstancy of both the human body and human existence.[7] This perspective plays a crucial role in Seneca's *Moral Letters* (*Epistulae*, or *Ep.*), a compilation of 124 prose essays that outline Seneca's brand of Stoicism and offer advice, addressed to his friend Lucilius but intended for wider consumption, about how to abide commonplace challenges and relatable forms of adversity – all with the goal of attaining the equanimity of a Stoic sage. Seneca acknowledges the difficulty of such challenges in *Letter 58*, where he tersely defines a human being as a 'substance that is fluid and perishable and exposed to every influence' (*Ep.* 58.24; cf. *Ep.* 58.27). Seneca proceeds to describe the universe itself as subject to incessant forces of flux and impermanence, which only exacerbate the precarious conditions in which human beings strive to care for their bodies and conduct their lives. This worldview hinges upon principles of *sympatheia*,[8] a Stoic doctrine which held that all of the elements of the physical universe, including human beings, exist in a constant and mutual state of tension and interactivity, producing pervasive conditions of flux and instability. Despite his sympathetic physics and his acute awareness of these underlying vulnerabilities, Seneca's perspective is not, as we will see below, psychologically sympathetic to the expression of physical or emotional pathos. Seneca normalises the inherent frailties of the human body and human beings' susceptibility to distress and erratic forces beyond their control, and yet he disdains vulnerability and exhorts his readers to transcend its influence. In this way, Seneca obstinately tests the limits of what is humanly possible, encouraging a *modus vivendi* that modern readers may find paradoxical and potentially toxic in the dissonance between its metaphysical realities and its moral directives.[9]

In spite of these turbulent circumstances, Seneca calls for his readers to maintain their composure and exhibit unflappable endurance, and he drives home his points with language that is laden with connotations of stereotypical masculinity and 'virtue'. These connotations are linked together in *Letter 67*, in which Seneca advises Stoic resolve in response to ill health and other forms of suffering. In one passage, Seneca urges readers to follow his example and not suffer illness in an 'unmanly' way ('si aegrotandum fuerit . . . nihil effeminate faciam', *Ep.* 67.4). In the following sentence, he associates virtue with the endurance of hardships ('virtus, qua perferuntur incommoda', *Ep.* 67.4). The use of *effeminate* in this context exposes a highly gendered formulation of *virtus*, particularly since the word *vir*, a common Latin word that can denote a 'man' or 'male person', is embedded within it and the two words are etymologically related[10] (even though *virtus* is grammatically feminine).[11] Seneca conceives of *virtus* in similar terms in *Letter 13*, in which he argues that fear is a baseless emotion and one that is capable of being suppressed. Shortly after proclaiming that 'virtue adds much to itself through affliction' ('multum enim adicit sibi virtus lacessita', *Ep.* 13.3), he avows that 'we [i.e. Stoics] speak of all those things that elicit cries and groans as trivial and disregardable' ('nos enim dicimus omnia ista, quae gemitus mugistusque exprimunt, levia esse contemnenda', *Ep.* 13.4).[12] The ability and willingness to withstand anguish without exhibiting a physical or emotional response are therefore integral to Seneca's notion of moral virtue.

Seneca draws an even more explicit connection between this conceptualisation of virtue and his ideal form of masculinity in *Letter 98*, in which he enjoins his audience to remain boldly defiant against the uncertainties and travails of human life:

> Licet reverti in viam, licet in integrum restitui: restituamur, ut possimus dolores quocumque modo corpus invaserint perferre et fortunae dicere 'cum viro tibi negotium est: quaere quem vincas'.

> It is possible to return to the path; it is possible to be restored to wholeness; let us be restored, in order that we may be able to endure pain, in whatever way it may assail the body, and say to Fortune: 'since it is difficult to deal with a man, seek someone whom you can conquer!' (*Ep.* 98.14)

While associating wholeness, invulnerability and invincibility with masculinity ('cum viro tibi negotium est'),[13] Seneca insinuates that individuals who are not *viri* would be less capable of enduring pain and thus easier for Fortune to 'conquer'. As I elaborate below, these stereotypical perspectives concerning endurance and vulnerability play a fundamental role in Seneca's construction of femininity, as well as his views regarding enslaved persons and children (whether male or female). In the parlance of modern toxic masculinity, Seneca suggests that one only needs to 'man up' in order to overcome life's troubles and adversities. Seneca further equates stalwart resistance to suffering with virility and virtue in *De Constantia Sapientis* (*On the Firmness of the Wise Man*), a text whose very title esteems obduracy and endurance. This title could, in fact, be translated *On the Firmness of the Wise Person*, as the Latin does not specify 'man', but this is clearly the default assumption with which Seneca operates. In this moral essay, Seneca employs a plethora of militaristic metaphors to lionise the imperturbability of the fully actualised Stoic sage. He underscores, for instance, the importance of maintaining composure in the face of hardship by commanding, in highly gendered rhetoric, his readers never to retreat upon the advance of hostile forces: 'Defend the post assigned to you by nature. Do you ask what this post is? A man's!' ('adsignatum a natura locum tuere. Quaeris quis hic sit locus? Viri!' *De Constantia Sapientis* 19.3) Such rhetoric is striking not only because it indicates that steadfastness is a masculine trait, but because it also asserts that this trait is endowed in *viri* by nature, and not a social or cultural convention.

Other sections of *On the Firmness of the Wise Man* characterise virtue itself as similarly steadfast and impervious:

> libera est, inviolabilis, immota, inconcussa, sic contra casus indurat, ut ne inclinari quidem, nedum vinci possit; adversus adparatus terribilium rectos oculos tenet, nihil ex vultu mutat, sive illi dura sive secunda ostentantur.

> [virtue] is free, inviolable, unmoved, unshaken and it is so hardened against misfortunes that it is not able to be bent, much less broken . . . nothing changes its expression, whether harsh or favourable circumstances are shown to it. (*De Constantia Sapientis* 5.4–5)[14]

Through this personification, Seneca sharpens the connection between his concept of virtue and the rigid characteristics of a Stoic sage. In his estimation, the ideal Stoic will fully embody the characteristics of virtue,[15] transcending the uncertainties and blows of Fortune to achieve a state of solidity, stability and security. Conversely, a person who is still in the process of learning how to be a Stoic 'still sways or moves slightly', as Aron Sjöblad has shown in his analysis of the conceptualisation of wisdom in Seneca's letters.[16] Seneca does not only rely upon metaphorical language alone to impress these points upon his readers; he repeatedly declares that the Stoic *sapiens* is, by definition, safe and impervious to both injury and insult ('tutus est sapiens nec ulla affici aut iniuria aut contumelia potest', *De Constantia Sapientis* 2.3, cf. 2.1; 3.3–5; 6.3–4; 7.3; 10.3; 13.1). At the same time, he implies that male individuals naturally possess a greater potential to exact insults upon those who lack Stoic resolve, going so far as to label the mere thought of being insulted by a woman a sort of 'madness' ('tanta quosdam dementia tenet, ut sibi contumeliam fieri putent posse a muliere', *De Constantia Sapientis* 14.1). While gendering the capacity to withstand insults dispassionately as masculine, he also genders the insults themselves based upon their source, intimating that aspersions cast by a *mulier* are essentially incapable of doing harm.

In addition to outlining virtue in the abstract, Seneca cites several specific figures as concrete models for his readers to emulate, all of whom represent ideals that are hypermasculine and frequently impossible to attain. This includes the Athenian philosopher Socrates, whom Seneca glorifies for his ability to tolerate a life of poverty, to perform military service (a social sphere patently coded as masculine) and to accept death unflinchingly (*Ep.* 104.27–8, cf. 104.22).[17] In a manner typical of Stoic texts,[18] Seneca also sprinkles in misogynistic rhetoric when commending Socrates' ability to endure 'a wife rough in manners and impudent in speech' ('uxorem . . . moribus feram, lingua petulantem', *Ep.* 104.27). In the same letter, Seneca celebrates the Roman statesman Cato the Younger for similar reasons, including his sangfroid disposition, his readiness to face death, and the fact that he lived during an era in which civil warfare (or the threat thereof) was constant (*Ep.* 104.29; cf. 104.22). Cato is also the subject of Seneca's discussion when he first asserts that a true Stoic sage is immune to both injury and insult in *On the Firmness of the Wise Man* (2.1–3). To be sure, one may find much to admire in personal qualities of bravery and resoluteness, but they quickly become toxic when expected in absolute terms or when the discourse becomes gendered, moralising and/or pathologising.

In addition to pointing out the moral resolve of other historical figures closely identified with Stoicism, such as Zeno, Chrysippus and Posidonius (*Ep.* 104.22), Seneca lauds individuals whom modern readers would regard as mythological or literary. He relates, for example, that Stoics regard Ulysses (Odysseus) and Hercules as wise men because of their famed capacity to endure prolonged journeys and labours, their renunciations of pleasure and their abilities to surmount fear (*De Constantia Sapientis* 2.1). These exempla would have rendered the moral ideals of Stoicism more comprehensible to Seneca's contemporary audience, as the mere mention of such names would have summoned up impressions of steadfastness. At the same time, the grandiosity of these characters' missions, the implausibility of their undertakings, and their semi-divine status evinces ideals that are mythic and beyond the grasp of attainment for real mortal men.

Just as Seneca associates constancy and invulnerability with masculinised virtue and a litany of male individuals, in stark binary contrast he aligns

unsteadiness and susceptibility to harm with a prescribed notion of femininity. This polarisation is particularly evident in the opening section of *On the
Firmness of the Wise Man*, where Seneca explicitly characterises Stoics as masculine, and non-Stoics as intrinsically feminine:

> Tantum inter Stoicos, Serene, et ceteros sapientiam professos interesse
> quantum inter feminas et mares non immerito dixerim, cum utraque
> turba ad vitae societatem tantundem conferat, sed altera pars ad obse-
> quendum, altera imperio nata sit. Ceteri sapientes molliter et blande, ut
> fere domestici et familiares medici aegris corporibus, non qua optimum
> et celerrimum est medentur sed qua licet; Stoici virilem ingressi viam non
> ut amoena ineuntibus videatur curae habent, sed ut quam primum nos
> eripiat et in illum editum verticem educat, qui adeo extra omnem teli
> iactum surrexit, ut supra fortunam emineat.

> I might justifiably say, Serenus, that there is as great a difference between
> the Stoics and other schools of philosophy as there is between men and
> women; although each set contributes to the fellowship of life equally,
> one group has been born to obey, and the other to command. Other
> philosophers operate softly and gently, like intimate family physicians
> who treat sick bodies in what is neither the best nor quickest way. Stoics,
> having set upon the masculine way, do not care that it may seem attrac-
> tive to those who proceed upon it, but care rather for how it might deliver
> us as soon as possible and lead us forth to that lofty summit which rises
> so far above the reach of any weapon that it towers above Fortune itself.
> (*De Constantia Sapientis* 1.1)

This passage lays bare the profoundly gendered nature of Seneca's perspective,
which not only colours his views on social roles but also infiltrates his perception
of abstract concepts like softness and gentleness, ways of being and approaches
to philosophy and medicine.[19] Extolling Stoicism as 'the masculine way' (*virilem
. . . viam*), Seneca maligns and feminises philosophers who are not adherents of
Stoicism[20] for their supposed passivity and obedience ('pars ad obsequendum'),
their 'soft' manner of action (*molliter*) and their ineffective medical practices
('ut fere domestici et familiares medici aegris corporibus'), which hints at
a broader predisposition to ineffectuality and suffering.[21] Through this constellation of characteristics, Seneca paints the 'feminine way' as vulnerable and
subject to domination by its more 'masculine' counterparts.[22]

Senecan prose is rife with rhetoric that equates femininity with 'softness',
personal comfort and excessive extravagance. In *Letter 51*, for instance, he
inveighs against the famous baths at the city of Baiae – a recognised symbol
of comfort and leisure in the ancient world – professing that the 'mind must

be hardened' ('indurandus est animus', *Ep.* 51.5) against such indulgences. In keeping with the lines he draws between self-deprivation, hardness and masculinity, Seneca avers that a proper Stoic 'will know that nothing should be done luxuriously, nothing softly' ('sciet nihil delicate, nihil molliter esse faciendum', *Ep.* 51.6). Here, Seneca pejoratively employs two adverbs, *delicate* and *molliter*, that have clear connotations of effeminacy.[23] The element of asyndeton in this phrase further underlines the link it makes between luxuriousness, 'softness' and implied effeminacy.[24] Seneca thus demands that his readers eschew what today we might call 'self-care', denigrating such practices as indolent and feminising.[25] *Letter 51* also maintains that living in an 'overly pleasant environment emasculates the spirit' ('effeminat animos amoenitas nimis', *Ep.* 51.10) and saps people of their vigour – a sentiment which is accentuated by the blatantly gendered verb *effeminat*. Seneca even applies this logic and rhetoric to the world of animals, observing that animals which pasture in 'soft and marshy meadows' ('in molli palustrique pascuo') become weaker and less capable of travelling on roads (*Ep.* 51.10). On the other hand, he presumes that harsh, rugged terrains strengthen the hooves of animals, and in the same way fortify the constitution and character of human beings ('severior loci disciplina firmat ingenium . . .', *Ep.* 51.11).[26] In *Letter 95*, Seneca nostalgically claims that human beings were in fact tougher in the past (here he may have in mind figures like Socrates and Cato), before becoming enervated by new-fangled luxuries and forms of so-called healing (*Ep.* 95.18f.).

Seneca finds the 'softness' of femininity objectionable not merely because it breeds moral lassitude, but also because it makes the physical body more susceptible to injury, infirmity and victimisation.[27] In a passage from *Letter 95* in which he reviles women who live immodestly and pursue pleasure, he debases all women as *pati natae*, or 'born to suffer' (*Ep.* 95.21), which reveals the inverse of his claim that men are naturally firm and unyielding (*De Constantia Sapientis* 19.3). The semantics of *pati* are particularly telling, simultaneously evoking exposedness to suffering (recalling the ineffective, feminised medical treatment in the opening passage of *On the Firmness of the Wise Man*), as well as passivity, submissiveness and penetrability[28] – all of which fit into Seneca's repellent construction of femininity. Craig Williams has discussed the close etymological connection between the verb *pati* and *pathicus, -a, -um*, an adjective used (often derogatorily) in reference to a person who is sexually penetrated (such as the receptive partner in a pederastic relationship) and in that sense 'submissive'.[29] I contend that these connotations are present in Seneca's use of *pati* in this passage, highlighting both the sexual subordination of women, which Seneca regards as natural (alternate possible translations include 'born to be submissive' and 'born to be penetrated'),[30] as well as women's inherent receptivity to the assaults of disease, injury and the blows of Fortune. Conversely, one may detect a link between sexual impenetrability and the Stoic sage's situation of safety and security, metaphorically expressed as being 'above the reach of any weapon' ('extra omnem teli iactum', *De Constantia Sapientis* 1.1).[31] Seneca makes this connection even more vivid when he declares that the wise man cannot be injured by any number of darts hurled towards him, 'since he is able to be penetrated by none' ('cum sit nulli penetrabilis', *De Constantia Sapientis* 3.5). This construction of masculinity aligns with what Jonathan Walters has termed the 'impenetrable penetrator' role that all 'real men' were, according to Walters, expected to adhere to in Roman society.[32]

Women also deviate from Seneca's Stoic ideal because of their supposed inability to control their emotions. He presents femininity as synonymous with emotionality, and as prone to expressions of sorrow[33] and anger.[34] His essay *On Anger*, for instance, personifies anger as a weak, sickly and helpless entity, and in the next breath derides it as 'womanly and childish in nature' ('ita ira muliebre maxime ac puerile vitium est', *De Ira* 1.20.3),[35] viewing anger as antithetical to full-fledged manhood.[36] This is one of several instances in which Seneca links emotionality with the purported attributes of children (e.g. *De Constantia Sapientis* 5.2), including young enslaved persons (e.g. *De Constantia Sapientis* 12.1–3),[37] revealing an intersectional element in his construction of femininity – and consequently his construction of masculinity.[38] This language of slavery also contrasts with Seneca's depiction of *virtus* as 'free' (*libera*) in *De Constantia Sapientis* 5.4–5. Indeed, just as Seneca and other classical authors rarely ascribe *virtus* to women (as noted above), they also rarely ascribe *virtus* to children or enslaved persons.[39]

Cedric Littlewood uncovers a similar interplay of gender, status and power in Seneca's mythological tragedy *Thyestes*, arguing that this play, which ostensibly lacks female characters, feminises all of its characters through their Stoic failings, including the sustainment of bodily harm, surges of emotion and personal subjugation.[40] While an analysis of Seneca's tragedies is beyond the scope of this chapter, their characterisation techniques and interpersonal power dynamics at times also reflect the gendered constructs and rhetoric that permeate Seneca's philosophical essays.[41] Further analyses could discuss similar manifestations of toxic masculinity in Senecan tragedies such as *Phaedra* and *Medea*, which stereotypically portray their eponymous female characters as emotionally volatile,[42] and *Hercules Furens*, in which the seemingly uber-masculine[43] titular character is reduced to tears by an emasculating attack of madness induced by the female goddess Juno.[44]

TOXIC PARALLELS FROM THE MODERN WORLD

Far from being a relic of the past, the ideological and rhetorical legacies of Senecan Stoicism pulsate at present with a disconcerting and escalating frequency. In August 2018, the American Psychological Association (APA) released, for the first time in its 127-year history, 'Guidelines for Psychological Practice with Boys and Men', which emphasise the continuing importance of helping boys and men 'understand how components of traditional masculinity such as emotional stoicism,[45] homophobia, not showing vulnerability, self-reliance and competitiveness' can negatively impact their interpersonal relationships and their own mental health.[46] This constellation of traits overlaps with the goals and preoccupations of Stoicism outlined in Senecan prose. The APA Guidelines also underscore how 'male stoicism' tends to stigmatise the seeking of care for mental health in the first place,[47] causing many cases of conditions such as depression to remain undiagnosed 'in part because internalising disorders do[es] not conform to traditional gender role stereotypes about men's emotionality'.[48] Whereas Seneca construes the expression of emotions and vulnerability as a sort of feminising illness, the APA in turn pathologises attitudes and behaviours identifiable with Stoicism and traditional masculinity while attesting to their prevalence in contemporary society.

One specific piece of rhetoric that distils the emotional detachment, insensitivity and chauvinism of Seneca's rhetoric into a single phrase is the now-widespread term 'special snowflake' (or simply 'snowflake'). One of the earliest and most influential uses of the term (with its current semantics and connotations)[49] occurs in the popular film *Fight Club*[50] (1999; based upon Chuck Palahniuk's 1996 novel of the same name), in which a nihilistic, proto-fascist group of men form an underground society centred around bare-knuckle pugilism along with other acts of violence and vandalism. The group inculcates in its members a brutal standard of physical and emotional imperviousness, as reflected in its mantra: 'You are not special. You are not a beautiful or unique snowflake. You are the same decaying organic matter as everything else. We are all part of the same compost pile.' Delivered in a context of hypermasculine conformity and aggression, this use of 'snowflake' pejoratively connotes physical vulnerability, emotional fragility and individuality (or deviation from normative societal expectations) – nuances that are reminiscent of Seneca's uses of *delicate* and *molliter*. Those who do not 'man up' and accept a fight when challenged by other group members are shunned and ridiculed, sometimes with misogynistic rhetoric.[51] At one point in the film, the character Tyler Durden insults the Narrator (also known as Jack)[52] for the mild-mannered personality he exhibits prior to his indoctrination into the fight club: 'A generation of men raised by women. Look what it's done to you.'[53] Durden's misogynistic, essentialising rhetoric calls to mind the use of the term 'Snowflake Generation' to express generic disapproval for young people (particularly millennials and members of Gen-Z) whose behaviour purportedly differs from that of previous generations.[54]

Recent years (especially the latter half of the 2010s) have seen a sharp rise in the use of 'special snowflake' as a weaponised insult in the United States and the United Kingdom, particularly by partisans of the far right[55] in their invective against people who do not subscribe to their worldview, one which is profoundly shaped by male stoicism. Jennifer M. Goldstein has traced the evolution of 'special snowflake' from a moderately insulting term used to ridicule people for alleged delusions of uniqueness to a rather vicious slur with broader and more politicised uses, to the point that 'it's hard to think of [an insult] that so clearly conveys so many [supposed] flaws at once: Fragility and self-importance, weakness and self-delusion'.[56] Such 'flaws' coincide with the catalogue of short-comings Seneca ascribes to non-Stoics at the beginning of *On the Firmness of the Wise Man*, with the possible exception of 'self-importance' (although there is a possible hint of that reproach in Seneca's condemnation of luxury and self-pampering in *Letter 51* and *De Constantia Sapientis* 10.3). Dana Schwartz's analysis of the 'snowflake' rebuke discerns a similarly broad semantic range: '[it] is an all-purpose dismissal, as easily applied to Meryl Streep speaking about empathy at the Golden Globes as it is to protesters marching against an unconstitutional Muslim ban. . . . Snowflake is an ad hominem attack. . . . You're a wuss, and so your argument is invalid.'[57] In addition to tracing the breadth of the term, Schwartz hits upon two other fundamental, interrelated aspects of its use. First, she recognises its inherently bullying nature – a characteristic it shares with male stoicism as described by the APA,[58] and with Seneca's belittling rhetoric against those who do not fulfil his Stoic standards. Schwartz also detects a recursive element in the bullying force of the term, as it does a twofold harm first by taunting its target for their vulnerability, and then by mocking any expression of offence as evidence of said vulnerability.[59] This quality resembles Seneca's penchant for insulting people who are susceptible to insult or injury, rendering any complaint or objection to his arguments as only proof of his point. In both cases, the compounding nature of the insult and potential for retraumatisation are akin to victim-blaming, a pernicious practice which has been used in attempts to justify innumerable forms of social injustice in both Greco-Roman antiquity and the modern world.

'Special snowflake' also wields gendered elements of abuse that recall the misogynistic rhetoric Seneca directs at those who are not fully actualised Stoics. Just as Seneca disparages non-Stoics by suggesting they follow 'the feminine way', champions of the 'snowflake' insult often use it to demean individuals who do not adhere to traditional masculinity or traditional gender roles, including their responses to insults and abusive language. As Seneca claims in *On the Firmness of the Wise Man*:

> Nimio otio ingenia natura infirma et muliebria et inopia verae iniuriae lascivientia his commoventur, quorum pars maior constat vitio interpre-tantis. Itaque nec prudentiae quicquam in se esse nec fiduciae ostendit qui contumelia afficitur. . .

Due to excessive leisure, dispositions which are naturally weak and effeminate, and self-indulgent in the absence of a real injury, are disturbed by these [insults], the greater part of which lies in the person who so interprets the 'fault'. Therefore any man who is bothered by an insult shows that he is lacking in sense and not confident in himself... (*De Constantia Sapientis* 10.3)

'Snowflake' boils all of this rhetoric down into a single term of abuse, implicitly alleging that the very possibility of feeling insulted stems from a combination of thin-skinned insecurity, weak-willed cowardice and excessive free time (with an implied incapacity for 'real work') which is filled by conjuring up imagined offences, delusions of self-importance and irrationality – all of which it codes as effeminate.[60] The layers of meaning in this multi-pronged insult lay bare an entire worldview. In the same way that Seneca applies his gendered rhetoric to the philosophical categories of Stoics and non-Stoics, 'snowflake' maps into gendered political groupings: as Schwartz succinctly puts it, the term's 'purpose is dismissing liberalism as something effeminate, and also infantile'.[61] These specific, intersectional facets of the term are analogous to Seneca's representation of non-Stoics as simultaneously womanly and childlike. Conversely, there is the implication that those who are *not* snowflakes, especially those who brandish the term as an insult, epitomise emotional stability[62] and masculinity.

With its capacity for unfiltered communication, the world of the internet has enabled rampant (and often anonymous) flinging of insults, trolling and online shaming, often directed at vulnerable members of society. As Donna Zuckerberg has discussed, these abuses have been common in far-right online communities, which are also quick to embrace aspects of Stoic philosophy, including its outlooks on vulnerability, emotionality and masculinity.[63] Indeed, these communities are predominantly male (and hence part of the 'manosphere'),[64] patriarchal in sociopolitical orientation, and keen to use the insult 'snowflake' as well as other emasculating epithets like 'beta'[65] and 'cuck'.[66] As such, the gendered rhetoric of Stoicism resonates with their ideologies and discursive habits, including their tendency to dismiss objections to their invective as further indications of effeminate hypersensitivity and effete 'political correctness'.[67] The semantics of the Latin adjective *mollis* are similar, with possible translations that include 'effeminate' as well as 'easily influenced', 'impressionable', 'susceptible' and 'sensitive'.[68] While the use of 'snowflake' often aims to silence and exacerbate the harm it does to opposing voices,[69] the manosphere idealises these harsh approaches to dialogue as a return to a more direct, hardened virile past,[70] not unlike the bygone era of masculine grit that Seneca pines for in *Letter 95*. Furthermore, the manosphere abounds with assertions of male entitlement to social and sexual dominance, including threats of rape and defences of rape culture,[71] and these abhorrent affronts parallel Seneca's multilayered degradation of women, as encapsulated in the polysemic reproach *pati natae* (*Ep.* 95.21).

During the COVID pandemic, the quintessentially Stoic fixation with emotional and bodily invulnerability has manifested itself in a literally toxic aversion to mask-wearing and other public health measures, particularly among men in the United States.[72] Despite overwhelming scientific evidence that mask-wearing is effective at limiting the transmission of COVID and a major positive for public health,[73] there has been resistance to this practice even during the most severe phases of the pandemic – a trend (sometimes referred to as 'toxic mask-ulinity') which several studies and numerous editorials[74] have attributed to identification with norms of masculinity such as narrow and misplaced ideas of 'toughness'.[75] As Anand Giridharadas observes, 'There has been a very dominant strain of men who clearly feel that wearing a mask would so expose their vulnerability that they would rather risk death from the virus.'[76] This macho insistence upon maintaining a veneer of invincibility and refusing to change one's habits even in the face of a deadly, highly contagious pandemic recalls Seneca's gendered personification of Stoic virtue as a steadfast, impenetrable figure who never 'changes its expression, whether harsh or favourable circumstances are shown to it' (*De Constantia Sapientis* 5.4–5). Moreover, Seneca's conception of virtue as free, inviolable and autonomous tellingly coincides with anti-maskers' rallying cries of 'freedom' and their rhetorical refusals to let the virus 'dominate' them[77] or change their way of life. In contrast, they tend to berate those who submit to public health advisories as cowardly, submissive and effeminate – in their discourse, 'snowflakes'. Emasculating and pathologising recognitions of shared vulnerability and bona fide efforts to curb the spread of disease, such rhetoric and behaviour have proven particularly toxic in their disregard for the common good and their exacerbation of political divisiveness.

Senecan prose displays a profound preoccupation with the fragility of the human body and human existence, but at the same time is contemptuous of those who cannot stoically eclipse the exigencies of the human condition. These unempathetic and paradoxical precepts, along with the misogynistic rhetoric Seneca uses to impart them, lie at the crux of Seneca's type of toxic masculinity. He reviles 'the feminine way' as a path of feebleness, emotionality, fickleness, indulgence, moral degeneracy, ineptitude, subordination, and sickness, while idealising the antithesis of these qualities as the pinnacle of masculinity, and in the process reveals a mode of thinking not far removed from the worldview represented by 'snowflake' invective. Like its Stoic antecedents, 'snowflake' inscribes a binary and inegalitarian approach in its constructions of gender, which it insidiously applies to other perceived patterns in social behaviour and aspects of nature, disdaining anything that evinces vulnerability. At their core, both manners of rhetoric aspire to 'make men great again' while unempathetically belittling those who do not adhere to traditional masculinity or traditional gender roles. In an era in which an entire age group has been labelled the 'Snowflake Generation' as a slight to its reputation for emotional sensitivity, and in which entire segments of the population have been insulted as 'unmanly' for proactively protecting the health of themselves and those around them, Seneca's rhetoric is resoundingly familiar, and the ability to recognise, parse and respond to it takes on a heightened significance and urgency.

NOTES

1. I thank the editors of this volume, Aven McMaster and Melanie Racette-Campbell, for their helpful and expeditious comments on this chapter.
2. The ancient Greek terms 'stoic' and 'stoicism' hearken back to the *Stoa Poikile* (ἡ ποικίλη στοά), or 'Painted Porch', a colonnade in the Athenian *agora* where Zeno, the founder of Stoicism, held philosophical discussions with his followers.
3. I refer to Reynolds' 1965 textual edition for Seneca's *Moral Letters*, and Reynolds 1977 for *On the Firmness of the Wise Man* and *On Anger*. All translations are my own.
4. On this reputation (including critiques of it), see Manning 1973, esp. 170, 172–4; Hill 2001, 26ff; Zuckerberg 2018, esp. 48, 70; 206 n. 49, 207 n. 63.
5. Sellars 2014, 2; see also 135–58 on the legacy of the Stoics.
6. Or '*vir*-ulent', if you like.
7. Goyette 2021, esp. 272–4.
8. For an ancient account of *sympatheia* in the Stoic system of thought, see Diogenes Laertius' *Life of Zeno*, esp. 7.140. For modern scholarship on *sympatheia* in Seneca and the Stoic tradition, see Pratt 1948, 46–8 and Rosenmeyer 1989, 106–9 et passim.
9. On the tension between the physics and ethics of Seneca's writings, see Scott 1999, esp. 63–8, and Edwards 1999, 255.
10. Ernout and Meillet 1932, s.v. *vir*; Glare 2012, s.v. *vir*. It is therefore unsurprising that *virtus* is rarely attributed to women in Latin literature (despite the Romans' personification of *Virtus* as a female deity). Zuckerberg (2018, 74) similarly observes that 'virtue itself is always coded in ancient texts as male'.
11. On the complex and frequently arbitrary relationship between grammatical gender and sexual physiology in the Latin language, see Corbeill 2015.
12. Cf. *Ep. 78*, where Seneca uses similarly gendered and moralising rhetoric concerning the suppression of pain and suffering: 'ideo vir magnus ac prudens animum diducit a corpore et multum cum meliore ac divina parte versatur, cum hac querula et fragili quantum necesse est' (*Ep.* 78.10).
13. Martorana's chapter in this volume detects a similar presentation of masculinity in Book 3 of Ovid's *Heroides*.
14. Cicero offers a comparable depiction of *virtus* in *Philippicae* 4.13.
15. Seneca personifies and characterises *philosophia* in similar terms in *Ep. 53* (esp. sec. 12).
16. Sjöblad 2015, 37; cf. *Ep.* 35.4.

17. On the Stoic valorisation of Socratic ethics and attitudes towards the emotions, see also Sherman 2005, 34, 134.

18. Zuckerberg 2018, esp. 48, 74–5.

19. Additionally, Graver (1998) observes in Seneca's *Letters* a tendency to apply gendered labels (e.g. *virilis contextus* or *compositio virilis*) to styles of writing and manners of rhetoric.

20. Berno (2018, 77) posits that Seneca has Epicurean philosophers in mind here.

21. On Seneca's construction of femininity in this passage, see also Williams 2010, 264–5.

22. Cf. my above discussion of the masculine-coded path that Seneca describes in *Ep.* 98.14. See also Edwards 1999, 262.

23. On the semantics of *molliter* and related nouns and adjectives, Williams (2013, 247) describes *mollis* and *vir* to be 'xenonyms', or words that result in a semantic clash and that are unlikely to occur in conjunction with each other.

24. Cf. Seneca's feminisation and moral denunciation of leisure in *De Constantia Sapientis* 10.3.

25. Cf. *Ep.* 108.16, where Seneca again casts bathing as a practice that is feminising and counterproductive.

26. Similar rhetoric occurs in *Ep.* 95.18. Comparable rhetoric is also evident in the Hippocratic medical treatise *On Airs, Waters, Places* (see esp. secs 19–22) in which the author argues that the ruggedness or smoothness of an environment determines the physical constitution and psychological characteristics of its inhabitants. This view has marked implications for matters of gender and ethnicity, as the author imagines that a smooth, gentle environment, such as that of the Scythians, can cause men to lose their virility and thence conduct their lives as women.

27. These perspectives are also characteristic of Greco-Roman medical tradition, which often represents female bodies as moist, unfirm and unstable in comparison with male bodies (King 2002, 28ff.).

28. Glare 2012, s.v. *pati*.

29. Williams 2010, 196; Williams 2018, 465–6.

30. Walters 1997, 32–3.

31. Williams 2010, 414 n. 42.

32. Walters 1997, 30.

33. E.g. *Consolatio ad Helviam* 16.1. On Seneca's tendency to associate femininity with 'excessive' grief, see Sherman 2005, 134–6; Wilcox 2006.

34. Berno 2018, 160.

35. Seneca also frequently connects the experience of anger with animality (Sjöblad 2015, 20).

36. Seneca similarly links blushing and its attendant emotions with youthfulness, as well as vulnerability, violation and disembodiment (*Ep.* 11.2). On these connections, and similarities between anger and blushing in the Roman imagination, see Barton 1999, esp. 214–16; 221–3.

37. Cf. Manning 1973, 171. Ager's chapter in this volume discusses comparable applications of rhetoric that associate women with servility in ancient magical spells.
38. As Gunderson (2000, 7) observes, the word *vir* can mean 'husband' or 'soldier' and thus denotes not only a male person, but a 'real man, a manly man' who (in contrast with women and children) occupies a position of authority, responsibility, enfranchisement and often military experience.
39. McDonnell 2006, 160.
40. Littlewood 1997, esp. 69–86.
41. Littlewood 1997, esp. 72.
42. Robin 1993, esp. 108, 112–13, 117.
43. Cf. *De Constantia Sapientis* 2.1 (discussed above).
44. While the relationship between these Senecan genres is complex, over the last few decades scholars have given increased attention to how Seneca's philosophical prose can provide insight into Senecan tragedy, and vice versa (e.g. Nussbaum 1994, esp. 448–53; Chaumartin 2014, esp. 657–60, 668–9; Fischer 2014, 745–68).
45. Cf. Lilly 2016, 26, 28, 117, 133.
46. American Psychological Association 2018, 11; cf. Brooks 1998 and Smiler 2016.
47. American Psychological Association 2018, 18; cf. Kupers 2005, esp. 720–2.
48. American Psychological Association 2018, 3; cf. Fitzsimmons 2019.
49. Merriam-Webster (n.d.) notes other historical uses of 'snowflake' as an insult with semantics and connotations that do not overlap as closely with recent usage: in the 1970s, 'snowflake' could be used to insult either a 'white man or a black man who was seen as acting white', and in the 1860s it was used to scorn those who opposed the abolition of slavery (implying that they valued white people over black people); cf. Goldstein 2017 and Miller 2017.
50. Miller 2017; Schwartz 2017.
51. The fight club's gender dynamics resemble those which are typical of all-male prisons, in which toxic masculinity frequently proliferates, discouraging the expression of any kind of vulnerability (Kupers 2005, esp. 718, 720).
52. As the film later reveals, Tyler Durden and the Narrator are in fact one and the same person; the character has dissociative identity disorder and thus his two, often opposing personalities could be read as a struggle between the poles of male stoicism and a way of being that is less aggressive and more vulnerable.
53. A more comprehensive analysis of the gender politics of the film is beyond the scope of this chapter, but the film's contemptuous and dehumanising treatment of women should be noted. One scene relates how members of the fight club surreptitiously collect human fat dumped outside of a liposuction unit, use it as tallow in the making of soap and then '[sell] rich women their own fat back to them'. In such ways, these characters participate in the literal disembodiment and commodification of the female body. Furthermore, the only prominent female character in the film, Marla, is portrayed as mentally unstable and is highly sexualised.

54. Nicholson 2016; Collins Dictionaries (2016) named 'Snowflake Generation' one of its ten words of the year in 2016. In East Asia, a parallel generational term, 'Strawberry Generation', has been used to insult people who express vulnerabilities (and thus 'bruise easily') for more than a decade (*New York Times* 2008).
55. Miller (2017) observes that 'snowflake' is 'one of the alt-right's favorite insults'.
56. Goldstein 2017.
57. Schwartz 2017. Pushing back against a social media bully who attempted to insult him as a 'snowflake' on Twitter, the actor John Cleese encapsulated the term more caustically: 'Yes I've heard this word. I think sociopaths use it in an attempt to discredit the notion of empathy.' Cf. Adejobi 2018.
58. The APA's Guidelines (2018, esp. 11 and 14) draw attention to the connections between male stoicism and bullying (including cyberbullying), homophobia and sexual harassment; cf. Fitzsimmons 2019.
59. As Yagoda (2016) puts it: 'Bullies have long recognized "crybaby" as a very effective, perhaps unmatched, insult, mainly because any defense can be framed as more crying! The same is true of *buttercup* and *snowflake*.' Or in the words of Nicholson (2016): 'if you, the snowflake, are offended, you are simply proving that you're a snowflake. It's a handcuff of an insult and nobody has the key.'
60. Goldstein (2017) parses these nuances in her discussion of an offensive definition of 'snowflake' that appeared on the popular website urbandictionary.com in June 2016 (and has since been altered or removed): 'An entitled millennial SJW-tard who runs to her "safe space" to play with stress toys and coloring books when she gets "triggered" by various innocuous "microaggressions" [*sic*].'
61. Schwartz 2017.
62. As Zuckerberg (2018, 83) perceptively states: 'To the Red Pill Stoic . . . impassioned dedication to social progress means that one has not yet achieved emotional equilibrium.'
63. Zuckerberg (2018, esp. 46–7, 70, 87) notes that contemporary interest in Stoicism is burgeoning among broad cross-sections of society, but emphasises that interest is particularly on the rise within far-right online groups; see also Lilly 2016, 59–60.
64. A now widespread term formed as a sardonic play on the word 'blogosphere'.
65. A term for a man who is perceived as 'weak and emasculated' (Roy 2016).
66. Derived from 'cuckold', and used as a term of rebuke for an individual (especially a Republican politician) who is perceived to be veering too close to liberal ideals, and thus 'emasculated' (Roy 2016), or for a 'weak man whose girlfriend cheats on him, usually with black men' (Ging 2019, 12).
67. Hess (2017) perceives an irony in these dismissals: 'The truth is that people who use "snowflake" as an insult tend to seem pretty aggrieved themselves – hypersensitive to dissent or complication and nursing a healthy appetite for feeling oppressed.'
68. Glare 2012, s.v. *mollis*.
69. Cf. Ging 2017, 9.
70. Lilly 2016, 86.

71. Ging 2017, 6, 8, 9, 10, 17 n. 2.
72. According to a Gallup survey on the demographics of mask-wearing in the United States which was published on 13 July 2020, 54 per cent of women reported that they always wore masks outside of their homes, compared with only 34 per cent of men (Brenan 2020).
73. Palmer and Peterson 2020.
74. E.g. Abad-Santos 2020; Gupta 2020; Pauly 2020.
75. Palmer and Peterson 2020.
76. Giridharadas 2020.
77. Following his own bout of COVID, Donald Trump encouraged his supporters by saying 'don't let it dominate your lives' (Gupta 2020).

CHAPTER 16

Toxic Manhood Acts and the 'Nice Guy' Phenomenon in Ovid

Melissa Marturano

Nearly all of Ovid's books of poetry highlight narrators and characters who, to ensure dominance, commit toxic and regressive acts of manhood, including their support of, and participation in, sexualised and intimate partner violence. Men take part in nearly a hundred acts of sexualised abuse in the poet's corpus.[1] The violence Ovid portrays is not only representative of his own Roman misogynistic and patriarchal context, but also resembles the pervasive levels of male violence against women we experience in North America and other parts of the Global North today (within which I am limiting my analysis). For this reason, many feminist Ovidian scholars have made connections between his work and our own misogynistic present.[2] As of yet, however, no scholarly work has explored at length the role of the 'nice guy' phenomenon in Ovid and its connections to male violence and the poet's larger project.

NICE GUYS, VIOLENCE AND MANHOOD ACTS

The term 'nice guy', first used in this sense by online feminists such as 'Heartless Bitch International' (2002), can refer to men who style themselves as chivalrous, generous and even compassionate towards the women they pursue sexually. Some adopt the pretence of niceness in the explicit hope of gaining sexual success, while others sincerely believe themselves to be 'nice'. In both cases, they view their own niceness as part of a larger heterosexual transaction, in which their purportedly 'less threatening masculinity' – to use the words of Michele White (2019) – merits sexual rewards from grateful women.[3] Currently, there are few academic pieces on the phenomenon, but recent scholarship has been catching up.[4] This is true even in our field, as Donna Zuckerberg (2018) has analysed the role of 'beta males' and 'incels', often equivalent to and conflated with 'nice guys', in the 'manosphere', a constellation of misogynist men online.[5] My analysis of the phenomenon is influenced by the popular definition enshrined, fostered and criticised on the internet and in the media and by the scholarship of White (2019) on 'nice guys' and that of Manne (2018), Schrock

(2009), Schwalbe (2009; 2014) and Kimmel (2013), who all investigate the connections among men, misogyny, entitlement and restorative violence when one's status as a man is threatened. My understanding will, moreover, be a feminist one: there is a difference between how feminists perceive these men and how they perceive themselves. Feminists see these men as entitled and misogynistic, but nice guys see themselves as aggrieved and fooled by lying women who claim they want men like them but instead choose other men or men who do not exhibit such behaviour. In the current chapter, I will show that this phenomenon has persisted for millennia, and that our modern perspectives on it can illuminate its earlier representations in Roman literature. I hope to initiate more scholarship on the ways ancient men – or at least the ones who are depicted in Ovidian literature – perceive themselves and their violence in relation to women. By studying the poet in this way, we are able to better and more critically reflect on a similar patriarchal reality that still affects the lives of women today: men dominating women violently, often in sheep's clothing. The connections among Ovid's poetry, the past and our present can seem distant, but as Zuckerberg (2018) has shown, many men today have already made these connections as they read, cite and turn to the poet to make sense of themselves and to justify their misogynistic behaviours and violence.[6]

A feminist understanding of nice guys recognises that the seeming chivalry of these men endures only as long as they receive sex in return for their niceness, perpetuating the notion that women owe their attention, bodies and devotion to men, which Manne (2018) has articulated as the cornerstone of misogyny and its surveillance and maintenance. Women, under her definition of misogyny, must be boundlessly giving of their bodies, labour and support. If 'they do not give enough of themselves', they can be punished brutally with violence (Manne 2018, 23). Manne frames misogyny not as the dehumanisation of women (the more common approach in feminist scholarship and sociology), but as the feeling of entitlement over the humanity of women. Accordingly, gender socialisation can be understood as the process by which men under patriarchal mandates come to expect access to women's bodies, and by which women are compelled to believe that sex is compulsorily owed to men (Millbank 2012).

The entitlement inherent in nice guy ideology can have dangerous consequences, as many of these men have adopted violence against women when denied the sexual gratification they feel they deserve.[7] Nice guys are supported by socialisation patterns that sanction the use of violence in the aftermath of rejection, as a means to resolve conflict or to restore their social position as men (Keith 2017, 445–92). This pattern was infamously enacted by Elliot Rodger, who murdered several women and (perceived) male rivals in a mass shooting in 2014, stating that he was goaded into violence by the women who rejected him sexually despite his kindness. Rodger in many ways represents the quintessential nice guy, a self-proclaimed 'perfect [and] supreme gentleman' who responds violently when his niceness fails to result in sex.[8] Often nice guys only fantasise about responding with violence if their emotional manipulation of women does not succeed, but other times this violence becomes all too real.[9]

This use of violence has significant implications for the production of men and their gender. Men, in order to prove that they are men and to cement their gender, engage in what sociologists Schrock and Schwalbe define as 'manhood acts', or actions and cultural practices 'aimed at claiming privilege, eliciting deference, and resisting exploitation, which are inherently about upholding patriarchy and reproducing gender inequality' (2009, 281; 287). Such actions allow men to define themselves as men and to attach themselves to dominance and the gendered position that provides them with power (Schwalbe 2014, 55–9). Many of these manhood acts are violent and valorise the notion that women owe men sex.[10] These acts are often perpetrated when someone feels their status as a man has been jeopardised, thereby becoming 'restorative' and 'retaliatory' in nature (Kimmel 2013, 77; Kimmel and Wade 2018). When nice guys, despite their calculated compassion, have been denied access to women's bodies (an entitlement that fundamentally defines them as men, or superior to women), they resort to violence to regain their imperilled positions as men and to retaliate against those who threatened it (Kimmel 2013; Schwalbe 2014; Myketiak 2016; Manne 2018). They may even conclude that their niceness, a feminine quality, has effeminised them, necessitating even more compensatory violence.

The restorative violence of nice guys and that of the ancient literary analogues we will see can be understood as expressions of 'toxic masculinity', a nexus of culturally and socially constructed traits which harm others and society more generally, which can include feeling wounded and violent sexual entitlement. But it is perhaps evident that I have so far avoided that term to frame my exploration of nice guys. This choice is intentional. I am sympathetic to Schwalbe (2014) and his work on the problematic relationship with 'masculinity' in gender studies and sociology to examine and elucidate the (often violent) actions of men. He argues that masculinity has lost power as a concept for grappling with male power as it foregrounds a multiplicity of performances rather than the violent actions and practices that unite and make men collectively and institutionally. It has become a non-threatening abstraction, detached from the social position of men and divorced from material acts of violence against women (and other men). Schwalbe stresses instead that we should study what men (or the representations of them) actually do to produce, maintain and perpetuate dominance over women and claim the gendered position that bestows that power. Emphasising masculinity rather than the acts of men risks exonerating them of their responsibility for violence, when their gendered position and identity is intimately connected to exploitation, power and violence. The study of masculinity can make invisible what men enact materially, particularly against women, in order to preserve their power and separates violence from male agents. Furthermore, as feminists, it may be better to challenge the distinction between toxic masculinity and whatever remains, and to instead ask if claiming one's social position as a man (ancient or modern) is inherently toxic; even if men do not commit violence themselves, they benefit from its continued potency.[11] For my purposes, focusing on men and their actions – instead of masculinity – adds a materiality to a discussion that must be material since we are addressing violence primarily against women. Like Schwalbe, I do not invoke masculinity as a cause for violence, but instead what men do.[12] The behaviour of violent nice guys is 'toxic', but I urge all of us to turn back to men's actions, rather than the folk concept of masculinity, in order to more fully understand the violent entitlement of men such as Elliot Rodger and the representations of Roman and mythological men we see in Ovid.[13]

THE *PRAECEPTOR AMORIS* AND NICE GUY IDEOLOGY

The same trajectory of emotional manipulation and entitlement escalating to sexual violence via manhood acts that we see from modern nice guys appears in Ovid's *Ars Amatoria* (*Ars*), *Heroides* (*Her.*) and *Metamorphoses* (*Met.*). I argue that Ovid introduces prototypes of this phenomenon and its entitlement and violence. By viewing these accounts through modern perspectives on the nice guy, we can better inform our (feminist) readings of Ovid's works, while exploring earlier stages of this particular strain of misogyny. Toward this end, I first consider the *Ars*, a parodic work of didactic poetry purporting to teach the 'art of love' first to men and then to women, which provides through example the ideology for Roman 'nice guys'. The narrator, the self-styled *praeceptor amoris* ('instructor of love'), teaches his male readers how to more systematically, effectively and cynically take on the characteristics and practices of the male protagonists in Augustan-era elegiac poetry as he likewise lays bare to us the endemic violence against women found in this genre. But his portrayal of an achievable *eros* (love) for men is deeply troubling. *Ars* Books 1 and 2 – and this must be said bluntly – are guides for teaching his male students to abuse, brutalise and rape women, as argued by Richlin (2014) and Desmond (2006). In service to his stated goal of helping men start relationships with women and then sustain them, the *praeceptor* instructs his students how to have sex with women at any cost by exploiting their entitlements and systematic power over women in his patriarchal Roman context. We learn in the *Ars* that the narrator trains his students in an 'erotics of domination' (to quote the words of Greene 1998) and that his strategies for *eros* are steeped in violent misogyny, including what I call 'proto–nice guy ideology' and its attendant and violent manhood acts, as his narrator and his teachings advocate for economically, emotionally and physically abusing women.

The *Ars* encourages men to simulate the persona of a nice guy who is devoted to the woman he is pursuing, but it is evident that the narrator views this niceness as a pretence, as part of a strategic ploy, one that barely masks the violent foundations of heteroerotic sex in Rome. The niceness is a means to an end, but if these emotionally manipulative tactics – such as flattering women (1.437–58; 2.295–314), buying them gifts (1.405–36; 2.261–85), or crying and begging for their attention (1.437–42, 455–504, 659–63) – do not succeed in obtaining a sexual reward, Ovid's *praeceptor* urges his male students in 1.664–704 to respond with sexualised violence against women. These tactics of manipulation can be found in every work of the Augustan elegiac genre, especially in their use of the *servitium amoris* ('slavery of love') trope, but all elegiac narrators ultimately find, as the *praeceptor* advises here, that violence is the solution.[14] Sexual abuse becomes a method for men to manifest their entitlement and positions as men, and in addition, becomes an acceptable and integral part of what they characterise as 'seduction'. The narrator even reminds his students that men do not deserve any sex unless they take everything they want and perpetrate violence ('Oscula qui sumpsit, si non et cetera sumet,/haec quoque, quae data sunt, perdere dignus erit', 'If the one who has taken kisses will not take the rest, these things which were given as well, he will deserve to lose,' 669–70).[15]

In the context of this advice, Ovid cites the myth of Achilles and Deidamia (1.681–706), in which the hero, dressed in women's clothes on the island of Skyros to hide from Trojan War conscription, rapes the heroine. Ovid cites heroes to demonstrate that *eros* is a game to be won (Zuckerberg 2018, 100), but he also cites this myth to show the necessity of violence in establishing one's standing as a man over a woman. Since the male students of the *praeceptor amoris* have temporarily been effeminised by the submissive practices he proposed earlier to gain women's favour, they should later assert they are still men through violence. The narrator writes of the myth that: 'Haec illum stupro comperit esse virum' ('This woman [Deidamia] discovers that he is a man through *stuprum*' 1.698). What is more, Ovid's use of this myth illustrates the belief that women – as part of the game of *eros* – desire violence and rape (Boyd 2012, 533). Men should exert force to take what they have earned without fear, for that very violence is in fact sexually arousing to women, even if social mores around sex and women compel them to pretend otherwise ('Viribus illa quidem victa est, ita credere oportet:/Sed voluit vinci viribus illa tamen', 'it is thus necessary to think that she was truly won by force, but nevertheless she wanted to be won by force' 1.699–700). In the end, Ovid's retelling affirms that Deidamia enjoyed Achilles and his violent act of manhood against her. According to the narrator, women might call normative, heterosexual relations *vis* (violence), when it is not *vis* in reality.[16] He insists here that women like Deidamia only feign resistance to male aggression as a way to maintain the appearance of their chastity and their feminine, societal reputations, thereby encouraging men to avail themselves of this excuse to realise their sexual desires.

The violent principles of *eros* established in the *Ars* suffuse other parts of Ovid's corpus, with this didactic poem informing the tools and praxis for later characters' violent efforts. The sexual abusers who emerge in the poet's work repeatedly implement this amatory pedagogy. In particular, as the *praeceptor* advises, they attempt to flatter and emotionally manipulate their victims in order to obtain sex, resorting to violence when these plans fail, thereby displaying proto–nice guy ideology predicated on both psychological manipulation and violence. For example, in the first story of sexual abuse in the *Metamorphoses*, the god Apollo attempts to exhibit his niceness by flattering and feigning concern for the nymph Daphne but moves on to violence after his use of kindness does not succeed (1.504–24). Zissos and Gildenhard (2007, 25–6) find that later in the work, Tereus, the king of Thrace, heeds the instructions of the *praeceptor* before his rape of princess Philomela, in his application of contrived weeping to bring his violent and erotic goals to fruition (*Met.* 6.471; *Ars* 1.659–63).[17] The use of these methods of seduction and then the escalation to violence is, in fact, a well-established pattern in Ovid's works.[18] In my mind, this is more than just the poet's pervasive interest in intratextuality and allusion to other pieces of his corpus,[19] it is rather the propagation of a prolonged violent and misogynistic poetic discourse. Below I have chosen two examples of male characters who make use of aspects of proto–nice guy ideology, and who resort to violence when their performance of niceness does not convince or compel women to grant them their sexual desires. These examples illustrate the parallels between contemporary nice guy ideology and how Ovid represents startlingly similar male behaviours and actions in his works.

ACONTIUS AND CYDIPPE

In the second iteration of the *Heroides* in which heroes and heroines write to one another, with the men always initiating the epistolary discourse, Ovid shows us Acontius, a youth made famous by a Callimachus poem (Fragments 67–75). When *Her.* 20 opens, we learn that with the help of the goddess Diana he has tricked Cydippe, an Athenian maiden, into reading a vow inscribed on an apple thrown before her feet while visiting the temple of the goddess at Delos.[20] The vow ('I swear by Diana that I will marry Acontius') causes Cydippe to become increasingly ill as she resists Acontius, and ultimately compels her to marry him (and thus, have sex with him) against her will (*Her.* 20.1–4; 21.113–14; 21.13–15). Throughout the letter, as he reminds Cydippe of her vow and attempts to persuade her to capitulate to him fully, he follows some of the proto–nice guy rules of seduction that the *praeceptor amoris* advocates.

Acontius performs nice guy ideology by attempting to prove his devotion to the maiden. In the letter he writes Cydippe, he confesses his passion and even threatens to stand and weep before her eyes ('ante tuos liceat flentem consistere vultus/ et liceat lacrimis addere verba suis', 'may it be allowed for me crying to stand before you and to add words to my tears' 75–6), weeping being a specific tactic of niceness and emotional vulnerability recommended in the *Ars* (1.659–63). He frames waiting outside her house and stalking her as acts of kindness, concern, and submission because he is worried about the illness he and his vow from Diana have inflicted upon her ('Ne tamen ignorem, quid agas, ad limina crebro/ anxius huc illuc dissimulanter eo' 'So that I may not be ignorant of how you are doing, I incessantly walk, anxiously, secretly, here and there before your home' 129–30), and he even declares that Cydippe will praise how patiently he has waited and loved her ('ipsa tibi dices: "quam patienter amat!"' 88).

Cydippe, despite Acontius' overtures, resists him, particularly through trying to marry her original betrothed three times (*Her.* 21.155–72). But Acontius cannot accept this opposition. That his niceness is only a superficial veneer becomes apparent as he deploys the violence of his own position as a man (and the power of Diana) to get what he wants. For example, although he refuses to acknowledge that he is a sexual abuser and separates himself from violent rapists ('per gladios alii placitas/rapuere puellas', 'other men raped pleasing girls through swords' 20.37), he proclaims that he understands the sexualised violence employed by Paris ('Non sum, qui soleam Paridis reprehendere factum,/ nec quemquam, qui vir, posset ut esse, fuit', 'I am not one who is inclined to condemn what Paris did [to get Helen], nor any man who, in order to become a husband, was a man' 49–50) and Achilles ('Briseida cepit Achilles', 69). He tells Cydippe again and again throughout his appeal that Diana will violently punish her unless she succumbs, such as in lines 99–100: 'nihil est violentius illa,/ cum sua, quod nolim, numina laesa videt' ('Nothing is more violent than when [Diana] sees – which I hope does not happen – that her divine powers have been offended'). Acontius even compares Cydippe to prey that will be captured ('non omnia retia falles', 'you will not evade all the nets [of love]' 45), likening himself to the many sexual abusers and rapists in Ovid who take on the qualities of a hunter and predator.[21] He objectifies her further by exclaiming that parts of her body are his to possess, reacting to the proximity of Cydippe's betrothed to her instead of his own ('iste sinus meus est! mea turpiter oscula sumis! a mihi promisso corpore tolle manus!', 'That bosom is mine! You [Cydippe's betrothed] are shamefully stealing away my kisses! Take your hands away from the body promised to me!' 145–6).

Acontius vacillates in his letter between cajoling Cydippe with images of his passionate devotion and threatening her. Acontius is desperate – or at least pretends to be – but will rely on violence and its attendant manhood acts if necessary. These fluctuations and reversals of feeling are pervasive in the elegiac genre (of which the *Heroides* is an innovative extension), but they are not only emotional outpourings.[22] Instead, they are better understood as manifestations of proto–nice guy ideology and its reliance on violent manhood acts for men to perform their entitlement over women. By aggressively pursuing and stalking Cydippe, torturing her with the vow's illness, naming her as his property, threatening violence, and subjecting her to the violence of Diana, his doting goddess, Acontius illuminates the entitlement he feels to her sexuality and seeks to affirm himself as a man, a status he imagines is endangered by Cydippe's resistance.[23] Acontius always had one goal: to sexually dominate Cydippe against her will. His adoption of the nice guy persona and its subsequent violence were both a means to an end and extensions of his desire, and what is more, both were ultimately demonstrations of his manhood.

GALATEA AND POLYPHEMUS

Polyphemus in Ovid's epic *Metamorphoses* Book 13 differs from the Cyclops infamous for his 'welcome' of Odysseus in Homer. Ovid's Cyclops is in part inspired by the singing, poetic one we find in Theocritus *Idyll* 11, where he declares his love for the sea nymph Galatea. Ovid changes this myth by allowing the nymph herself to narrate the story of the Cyclops' wooing and later violence, as a way to warn her fellow nymph, Scylla, about the consequences of spurning male advances. The Cyclops first attempts to seduce Galatea in four ways: flattering her through song (just as Acontius flatters Cydippe through a letter) (13.789–97), illuminating the extent of his personal wealth (13.810–30), boasting of his divine connections to his father Neptune (854–6), and reminding her of his own beauty, which he says is similar to that of Jupiter and Sol (843–53). All three stances – the flattery, the financial posturing and the focus on appearance – arise as suggestions in the *Ars* (1.505–24), again revealing the persistence of the ideologies of *praeceptor amoris* in other sexualised interactions in Ovid's corpus. But Polyphemus most closely aligns himself with the tenets of both the proto– and modern nice guy ideologies we have discussed through his flattery and promises of (economic) devotion to Galatea.[24] Gloating about what he can offer Galatea economically shows that he is not only an artistic, faithful man who sings for her, but also someone who wants to display what he could offer her as a man. By taking on all four of the positions outlined above and moving through many different strategies endorsed by the *praeceptor* so quickly, it is clear that Polyphemus, like Acontius, is desperate to achieve his sexual goals and decides to count on varied displays and acts of manhood – including performative niceness and loyalty – to convince the resistant Galatea to be his sexually.

But the nymph is not convinced (13.869), and Polyphemus becomes enraged, envisioning how he will tear her lover, Acis, limb from limb ('viscera viva traham divulsaque membra per agros/perque tuas spargam . . . undas', 'I will rip out his guts while he is still alive and I will scatter his severed limbs through the fields and your waters' 865–6). We learn that these are not mere empty threats in reaction to the sexual rejection, as Polyphemus almost murders Acis (870–97). With the Cyclops, as with Elliot Rodger, it is important to note that their manhood acts terrorise not only women, but also other men who they feel imperil their manhood. Misogyny and patriarchal power rest upon the domination of women and other men (Manne 2018, 75). Galatea has effeminised Polyphemus further than he already did himself (through his submission and fixation on his appearance) by rejecting him, and he must regain his standing as a man violently.[25] The dangers Polyphemus presents and the violence of which he is capable, despite the kinder persona he has taken on to seduce Galatea, is furthermore shown through Ovid's allusions to Polyphemus' epic character in Homer and the contradictions he poses in the seemingly peaceful pastoral landscape (Farrell 1992 and Mack 1999).[26] The manhood acts he perpetuates are not just any type of violence, but an epic one. Acontius takes on a similar approach: he is a concerned lover, he writes Cydippe a loving, ingratiating and pleading letter, but he turns to the epic world by analogising himself to Achilles and Paris to help her grasp what he will do if she continues to rebuff him. She will experience epic violence, too. Like the other nice guys we have encountered, Polyphemus first hopes he will achieve sex through displays of devotion, but quickly turns to the male violence on which he knew he could rely.[27]

CONCLUSION

Our modern understanding of how men strategically employ niceness in order to attain sex and that strategy's proximity to entitlement and restorative violence, or the nice guy phenomenon, allows us to make better sense of the behaviours of characters in Ovid who act in similar ways. At the same time, it illuminates the persistence of such violent and toxic manhood acts from antiquity to today. But another question remains (one which always surfaces in discussions of Ovid's representations of women): Why does the poet depict these manhood acts of nice guy ideology and violence? Ovid's sympathy (or not) for women and his purpose in so systematically representing violence against women by men is a source of perennial contention among feminists and Ovidian scholars. Most such scholars maintain that he does so to intentionally criticise these manhood acts and the misogyny of his time (examples include James 2012 and Liveley 2012); others say that he revels in said misogynistic violence (Richlin 2014 and Ranger 2023).[28] The division, overall, leads many to assert that his writings can be used to resist that violence and some others to assert his that writings too foundationally uphold it.

We can never know Ovid's intentions, but even so, we can gauge with more certainty the impact of his words on his audience and on our own times. Projansky (2001, 2) argues that narratives of sexualised violence 'are themselves functional, generative, formative, strategic, performative, and real' – or in other words, have material effects on society and can work to normalise violence. And thus, it is a mistake not to interrogate the teachings and scenes of sexualised violence in Ovid despite his many parodies of elegiac, didactic and epic poetry. Zuckerberg, when considering how Ovid and his narrator's endorsement of sexualised violence in the *Ars* is used by male pickup artists today (often within online forums in the manosphere) to justify predatory behaviour towards women and even rape, has also argued that 'treating the premise of the poem as fundamentally playful or subversive . . . becomes irresponsible when there is a community using it today to normalise an attitude towards [sexual consent] that would not be out of place in Rome' (2018, 95). The context of us reading Ovid's work today matters.

Moreover, it must be said that it is much more likely Ovid was not sympathetic to women, owing to the sheer magnitude and graphic nature of violence he depicts against them, and the paucity of outlets he gives women to meaningfully resist without experiencing further violence. For example, women resist rape in the *Metamorphoses* but only to experience the violence of bodily change, such as in the case of Daphne (1.544–67). Even if we can concede that Ovid is ambiguous about women and his sympathy to them, the poet's very ambiguity should be troubling to us. Richlin (2014), Keegan (2002) and Ranger (2023) urge scholars to always acknowledge that problematic ambiguity: if they do not, they risk sustaining the misogynistic, masculinist ideologies of Ovid's time and further entrenching our own contemporary misogyny.

But wherever the truth is about Ovid's sympathy towards women or my belief that Ovid wrote misogynistic projects, his poetry nevertheless helps us to better discern the origins and ongoing survival of misogyny and violent manhood acts for women today.[29] His works reflect ourselves, as well, because of how men continue to act and what women continue to suffer under them. Nice guys and their restorative acts of violence have a transhistorical constancy and significance. Ovid's poetry exposes how little has changed in 2000 years and how sex, gender and sexuality are similarly and perniciously created in the ancient world and the Global North today. Although the context is different and the 'straight line' we often assume we see between us and the Romans is 'an ideologically motivated strategy' (Zuckerberg 2018, 147), our own misogyny and the discourse around it rest on related principles and constructs. It is not a question of if Ovid is influencing us, it is how he is doing so. As we explore the foundations of Western misogyny and violent manhood acts that allow women to be surveilled, punished and dominated, we are better equipped to challenge how they continue to be justified in our world, and we are better equipped to fight the misogyny that persists all around us.[30]

NOTES

1. See Richlin 2014; James 2016; and Marturano 2017.
2. In particular see most recently in more traditional publications James 2016; Zuckerberg 2018; Enterline 2021; and Libatique 2021; in online literary journals, see: Beek 2016; Johnson 2016; McCarter and Tolentino 2019; and Parrish's interview with McCarter 2018. Martorana in this volume sees Ovid as a source for knowing about both our past and present.
3. The stereotypical 'nice guy' who we find in popular culture and the growing feminist scholarship is heterosexual, especially the one who turns to violence against women, as we will see below. But this concept could be applied to queer men more broadly as people adopting the qualities of niceness to achieve a sexual end. An ancient analogue that comes to mind is Eumolpus in the *Satyricon* 85–7, who lavishes gifts upon his targeted *eromenos* (beloved).
4. Recently Nesbø has published a 2021 master's thesis on the phenomenon in literature and film media, and White's 2019 monograph explores how they form and find identity in online communities. But as a result of this general lack of formal academic research, there is not a stable definition of the 'nice guy'. What is more, academics themselves are guided by the definitions settled upon by feminist communities online.
5. Ager and Goyette in this volume, too, cast a light on the connections between the manosphere (and alt-right) at large and antiquity. The manosphere is the ever-growing locus of misogyny and wider bigotry that is not only deep and reactionary, but – as is becoming clearer day by day – is supportive of violence against women and other marginalised groups (for more, see Ford 2018 and Haase 2021).
6. Enterline (2021), in her analysis of the reception of Ovid and masculinity in Renaissance literature, has echoed the wider concerns of Zuckerberg, particularly on Ovid's impact on and use in the manosphere.
7. The examples are, unfortunately, countless. For more everyday examples of such violence, read Ford's 2018 analysis of the former tumblr blog, entitled 'When Women Refuse', where the editors collected piece of evidence after piece of evidence of the destructive ramifications of rejecting men and their sexual entitlement.
8. This quote can be found in his video entitled 'Redemption' uploaded on 23 May 2014, before the mass shooting. Elliot made a separate manifesto entitled 'My Twisted World: The Story of Elliot Rodger'.
9. Morales in *Antigone Rising* (2020), although she does not discuss the nice guy phenomenon, connects the violence of Elliot Rodger to antiquity and claims that he is one part of a long-standing tradition of violent misogyny. Like the ancient men who envisioned themselves punishing Amazons for their sexually illicit behavior, so did Rodger.

10. A non-violent example might include installing oneself as the economic breadwinner in a household, but that could turn into the violence of economic domination and manipulation of women.

11. Ezzell (2014) contends, similarly to Schwalbe and myself, that there is no healthy 'masculinity' because it rests fundamentally on inequality and dominance. Such a foundation renders it all 'toxic'.

12. For current sociological studies that apply Schwalbe's framework of 'manhood acts' and that view gender as an action, see Moloney and Love 2018 and Haase 2021; both pieces emphasise the enactment of virtual manhood acts in homosocial online communities like the manosphere.

13. Schwalbe (2014) asks us to remember that the prioritising of masculinity in gender studies has caused us to drift away from important radical (but not trans-exclusionary), feminist thought that centres on how men and women are produced, created and maintained as both subject positions and as a material reality and how men make themselves dominant over women through institutional and collective violence. See the influential work of earlier radical feminists such as Dworkin (1983) and MacKinnon (1989) and newer work in the radical feminist tradition or inspired by its tenets such as Mardorossian 2014; and Stringer 2014.

14. Tibullus 1.10 and Propertius 3.8 are some of the most salient examples of other elegiac narrators using violence after heralding their devotion and submission to their *dominae* (mistresses). Roman love elegy, despite the pretence and trope of the *servitium amoris* – in which the male narrator takes on the persona of a *servus* (slave) and the female love interest becomes the *domina* – has always glorified men's sexual domination of women. As many scholars, especially James (2003, 145–50), have explored, the *servitium amoris* and its posture of male inferiority to a controlling *domina* is an exploitative ruse which seeks to hide where the real erotic power lies and how the male narrators dominate the *puellae* (girlfriends) of elegy sexually. Greene (2012, 358) suggests that the *servitium amoris* allows the elegiac poets to take on alternate modes of a superficially submissive male identity, while still enjoying the benefits of a more traditional one. Ovid repeatedly exposes the position's pretexts, such as in *Amores* 1.7, in which the narrator strikes his *domina* and compares her to an enslaved captive of an *imperator*.

15. All translations of Ovid's Latin are my own.

16. Richlin (2014, 148), while analysing this passage, rightly claims that by prioritising the male point of view in this scene of rape, the *praeceptor* and Ovid the poet render the 'women's emotions . . . consistently unreal'.

17. Ovid from the outset shows that Tereus is brutal and inhumane and attributes his violence to something inherent about his birth and nation. He is a Thracian who kidnaps, rapes and mutilates a Greek woman and the poet leans into the contact between barbarity and civilisation to investigate the nature of violence, its inevitability and the effects of Thrace's barbarity on the violence of Procne and Philomela (see e.g. Gildenhard and Zissos 2007 for more on the implications of Tereus' 'barbarity'). But for our purposes, Tereus, and Ovid's emphasis on his

inherent propensity towards violence, helps us to better appreciate the pretence of ancient and modern nice guys and how their actions throughout Ovid's works barely conceal the violence underneath and its socialisation and approval, the violence from which they can always draw to achieve their sexual goals.

18. This poet's corpus is unique because of how extensively he writes about sexual abuse. Readers can discern patterns (of staggering magnitude) in his narratives of rape, most particularly in his epic the *Metamorphoses*. For more on these patterns, see Richlin 2014; James 2016; and Marturano 2017 and 2023.

19. For more on Ovidian intratextuality, see recently Fulkerson and Stover 2016 and Thorsen 2018.

20. In this myth, the virgin Diana does not help the virgin Cydippe, but rather the man who hopes to seize her virginity. Diana has often shown herself to be on the side of patriarchy, most plainly in the myth of Callisto, in which she punishes the nymph for being raped by Jupiter and expels her from her protective band of nymphs. For more on Diana's misogynistic acts, see Marturano (2017 and 2023) and my exploration of 'sororophobia'.

21. Ovid uses figurative language (primarily similes) to connect mortal and divine sexualised violence to predatory interactions between animals, with the male as the predatory figure and the female as the prey figure (with few exceptions). These similes imitate ones found in Homer's *Iliad* that highlight the fear of soldiers in battle who are fleeing death such as in *Iliad* 22.139–42, 22.308–19, 22.263–4. In these similes, the female rape victim fears the pursuit of the male predator just as the rabbit fears the dog or the sheep fears the wolf. Furthermore, for Ovid in the *Metamorphoses* and *Fasti*, the animalisation of female figures, especially in his use of predator and prey imagery during rape and other acts of sexual abuse, reflect the later transformation of countless female figures into animals.

22. Martorana, a contributor to this volume, mentioned to me in correspondence that elegy itself is a genre rooted in reversals, such as in the *militia amoris* (army of love) trope in which the male narrators, although often opposed to writing epic, analogise themselves and their sexual pursuits to soldiers in war, or in other words, reverse the terrain of what we normally deem militaristic. For example, Ovid in *Amores* 1.3 stages a Roman triumph, an inversion of a militaristic norm (at that time reserved for the imperial family) in which his narrator becomes a slave of the victorious god Amor. We can also see the reversals intrinsic to the genre in the performative gender roles of the *servitium amoris* trope considered above. A feminist approach to this reversal in Roman elegy began with Hallet's groundbreaking 1973 article which read against the grain about the role of women in the genre, although the extent and purpose of this reversal of power has been questioned (see Greene 2000, Wyke 2002, James 2003).

23. Cydippe's own letter discloses (*Her.* 21), according to Rimell 2006, a host of polysemous desires for Acontius, where she both despises and yearns for him, Rimell espousing an understanding of Ovid which is not always hierarchal, but relational. Cydippe confesses her feelings for him (*Heroides* 21.204), and she depicts her beauty to Acontius (for example, she compares herself to an apple,

216). But she simultaneously hopes that her body repulses him (221–2). She condemns how Acontius has made her a *miserabile corpus* ('miserable body'), the great *tropaeum* ('military trophy') for his ingenuity (213–17). Cydippe, moreover, is emaciated, ill and suffering because of him, and near the very end of her letter, she hopes that will change his mind about pursuing her (221–6). For these very reasons, a belief in the fundamental 'polysemy' of this relationship can only go so far. The violence and sexual domination Acontius wields over Cydippe as a man and the rape she experiences should be the priority in any examination of their relationship, despite the niceness he performs. She must yield to him for her own survival. If she does not marry Acontius—as she is well aware from her own experience and his boasting (20.109–10)—she will succumb to the illness consuming her body (21.170–2). Cydippe's confession of feelings and other evidence for her attraction cannot distract us from the sexualised violence he perpetrates: her eventual surrender, in mind and body, to her abuser, comes after months of (divinely influenced) coercion as Acontius not only makes her ill, but stalks her as well. Her desires for her abusive suitor derive from his and Diana's coercion, which directly challenges her avowed affection.

24. For Polyphemus' alignment with toxic manhood acts and the 'nice guy' phenomenon in the classroom from a feminist pedagogical perspective, see my piece from 2020 in *Classical Outlook*.

25. Salzman-Mitchell (2005, 188) interprets this manhood act of Polyphemus similarly.

26. Farrell (1999) and Mack (1999) cite the weapons he uses, the magnitude of his body and the violence he committed previously. Furthermore, the trope of the *locus amoenus*, the setting of this myth and the majority in Ovid's *Metamorphoses*, indicates that violence is not external, but rather rooted in the pastoral landscape. See Spencer 2010.

27. Although Galatea escapes physical and sexualised violence herself, there are many indications that the Cyclops will become her rapist (he, for example, takes on the boasting speech of sexual abusers like Apollo and Jupiter, *Met.* 1.504–24; 589–97; 13.808–30), but the violence he commits in the poem itself is instead against the sexual rival. There are several instances in the epic when Ovid creates suspense around an impending rape, only to displace the violence into another outlet, such as in the tales of Narcissus and Echo (3.339–510) and Vertumnus and Pomona (14.623–771).

28. A synthesis of arguments for more pessimistic, resisting readings and more optimistic, releasing readings can be found summarised in Salzman-Mitchell 2005, 17–21; McAuley 2016, 26; Rimmel 2018; Sharrock 2020; Marturano 2023; and Ranger 2023. In addition, Ranger and Richlin (2014, 33) discuss the liberal (as opposed to radical) feminist wave of scholarship after Richlin's first publication of 'Reading Ovid's Rape' in 1992, which in various ways attempted to reclaim Ovid and his representations of women. Rimmel (2018) endeavours to find the space between the liberal and radical feminist critiques. Sharrock, likewise, attempts an optimistic and pessimistic reading of metamorphosis, empathy and objectification in the poet's epic, even if she struggles with the

ethics and even morality of such a reading. In the same article, Sharrock (2020, 36) observes that general consensus among feminist scholars is that Ovid's work contains male chauvinism and violence (resisting), but the poet himself does not espouse those views (optimistic). I am not entirely convinced by liberal, optimistic feminist scholarship or that the totality of the poet's misogyny can be overlooked or complicated, even if there are glimmers of sympathy such as Cydippe having the last word over Acontius in the *Heroides* or Galatea having the opportunity to tell us her own tale of sexual abuse. Like Richlin and Ranger, I fear that an unwillingness to call Ovid a misogynist leads us to miss the forest for the trees. Enterline (2021, 298) believes that Ovid, especially his *Ars Amatoria*, is being misappropriated and then used as justification by male misogynists in the manosphere because they mistakenly read 'Ovidian masculinity [as] straight, rapacious, essentially unchanging', neither grasping the poet's irony and subversion nor his nuance as the *praeceptor amoris* (and elsewhere). But is Richlin erroneously reading Ovid without the necessary context or nuance? Do those who follow in her wake, such as myself and those outside of Classics (Kahn 2005 and Desmond 2006) who see the *Ars Amatoria* as a rape manual, make the same error as the misogynists in the manosphere? Is such an appropriation by misogynists enough to make us reconsider our optimism on Ovid's views on women?

29. Libatique (2021) expresses a similar sentiment in his analysis of Ovid, sexual power and violence, and objectification in the wake of #metoo, although he is a more optimistic reader of Ovid than myself.

30. I would like to thank Christina Nadler, Ena Markovic, Cristina Ferrandez, Noah Frederick, Lyn Rosen and above all, Esther Burson for reading this article and for talking over its thornier issues with me at length. You all – whether academics or classicists or not – helped me to achieve the clarity I needed.

CHAPTER 17

Violence, Victimhood and the Rhetoric of Erotic Curses

Britta Ager

διὸ ἄνασσα, ἱκετῶ· ἄξον τὴν δεῖνα, ἣν δεῖνα, τάχιστα μολοῦσαν ἐλθεῖν
ἐν προθύροισιν ἐμοῦ τοῦ δεῖνος, οὗ ἡ δεῖνα, φιλότητι καὶ εὐνῇ, οἴστρῳ
ἐλαυνομένην, κεντροῖσι βιαίοις ὑπ' ἀνάγκῃ, σήμερον, ἄρτι, ταχύ.

Wherefore, Lady, I beseech you: attract
NN,[1] whom NN bore, to come with haste
To my doorstep, me, NN, whom NN bore,
And to the bed of love, driven by torment,
Under compulsion from the powerful goads –
today, right now, quickly.[2]

Among the more startling evidence for ancient gender relations are *defixiones* such as this, the binding spells with which ancients attacked rivals and enemies. *Defixiones* appeared in Greece in the fifth century BCE, probably inspired by earlier Egyptian and Near Eastern traditions of cursing, and were in widespread use into late antiquity. Surviving examples include texts in Greek, Latin, Demotic and Coptic. They are found in ancient spellbooks in the form of recipes into which a magician may insert personalised details and as fully enacted spells written on lead tablets, papyri and ostraka personalised with the names of the spellcaster and target.[3] A large number of the surviving binding spells deal with erotic matters: the acquisition of lovers, the separation of couples and sometimes both at once.

Defixiones which attempt to unite or divide lovers – sometimes nostalgically called love spells, but more accurately erotic curses – were a popular way of overcoming sexual disappointment in classical antiquity and were used by both men and women. Spells cast with the intention of forcing a victim to desire the spellcaster show many gender configurations of caster and target: the largest number of enacted curses involve men attempting to attract women, a smaller but still sizeable proportion are written by women to attract men, and a handful of homoerotic curses are preserved in which women try to attract women or men try to attract men.[4]

While some scholars such as Matthew Dickie and Eleni Pachoumi have pushed back against the idea that erotic curses were more often used by men than women,[5] the magical papyri usually treat a man attracting a woman as the default arrangement: the ὁ/ἡ δεῖνα ('so-and-so') formula, used in spell formularies to indicate 'blanks' in which the user should insert names, is usually found with the masculine form used for the caster in erotic spells and the feminine for the victim. Some papyri do indicate that either a man or a woman might be the target,[6] and a user might adjust a spell recipe to suit any gender configuration. In support of the latter point, Dickie points to pairs of curses which were copied from the same recipe but which show different gender patterns for the victim and caster.[7] However, these arguments do not undercut the expectation in ancient spell books that erotic spells will be predominantly used by men to target women or the fact that, when the gender of the user and target can be identified in enacted curses, the largest number follow this pattern.

In this paper, I will be primarily concerned with the curse tablets in which men cast erotic attraction spells on women, and only tangentially with other categories, since this subgroup of erotic *defixiones* shows some quirks of rhetoric which are worth discussing in the context of toxic masculinity. Curses in which men target women show a higher degree of violence than other erotic spells, subjugating and degrading language, and fantasies of enslavement and humiliation. While some of these same characteristics occur in other erotic curses, they are used more regularly and take on special significance here, since within this subgroup gendered rhetoric is deployed in a way that is not interchangeable between the spells with male spellcasters and the ones with female spellcasters. Images of victims being dragged by the hair, for instance, are only aimed at female victims.

I will discuss the 'toxic' aspects of toxic masculinity in terms of how erotic curses attempt to negotiate, subvert and gloss over the ways in which the writers' demands for women's bodies and attention are inappropriate even by ancient standards, and how the formulaic language of the curses encourages curse users to think of sexual relations between men and women in terms of violence and possession. The writers simultaneously exploit ancient gender norms which tell men that they should be sexually and socially dominant over women, by force if necessary, and reject the same standards insofar as the writers deny other men's previous 'ownership' of the same women. The erotic curses recognise the writers' desire for the target to the exclusion of all else, and to the detriment of both the targeted women and, in ancient terms, that of other men and society at large.

THE PROBLEM OF VIOLENCE IN THE EROTIC CURSES

Most of the ancient *defixiones* express a desire for harm and misfortune to afflict their victims: for charioteers to crash, thieves to die, businesses to fail and personal enemies to waste away. The mildest hope for opponents to be prevented from taking some action, such as testifying against the writer in court. The erotic curses are no exception, and often articulate vivid wishes for tortures to be inflicted on the target of desire until they sexually submit to the user. A few examples include a tablet in which a man named Sarapammon asks a ghost to 'drag her by the hair and heart until she does not keep away from me';[8] a recipe in a spell book which instructs 'bring her under torture . . . obey me and rouse NN on this night and take the sweet sleep away from her eyes, and cause her miserable anxiety and fearful pain';[9] and another which commands 'strike her from her heart to her belly, from her belly to her intestines, from her intestines to her womb'.[10] The curses are addressed to gods or to ghosts who are expected to enact the spellcasters' wishes. Typical torments which the spellcasters hope to inflict on the person they desire include burning, fever, insomnia, hunger, thirst, whipping, dragging, frenzy and dizziness. As has been pointed out, many of the torments which erotic curses seek to inflict, such as sleeplessness and fever, were also symptoms of love sickness in antiquity; the *defixiones* thus try to induce love by inducing its symptoms.[11]

Scholars have been puzzled by the juxtaposition of sexual desire and extreme violence directed at the same targets in these spells. John Gager suggests that the fundamental use of the spells is cathartic: by articulating violent desires, the frustrated spellcaster finds relief for their feelings.[12] John Winkler takes a similarly psychological approach, but sees the tortures of the victims as a projection of the spellcaster's own distress at their unreciprocated yearning.[13] Henk Versnel objects to what he sees as an academic refusal to come to grips with an ugly side of classical culture, and urges scholars of ancient magic to take the violent desires articulated in these spells literally: that ancient spellcasters did, in fact, want their victims whipped, burned and starved.[14]

Versnel is correct that modern readers have been less squeamish about believing that the violent wishes in curses against thieves, for example, are literal; when a curse tablet asks that a thief be made to pour out his own blood into the bronze bowl which he stole (Tomlin 44), we have little trouble believing that to be sincere. But while Versnel's broad point about projecting our discomforts onto antiquity is salutary, it avoids grappling with the root of the bewilderment with erotic curses, where there is a more complex interpretive problem than he acknowledges. Many curses seek to force their targets into long-term relationships; all want at least a relationship long enough to consummate.[15] When curses ask that a woman be whipped or burned, they often include the caveat 'until she relents', but what are we to do with a curse which demands 'consume her brain with burning . . . burn her insides and turn them inside out, drain her blood out, until she comes to me'?[16] The spellcaster cannot literally want the woman to be exsanguinated and turned inside out before trotting off to join him in bed.

Such murderous expressions of desire allow men to imagine dominating, controlling and punishing women until they are not only sexually compliant, but lusting after the writers. Versnel makes the point that there is a real satisfaction for the writer in the 'panning-shot' imagery which lingers over detailed descriptions of a target, their limbs, and the pain to be inflicted there.[17] The usual reading of the function of the violent rhetoric in these curses is, as seen, psychological: by pouring out their complaints to the gods and describing the tortures they want to impose on the person who has caused their distress, the spellcaster either satisfies their genuine hatred of the victim, cathartically relieves their erotic frustrations, or attempts to magically project their own pain onto the object of their desire.[18] In this chapter, I am less interested in a psychological analysis of the effect of erotic curses on their users than in a rhetorical analysis of the logic and phrasing of erotic spells in which women are targeted. The conceit that men were naturally sexually dominant, and that for them to be sexually dependent on women's acquiescence was an inversion of proper relations, made curses an easy rhetorical device for men to adopt since curses in general were phrased as tools for righting injustices and unnatural situations. Erotic curse writers exploit this familiar template of victimhood to frame themselves as the wronged parties, while the already violent language of curse-writing, where the pain and incapacitation of the victims was intended as a way of righting injustices, was a natural fit for curses dealing with sexual compulsion; in a worldview in which assault was considered a more natural response to sexual frustration than to legal setbacks, violent erotic curses are in many ways a more natural development than judicial ones. The erotic spells in which men target women show two particularly gendered exploitations of the rhetoric of cursing: attempts to frame the men writing them as victims in order to gain divine assistance, and visualisations of the women targeted being humbled and acquiescent in a magical attempt to will that state of affairs into reality.

COMPLAINTS AND PLEAS TO THE GODS

The men who use erotic curses address them to various supernatural powers: gods, ghosts and other entities who might be persuaded, threatened or tricked into enacting the user's curse, and who must be supplicated in appropriate fashion. In a society whose patriarchal structures were seen as natural and inevitable, the gods were expected to be willing to enforce them; thus the men using attraction spells appeal to deities in ways which emphasise the justice of the men's claims. How did the writers plead their cases to the gods?[19] The language of the spells shows great concern to establish that the writers have been victimised by the women they target, to elicit sympathy from the listening deities, and to justify their aggression towards the targets, whose alleged bad behaviour, the writers argue, should be punished via the erotic attacks they ask the gods to cause. These men use a number of rhetorical strategies to elicit divine assistance.

A few writers describe their own desire and longing in dramatic terms in the *defixiones*.[20] One pleads in a hymnic address to ghosts that they 'bring success to him who is in torment' (αὐτὸν . . . βασάνοις ἐχόμενον) and refers to his own 'tears and bitter groans' (δάκρυσιν . . . καὶ στενάγμασιν πικροῖς).[21] A melodramatic Coptic text attributed to Cyprian of Antioch complains that thanks to his erotic suspense:

> My heart has grown bitter. I have grown pale. My flesh shudders; the hair of my head stands on end. I am all afire. I have lain down to rest, but I could not sleep; I have risen, but I found no relief. I have eaten and drunk in sighing and groaning. I have found no rest either in soul or in spirit for being overwhelmed by desire. My wisdom has deserted me; my strength has been sapped.[22]

A few project the user's distress into the mythological realm, such as a Coptic spell which has the magician speak in the person of Horus, complaining to his mother Isis that a woman has rejected his advances, and so he has wept and sighed 'until the tears of my eyes covered the soles of my feet'.[23] The exaggerated complaints are typical of toxic manifestations of masculinity in which men describe themselves as embattled, repressed victims of an unnatural social order in which their masculinity is threatened by women, other men and society at large.[24]

An attraction spell recipe in which a magician implores and commands Aphrodite to help him shows a complex expression of male victimhood.[25] The ritual involves a compulsive hymn and offering to the goddess, which are intended to force her to aid the magician. Compulsive magical rituals aimed at the gods are common in the spell books and involve special foul-smelling incense blends, unusual sacrifices and offerings, and threats; they are to be resorted to after normal supplications have failed to attract divine help. In this case the magician is to burn incense made from myrrh, wormwood and a dove's blood and fat, make an offering of a vulture's brain, and utter a hymn of compulsion in which he threatens to bind Aphrodite's lover Adonis in Hades if she does not help him. The hymn includes a *historiola*, a paradigmatic story which the magician recites as part of a spell in hopes that the universe can be persuaded to follow the same pattern in his case.[26] The *historiola* of this ritual describes how Aphrodite magically attracted an unwilling man to her bed; thus, the speaker says, he wants the goddess to help him attract the object of his desire to his own bed.[27] The interest here lies in the reversal of genders; although the spell recipe is phrased for a man to attract a woman (and includes rhetoric for coercing a further woman, Aphrodite), the *historiola* changes the paradigmatic aggressor to female and the victim to male. The implication, conscious or not, is that the male user, or perhaps men in general, have been aggressed against by love – his desire for the woman he seeks to attract is proof that the user has already been attacked, and his retaliation is only fair.

A number of curses insert explicit comments on the behaviour of the woman who is targeted, suggesting that not only has the man been pained by love, but he has been actively wronged by his victim, who forces him to desire her and yet refuses him. On one level, this can be seen as a cathartic venting of the user's irritation at his target's intractability, but the point is also to prove to the gods that the woman is a valid target deserving of retribution for her rejection of him (or perhaps her simple unawareness of or inaccessibility to him). Male sexual frustration and frustrated dominance is thus narcissistically cast as a cosmic problem which the gods ought to help resolve. Men's complaints about women's behaviour towards them range from the simple and formulaic to the elaborate and personalised. In an enacted spell, a man named Hermeias writes:

Ἄνουβι . . . <ἀ>νάπαυσον αὐτὴν τῆς ὑπερηφανείας καὶ τ[οῦ] λογισμοῦ καὶ τῆς αἰσχύνης. ἄξον δ[έ μ]οι αὐτὴν ὑπὸ τοὺς ἐμοὺς πόδας . . . ἕως ἂν ὑπό σου μαστιζομένη ἔλθη ποθοῦσά με, τὰς χεῖρας ἔχουσα πλήρεις, μετὰ μεγαλοδώρου ψυχῆς καὶ χαριζομένη μοι ἑαυτὴν καὶ τὰ ἑαυτῆς [κ]αὶ ἐκτελοῦσα, ἃ καθήκει γυναιξ[ὶν πρὸς ἄνδρ]ας.

Anubis . . . Make [Tigerous] cease from her arrogance, calculation and her shamefulness. Drive her to me, under my feet . . . until, whipped by you, she comes wanting me, with full hands, with a generous soul and graciously giving me both herself and her possessions and doing what is right for women in regards to men.[28]

Hermeias does not simply want Tigerous; he wants her to entirely alter her behaviour, to cease what he sees as the unnatural inversion of their positions in which she, a woman, has the upper hand over him. We are not told what her 'arrogance, calculation and shamefulness' consist of, but her refusal of Hermeias' advances are certainly part of it; he wants to re-establish normative gender relations in which she behaves as is 'right' for a woman. Hermeias' spell amounts to a complaint that the world is out of joint and order needs to be reasserted. Another spell includes a rather passive-aggressive comment that one Theodotis should 'no longer' (μηκέτι) try anything with another man.[29]

Versnel points to rhetorical similarities between the love curses and judicial curses; in both, the user wants to portray themselves as suffering a wrong which the gods should help to rectify.[30] Judicial curses against thieves, murderers and the like and prayers for restitution were considered far less antisocial than many types of magic, and were sometimes openly deployed without fear of social disapproval or legal censure.[31] In one striking example, a marble tablet from Rheneia commemorates the death of a woman named Heraklea, whose relatives believed her to have been murdered.[32] The tablet is engraved with hands lifted in supplication and entreats a god to punish Heraklea's murderers and their children with the same fate that she suffered in language very similar to that found in other *defixiones*. Far from being stealthily deployed, this was set up in public for all to read. By borrowing the formal characteristics of a socially licit curse form, such as the exhaustive listing of body parts to be cursed, the writers of the much less licit erotic curses hope to appropriate the aura of respectability and justified anger attached to the former.

FANTASIES OF TORTURE AND HUMILIATION

Other spells use a different tactic. Rather than emphasising the abject victim-hood of the caster and the evil of the target, they visualise the man as domi-nant and overmastering and the woman as subjugated, humiliated and tamed, hoping thereby that this may be realised through supernatural aid. The women are aspirationally framed as enslaved, servile, or as animals, and as subject to the sort of violence commonly inflicted on slaves and beasts of burden in the ancient world. Ammonion's curse on Theodotis wishes for her to be enslaved (δεδουλαγωγημένη); another asks 'force her, NN, to be serviceable to me' (συνανάγκασον τὴν δεῖνα ὑπουργὸν εἶναί μοι); Cyprian's spell on Justina asks for her to be brought to him in 'humility and subjection'; Hermeias' spell on Tigerous wants her attracted 'beneath my feet' (ὑπὸ τοὺς ἐμοὺς πόδας).[33] If the previous group of spells complain about men's rejection and helplessness in the face of the objects of their affection, this is the inverse, allowing the casters to fantasise about regaining what they see as their rightfully dominant place in the relationship they desire, as well as punishing their targets for their own perceived humiliations.

Language of subjection is not limited to the tablets in which men attract women. One erotic *defixio* which specifically articulates a wish for the victim to be enslaved (ποίησον αὐτὸν ὡς δοῦλον) to the caster is the curse of a woman named Domitiana on a man, Urbanus.[34] However, many *defixiones* written by men contain images of violence inflicted on the targets which suggest enslave-ment. Whipping, for instance, is one of the tortures which several spells wish to inflict on their targets; as a means of corporal punishment typically reserved for slaves, these spells have overtones of humiliation and subjugation as well as simple torture. The ritual involving a compulsive hymn to Aphrodite, for example, asks for the target to be driven with goads, in a passage in which the target's subjugation is parallel to the tortures the caster will inflict on Adonis if Aphrodite does not oblige.[35] Another links whipping with the insomnia to be inflicted: if the victim tries to sleep, the gods are to 'spread cords with thorns under her, and spikes upon her temples'.[36] Theon's curse on Euphemia wants her to come before his feet and to be bound with 'indissoluble, strong, adamantine fetters' (δεσμοῖς ἀλύτοις, ἰσχυρῦς, ἀδαμαντίνοις) to love him.[37] However metaphorically we take this, the imagery of bondage is still striking.

The spells occasionally wish for a victim to be dragged by her hair, a form of violence which carries both gender and status markers. 'Tell the divine spirit to go off to her, NN, to bring her by her hair, by her feet,' asks one spell in the papyri;[38] a 'Wondrous spell for binding a lover' requests that the gods 'drag NN by her hair, by her heart, by her soul, to me, NN'.[39] That the hair is of equivalent importance here with the heart and soul highlights the symbolic weight it bears in the erotic papyri. Long hair, then as now, was a symbol of femininity; long hair on men or boys was a marker of servitude, particularly of slaves expected to provide sexual services. To seize someone of any gender by the hair, or to otherwise violently or possessively touch their hair, is marked in ancient culture as something done by masters to slaves.[40] In the Cupid and Psyche episode of Apuleius' *Metamorphoses*, for instance, when Psyche is claimed by Venus as a slave she is seized by the hair and dragged into Venus' house to be whipped and tortured in a scene of erotic pain infliction with obvious parallels to the *defixiones*.[41] An elaborate ritual entitled the 'Sword of Dardanos' echoes the same tradition as Apuleius when it tells the magician to engrave a magnet with an image of Aphrodite, Psyche and Cupid; Aphrodite should be riding Psyche and pulling her hair, while Eros burns her with a torch.[42] This magnetic Psyche amulet suggests that the woman is not only a slave, but perhaps an animal as well, one to be ridden and tamed by Eros and Aphrodite's punishments. Some Coptic spells make explicit animal comparisons: 'I desire that N. daughter of N. spend forty days and forty nights hanging on me like a bitch for a dog, like a sow for a boar,' reads a typical example.[43]

The users of these spells attempt to inflict a lower status on their targets as much as they do pain. By rhetorically placing themselves in the position of a master disciplining a slave, rather than a man attempting to win the affections of a woman who can refuse him, the user encourages the gods to enforce what he now asserts to be appropriate relations between them. Like the *historiolae*, it articulates a pattern which the magician hopes the spell will make reality. It also helps to gloss over the transgressive nature of the spellcasters' requests. The writers of curses are, often, attempting to illicitly obtain women who are not supposed to be sexually available: other men's wives, daughters, sisters and slaves.

While the identity and status of the women who are targeted is debated – and there is unlikely to be a single answer – a number of spells include wishes to separate the target from family members who include parents, siblings, husbands and children.[44] In attempting to claim other men's property, this behaviour is transgressive even by ancient standards and threatens the standards of hegemonic masculinity, which place intense importance on chastity and sexual fidelity in women. These strictures bar the curse users from their targets and frustrate the expectation of sexual satisfaction for men which is at the core of Greco-Roman masculinity, thus pitting men who desire women, who are encouraged to think their desires should be met, against men who already have women, who are encouraged to guard their female relations from such attacks. The language of the erotic curses is an attempt to make an end run around the disapproval which attempting to seduce such a woman incurs. Recasting the victims as their own slaves rather than as sexually claimed free women or the property of other men avoids undercutting the users' rhetorical assertions of victimhood.

While all the erotic curses share broad similarities, parsing them by the pattern of the users and targets illuminates features of the language, such as the animal comparisons and images of violence such as hair-dragging, which seem to be predominantly aimed at women. Even if a spell which contains language such as 'drag her by the hair and heart' can theoretically be adapted for use by a woman against a man, the language would have very different overtones in such a case, and it is probably not an accident that all examples of hair-dragging threats in the extant *defixiones* are aimed at women. While discussion of the curses has often focused on their formulaic language and their shared features, study of how the rhetoric of specific spells chooses, adapts or deviates from the usual formulae suggests that men and women may have deployed somewhat different erotic curses, intersecting with larger ancient tropes regarding gender. The curses used by men to attract women simultaneously assert the users' victimhood and envision the users as dominant and powerful; while much could be said about the satisfactions of these fantasies, which allow the casters to both indulge in the recounting of their own perceived ill-treatment and to mentally correct it by imagining their retaliation, this is also a calculated rhetorical strategy to garner divine sympathy and aid from gods who are expected to step in to restore normative gender relations, if not normative social relations, by providing the caster with the woman they desire, regardless of other hegemonic male claims to her.

Traditional approaches to erotic curses have emphasised the potential psychological and emotional benefits of performing such spells, particularly the cathartic release of anger and frustration which many scholars have seen as typical of and perhaps as a conscious or unconscious goal of these rituals. However, the carefully constructed images of victimised, humiliated men in need of supernatural compensation, and the violent denigration of their female targets and accompanying wishes for pain and humiliation upon them, suggest that the rhetoric of these spells should be seen as a carefully constructed performance rather than a genuine, unmediated outpouring of male sadness. The entitlement at the core of such manifestations of toxic masculinity does not preclude calculated strategies about how best to satisfy it, and the users of these spells can both feel truly entitled to the women they want and aware that their desires must be presented vis-à-vis the claims of traditional, hegemonic Greco-Roman masculinity.

NOTES

1. 'NN' is conventionally used to translate ὁ/ἡ δεῖνα ('so-and-so'), a formula used in the spell books to indicate where the names of the actual spellcaster, target, and other specific individuals should be inserted when the spell is used.
2. *PGM* IV.2891–942 ll. 2907–12.
3. *Defixio* (and the Greek equivalent, *katadesmos*) are often used to indicate the lead curse tablets on which binding spells are often written. For simplicity, in this piece I follow Faraone (1991) in using the term for the entire corpus of binding curses, regardless of medium or whether they are recipes for spells, or spells which were actually enacted.
4. For a catalogue of known erotic tablets and relevant statistics, see Pachoumi 2013, 294–325.
5. Dickie 2000, 563–83 and Pachoumi 2013.
6. E.g. *PGM* XXXVI.69–101.
7. Dickie 2000, 565–6.
8. *SuppMag* 47 ll. 23–4: 'ἕλκε αὐτὴν τῶν τριχῶν, τῶν σπλάγχνων, ἕως μὴ ἀποστῇ μου'. Translations are my own unless otherwise noted.
9. *PGM* IV.1390–1495 ll. 1412–28: 'ἄξατε οὖν αὐτὴν βασανιζομένην . . . ἐπακούσατέ μου καὶ ἐξεγείρατε τὴν δαῖνα ἐν τῇ νυκτὶ ταύτῃ καὶ ἀφέλεσθε αὐτῆς τὸν ἡδὺν ὕπνον ἀπὸ τῶν βλεφάρων καὶ δότε αὐτῇ στυγερὰν μέριμναν, φοβερὰν λύπην'.
10. *PDM* xiv.636–69 (trans. Janet H. Johnson).
11. See e.g. Versnel 1998.
12. Gager 1992, 81–2.
13. Winkler 1991.
14. Versnel 1998.
15. E.g. *SuppMag* 47 l. 26, which Sarappamon wants Ptolemais to be filled with love and obedient 'for all the time of my life' (εἰς τὸν ἅπαντα χρόνον τῆς ζωῆς μου); and a similar wish in *SuppMag* 51 l. 9. Cf. *PGM* CI.1–53 l. 49, which hopes for both 'unending love' (ἔρωτα ἀκατάπαυστον, l. 49) in his target but also, unusually, for his victim to desire him for a specific ten-month time period (ll. 36–7).
16. *PGM* IV.1496–595 ll. 1543–6: 'κατάκαυσον τὸν ἐγκέφαλον, ἔκκαυσον καὶ ἔκστρεψον αὐτῆς τὰ σπλάγχνα, ἔκσταξον αὐτῆς τὸ αἷμα, ἕως ἔλθῃ πρὸς ἐμέ'.

17. Versnel 1998.
18. Versnel 1998, Gager 1992, 81–2 and Winkler 1991, respectively. While the supposed cathartic benefits of magic are often discussed, I wonder how often spells like these instead worked to reaffirm and strengthen the magician's anger and sense of grievance.
19. Magical procedures for obtaining divine aid through force or tricks are also used in erotic spells, but are largely outside the scope of this paper.
20. Winkler (1991, 226) argues that the spells tend to suppress mention of the user's erotic torment in order to project it onto the victim; I find this unconvincing. While the user's feelings are described in a small minority of tablets, these are numerous enough to regard as more than exceptions.
21. *PGM* IV.1390–495 ll. 1405–7. The spell appeals to the spirits of those who died young or by violence, and the magician's expression of his own woe, although it arises from a different cause, appears designed to make common cause with the unhappiness of the ghosts.
22. *CTRP* 73, trans. Howard M. Jackson. The 'Spell of Cyprian' comes from an eleventh-century papyrus text (Heidelberg P. Kopt. 684) which preserves what appears to be a late antique spell. It is based on the fourth-century *Confession of Cyprian of Antioch*, a popular narrative about a pagan magician, Cyprian, who converted to Christianity after his magic failed to obtain the Christian woman, Justina, with whom he had fallen in love. This passage from the eleventh-century text is not part of the actual incantation which Cyprian claims to have spoken, but is in the narrative introduction to it, much as the *PGM* spell texts often include narrative sections within which the incantations and other procedures are contained. On the 'Spell of Cyprian', see Bilabel and Grohmann 1934, 304–25.
23. *CTRP* no. 72, trans. Neal Kelsey.
24. Tereškinas 2018, 139–48.
25. *PGM* IV.2891–942.
26. On *historiolae* in magic, see Frankfurter 1995, 457–76 and Sowers 2017, 426–48.
27. *PGM* IV.2891–942 ll. 2933–7.
28. *PGM* XVIIa.1–25 ll. 3–20.
29. *SuppMag* 38 l. 9.
30. Versnel 1998, 264.
31. See Versnel 1991, 214–43 and the examples in Ogden 1992, 175–99.
32. Gager 1992 no. 87 = Launey and Roussel 1937, no. 2532.
33. *SuppMag* 38 l. 10; *PGM* IV.296–466 ll. 381–2; *CTRP* 73 ll. 195–200 (trans. Howard M. Jackson); *PGM* XVIIa.1–25 ll.8–9.
34. *DT* 271 ll. 43–4.
35. *PGM* IV.2891–942 ll. 2902–12. The spell threatens to fetter Adonis with steel chains and bind him to a wheel of Ixion; although whipping is not explicit, binding the victim to a wheel for a beating was a common early Greek form of torture which is echoed in a number of love spells, on which see Faraone 1991.
36. *PGM* XXXVI.134–60 ll. 151–2: 'ἐαν δὲ θέλῃ κοιμᾶσθαι, ὑποστρώσατε αὐτῇ σιττύβας ἀκανθίνας, ἐπὶ δὲ τῶν κοτράφων σκόλοπας'.

37. *SuppMag* 45 l. 44.
38. *PGM* VII.862–918 ll. 886–7: 'κέλευσον ἀγγέλῳ ἀπελθεῖν πρὸς τὴν δεῖνα, ἄξαι αὐτὴν τῶν τριχῶν, τῶν π[ο]δῶν'.
39. *PGM* IV.296–466 ll. 376–7: 'ἕλκε τὴν δεῖνα τῶν τριχῶν, τῶν σπλάγχνων, τῆς ψυχῆς πρὸς ἐμέ, τὸν δεῖνα'. A copy of this recipe was followed by Sarapammon in his curse on Ptolemais (*SuppMag* 47); Sarapammon's enacted spell asks for Ptolemais to be dragged by the hair and internal organs.
40. Cf. masters using slaves' hair to wipe their hands in Petronius *Satyricon* 27 and 57. See Pandey (2018, 454–88) for hair and domination in Roman elegy, and Cosgrove (2005, 675–92) for biblical examples.
41. On this scene and the *defixiones* see Ager 2019, 317–43.
42. *PGM* IV.1716–870.
43. *CTRP* 72. Cf. *CTRP* 73–5, 78.
44. See for example *PGM* LXI.1–38, *PGM* XIXa.1–54 and *DT* 230.

CHAPTER 18

'Legitimate Rape' and Toxic Masculinity from Todd Akin to Soranus

T. H. M. Gellar-Goad

E leven twenty-four a.m., on a Sunday, in St Louis, Missouri. KTVI-TV, Fox channel 2, has just uploaded an interview on its website. The star: Todd Akin, the Republican nominee for the state's United States Senate race, challenger to incumbent Senator Claire McCaskill. It is August 19th, 2012. Akin does not yet realise it, but his Senate bid is now over.

Why? During the interview, Akin had been asked about his position on abortion rights, to which he is firmly opposed, even to exceptions for pregnancies resulting from rape and incest. The key phrase in his response will become (in)famous in the weeks to come: 'It seems to be, first of all, from what I understand from doctors, it's really rare. If it's a legitimate rape, the female body has ways to try to shut the whole thing down.' After the interview has gone live, Twitter erupts in outrage, McCaskill quickly releases a statement condemning Akin's remarks, Akin claims he misspoke but does not actually change his position, and the Republican presidential nominee, Mitt Romney, issues not one but two statements denouncing what Akin said.[1]

Akin went down to defeat that November. McCaskill coasted to re-election in a race that the demographics and political climate suggested she should have lost – as, in fact, she subsequently did during her next re-election campaign, in 2018, to a less toxic Republican opponent, Josh Hawley, now famous for supporting the January 6, 2021 insurrection. The 2018 campaign was haunted by the spectre of Akin: dozens of news stories contrasted McCaskill's newer challenger with Akin and warned that one Akin-like moment could upend Republican hopes of taking McCaskill's seat once more.

Akin's words are now a classic example of a 'Kinsley gaffe'. Gaffes occur when politicians unintentionally say something that causes them political problems. A Kinsley gaffe is a particular subspecies: when politicians slip up and say what they actually think.[2] Akin believed that a woman who had been raped could only get pregnant if she had, in actuality, wanted to get raped – but he also knew that his belief was far outside the American political mainstream, and thus that he should talk around his views, should dissemble, should use code and intimation and dog-whistles. But in the KTVI-TV interview, Akin told the truth about his positions. Thence the gaffe. Within a year after the controversy erupted, 'Akinise' had come to describe a political tactic whereby a Democrat would compare a Republican opponent's words to Akin's 'legitimate rape' comments.[3]

Akin was expressing a factually baseless belief;[4] but it was not an idea he innovated.[5] And his comments were part of such a trend of 2012 election-cycle 'rape and pregnancy controversies' that Wikipedia has a page devoted to it,[6] and a poem was published that year with the title 'Three Republican Candidates Discourse on the Subject of Rape'.[7] Akin also was participating in a tradition dating back at least to the early second century CE, to the Greek medical writer Soranus of Ephesus, whose treatise on gynaecology is filled with quack-science gems akin to Akin's. The two texts – Soranus' treatise and Akin's interview – are nodes on a thread of toxic masculinity[8] stretching from the ancient Greek world to the modern United States, chronologically distant but ravelling from the same cloth, as I will show. Yet at the same time, as I argue in this chapter, there is a key difference of opinion between Akin and Soranus, a difference that makes Akin's comments more sinister by contrast.

RAPE DENIAL AS TOXIC MASCULINITY

It might seem self-evident that rape denial and apologia, inasmuch as they are part of rape culture, are intertwined with toxic masculinity.[9] Yet the connection between these sorts of rape denials and toxic masculinity is not often made explicitly, and it merits a brief walkthrough to connect the dots between the two phenomena. Most straightforwardly: excusing or minimising sexual assault absolves rapists of culpability for their mistreatment of women, and thus bolsters a form of masculinity that subordinates women's consent and wellbeing to men's pleasure. At the same time, much sexual violence is not about sex so much as it is about power (see, e.g., Filipovic, 'Rape is about Power'), and the dismissal of reports of sexual assault reinforces the sexist power dynamics of patriarchal societies. As Connell and Messerschmidt note, with reference to 'hegemonic masculinity', a term related to toxic masculinity: 'There exists considerable evidence that hegemonic masculinity is not a self-reproducing form, whether through habitus or any other mechanism. To sustain a given pattern of hegemony requires the policing of men as well as the exclusion or discrediting of women.'[10] So attacks on women's credibility and agency, in addition to attacks on their bodies and psyches, are a necessary component of hegemonic or toxic masculinity. Attenborough, in a study of news coverage of rape allegations, notes how frequently the media discusses rape in terms that allow a woman to claim she has been raped, but juxtapose her testimony with descriptions of what is alleged to have happened in terms that suggest she was not really raped.[11] This sort of discussion, Attenborough argues, encourages media consumers to believe the sort of discrediting of women on which the hegemony of toxic masculinity depends.

One of the effects of rape denialism is to reinforce the violence inherent in toxic masculinity. As Marcotte notes, 'toxic masculinity is a specific model of manhood, geared towards dominance and control . . . [which] sees sex as an act not of affection but domination, and which valorises violence as the way to prove one's self to the world'.[12] As a result of this valorisation, 'men are more likely to act violent when their masculinity and male privilege are threatened . . . and one common way for men to assert their dominance is through sexual assault and harassment'.[13] Rape denial assuages the threat to men's masculinity at the same time as it excuses or even justifies men's acts of sexual assault. And it also normalises the behaviour, with the result that men are engendered to believe that coercive and non-consensual sex is acceptable, or even expected, a prerogative they have (and must exercise) as men.

The particular aspect of hegemonic masculinity's toxicity that I address in this chapter is its harm to non-masculine others, specifically women. In the logic of toxic masculinity, biological sex is binary, is determinative of gender, maps directly onto only one admissible sexuality (viz., heterosexuality), and is the primary factor constituting gender roles, ability, power, privilege and the relationship between humans and the non-human natural world. This gender binary and essentialism of sex and gender is the toxic fruit of a poisonous tree with ancient roots: as Laqueur shows, ancient ideas of humans as a single sex, with woman an inversion of man (so, e.g., Aristotle's notion of woman as a deformed, incomplete, or mutilated man, *GA* 2.3, 737a25) blossomed into the modern bipolar opposition of 'male' and 'female'.[14] The opposition is, like gender itself, a social construct, one that suppresses the natural occurrence of a broad spectrum of sexual and gender diversity, as Fausto-Sterling argues extensively.[15]

The patriarchal sexual ideologies of a toxically masculine society place control of sex drive and responsibility for pregnancy with the women but grant control over outcomes and women's bodies to men. Women's bodies are important first and foremost in this sort of system as sites of reproduction: as baby factories. While sexual pleasure is a valued good for men, for women it is treated as irrelevant or, on occasion, as counter(re)productive. The primacy placed on the desires and control of men and on the begetting of children outweighs anything else. Hence the denial that any pregnancy could be undesired or conceived without consent and the idea of 'legitimate rape', which can even enter the beliefs of a person who genuinely feels empathy for survivors of sexual assault.

Todd Akin and Soranus of Ephesus are both case studies for these ideologies of toxicity, unmoored from reality. The motivations behind their separate denials of rape are similar, inasmuch as they are structured by a reproductive political agenda. In each case, too, the man talking about rape erases the (hypothetical) man who has perpetrated it: we hear only of the woman's supposed desire and of the physical consequences, nothing of the aggressor. Neither Akin nor Soranus is satisfied with believing women: neither can accept that if a woman says she was raped, then it was rape. The details of the physiological accounts presented by Akin and Soranus differ, however, and more significantly the vectors of their toxic masculinity are not the same, even if the ideas are similar. For Akin, 'legitimate rape' is narrowly a logical entailment of his religiously founded anti-abortion extremism, a partisan position that participates in a wider repressive and misogynistic political agenda. For Soranus, on the other hand, it is a broader question of power: the power for citizen men to discern between fact and fiction, to propagate their bloodlines and to micromanage citizen women's bodies.[16]

Looking at a Greek medical text alongside an American political campaign illustrates the usefulness of the 'toxic masculinity' rubric for contextualising beliefs about sex and reproduction within the power dynamics of patriarchal societies. Despite the divergences in Akin's and Soranus' explanations of pregnancy after sexual assault, with one locating women's supposed libidinal faculties in the body and the other in the mind, we see women trapped in a toxic catch-22. Whether body or mind, either way they lose. And the overarching concept of 'toxic masculinity' helps remind us that these rape denials belong to a larger constellation of misogyny ancient and modern, from Semonides and Ovid's *praeceptor amoris* to the Reagan, Bush and Trump White Houses and the alt-right (cf. Zuckerberg, *Not All Dead White Men*).

SORANUS ON RAPE AND PREGNANCY

Soranus is a chief extant member of the ancient medical tradition termed 'methodism', which holds that good health and all ailments can be explained and cared for on the heuristic of constriction or relaxation (or 'stricture' and 'flux') in the body and its component systems; accordingly, methodist remedies focus on stringent or laxative treatments.[17] As a methodist, Soranus deprecates case study and judgements based on experience in preference of a grand-theory approach.[18] Soranus' gynaecological treatise *Gynaikeia* is, after Galen, the most substantial and important surviving gynaecological work from antiquity, and seems to have been more influential than Galen on ancient gynaecology in the Greek east.[19] *Gynaikeia* does not discuss fertilisation or embryology at length because Soranus wrote a separate treatise, now lost, about that topic.[20]

Gynaikeia 1.37 is the passage in contact with Todd Akin's 2012 comments. I quote extensively to allow for a fully contextualised discussion:

ὡς γὰρ χωρὶς ὀρέξεως οὐκ ἐνδεχόμενον ὑπὸ τῶν ἀρρένων τὸ σπέρμα καταβληθῆναι, τὸν αὐτὸν τρόπον χωρὶς ὀρέξεως ὑπὸ τῶν θηλειῶν οὐκ ἐνδεχόμενον αὐτὸ συλληφθῆναι. καὶ ὡς ἡ τροφὴ χωρὶς ὀρέξεως

καταποθεῖσα καὶ μετά τινος ἀποστροφῆς οὐ καλῶς κατατάσσεται καὶ
τῆς ἐπιβαλλούσης <ἀπο>τυγχάνει πέψεως, οὕτως οὐδὲ τὸ σπέρμα
δύναται ἀναληφθῆναί τε καὶ κρατηθὲν κυοφορηθῆναι δίχα τοῦ
παρεῖναι πρὸς συνουσίαν ὁρμὴν καὶ ὄρεξιν. καὶ γὰρ εἴ τινες βιασθεῖσαι
συνέλαβον, ἔστι καὶ ἐπὶ τούτων εἰπεῖν, ὅτι τὸ μὲν τῆς ὀρέξεως πάντως
πάθος καὶ ταύταις παρῆν, ἐπεσκοτεῖτο δὲ ὑπὸ ψυχικῆς κρίσεως.

For just as it isn't possible for sperm to be discharged by males without
desire, in the same way it isn't possible for it [i.e. sperm] to be conceived
by females without desire. And just like food swallowed down without
desire and with some aversion isn't ingested well and fails in the following
process of digestion, so also the sperm can't be taken up and, if taken,
can't be carried through to pregnancy,[21] without the presence of an urge
for intercourse and desire. For even if some women conceive after being
raped, for them there's this to say: that even in these women the quality of
desire was present at any rate, but it was overshadowed by the judgement
of the psyche.[22]

Soranus, lacking the wherewithal to assess women's reproductive systems on
their own merit,[23] has recourse to analogy. Women's conception is like men's
ejaculation and like human digestion.[24] The first comparandum conflates sexual
pleasure with conception; Soranus' assumption that women's sex organs function as a kind of interiorised mirror of men's is common in ancient medical
texts.[25] But the analogy is itself inaccurate. Sexual desire in men is not a necessary prerequisite for ejaculation either. Similarly with the second comparison:
hunger, or desire for food, is not in fact necessary for digestion. Even if the
analogies were accurate, however, they are still inapposite. Soranus does not
prove the relevance of the comparisons he makes, or the transferability of the
principles underlying them.

For Soranus, conception is a psychosomatic phenomenon. The process
depends on physiological responses to psychological experiences. The 'urge
for intercourse' ('πρὸς συνουσίαν ὁρμή') combined with desire (ὄρεξις)
prepares the uterus to be receptive; the term ὁρμή may suggest an instinctual or
autonomous response rather than a conscious one, while the desire is a consciously
experienced emotion. Given the assumptions Soranus makes about conception,
pregnancy resulting from rape – by definition, undesired sex – presents a
conundrum. Soranus' solution is to present a calculus of different competing
psychological impulses, 'the quality of desire' ('τὸ . . . τῆς ὀρέξεως . . . πάθος')
and 'the judgement of the psyche' ('ψυχικὴ κρίσις'), whose conflict results in
either the engagement or failure of the body's mechanisms for conception. The
muddiness of Soranus' presentation here is complicated further by the manifold
connotations and denotations of the term πάθος. The πάθος of desire could

mean the 'quality of desire', as I translate it above, or the property of desire. But it could also refer to the 'emotion' or 'passion' of desire, with much clearer shades of intention and will on the rape survivor's part, or even the 'accident' or 'experience', in which case the desire would appear to be almost like an external phenomenon to which the woman is subjected whether she wants it or not, in parallel to the sexual assault itself.[26]

There is yet more to this toxic nexus in Soranian gynaecology. At *Gynaikeia* 1.10, Soranus claims that the orifice of the uterus dilates 'in the desire for intercourse, in order to receive sperm' ('ἐν τῇ ὀρέξει τῆς συνουσίας πρὸς παραδοχὴν τοῦ σπέρματος'), as well as for the excretion of menstrual fluid and during pregnancy.[27] Not long after Soranus' 'legitimate rape' passage, he asserts that, after conception, 'sperm [here meaning the embryo post-conception] escapes [the body] because of fear and grief and unexpected delight and, in general, by forceful upset of disposition' ('ἐξίεται γὰρ τὸ σπέρμα καὶ διὰ φόβον καὶ διὰ λύπην καὶ χαρὰν αἰφνίδιον καὶ καθόλου διανοίας ἰσχυρὰν ταραχήν', 1.46). An implication of this last assertion, lodged in a passage describing means of ending a pregnancy, is that even if a woman conceived after being raped, the pregnancy would not last for long: because if she was truly raped, she would be afflicted with emotions such as fright, sorrow and severe mental upset, and thus would evacuate the 'sperm'. In other words, one might say, 'the female body has ways to try to shut the whole thing down'.

AKIN AND SORANUS

The resonances of Akin's words with this heinous passage from Soranus' *Gynaikeia* are clear. Women, according to each of the two men, cannot become pregnant without desire. Thus pregnancy resulting from sexual violence is evidence that the victim desired the assault. It is victim-blaming, pure and simple. Each man's theory of conception furthermore supports his ideological position that abortion is unacceptable for women who do not want to be pregnant, and his broader, toxic view of women as fit first and foremost for reproduction.

In the immediate wake of the Akin gaffe, a number of bloggers made the connection between Akin's comments and Soranus'.[28] Many have done so via Laqueur, who adduces Soranus when discussing the assertion by eighteenth-century medical writer Samuel Farr that 'without an excitation of lust, or enjoyment in the venereal act, no conception can probably take place';[29] Laqueur also points out that '[t]he 1756 edition of Burn's *Justice of the Peace*, the standard guide for English magistrates, cites authorities back to the Institutes of Justinian to the effect that "a woman cannot conceive unless she doth consent".'[30]

Caldwell, 'Akin's Reproductive Ideas', emphasises that both Soranus and Akin adhere to the principle that sex should be for producing children and nothing else, and points out how, in both Soranus and Akin, an appeal to medical authority is used to try to control women's bodies. Whalen, 'Contemporary Views of Men's Views on Women's Anatomies', connects Akin's remarks to the Hippocratic corpus, specifically the comment at *On Generation* 5 that a woman who does not want to conceive can expel a man's sperm at will. Huntley and McClain, 'Legitimately Ancient Ideas about Rape', tie the Hippocratic *On Generation* and the Soranus passage together with Galen's comment (7.127.3–11) that a woman cannot conceive without orgasm[31] – and thus by extension could not conceive after being raped, a sentiment echoed by Aetius (16.26).

Of the various contemporary commentators who have linked Akin's words with Soranus', the most extensive examination of the intertext is provided by Greenfield, 'Consent and conception':

> In this context, it is worth remembering the historical precedent. When the second-century Soranus said that conception proves a woman's 'sexual appetite' was merely 'obscured by mental resolve', he assumed her mental response was less important than her sexual one. The same is true of the early modern legal assumption that 'a woman cannot conceive unless she doth consent'. Again, it appears, the pregnant body legally outweighs a woman's mind. She may think she did not want to have sex – or get pregnant – but her body contradicts this and is granted the legal upper hand.
>
> How different are these examples from Akin's suggestion that, 'if it's a legitimate rape, the female body has ways to try to shut that whole thing down'? As my twenty-one year old daughter Anna told me, there is no 'thinking woman' in this statement. Rather, the woman's body seems to do the only work. If her body really did not want to have sex, she would not have gotten pregnant in the first place. If she is now pregnant, her body must have both wanted to have sex and wanted to conceive, and she is now obligated to remain pregnant.

Greenfield misses, I think, an important distinction between Soranus on the one hand and both 'legitimate rape' and the early modern 'a woman cannot conceive unless she doth consent' on the other. Soranus claims that pregnancy is proof of the 'quality of desire', the pathos of desire (πάθος, as we saw above, can mean 'quality' or 'property', 'emotion' or 'passion', or even 'accident' or 'experience'). The early modern formula claims instead that conception is proof of consent. Concealed in the phrase 'legitimate rape', too, is the idea of consent. What makes rape – i.e. non-consensual sexual violence – 'legitimate' is the very fact that it is non-consensual. Soranus may ultimately be taken as appearing to conceive of non-consensual desire or, in other words, unwilling physical arousal,[32] but such nuance is lacking in both the early modern source and in Akin's comments.

So while Soranus, Akin and early modern jurisprudence all agree that pregnancy is proof of a woman's desire, Soranus diverges from the later authors in the mechanisms that lead to pregnancy in what all three might distressingly consider 'questionable cases' of sexual assault. For Soranus, a woman's body is in control, her conscious mind subordinate. Even if a woman's psyche says no, her body with its hidden, subconscious desire can overrule it. For modern proponents of this ideology, it is mind over matter. If the woman's psyche doesn't desire, then the body follows the mind's lead and 'shuts the whole thing down'. The 'legitimate rape' doctrine, therefore, is at once more modern and more repugnant. Unlike its Greek predecessor, which treats women as irrational creatures beholden to physical urges,[33] the modern viewpoint grants women sovereignty of mind. But while Soranus describes pregnancy resulting from rape as a triumph of the body over the mind, 'legitimate rape' attributes it to the mind's complicity. If Soranus asserted, 'she couldn't help it, her body wanted it', his modern counterpart might reply, 'the body could have helped it, but the mind wanted it'. What we see in Akin et al.'s conception of pregnancy after rape is victim-blaming par excellence that exceeds even the misogynistic models of ancient Greece and Rome.

TOXIC DOCTRINES ANCIENT AND MODERN

The toxic sludge of men's thoughts on rape and pregnancy is not limited to Todd Akin in modern Republican politics or to medical writers in the ancient world. As Ortega, 'Days without a GOP Rape Mention', attests, Republican politicians and rape-comment 'gaffes' have been an ongoing problem – one renewed as recently as late June 2022, when Yesli Vega, Prince William County Supervisor and Republican candidate for Congress, suggested that pregnancy resulting from rape was rare, 'Because it's not something that's happening organically. You're forcing it.'[34] The problem was brought to a fever pitch in that same month by the partisan decision of the corrupt Supreme Court of the United States to overturn *Roe* v. *Wade* and thus deprive people who may become pregnant of fundamental health and body rights, even in instances of rape, incest and pregnancies that threaten the life of the pregnant person.

And it is not difficult to find other moments in other ancient literature where a man suggests that forcible sexual assault is maybe not so non-consensual after all. Perhaps most prominent is a notorious passage of Ovid's *Ars Amatoria* (1.663–80) in which the *magister amoris*, who narrates the poem's guide on how to find available sex-labourers and trick or talk them into free sex, endorses sexual assault. The Ovidian speaker tells the narratee to take kisses even ungiven,[35] says a woman who fights back wants to be beaten in a fight,[36] authorises the use of force on the grounds that a woman likes force and enjoys giving up sex unwillingly,[37] and characterises rape as a gift to its survivors.[38] When your values rate women's bodily sovereignty lower than childbirth (as for Soranus and Akin) or men's pleasure (as for the *magister amoris*), sexual assault needs to be explained away, redefined as being, on some level, a mutual encounter.

The toxic masculinity about sexuality extends well beyond rape in pseudo-medical and political thinking both ancient and modern. Soranus tells us that 'not conceiving is much better than destroying what has been conceived' ('τοῦ {μὴ}[39] φθείρειν τὸ συλληφθὲν πολὺ μᾶλλον συμφέρει τὸ μὴ συλλαβεῖν', 1.61), a maxim echoed by modern right-wing pushes for education and healthcare regimes that prioritise maximal abstinence over open access to contraception and abortion.[40] In the same section of *Gynaikeia*, discussing means of avoiding conception during sex, Soranus recommends what we would now call the 'rhythm method' (of dubious efficacy) and 'pull and pray' (even more dubious). The sketchiness of his recommendations is compounded by the fact that he makes it the woman's responsibility to pull herself away from the man's penis before he ejaculates. At 1.33, Soranus notes that the best time to deflower a virgin is when she begins menstruating, usually in her fourteenth year of age, to which we might compare child-marriage in some fundamentalist Christian communities in the United States and 'age of consent' laws that permit marriage well below eighteen years of age in some American states.[41]

Perhaps most remarkable in the current sexual-political climate is *Gynaikeia* 1.30, where Soranus writes that ovulation is harmful to women just as ejaculation is harmful to men; he suggests as evidence for this assertion that chastity makes men healthier (and thus it will make women healthier, too).[42] We see here a kernel of the idea underpinning two quite different modern takes on chastity and men's health in particular. As Diefendorf, 'After the Wedding Night', demonstrates, many Christian men in the present-day United States who undertake pledges to be abstinent before marriage end up conceptualising their chastity as proof of 'strength' and 'manliness' in ways that reinforce hegemonic masculinity. Meanwhile, the notion that a man's abstinence from sex (and particularly from masturbation) will grant him enhanced strength and life force and virility is a long-held and long-discredited canard that has recently gained traction in certain online subcultures. The 'NoFap' and 'No Nut November' movements encourage men to avoid ejaculation and provide communities for men to discuss their struggles to remain abstinent.[43] But, as Manavis (2018) shows, the grisly underbelly of these men's chastity initiatives is one of intense, violent misogyny. Taylor and Jackson (2018) likewise trace how the rhetorical cesspool of NoFap-style chastity reinforces normative masculinity rather than challenging it. And the types who populate the NoFap forums turn out to be the usual suspects from the 4chan and Reddit internet fora, who endorse the sexist, objectifying model of the 'pickup artist'[44] and decry the supposed sexual economy that leaves some of them as involuntarily celibate, or 'incels'.[45] There is overlap, too, between this kind of toxic masculinity and the resurgence of internet-fuelled white supremacist extremism across the United States and Europe, from mass shootings to insurrection.[46] Underpinning all these strange and ghastly social phenomena, from Soranus to the 'incel' mass murderer Elliot Rodger, is a firmly held, unexamined commitment to the essentialism of sex and sexuality as ordering not only gender and gender roles but also power, privilege, and humans' relationship to nature and the divine.[47]

Something about all this toxicity that makes it so insidious is that it can coexist with seemingly contradictory beliefs and values, such as heartache for women who have survived sexual assault. In his apology statement, Todd Akin wrote, 'I misspoke in this interview and it does not reflect the deep empathy I hold for the thousands of women who are raped and abused every year.'[48] We should not be too hasty in discounting this claim of empathy as cynical or perfunctory, even when we learn that the next sentence of Akin's statement again rejected a woman's right to abortion in the case of rape.[49] Similarly, Porter, 'Compassion in Soranus' *Gynecology*', has shown that Soranus, in certain parts of *Gynaikeia*, shows profound compassion for women in medical distress. Compassion and empathy are not inconsistent with the misogynistic moral outlook declaring that women who conceive after rape really wanted it all along. The expression of heartfelt emotion acts as a temper to the venomous ideologies that lurk beneath – a dose of honey on the rim of a bitterly poisonous cup.[50]

NOTES

1. Moore (2012) offers a detailed timeline of the events.
2. See Goddard n.d., s. v. *gaffe*; named after Kinsley 2007.
3. So Lambrecht 2013.
4. See, for example, Holmes et al. 1996.
5. As Franke-Ruta (2012) explains, 'the idea that trauma is a form of birth control' has been expressed by anti-abortion Republican politicians dating back to 1980 and possibly earlier. In 1988, Pennsylvania state legislator Stephen Freind suggested that pregnancy caused by rape occurs at the rate of 'one in millions and millions and millions' because during sexual assault 'a woman secretes a certain secretion which has a tendency to kill the sperm'; he also, in defence of his position, cited anti-abortion propaganda based on Nazi concentration-camp experiments (see Drachler 1988). In 1995, United States Congressman Henry Aldridge, Republican of North Carolina, remarked in a Congressional committee meeting, '[t]he facts show that people who are raped – who are truly raped – the juices don't flow, the body functions don't work and they don't get pregnant' (quoted at Associated Press 1995). Four years later, the prominent anti-abortion pundit John C. Willke argued that pregnancy almost never occurs as a result of rape because the trauma of sexual assault will cause enough hormonal change in women that any pregnancy will either not take place or not remain viable (Willke 1999), a claim to be found in ancient medical texts as well, as I note

below. A year prior to the Akin gaffe, the House of Representatives (controlled by a Republican majority) had passed a bill, rejected by the Senate, that would have blocked federal healthcare funding for abortion in the cases of statutory rape (i.e. rape of underage children), non-violent rape, and rape of women who had been drugged; and would have required the Internal Revenue Service to demand documentation of rape from women who used tax deductions to pay for health insurance that covered abortions (see Somanader 2011). And a few months before Akin's own scandalous moment in the spotlight, Idaho state legislator Chuck Winder had suggested that doctors should scrutinise women's reasons for requesting abortions when they say the pregnancy was the result of rape (quoted at Bassett 2012).

6. See Wikipedia contributors, 'Rape and pregnancy statement controversies'.

7. Trillin 2012. The stanza on Akin: 'Legitimate rape, so we're told by Todd Akin, | Will not produce children but simply awaken | Defensive biology. That quickly locks | The system all down, just as safe as Fort Knox'.

8. For a history of the term 'toxic masculinity', including how it ironically originated in antifeminist 'deep masculinity' circles, see Gilchrist 2017. The 'toxicity' of toxic masculinity is multivalent: it poisons women and non-normatively-masculine men, and the larger society – and also the men who adopt this masculinity. Nevertheless, as Flood (2018) notes, '[m]asculinity may be 'toxic' for men, but it is also rewarding, providing a range of unfair and unearned privileges'. See also Salter 2019, for an argument that we ought to pay attention to the material, political and cultural realities underpinning toxically masculine behaviours, and that toxic masculinity is not the same across cultures and situations.

9. For a definition of the term 'rape culture' and its own connection to toxic masculinity, see e.g. Posadas 2017.

10. Connell and Messerschmidt 2005, 844. Connell and Messerschmidt focus on masculinities as paths to and of power.

11. Attenborough 2014, 199–201. See also Coates and Wade 2007 for a typology of 'discursive operations' that downplay rape.

12. Marcotte 2016. Cf. Friedman 2013, who writes: 'It's a masculinity that defines itself not only in opposition to female-ness, but as inherently superior, drawing its strength from dominance over women's "weakness", and creating men who are happy to deliberately undermine women's power; it is only in opposition to female vulnerability that it can be strong.'

13. Weiss 2016.

14. Laqueur 1990. The specific ideology that the vagina is an inverted penis is present not only in Graeco-Roman physiological thinking but also in classical Chinese thought: thus Nye 2004, 16.

15. Fausto-Sterling 2000.

16. Compare the work of Witzke (2022) on echoes of Augustus' legislation on marriage and childbirth in the Republican Party's abortion politics, culminating in the overturning of *Roe* v. *Wade* in June 2022.

17. See further Hanson and Green 1994, 988–1005; Jones-Lewis 2016, 492–3; *Oxford Classical Dictionary*, 4th ed., s.v. 'medicine', §5.3.

18. So King 1995, 199, 204.
19. See *OCD* 4th ed. 'Soranus of Ephesus, physician'. Maire (2008) examines the translation project of Mustio, whose *Gynaecia* in part provides a Latin rendering of portions of Soranus' treatise.
20. So Temkin 1956, xxx.
21. Soranus rarely (as here and at e.g. 1.18, 1.43) makes a clear distinction between pregnancy and conception (so Temkin 1956, 16 n. 33).
22. Throughout I use Ilberg 1927 for the text of Soranus; all translations are mine. Mustio's abridged Latin translation of *Gynaikeia*, produced in the late fifth century CE, omits this portion of Soranus: see e.g. Prenner 2012, 112–20.
23. Perhaps not surprisingly, Temkin (1956, xxx) refers to Soranus' 'ambivalent attitude toward science', an ambivalence reflected in the modern ideology I study in this chapter, as well. Soranus elsewhere gets fundamental facts about women's sexual organs wrong, as Temkin (xxxix) indicates: 'the lack of a clear distinction between nerves and tendons is confusing, and his belief that the seminal ducts in women ended in the bladder, as well as his denial of the existence of the hymen [at 1.17] is surprising'. So also Malinas et al. 1985, 162: Soranus' 'description de l'appareil génital [of women] est une combinaison d'observations d'une surprenante exactitude et d'erreurs qui nous paraissent extraordinaires tant elles sont inattendues' ('description of the genitals of women is a combination of observations of a surprising exactitude and errors which appear to us as extraordinary as they are unexpected').
24. Analogy is ubiquitous in *Gynaikeia* for explanations of the function of women's reproductive systems, particularly comparisons to men's reproductive systems and to other human body functions. In book 1, for assertions that women's genitalia are like men's, see e.g. 1.9, 12, 16, 25, 30 (discussed below), 33 and 37; and compare my brief discussion of the 'single-sex'/'inversion' theory of sex in the previous section of this chapter. Other points of comparison in the first book for women's sexual organs include e.g. the gums (1.28); the feet and eyes (31); the whole body (34, 38); the stomach (36, 53); muscles (46); bones (46 again); wounds (36, 46); perspiration and salivation (31); sweat, urine and faeces (65); vomiting (36, 46); drunkenness (26); seasickness (49); and venesection (42). Soranus' first book also repeatedly compares women's genitalia to cropland: so 1.35 (soil quality and fertility); 36 (seasons for sowing seed); 39 (not seeding flooded land); 40 (sowing only after cleansing the soil); 41 (seeds do not grow in winter); 42 (soil becomes exhausted from continuous production); and 53 (a woman's eating unhealthy food is for the foetus like a muddy water supply). I am reminded here of the traditional Greek formula for betrothal, spoken by the father to the soon-to-be husband, as preserved by, among others, Menander *Perikeiromene* 1013–14: 'ταύτην γνησίων | παίδων επ' ἀρότῳ σοι δίδωμι' ('I give this woman to you for the ploughing of citizen children'). At Soranus *Gynaikeia* 1.47, the reproductive system is compared to the construction of buildings, and at 1.57, the woman's uterus is compared to an eggshell.
25. See e.g. Galen *On the Usefulness of the Parts of the Body* 14.6, *On Seed* 2.1; see further Laqueur 1990, 25–9.

26. I return to the multiplicity of meanings of πάθος in the next section of this chapter.

27. Frustratingly for the enquiry at hand, Soranus at 1.24 writes, 'and it turns out that women forced into sex suffer/experience this' ('συμβαίνει δὲ τὰς τῇ συνουσίᾳ προσβιαζομένας τοῦτο πάσχειν'). But it is impossible to know what 'this' is: Ilberg 1927, ad loc. indicates a lacuna.

28. See e.g. Larbalestier 2012; Long 2012; Caldwell 2012; Huntley and McClain 2012; and Whalen 2013.

29. Laqueur 1990, 161.

30. Laqueur 1990, 161–2. Reinhart (2012) adduces biblical parallels for Akin's worldview: the requirement that survivors of rape marry their rapists (*Deuteronomy* 22.28–9; I would add the parallel of Menandrian New Comedy), the authorisation to sell a daughter into sex-slavery (*Exodus* 21.7–11), permission to coercively marry war captives (*Deuteronomy* 21.11), execution for rape survivors who did not cry out during the assault (*Deuteronomy* 22.23–4), and Moses' declaration of a virgin sex-slave as plunder for his soldiers upon the capture of a city (*Numbers* 31.18). The English magistrates and Todd Akin, but not Soranus, make it into Moss' 'History of the Orgasm' (2017).

31. For further discussion and citations, see Halperin 1990, 278–9 and nn. 80, 82.

32. One might compare this position with the established fact that a man who is raped may develop an erection or even ejaculate during the assault: see e.g. Bullock and Beckson 2011.

33. See further e.g. Soranus *Gynaikeia* 1.33.

34. Concepcion 2022. The news of the comments broke the exact day I was submitting my revised version of this chapter to the editors.

35. 'What man who has any sense wouldn't mix kisses in with flattering words? Even if she doesn't give [kisses], take them ungiven anyway' ('quis sapiens blandis non misceat oscula verbis? | illa licet non det, non data sume tamen', 1.663–4). Text of Kenney 1961 [1995], translations mine.

36. 'Perhaps at first she'll fight and say you're behaving badly – but she'll want herself to be beaten in the fighting' ('pugnabit primo fortassis, et 'improbe' dicet; | pugnando vinci se tamen illa volet', 1.665–6).

37. 'It's okay to use violence, your violence is pleasing to girls: they often want to have given unwillingly what's pleasing to them' ('vim licet appelles: grata est vis ista puellis: | quod iuvat, invitae saepe dedisse volunt', 1.673–4).

38. 'Whatever woman has been violated by a sudden sexual assault enjoys it, and your bad behaviour functions as the equivalent of a gift' ('quaecumque est veneris subita violata rapina, | gaudet, et improbitas muneris instar habet', 1.675–6). Kenney capitalises *Veneris*, as being the goddess Venus, but I take it as a mundane instance of *uenus* in reference to sexual intercourse.

39. Ilberg follows Ermerins in deleting μή, but notes that Rose conjectures μέν.

40. A push that has now met with monstrous success in the overturning of *Roe* v. *Wade*, with a call from some members of the illegitimate Supreme Court majority to overturn contraception rights safeguarded by *Griswold* v. *Connecticut*.

41. See e.g. Bee 2017. Soranus exposes the ironic hypocrisy of modern 'defenders of traditional marriage' against same-gender unions: 'traditional' marriage, we

should remember, was between an adult man and a girl who has just become fertile enough to reproduce.

42. On Soranus' praise of chastity, see Manuli 1982; Pinault 1992; and Hanson and Green 1994, 1027. Soranus' asseveration that chastity is healthy for a woman and that, by contrast, sexual activity is unhealthy casts a pall over the remainder of his work, which is devoted to getting women pregnant and childbearing. Thus Flemming (2000, 238) notes: 'for Soranus (and others among the *methodikoi*), to be a woman is to be reproductive . . . which is not healthy but useful; and it is towards this utilitarian end that Soranus directs his efforts. . . . [I]t should also be noted that there is little or no suggestion of any female choice or control over which category she will inhabit.'

43. 'Fap' is slang for masturbation. On the NoFap movement, see Ley 2015.

44. 'PUAs' even look to Ovid's *Ars Amatoria* for guidance: see Zuckerberg 2018, ch. 3.

45. See e.g. Weissmann 2018.

46. For an ethnography, see Zuckerberg 2018, ch. 1; and compare also Morales 2020, ch. 1.

47. Compare the encapsulation Coates (2012) creates of the implicit line of thinking about power that underlies Akin's comments: 'All of my rationales range from the totally subjective to the outright mythical. But I am the sovereign of the female body. On my word rumor becomes science, and the destruction of your life is repackaged as the defense of someone else's.'

48. Reported at e.g. Mak and Glueck 2012.

49. 'I believe deeply in the protection of all life and I do not believe that harming another innocent victim is the right course of action.'

50. I owe thanks to Caitlin Hines, Serena S. Witzke, Amik La Theirr, Jeffrey Henderson, Aven McMaster, Melanie Racette-Campbell and the anonymous reader for Edinburgh University Press.

CHAPTER 19

Toxic Masculinity in the First-Year Classics Classroom

Jayne Knight and Jonathan Wallis

G endered violence associated with 'toxic masculinity' is common in the sources and topics which we often teach to students encountering Classics for the first time. Drawing upon our experience as teachers of first-year cohorts, this chapter considers our responsibility as primary conduits for such material.[1] We employ a definition of toxic masculinity provided by Harris O'Malley writing for the *Good Men Project*: 'a narrow and repressive description of manhood, designating manhood as defined by violence, sex, status and aggression'.[2] Our case studies are drawn from a first-year Roman civilisation course taught at the University of Tasmania. We discuss how toxic masculinity pertains to three key topics that students encounter during this course: the rape of Lucretia, Catullus' erotic poetry, and Julius Caesar and the decline of the Republic. We offer reflections on our students' responses to these topics, and we consider how teachers might use the concept of toxic masculinity to facilitate student engagement with them. Especially in the wake of 2017's #MeToo movement, we suggest that our students' increasing familiarity with discourse about entitled and violent masculine cultures provides an opportunity for first-year Classics teaching, because it prompts teachers and students to consider the ways in which cultural gender norms and expectations can play a powerful role in shaping a society and its history.[3]

For many students worldwide, a first-year university course will be their first (and perhaps only) academic exposure to the ancient Greeks or Romans. We teach these courses with the hope that students will be inspired to pursue further study in Classics, and perhaps become Classics majors. It is therefore crucial to present material in a compelling and accessible way. But we must also be aware of how ancient sources resonate differently with new generations of students and refine our approaches accordingly. We have found that the ongoing discussion stemming from the #MeToo movement that reached mainstream prominence in late 2017 has had a particular effect in shaping the way students engage with the themes of gender, power and (sexual) violence that are common in a first-year Classics course. The changes we have witnessed in student reception of our first-year Roman civilisation course topics since 2017 prompted us to write this chapter.

Students studying Roman civilisation are confronted with depictions of gendered violence from the outset: early Roman history is punctuated by violence against women, perpetrated by men whose power is based upon 'violence, sex, status and aggression'. The rape of the Sabine women and the rape and suicide of Lucretia are pivotal moments in Rome's foundational narrative, so they are often taught early in a semester. But teachers need to introduce these topics with care, especially since it is easy to become desensitised to them after many years of exposure. Our first case study is Livy's narrative about Lucretia, a story central to Roman history and culture, but extremely difficult for students and teachers to grapple with.

LUCRETIA

With hindsight we admit to a certain naivety in the original planning of our new first-year course *Introduction to Ancient Rome* in early 2017.[4] This important course aims to introduce first-time Classics students to a range of Roman historical, literary, philosophical and material sources, and especially to the connections between these. We adopt a chronological approach to our sources, at least in terms of the periods being represented: we begin the semester with the Augustan-era texts of Livy and Virgil in order to examine the Roman foundational narratives of Aeneas, Romulus and Lucretia. In the first two iterations of this course, in 2017–18, we taught Livy first and Virgil second, in the belief that Livy's prose and rationalising narrative would be more approachable right at the beginning of the semester than the grand opera of Virgil's mythological epic. But this has meant that our first seminar for the course included overtly confrontational material: extended discussion of Lucretia's sexual assault by the elite figure of Sextus Tarquinius, and the way that Livy uses Lucretia's subsequent suicide as catalyst for Roman men to embrace civic liberty in the form of Republican government. Since 2019 we have integrated the story of Lucretia into the beginning of the course in a different way. We outline our current approach below, but first it is valuable to summarise the striking cultural shift which led to our redesign.

Lucretia's presence in the course's first iteration in 2017 was, in effect, 'traditional'. Despite an intention to teach Lucretia's story within a frame informed by current discussion of gendered issues inherent in sexual violence, we found that any independent symbolic significance of Lucretia was overwhelmed by the patriarchal logic in Livy's narrative of Republican foundation. In hindsight, the reasons for this are clear to see. Sexual assault is a challenging topic to discuss at any time, and especially with a group of young people meeting for the first time. It is also now apparent that, right at the beginning of semester, a new and inevitably tentative cohort of students were *en masse* unwilling to read against the culturally authoritative voice Livy possesses – in fact, we were struck by the way that students largely 'concurred' with (or, we suspect, 'echoed') Livy's patriarchal assessment of a woman's cultural worth as validated by Lucretia's 'heroic' suicide. Our 2018 class was very different, and yet made the inadequacy of our course design more obvious. Now almost a year after #MeToo, this cohort of students was far more willing to read Livy's story from Lucretia's perspective, and far more articulate in identifying and critiquing the toxically masculine culture represented by the entitled banter about female 'virtue' exchanged by the drunken young princes at the siege of Ardea. The increased willingness of our 2018 cohort to engage critically with the cultural dynamics present in the story of Lucretia was both striking and heartening, but it highlighted for us that to open our course with such a story – when there is no time for adequate preparation – was insensitive.

In 2019 we swapped the order in which we teach Livy and Virgil as our primary texts for introducing Roman foundation legends. First, by beginning the semester with the clearly fictionalised story of Aeneas' flight from Troy, we are better able to facilitate student engagement by contextualising Rome's foundation stories (including, now in the second week, the stories of Romulus and Lucretia) not as 'Roman history' but rather as cultural myths resembling our own. Second, we are now able to prepare the class for discussing the particular cultural myth of Lucretia in terms of both Roman and contemporary cultural discourses. All our classes are preceded by a short online video 'lecture'; our introductory video for the Livy seminar now concludes with the following statement:

> There's a more sombre note to finish on. In our readings this week we come upon the uncomfortable truth that the stories of Rome's foundation contain some deeply uncomfortable material. Romulus' grand story, for instance, is predicated on the killing of his own brother. His expansion of the city is brought about by the wholesale abduction of women from a neighbouring town – an assault that our historian Livy largely excuses. Most troubling of all, the catalyst for Rome's celebrated embrace of freedom in the form of a Republic is the sexual assault and suicide of a young woman. I would like to let you know in advance that we'll be examining this story and its cultural significance in the second half of our first seminar. In Livy's version, political power and sexual power go hand in hand, and this is a form of gendered tyranny that remains distressingly

familiar in our own culture. In the coming week, we'll certainly look at what this story meant to the Romans. But we'll also look at this symbolic use of women's bodies with twenty-first-century eyes – at the way that stories like Livy's romanticise a passive form of femininity that ultimately serves to legitimise male authority. And that's a very Roman story.

As foregrounded here, we now structure our Lucretia class in two parts. We first discuss Lucretia on Livy's terms, framed by an Augustan system of personal and civic values. We then look at how the reception of Lucretia articulates particular cultural attitudes and gender norms at different periods, culminating in her significance in our own post-#MeToo cultural context. Here the depictions of Lucretia in art, which we had originally included at the beginning of the seminar to demonstrate the enduring 'significance' of Lucretia's story (but in fact risked complicity in glamorising her assault) now introduce the second half of the seminar and include several overtly feminist artworks. In the first iteration of our reworked course in 2019, we had initial success in harnessing our students' increased awareness of the dynamics of toxic masculine culture to examine a story written over 2,000 years ago. Current focus on sexual aggression as an aspect of toxic masculinity provides an entry point for classroom analysis and discussion of Lucretia's story. The contemporary frame of toxic masculinity can be used to make sense of the dire consequences of Sextus Tarquinius' *mala libido*.

CATULLUS

Our experience has been that Catullus is a challenging but valuable inclusion in the first-year Roman civilisation syllabus. Early iterations of this course focused with only limited success on Catullus' 'Lesbia' poems, in the hope that the immediacy and eroticism of these poems would help our first-time classicists to bridge the 'distancing' that affects much ancient primary source material. With hindsight, our lack of success is not surprising. The remarkably persistent belief that 'Of all the Roman poets Catullus is most accessible to the modern reader'[5] is based on the presumption that Catullus 'was just like us',[6] and so assumes that the modern reader is young, male and privileged (and that sexual attitudes are transhistorical). In our comparatively diverse classes, students (many already intimidated by being presented with poetry) found the aggression of Catullan desire off-putting and his overt slut-shaming of Lesbia alienating. Our current version of this course embeds Catullus in discussion of late Republican society and politics, and here we have had far more success. The context of Roman history gives the poems a framing narrative, without which students had struggled when being asked to engage with them as 'art pieces'. The particular focus of this

narrative on sociopolitical disintegration has allowed students to engage pro-
ductively with Catullus' expressions of anger, frustration and disillusionment in
both his political and his erotic poems.

But the challenges remain. Catullus' sociopolitical poetry, no less than his
erotic material, is marked by sexually violent language, and by misogynistic and
'homophobic' humour. Both of these aspects are now well recognised in contemporary society as fundamental to the perpetuation of rape culture. Catullus' bitter
voicing of erotic entitlement in Poem 76, and his exhortation to himself to 'be
a proper man' in Poem 8 – where being a man is to reject perceptions of effeminacy – chime uncomfortably with contemporary definitions of 'toxic masculine'
behaviour. We make the point below that perceived correspondences between
Catullan discourse and our own cultural moment (especially its increased willingness to critique such discourse) provide an opportunity for productive discussion.
But we note first that the new prominence in our media of narratives about gendered and sexual violence connected with 'toxic masculinity' can and does make
classroom engagement with Catullus uncomfortable for many students. It has also
become apparent that teaching Catullus in the context of a first-year class needs
careful contextual framing to avoid implicitly endorsing a misapprehension of
classical material similar to that apparent in 'men's rights' advocates who appeal to
classical models in an attempt to justify destructive gender stereotypes.

We now introduce Catullus specifically in the context of a discussion of
Roman sexuality in the late Republican era. This allows us to foreground the link
in Roman male culture between sexual behaviour and social performance, and so
to frame the violence of Catullan poetry as a form of invective discourse similar
to what students encounter in Cicero's *First Catilinarian* earlier in the semester
(a prose text and more obviously a 'performance', which students find easier to
approach). Once we have contextualised these poems as cultural narratives about
sexual behaviour designed to assert or undermine social authority, we find our students – who are generally experienced in the rhetorical proving grounds of social
media – are well equipped to discuss the personal dynamics of Catullus' poetry. In
future classes, we intend to set a group discussion question using Catullus to compare the social use of sexual narratives in Republican Rome with our own cultural
context. We hope, first, that this will harness our students' contemporary familiarity with such narratives to provide a point of access to Catullan poetry, especially
as social performance. But we also hope it will allow us to establish important
differences (alongside the similarities) between Roman *amor* and post-Romantic
'love', and between constructions of masculine identity then and now.

Directly related to this, and similar to our experience with Lucretia, in 2018
we found that our students were more willing to 'call out' what they recognised
as the toxicity of Catullan discourse. This provides two further opportunities,
both of which we intend to pursue more formally with new cohorts. First, we will

leverage contemporary awareness that the 'toxicity' of certain masculine identities negatively affects men as well as women to approach the emblematic fragmentation and disillusionment of the Catullan persona. But we will also use the case study of Poem 29 (in which Catullus lambasts Caesar's politics as hyper-phallic entitlement and aggression) to encourage students to see Catullus himself 'calling out' the toxicity of Roman political culture – while also being complicit in its perpetuation.

JULIUS CAESAR

Julius Caesar is a popular figure with students, many of whom will have encountered him in some form by the time they enrol in a first-year university course. In our course, Caesar plays a leading role in the historical narrative leading to the decline of the Republic and the establishment of the Principate. About halfway through the semester, we devote a seminar to Caesar's actions as dictator. We conclude the seminar with a set of discussion questions which prompt students to consider the relationship between Roman values and the inherent instability of the Roman Republican system which was exploited by Caesar. We ask, 'To what extent did the value system of Roman Republican society contribute to its decline?' In 2018, students responded by noting the destructive character of Roman masculinity as embodied in the ideal of *virtus*. They pointed with considerable insight to the way a system that rewarded martial values in public life encouraged increasingly damaging competition between Roman men and led inevitably to the social and political devastation brought about by hyper-masculine figures like Caesar himself. This 2018 discussion was the first time we saw students employ the specific phrase 'toxic masculinity' to describe aspects of Roman society and culture, and it prompted us to reflect upon how we might be able to use this concept actively in future discussion activities, instead of waiting for students to raise it on their own.

Asking students to consider the overlap between facets of Roman *virtus* as it is represented in late Republican sources and modern definitions of toxic masculinity has the potential to generate critical discussion about how gender norms and expectations impacted Roman politics and society in destructive ways. It creates a bridge between ancient Rome and the present that allows students to explore the continuities between Rome and their own society while also taking stock of the differences. We have found that students are eager to participate in this kind of exercise. Class discussions about late Republican figures like Caesar, Sulla, Marius and Antony often spark comparisons with modern political figures and events, and this has only become more common since the 2016 US presidential election. The concept of toxic masculinity can provide structure for a discussion about the sociopolitical ramifications of 'narrow and repressive' definitions of manhood during the late Republic and today.

Famous Roman men like Caesar are often idealised and heroised by popular culture, and today the type of masculinity that Caesar embodied is celebrated by 'male supremacist' groups who advocate for the return of the patriarchal value system that they believe once made Western civilisation great.[7] Critical approaches to *virtus* and to the ways it was conceptualised and exhibited are therefore crucial in today's classroom. In order to challenge oversimplified or idealised perceptions of Roman masculinity, teachers can demonstrate how ideas about *virtus* changed over time, and how individual Roman writers, even those living at the same time, could hold different beliefs and attitudes about *virtus* and what kinds of behaviour it demanded. As scholars contributing to *Pharos* have pointed out, 'The hypermasculine and militaristic view of *virtus* . . . reflects only the way the term was used in the earliest history of Rome and not how the term's meaning changed over time. Rome's military expansion led to cultural exchange that broadened their concept of *virtus* from a gendered, militaristic meaning to a more general ethical category.'[8]

In the context of a class discussion about Julius Caesar and Roman masculinity, it can be helpful to provide students with a selection of excerpts drawn from primary sources that display different assessments of Caesar's *virtus*; for example, Catullus' scathing depiction of Caesar's hypermasculine rapacity in Poem 29, Caesar's speech to his men justifying his illegal entry into Italy in his *Bellum Civile*, Cicero's letters in the wake of Caesar's assassination, and Lucan's brutal characterisation of Caesar in *Pharsalia*.[9] Examining a selection of primary sources like these together brings into view the spectrum of perspectives that coexisted in antiquity about the masculine character and behaviour of a single figure like Caesar. In an activity like this, teachers can prompt students to interrogate whether the concept of toxic masculinity can be usefully applied to understand the representations of Caesar found in these sources.

CONCLUSION

Each of our case studies has shown how topics and sources that are commonly introduced in first-year-level Roman civilisation courses feature depictions of masculinity that fall under modern definitions of toxic masculinity. Livy's narrative about the rape of Lucretia showcases how masculinity defined by 'violence, sex, status and aggression' – the masculinity embodied by Sextus Tarquinius – promotes and perpetuates rape culture. Lucretia's story demands thoughtful framing that acknowledges the challenging nature of the source material, but when introduced properly, it provides a launching point for rich discussions about the interplay between gender, culture and politics both in ancient Rome and today. When introduced with careful historical and literary contextualisation, Catullus' poetry vividly illustrates the performative nature of ancient Roman masculinity, and many of his poems highlight in particular the 'toxic' elements of that masculinity, again providing stimulating material for discussion. Julius Caesar provides a case study in ancient representations of civic and martial masculinities. Reading the diverse body of sources written about his role in the civil strife that ended the Republic through the lens of toxic masculinity can be a rewarding exercise that challenges overly simplistic or idealised perceptions of Caesar's significance as a 'great man' of Roman history.

We have suggested that teachers can use the modern concept of toxic masculinity to facilitate and deepen student engagement with these ancient texts and topics. Students today are increasingly aware of the culturally constructed nature of gender, and they are curious about how gender was theorised, constructed and performed in the ancient world. Including discussions about gender as part of a first-year classical civilisation course shows students how studying the ancient past can enhance their understanding of present-day issues that are meaningful to them. It is often said that Classics is 'good to think with'. The frame of toxic masculinity can be a teaching tool that highlights the critical potential of classical studies in today's world.

Our experience has been that it is beneficial to introduce students to the diversity of viewpoints on masculine behaviour presented by ancient sources, ideally by facilitating direct engagement with a range of these sources in translation. Although some ancient sources appear to validate and encourage a 'narrow and repressive' version of manhood that is defined by violence, sex, status and aggression, other sources critique socially and politically destructive forms of masculinity, demonstrating that debate about gender and behaviour was active even in antiquity (although it was conducted in different terms). Inviting students to apply the frame of toxic masculinity to their analysis of ancient sources can be a beneficial use of anachronism, as it bridges the temporal gap between ancient Romans and ourselves, making the Romans seem more human in the process. At the same time, we suggest that it is necessary to provide thorough historical, cultural and literary contextualisation of primary sources in advance so that the stark differences between ancient Roman and modern cultures are not glossed over or washed out.

A social mission underpins university education – at our university, graduates are expected to recognise and critically evaluate issues of social responsibility, ethical conduct and sustainability. Teachers are responsible for presenting the elements of ancient culture and history which illustrate harmful masculine ideals and behaviours in a socially conscious way that encourages critical engagement with the past and its relationship to the present. Dialogue about how societies encourage and reward destructive models of masculinity is at the forefront of today's public discourse, and it can also have an impactful place in the first-year Classics classroom. We hope to have provided some useful thoughts and suggestions on how teachers can put the concept of toxic masculinity to work in their own first-year classrooms.

NOTES

1. Many classicists have drawn attention to the need for thoughtful approaches to teaching sensitive or controversial subject matter. See Rabinowitz and McHardy (eds) 2014. Strategies for teaching about rape have been the focus of many works; for example, Gloyn 2013. Genevieve Liveley and Sharon James' two chapters on teaching rape close the 2012 volume *A Companion to Roman Love Elegy*. Scholars have also turned to public scholarship to address the need for Classics courses to confront difficult issues, for example, Beek 2016. Sears (2017) emphasises the importance of a nuanced approach to teaching ancient sources like the *Iliad*, which are used by some to defend and promote a kind of masculinity embodied by the Homeric Achilles – a destructive masculinity that claims legitimacy and entitlement through violence.

2. O'Malley 2016.

3. The original movement was founded by activist Tarana Burke in 2006. In October 2017, the #MeToo hashtag went viral on social media in the wake of sexual violence accusations against American film producer Harvey Weinstein. People around the world began to use the #MeToo hashtag to share personal experiences of sexual violence and express solidarity with victims. According to the Pew Research Center, the hashtag was used more than 19 million times between 15 October 2017 and 30 September 2018, a figure that illustrates the movement's rapid rise to mainstream prominence. See Anderson and Toor 2018.

4. Our *Introduction to Ancient Rome* course combines the study of Roman history and literature and is taught as a weekly mixed-format seminar in which short lectures are paired with periods of discussion or activity. Each seminar is preceded by an introductory video lecture which students watch online. This format encourages deep, instructor-guided student engagement with sources and topics.

5. Godwin 2008, back cover. See also Daniel Garrison 2007, 503: 'If there were ever a Latin author perfectly suited for the college curriculum, Catullus is the gift from heaven' – although Garrison's point distinguishes college-level students as 'adult readers' from adolescent or teenage readers more likely to be interested only in Catullus' 'turbulent obsessions'.

6. Godwin 2008, Preface.

7. *Pharos* 2017. Donna Zuckerberg's *Not All Dead White Men* examines how far-right groups use ancient texts to support their misogynistic and white supremacist views online.

8. Ball et al. 2018.

9. When designing an activity like this, we recommend providing students with some contextual information about each source (such as, for example, authorship, date and genre) to help guide their analysis.

Bibliography

Abad-Santos, Alex. 'Performative Masculinity Is Making American Men Sick'. *Vox*, 10 August 2020. https://www.vox.com/the-goods/21356150/american-men-wont-wear-masks-covid-19.

Addis, Michael, and Geoffrey Cohane. 'Social Scientific Paradigms of Masculinity and Their Implications for Research and Practice in Men's Mental Health'. *Journal of Clinical Psychology* 61.6 (2005): 633–47.

Adejobi, A. 'Monty Python Actor John Cleese Denounces Twitter Troll over "Snowflake" Insult'. *Metro*, 9 July 2018. metro.co.uk//07/09/monty-python-actor-john-cleese-denounces-twitter-troll-over-snowflake-insult-7694871.

Aerts, W. J. *Michaelis Pselli Historia Syntomos. Corpus Fontium Historiae Byzantinae.* Vol. 30. Series Berolinensis. Berlin/New York: De Gruyter, 1990.

Ager, Britta. 'Necromancy, Divine Encounters, and Erotic Magic in Cupid and Psyche'. *American Journal of Philology* 140 (2019): 317–43.

Aguirre, M. 'La Difesa Della Razza (1938–1943): Primitivism and Classicism in Fascist Italy'. *Politics, Religion and Ideology* 16.4 (2015): 370–80.

Allison, June W. *Word and Concept in Thucydides.* Atlanta: Scholars Press, 1997.

Alston, Richard. 'Arms and the Man: Soldiers, Masculinity, and Power in Republican and Imperial Rome'. In Foxhall and Salmon 1998, 205–23.

American Psychological Association. 'APA Guidelines for Psychological Practice with Boys and Men', 2018. https://www.apa.org/about/policy/boys-men-practice-guidelines.pdf.

Ampolo, C. 'Introduzione'. In C. Ampolo and M. Manfredini, eds. *Plutarco: Le Vite Di Teseo e Romolo.* Milan: Mondadori, 1988, ix–lv.

Anderson, Monica, and Skye Toor. 'How Social Media Users Have Discussed Sexual Harassment Since #MeToo Went Viral'. *Fact Tank (Pew Research Center)*

(blog), 11 October 2018. https://www.pewresearch.org/fact-tank/2018/10/11/
how-social-media-users-have-discussed-sexual-harassment-since-metoo-went-
viral/.

Anderson, William. 'Plautus' "Trinummus": The Absurdity of Officious
Orality'. *Traditio* 35 (1979): 333–45.

Arnold, J. H., and S. Brady, eds. *What Is Masculinity? Historical Dynamics from
Antiquity to the Contemporary World*. Houndmills and New York: Palgrave
Macmillan, 2011.

Arthurs, J. *Excavating Modernity: The Roman Past in Fascist Italy*. London and
Ithaca, NY: Cornell University Press, 2012.

Associated Press. 'Lawmaker Says Rape Can't Cause Pregnancy'. *SFGate*, 21
April 1995. https://www.sfgate.com/news/article/Lawmaker-Says-Rape-Can-
t-Cause-Pregnancy-3036411.php.

Astin, Alan E. *Cato the Censor*. Oxford: Clarendon Press, 1978.

Attenborough, Frederick. 'Rape Is Rape (Except When It's Not): The Media,
Recontextualisation and Violence against Women'. *Journal of Language
Aggression and Conflict* 2.2 (2014): 183–203.

Austin, C., and S. D. Olson. *Aristophanes: Thesmophoriazusae*. Oxford: Oxford
University Press, 2004.

Ball, Siobhan, Maud W. Gleason, Erich S. Gruen, Alexander Hardwick, Robert
Kaster, Myles McDonnell and Craig A. Williams. 'Scholars Respond to
Misogynist Nostalgia for Roman Masculinity'. *Pharos* (blog), 5 March 2018.
https://pharos.vassarspaces.net/2018/03/05/scholars-respond-to-miso
gynist-nostalgia-for-roman-masculinity.

Balmaceda, C. *Virtus Romana: Politics and Morality in the Roman Historians*.
Chapel Hill: University of North Carolina Press, 2017.

Balot, Ryan K. *Courage in the Democratic Polis: Ideology and Critique in Classical
Athens*. New York: Oxford University Press, 2014.

Baltussen, H. 'A Grief Observed: Cicero on Remembering Tullia'. *Mortality* 14
(2009): 355–69.

———, ed. *Greek and Roman Consolations: Eight Studies of a Tradition and Its
Afterlife*. Swansea: Classical Press of Wales, 2013.

Banet-Weiser, Sarah, and Kate Milner Miltner. '#MasculinitySoFragile: Culture,
Structure, and Networked Misogyny'. *Feminist Media Studies* 16.1 (2015):
171–4.

Bannon, C. J. *The Brothers of Romulus: Fraternal Pietas in Roman Law, Literature,
and Society*. Princeton: Princeton University Press, 1997.

Barchiesi, A. *Epistulae Heroidum 1–3*. Firenze: Le Monnier, 1992.

Barlow, Jonathan. 'Scipio Aemilianus and Greek Ethics'. *Classical Quarterly*
68.1 (2018): 112–27.

Barton, Carlin. 'The Roman Blush: The Delicate Matter of Self-Control'. In
Porter 1999, 212–34.

————. *Roman Honor: The Fire in the Bones*. Berkeley: University of California Press, 2001.

Bartsch, Shadi. *Actors in the Audience: Theatricality and Doublespeak from Nero to Hadrian*. Cambridge, MA: Harvard University Press, 1994.

Baskins, Cristelle L. '(In)Famous Men: The Continence of Scipio and Formations of Masculinity in Fifteenth-Century Tuscan Domestic Painting'. *Studies in Iconography* 23 (2002): 109–36.

Bassett, Laura. 'Chuck Winder, Idaho Lawmaker, Suggests Women Use Rape As Excuse For Abortions'. *Huffington Post*, 20 March 2012. https://www.huffingtonpost.com/2012/03/20/chuck-winder-rape-abortions_n_1366994.html.

Bassi, K. *Acting Like Men: Gender, Drama, and Nostalgia in Ancient Greece*. Ann Arbor: University of Michigan Press, 1999.

————. 'The Semantics of Manliness in Ancient Greece'. In Rosen and Sluiter 2003, 25–58.

Bauman, Richard A. *Women and Politics in Ancient Rome*. London: Routledge, 1992.

Beek, Anna Everett. 'Ovid's Afterlife: Mythical Rape and Rape Myths'. *Eidolon*, 22 April 2016. https://eidolon.pub/ovid-s-afterlife-4f708df9d244.

Ben-Ghiat, Ruth. 'Envisioning Modernity: Desire and Discipline in the Italian Fascist Film'. *Critical Inquiry* 23.1 (1996): 109–44.

————. *La Cultura Fascista*. Bologna: Società editrice il Mulino, 2000.

————. 'Italian Fascism's Empire Cinema: Kif Tebbi, the Conquest of Libya, and the Assault on the Nomadic'. In Sandra Ponzanesi and Marguerite Waller, eds. *Postcolonial Cinema Studies*. London and New York: Routledge, 2012, 20–31.

Bennet, L., and W. Tyrrell. 'Sophocles' *Antigone* and Funerary Oration'. *American Journal of Philology* 111.4 (1990): 441–56.

Berg, H. 'Masculinities in Early Hellenistic Athens'. In Arnold and Brady 2011, 97–113.

Berlant, Lauren, and Michael Warner. 'Sex in Public'. *Critical Inquiry* 24.2 (1998): 547–66.

Bernal, Martin. *Black Athena: The Afroasiatic Roots of Classical Civilization*. New Brunswick, NJ: Rutgers University Press, 1987.

Berno, Francesca Romana. *L. Annaeus Seneca: De Constantia Sapientis: La Fermezza Del Saggio*. Napoli: Paolo Loffredo Editore, 2018.

Bevegni, Claudio. *Eudocia Augusta: Storia Di San Cipriano*. Milan: Adelphi, 2006.

Bielman, Anne. 'Female Patronage in the Greek Hellenistic and Roman Republican Periods'. In Dillon and James 2012, 238–48.

Bilabel, Friedrich, and Adolf Grohmann. *Griechische, Koptische, Und Arabische Texte Zur Religion Und Religiösen Literatur In Ägyptens Spätzeit*. Heidelberg: Heidelberg University Press, 1934.

Bodson, Liliane. 'Attitudes toward Animals in Greco-Roman Antiquity'. *International Journal for the Study of Animal Problems* 4.4 (1983): 312–20.

Bosson, J. K., R. M. Burnaford, D. Cohen, J. A. Vandello and J. R. Weaver. 'Precarious Manhood'. *Journal of Personality and Social Psychology* 95.6 (2008): 1325–39.

Boswell, John. *Same-Sex Unions in Premodern Europe*. New York: Villard Books, 1994.

Bourdieu, Pierre. *Masculine Domination*. Stanford: Standford University Press, 2001.

Bowie, A. M. *Herodotus: Histories Book VIII*. Cambridge: Cambridge University Press, 2007.

Boyd, Barbara. 'Teaching Ovid's Love Elegy'. In Gold 2012, 526–40.

Brakke, David. 'Ethiopian Demons: Male Sexuality, the Black-Skinned Other, and the Monastic Self'. *Journal of the History of Sexuality* 10.3/4 (2001): 501–35.

Bremmer, J. 'Romulus, Remus and the Foundation of Rome'. In J. N. Bremmer and N. H. Horsfall, eds. *Roman Myth and Mythography*. London: Institute of Classical Studies, 1987, 25–48.

Brennan, T. Corey. 'Perceptions of Women's Power in the Late Republic'. In Dillon and James 2012, 354–66.

Brooks, David. 'Opinion: Before Manliness Lost Its Virtue'. *New York Times*, 1 August 2017. https://www.nytimes.com/2017/08/01/opinion/scaramucci-mccain-masculinity-white-house.html.

Brooks, G. R. *A New Psychotherapy for Traditional Men*. San Francisco: Jossey-Bass, 1998.

Brown, Andrew. *Sophocles: Antigone*. Warminster: Aris and Phillips, 1987.

Brown, Peter. *Power and Persuasion in Late Antiquity: Towards a Christian Empire*. Madison: University of Wisconsin Press, 1992.

———. *The Rise of Western Christendom: Triumph and Diversity AD 200–1000*. Chichester: Wiley-Blackwell, 2013.

Bullock, C. M., and M. Beckson. 'Male Victims of Sexual Assault: Phenomenology, Psychology, Physiology'. *Journal of the American Academy of Psychiatry and the Law* 39.2 (2011): 197–205.

Burke, John. 'Inventing and Re-Inventing Byzantium: Nikephoros Phokas, Byzantine Studies in Greece, and "New Rome"'. In Ingela Nilsson and Paul Stephenson, eds. *Wanted, Byzantium: The Desire for a Lost Empire*. Uppsala: Uppsala Universitet, 2014, 9–42.

Butler, Judith. *Gender Trouble: Feminism and the Subversion of Identity*. New York: Routledge, 1990.

———. *Bodies That Matter: On the Discursive Limits of 'Sex'*. New York: Routledge, 1993.

————. *Antigone's Claim: Kinship between Life and Death*. New York: Columbia University Press, 2000.

Cagnetta, Mariella. *Antichisti e Impero Fascista*. Bari: Dedalo libri, 1979.

Cairns, Douglas L. *Aidos: The Psychology and Ethics of Honour and Shame in Ancient Greek Literature*. Oxford: Clarendon Press, 1993.

————. *Sophocles: Antigone*. London: Bloomsbury, 2016.

Calder, Louise. *Cruelty and Sentimentality: Greek Attitudes to Animals, 600–300 BC*. London: Archaeopress, 2011.

Caldwell, Lauren. 'Akin's Reproductive Ideas Relate to Romans'. *Hartford Courant*, 24 August 2012. https://www.courant.com/news/connecticut/hc-xpm-2012-08-24-hc-op-caldwell-akin-taps-ancient-roman-medical-kno-20120824-story.html.

Capogrossi Colognesi, L. 'Tollere Liberos'. *Mélanges de l'École française de Rome* 102 (1990): 107–27.

Caprotti, Federico. *Mussolini's Cities: Internal Colonialism in Italy 1930–1939*. Youngstown, NY: Cambria Press, 2007.

Carabba, Claudio. *Il cinema del ventennio nero*. Florence: Vallecchi, 1974.

Carlà-Uhink, F. 'Between the Human and the Divine: Cross-Dressing and Transgender Dynamics in the Graeco-Roman World'. In D. Campanile, F. Carlà-Uhink and M. Facella, eds. *TransAntiquity: Cross-Dressing and Transgender Dynamics in the Ancient World*. London and New York: Routledge, 2017, 3–37.

Cartledge, Paul. *Agesilaos and the Crisis of Sparta*. London: Duckworth, 1987.

————. 'The Machismo of the Athenian Empire – or the Reign of the Phallus?' In Foxhall and Salmon 1998, 54–67.

————. *Spartan Reflections*. Berkeley: University of California Press, 2001.

————. *The Spartans: The World of the Warrior-Heroes of Ancient Greece*. New York: Overlook Press, 2003.

Castelli, Elizabeth. 'Virginity and Its Meaning for Women's Sexuality in Early Christianity'. *Journal of Feminist Studies in Religion* 2 (1986): 61–88.

Chaumartin, François-Régis. 'Philosophical Tragedy?' In Damschen and Heil 2014, 653–69.

'Child Brides'. *Full Frontal*, 14 June 2017. https://www.youtube.com/watch?v=B0lwiInZG1E.

Chrystal, P. *Women at War in the Classical World*. Barnsley: Pen and Sword, 2017.

Churchill, J. Bradford. 'Ex Qua Quod Vellent Facerent: Roman Magistrates' Authority over Praeda and Manubiae'. *Transactions and Proceedings of the American Philological Association* 129 (1999): 85–116.

Clarke, John. 'Hypersexual Black Men in Augustan Baths'. In Natalie Kampen, ed. *Sexuality in Ancient Art*. Cambridge: Cambridge University Press, 1996, 184–98.

Clarke, W. M. 'Achilles and Patroclus in Love'. *Hermes* 106.3 (1978): 381–96.

———. 'Manhood and Heroism'. In R. L. Fowler, ed. *Cambridge Companion to Homer.* Cambridge: Cambridge University Press, 2004, 74–90.

Classen, C. J. 'Romulus in Der Römischen Republik'. *Philologus* 102 (1962): 173–204.

Cleese, John. 'Yes I've heard this word. I think sociopaths use it in an attempt to discredit the notion of empathy'. *Twitter,* 8 July 2018. https://twitter.com/johncleese/status/1015886273482027014?lang=en.

Coates, Linda, and Allan Wade. 'Language and Violence: Analysis of Four Discursive Operations'. *Journal of Family Violence* 22 (2007): 511–22.

Coates, Ta-Nehisi. 'Rape, Abortion, and the Privilege of Magical Thinking'. *The Atlantic,* 20 August 2012. https://www.theatlantic.com/politics/archive/2012/08/rape-abortion-and-the-privilege-of-magical-thinking/261313/.

Cohn, Carol, and Cynthia Enloe. 'A Conversation with Cynthia Enloe: Feminists Look at Masculinity and the Men Who Wage War'. *Signs* 28.4 (2003): 1087–1107.

Collins Dictionaries. 'Top 10 Collins Words of the Year 2016'. *Language Lovers* (blog), 3 November 2016. https://www.collinsdictionary.com/word-lovers-blog/new/top-10-collins-words-of-the-year-2016,323,hcb.html.

Concepcion, Summer. 'Spanberger's GOP Challenger Downplays Possibility of Pregnancy after Rape'. *Talking Points Memo,* 27 June 2022. https://talkingpointsmemo.com/news/yesli-vega-virginia-senate-campaign-pregnancy-rape.

Connell, R. W. 'Class, Patriarchy, and Sartre's Theory of Practice'. *Theory and Society* 11 (1982): 305–20.

———. *Which Way Is Up? Essays of Sex, Class and Culture.* Sydney: Allen and Unwin, 1983.

———. *Gender and Power: Society, the Person, and Sexual Politics.* Redwood City, CA: Stanford University Press, 1987.

———. *Masculinities.* Sydney: Allen and Unwin, 1995.

———. *Masculinities.* 2nd ed. Berkeley: University of California Press, 2005.

———. 'Margin Becoming Centre: For a World-Centred Rethinking of Masculinities'. *NORMA: International Journal for Masculinity Studies* 9.4 (2014): 217–31.

———. 'The Study of Masculinities'. *Qualitative Research Journal* 14.1 (2014): 5–15.

Connell, R. W., and James W. Messerschmidt. 'Hegemonic Masculinity: Rethinking the Concept'. *Gender and Society* 19.6 (2005): 829–59.

Cooper, Kate. *Band of Angels: The Forgotten World of Early Christian Women.* New York: Overlook Press, 2013.

Corbeill, Anthony. *Controlling Laughter: Political Humor in the Late Roman Republic.* Princeton: Princeton University Press, 1996.

————. *Sexing the World: Grammatical Gender and Biological Sex in Ancient Rome*. Princeton: Princeton University Press, 2015.

Cornell, T. J. 'Aeneas' Arrival in Italy'. *Liverpool Classical Monthly* 2 (1977): 77–83.

Cornwall, A., and N. Lindisfarne. 'Dislocating Masculinity: Gender, Power, and Anthropology'. In A. Cornwall and N. Lindisfarne, eds. *Dislocating Masculinity: Comparative Ethnographies*. London: Routledge, 1994, 11–47.

Cosgrove, Charles H. 'A Woman's Unbound Hair in the Greco-Roman World, with Special Reference to the Story of the "Sinful Woman" in Luke 7:36–50'. *Journal of Biblical Literature* 124.4 (2005): 675–92.

Cottom, Tressie McMillan. *Thick: And Other Essays*. New York: New Press, 2018.

Crane, Gregory. *The Blinded Eye: Thucydides and the New Written Word*. Lanham, MD: Rowman and Littlefield, 1996.

————. *Thucydides and the Ancient Simplicity: The Limits of Political Realism*. Berkeley: University of California Press, 1998.

Creighton, G., and J. L. Oliffe. 'Theorising Masculinities and Men's Health. A Brief History with a View to Practice'. *Health Sociology Review* 19.4 (2010): 409–18.

Creighton, G., J. L. Oliffe, S. Butterwick and E. Saewyc. 'After the Death of a Friend: Young Men's Grief and Masculine Identities'. *Social Science and Medicine* 84 (2013): 35–43.

Cunliffe, Barry. *The Ancient Celts*. Oxford: Oxford University Press, 1997.

Curtis, L. 'War Music: Soundscape and Song in Vergil, *Aeneid* 9'. *Vergilius* 63 (2017): 37–62.

Damschen, Gregor, and Andreas Heil, eds. *Brill's Companion to Seneca: Philosopher and Dramatist*. Leiden and Boston: Brill, 2014.

Davidson, James. *Courtesans and Fishcakes: The Consuming Passions of Ancient Athens*. Chicago: University of Chicago Press, 1997.

————. 'Dover, Foucault and Greek Homosexuality'. *Past and Present* 170 (2001): 3–51.

————. *The Greeks And Greek Love: A Radical Reappraisal of Homosexuality in Ancient Greece*. London: Weidenfeld and Nicolson, 2007.

Davies, Paul. 'Equality and Distinction within the Spartiate Community'. In Powell 2018, 480–99.

Davies, Stevan L. *The Revolt of the Widows: The Social World of the Apocryphal Acts*. Carbondale: Southern Illinois University Press, 1980.

De Grazia, V. *How Fascism Ruled Women: Italy 1922–1945*. Berkeley: University of California Press, 1992.

De Libero, L. 'Precibus Ac Lacrimis: Tears in Roman Historiographers'. In Fögen 2009, 209–34.

De Sanctis, G. 'Il salto proibito. la morte di Remo e il primo comandamento della città'. *Studi e Materiali Di Storia Delle Religioni* 75 (2009): 65–88.

De Ste Croix, G. E. M. 'Trials at Sparta'. In Michael Whitby, ed. *Sparta*. Edinburgh: Routledge, 2002, 69–78.

Deacy, Susan, José Malheiro Magalhães and Jean Menzies, eds. *Revisiting Rape in Antiquity: Sexualised Violence in Greek and Roman Worlds*. London: Bloomsbury, 2023.

Debnar, Paula A. 'Diodotus' Paradox and the Mytilene Debate (Thucydides 3.37–49)'. *Rheinisches Museum für Philologie* 143.2 (2000): 161–78.

Delcourt, A. *Lecture des Antiquités Romaines de Denys d'Halicarnasse*. Brussels: Académie Royale de Belgique, 2005.

Demetriou, Demetrakis Z. 'Connell's Concept of Hegemonic Masculinity: A Critique'. *Theory and Society* 30.3 (2001): 337–61.

Dench, Emma. *From Barbarians to New Men: Greek, Roman, and Modern Perceptions of Peoples from the Central Apennines*. Oxford: Oxford University Press, 1995.

Des Bouvrie, Synnøve. *Women in Greek Tragedy: An Anthropological Approach*. Oslo: Norwegian University Press, 1990.

Desmond, Marilynn. *Ovid's Art and the Wife of Bath: The Ethics of Erotic Violence*. Ithaca, NY: Cornell University Press, 2006.

Dickie, Matthew W. 'Narrative Patterns in Christian Hagiography'. *Greek Roman Byzantine Studies* 40 (1999): 83–98.

———. 'Who Practiced Love-Magic in Classical Antiquity and in the Late Roman World?' *Classical Quarterly* 50.2 (2000): 563–83.

Diefendorf, Sarah. 'After the Wedding Night: Sexual Abstinence and Masculinities over the Life Course'. *Gender and Society* 29.5 (2015): 647–69.

Dillery, J. *Xenophon and the History of His Times*. London: Routledge, 1995.

Dillon, John. *The Middle Platonists*. 2nd ed. Ithaca, NY: Cornell University Press, 1996.

Dillon, Sheila, and Sharon L. James, eds. *A Companion to Women in the Ancient World*. Chichester: John Wiley and Sons, 2012.

Dinshaw, C. *Getting Medieval: Sexualities and Communities, Pre- and Postmodern*. Durham, NC and London: Duke University Press, 1999.

Dixon, Suzanne. *Reading Roman Women: Sources, Genres, and Real Life*. London: Duckworth, 2001.

Donaldson, M. 'What Is Hegemonic Masculinity?' *Theory and Society* 22.5 (1993): 643–57.

Doniger, Wendy. *The Ring of Truth and Other Myths of Sex and Jewellery*. Oxford: Oxford University Press, 2017.

Dorati, Marco. 'Acqua e fuoco nella "Lisistrata"'. *Quaderni Urbinati di Cultura Classica* 63.3 (1999): 79–86.

Dover, Kenneth James. *Greek Homosexuality*. Cambridge, MA: Harvard University Press, 1978.

Drachler, Stephen. 'Friend Backs off From Rape Statement'. *Morning Call*, 30 March 1988. https://web.archive.org/web/20161221181954/http://articles.mcall.com/1988-03-30/news/2610418_1_anti-abortion-abortion-control-pregnant.

Dressler, Alex. *Personification and the Feminine in Roman Philosophy*. Cambridge: Cambridge University Press, 2016.

Ducat, Jean. *Spartan Education: Youth and Society in the Classical Period*. Wales: Classical Press of Wales, 2006.

Duff, Timothy E. *Plutarch's Lives: Exploring Virtue and Vice*. Oxford: Oxford University Press, 1999.

Dugan, J. *Making a New Man: Ciceronian Self-Fashioning in the Rhetorical Works*. Oxford: Oxford University Press, 2005.

Dworkin, Andrea. *Right-Wing Women: The Politics of Domesticated Females*. London: Women's Press, 1983.

Dyck, Andrew R. *A Commentary on Cicero, De Officiis*. Ann Arbor: University of Michigan Press, 1996.

Eagleton, Terry. *Ideology: An Introduction*. New York: Verso Press, 1991.

Earl, Donald. *The Moral and Political Traditions of Rome*. Ithaca, NY: Cornell University Press, 1967.

Edwards, Catharine. *The Politics of Immorality in Ancient Rome*. Cambridge: Cambridge University Press, 1993.

———. 'Unspeakable Professions: Public Performance and Prostitution in Ancient Rome'. In Hallett and Skinner 1997, 66–98.

———. 'The Suffering Body: Philosophy and Pain in Seneca's Letters'. In Porter 1999, 252–68.

Eecke, M. ver. *La République et le roi: Le mythe de Romulus à la fin de la République romaine*. Paris: De Boccard, 2008.

Enterline, Lynn. 'Envoy'. In Garrison and Stanivukovic 2021, 287–302.

Ernout, Alfred, and Antoine Meillet. *Dictionnaire étymologique de la langue latine*. Paris: Imprimerie Durand, 1932.

Evans, Jessica. 'Rhetorical Masculinity in Stasis: Hyper-Andreia and Patriotism in Thucydides' *Histories* and Plato's *Gorgias*'. In Sophia Papaioannou, Andreas Serafim and Kyriakos N. Demetriou, eds. *The Ancient Art of Persuasion across Genres and Topics*. Vol. 12. International Studies in the History of Rhetoric. Leiden: Brill, 2020, 12: 209–24.

Evans, Rhiannon. *Utopia Antiqua: Readings of the Golden Age and Decline at Rome*. London and New York: Routledge, 2008.

Ezzell, Matthew B. '"I'm in Control": Compensatory Manhood in a Therapeutic Community'. *Gender and Society* 26.2 (2012): 190–215.

————. 'Healthy for Whom? Males, Men, and Masculinity: A Reflection on the Doing (and Study) of Dominance'. In Pascoe and Bridges 2015, 188–97.

Fabre-Serris, J., and Alison Keith, eds. *Women and War in Antiquity*. Baltimore: Johns Hopkins University Press, 2015.

Fantuzzi, M. *Achilles in Love*. Intertextual Studies. Oxford: Oxford University Press, 2012.

Faraone, Christopher. 'The Agonistic Context of Early Greek Binding Spells'. In Faraone and Obbink 1991, 214–43.

Faraone, Christopher, and Laura K. McClure, eds. *Prostitutes and Courtesans in the Ancient World*. Madison: University of Wisconsin Press, 2006.

Faraone, Christopher, and D. Obbink, eds. *Magika Hiera: Ancient Greek Magic and Religion*. New York: Oxford University Press, 1991.

Farrell, Joseph. 'Dialogue of Genres in Ovid's "Lovesong of Polyphemus" (Metamorphoses 13.719–897)'. *American Journal of Philology* 113 (1992): 235–68.

Fausto-Sterling, Anne. *Sexing the Body: Gender Politics and the Construction of Sexuality*. New York: Basic Books, 2000.

Fedeli, P. 'Le riscritture del mito: il pianto di Briseide e di Andromaca (Prop. 2,8; 2,9; 2,20)'. *Euphrosyne* 32 (2004): 157–71.

————. *Properzio. Elegie, Libro II: Introduzione, testo e commento*. Cambridge: Francis Cairns, 2005.

Feig Vishnia, Rachel. *State, Society, and Popular Leaders in Mid-Republican Rome, 241–167 BC*. London: Routledge, 1996.

————. 'Ancient Rome in Italian Cinema under Mussolini: The Case of Scipione l'Africano'. *Italianist* 28.2 (2008): 246–67.

Fertik, Harriet. 'Sex, Love, and Leadership in Cicero's *Philippics* 1 and 2'. *Arethusa* 50.1 (2017): 65–88.

Festa, Nicola. *Saggio sull' "Africa" del Petrarca*. Palermo, Rome: Libraio della real casa, 1926.

Festugière, A. J. *La révélation d'Hermès Trismégiste, Vol. 1: L'astrologie et les sciences occultes*. Paris: Lecoffre, 1950.

Filipovic, Jill. 'Rape Is about Power, Not Sex'. *Guardian*, 29 August 2013. https://www.theguardian.com/commentisfree/2013/aug/29/rape-about-power-not-sex.

Fischer, Susanna E. 'Systematic Connections between Seneca's Philosophical Works and Tragedies'. In Damschen and Heil 2014, 745–68.

Fisher, Nicolas R. *Hybris: A Study in the Values of Honour and Shame in Ancient Greece*. Warminster: Aris and Phillips, 1992.

————. 'Violence, Masculinity and the Law in Classical Athens'. In Foxhall and Salmon 1998, 68–97.

Fitzgerald, William. *Slavery and the Roman Literary Imagination*. Cambridge and New York: Cambridge University Press, 2000.

Fitzsimmons, T. 'American Psychological Associations Links "Masculinity Ideology" to Homophobia, Misogyny'. *NBC News*, 8 January 2019. https://www.nbcnews.com/feature/nbc-out/american-psychological-association-links-masculinity-ideology-homophobia-misogyny-n956416?cid=sm_npd_nn_tw_ma.

Flemming, Rebecca. *Medicine and the Making of Roman Women: Gender, Nature, and Authority from Celsus to Galen*. Oxford: Oxford University Press, 2000.

Flood, Michael. 'Toxic Masculinity: A Primer and Commentary'. *XY Online*, 7 July 2018. https://xyonline.net/content/toxic-masculinity-primer-and-commentary.

Flower, Michael, ed. *Cambridge Companion to Xenophon*. Cambridge: Cambridge University Press, 2017.

———. 'Xenophon as a Historian'. In Flower 2017, 301–22.

Fögen, T., ed. *Tears in the Graeco-Roman World*. Berlin: Walter De Gruyter, 2009.

———. 'Tears in Propertius, Ovid and Greek Epistolographers'. In Fögen 2009, 179–208.

Foley, Helen P. 'The Conception of Women in Athenian Drama'. In Helen P. Foley, ed. *Reflections of Women in Antiquity*. New York and London: Routledge, 1981, 127–68.

Ford, Clementine. *Boys Will Be Boys: Power, Patriarchy and the Toxic Bonds of Mateship*. Melbourne: Allen and Unwin, 2018.

Foucault, Michel. *The Use of Pleasure*. Translated by Robert Hurley. Vol. 2. *The History of Sexuality*. New York: Vintage, 1985.

———. *The Care of the Self*. Edited by Robert Hurley. Vol. 3. *The History of Sexuality*. New York: Vintage, 1986.

Fox, M. J. 'The Idea of Women in Peacekeeping: Lysistrata and Antigone'. *International Peacekeeping* 8.2 (2001): 9–22.

Fox, Matthew. 'History and Rhetoric in Dionysius of Halicarnassus'. *Journal of Roman Studies* 83 (1993): 31–47.

———. 'The Constrained Men'. In Foxhall and Salmon 1998, 6–22.

Foxhall, L., and J. Salmon, eds. *Thinking Men: Masculinity and Its Self-Representation in the Classical Tradition*. London and New York: Routledge, 1998.

———, eds. *When Men Were Men: Masculinity, Power, and Identity in Classical Antiquity*. London and New York: Routledge, 2011.

Franiuk, Renae, and E. Ashley Shain. 'Beyond Christianity: The Status of Women and Rape Myths'. *Sex Roles* 65 (2011): 783–91.

Franke-Ruta, Garance. 'A Canard That Will Not Die: "Legitimate Rape" Doesn't Cause Pregnancy'. *The Atlantic*, 19 August 2012. https://www.theatlantic.com/politics/archive/2012/08/a-canard-that-will-not-die-legitimate-rape-doesnt-cause-pregnancy/261303/.

Frankfurter, David. 'Narrating Power: The Theory and Practice of the Magical Historiola in Ritual Spells'. In M. Meyer and P. Mirecki, eds. *Ancient Magic and Ritual Power*. Leiden: Brill, 1995, 457–76.

———. 'The Perils of Love: Magic and Countermagic in Coptic Egypt'. *Journal of the History of Sexuality* 10 (2001): 480–500.

Frazel, Thomas Dooley. *The Rhetoric of Cicero's 'In Verrem'*. Göttingen: Vandenhoeck und Ruprecht, 2009.

Friedman, Jaclyn. 'Toxic Masculinity'. *American Prospect*, 13 March 2013. https://prospect.org/power/toxic-masculinity/.

Fromentin, V. 'Les Moi de l'historien : récit et discours chez Denys d'Halicarnasse'. *Dialogues d'histoire ancienne* 4 (2010): 261–77.

Fulkerson, Laurel. *The Ovidian Heroine As Author: Reading, Writing, and Community in the Heroides*. Cambridge: Cambridge University Press, 2005.

Fulkerson, Laurel, and Tim Stover, eds. *Repeat Performances: Ovidian Repetition and the Metamorphoses*. Madison: University of Wisconsin Press, 2016.

Gaca, Kathy L. 'The Andrapodizing of War Captives in Greek Historical Memory'. *Transactions of the American Philological Association* 140.1 (2010): 117–61.

Gager, John. *Curse Tablets and Binding Spells from the Ancient World*. Oxford: Oxford University Press, 1992.

Gardner, Jane F. *Being a Roman Citizen*. London: Routledge, 1993.

Garland, L. *Byzantine Empresses: Women and Power in Byzantium, AD 527–1204*. New York: Routledge, 1999.

Garrison, Daniel. 'Catullus in the College Classroom'. In Marilyn Skinner, ed. *A Companion to Catullus*. Malden, MA: Wiley-Blackwell, 2007, 503–20.

Garrood, W. 'The Byzantine Conquest of Cilicia and the Hamdanids of Aleppo, 959–965'. *Anatolian Studies* 58 (2008): 127–40.

Gaughan, J. E. *Murder Was Not a Crime: Homicide and Power in the Roman Republic*. Austin: University of Texas Press, 2010.

Geertz, Clifford. *Works and Lives: The Anthropologist as Author*. Stanford: Stanford University Press, 1988.

Georgoudi, Stella. 'To Act, Not Submit: Women's Attitudes in Situations of War in Ancient Greece'. In Fabre-Serris and Keith 2015, 200–13.

Gilchrist, Tracy E. 'What Is Toxic Masculinity?' *Advocate*, 11 December 2017. https://www.advocate.com/women/2017/12/11/what-toxic-masculinity.

Gildenhard, Ingo, and Andrew Zissos. 'Barbarian Variations: Tereus, Procne and Philomela in Ovid (*Met.* 6.412–674) and Beyond'. *Dictynna* 4 (2007).

Ging, D. 'Alphas, Betas, and Incels: Theorizing the Masculinities of the Manosphere'. *Men and Masculinities* 20.10 (2017): 1–20.

Giridharadas, Anand. 'The Illness He Is'. *The.Ink* (blog), 5 October 2020. https://the.ink/p/the-illness-he-is.

Glazebrook, Alison. 'Sexual Rhetoric: From Athens to Rome'. In Hubbard 2014, 431–45.

Gleason, M. W. *Making Men: Sophists and Self-Presentation in Ancient Rome*. Princeton: Princeton University Press, 2008.

Glendinning, Eleanor. 'Reinventing Lucretia: Rape, Suicide and Redemption from Classical Antiquity to the Medieval Era'. *International Journal of the Classical Tradition* 20 (2013): 61–82.

Gloyn, Liz. 'She's Only a Bird in a Gilded Cage: Freedwomen at Trimalchio's Dinner Party'. *Classical Quarterly* 62.1 (2012): 260–80.

———. 'Reading Rape in Ovid's Metamorphoses: A Test-Case Lesson'. *Classical World* 106.4 (2013): 676–81.

Godwin, J. *Reading Catullus*. Liverpool: Liverpool University Press, 2008.

Goff, Barbara, ed. *Classics and Colonialism*. London: Duckworth, 2005.

Gold, Barbara, ed. *A Companion to Roman Love Elegy*. West Sussex: Wiley-Blackwell, 2012.

Goldberg, Charles. 'Priests and Politicians: Rex Sacrorum and Flamen Dialis in Middle Republican Politics'. *Phoenix* 69 (2015): 334–54.

Goldstein, J. M. 'The Surprising History of "Snowflake" as a Political Insult'. *Think Progress*, 19 January 2017. https://thinkprogress.org/all-the-special-snowflakes-aaf1a922f37b/.

Goold, G. P. *Ovid, Heroides, Amores*. Translated by G. Showerman. Cambridge, MA: Harvard University Press, 1977.

Gould, J. 'Law, Custom and Myth: Aspects of the Social Position of Women in Classical Athens'. *Journal of Hellenic Studies* 100 (1980): 38–59.

Goyette, Michael. 'Seneca's "Corpus": A Sympathy of Fluids and Fluctuations'. In Mark Bradley, Victoria Leonard and Laurence Totelin, eds. *Bodily Fluids in Antiquity*. New York: Routledge, 2021, 272–86.

Graf, Fritz. 'Women, War, and Warlike Divinities'. *Zeitschrift für Papyrologie und Epigraphik* 55 (1984): 245–54.

Gramsci, Antonio. *Selections from the Prison Notebooks of Antonio Gramsci*. Edited by Quintin Hoare and Geoffrey Nowell Smith. New York: International Publishers, 1971.

Graver, M. 'The Manhandling of Maecenas: Senecan Abstractions of Masculinity'. *American Journal of Philology* 119.4 (1998): 608–32.

Gray, Vivienne. *The Character of Xenophon's Hellenica*. London: Duckworth, 1989.

———. *Xenophon on Government*. New York: Cambridge University Press, 2007.

Graziosi, B., and J. Haubold. 'Homeric Masculinity: ΗΝΟΡΕΗ and ΑΓΗΝΟΡΙΗ'. *Journal of Hellenic Studies* 123 (2003): 60–76.

Greene, Ellen. *The Erotics of Domination: Male Desire and the Mistress in Latin Love Poetry*. Baltimore: Johns Hopkins University Press, 1998.

————. 'Gender Identity and the Elegiac Hero in Propertius 2.1'. *Arethusa* 33.2 (2000): 241–61.

————. 'Gender and Elegy'. In Gold 2012, 357–72.

Greenfield, Richard P. H., and Alice-Mary Talbot, eds. *Holy Men of Athos*. Cambridge, MA: Harvard University Press, 2016.

Greenfield, Susan Celia. 'Consent and Conception'. *Need to Know on PBS*, 23 August 2012. http://www.pbs.org/wnet/need-to-know/opinion/consent-and-conception/14573/.

Griffin, J. 'Augustan Poetry and the Life of Luxury'. *Journal of Roman Studies* 66 (1976): 87–105.

Griffith, M. *Sophocles' Antigone*. Cambridge: Cambridge University Press, 1999.

Grillo, Luca. 'Speeches in the Commentarii'. In Grillo and Krebs 2018, 131–43.

Grillo, Luca, and Christopher B. Krebs, eds. *Cambridge Companion to the Writings of Julius Caesar*. Cambridge: Cambridge University Press, 2018.

Gruen, Erich S. *Studies in Greek Culture and Roman Policy*. California: University of California Press, 1990.

————. *Culture and National Identity in Republican Rome*. Ithaca, NY: Cornell University Press, 1992.

Gunderson, Erik. *Staging Masculinity: The Rhetoric of Performance in the Roman World*. Ann Arbor: University of Michigan Press, 2000.

Gupta, Alisha Haridasani. 'How an Aversion to Masks Stems from "Toxic Masculinity"'. *New York Times*, 22 October 2020. https://www.nytimes.com/2020/10/22/us/masks-toxic-masculinity-covid-men-gender.html.

Haase, Christian Dieter. 'Virtual Manhood Acts within Social Networks: The Enactment of Toxic Masculinity on Reddit'. PhD diss., James Madison University, 2021.

Haimson Lushkov, A. *Magistracy and the Historiography of the Roman Republic. Politics in Prose*. Cambridge: Cambridge University Press, 2015.

Halberstam, J. *Female Masculinity*. Durham, NC: Duke University Press, 2018.

Haley, Shelley. 'Livy's Sophonisba'. *Classica et Mediaevalia* 40 (1989): 171–81.

Hallett, Judith P. 'The Role of Women in Roman Elegy: Counter-Cultural Feminism'. *Arethusa* 6.1 (1973): 103–24.

————. 'Fulvia: The Representation of an Elite Roman Woman Warrior'. In Fabre-Serris and Keith 2015, 247–65.

Hallett, Judith P., and Marilyn B. Skinner, eds. *Roman Sexualities*. Princeton: Princeton University Press, 1997.

Halperin, David M. 'Is There a History of Sexuality?' *History and Theory* 28.3 (1989): 257–74.

————. 'Why Is Diotima a Woman? Platonic Eros and the Figuration of Gender'. In David M. Halperin, John J. Winkler and Froma I. Zeitlin, eds.

Before Sexuality: The Construction of the Erotic Experience in the Ancient Greek World. Princeton: Princeton University Press, 1990, 257–308.

———. *How to Do the History of Homosexuality*. Chicago: University of Chicago Press, 2002.

Hamblin, J. 'Toxic Masculinity and Murder'. *The Atlantic*, June 2016. https://www.theatlantic.com/health/archive/2016/06/toxic-masculinity-and-mass-murder/486983/.

Hanink, Johanna. *How to Think about War: An Ancient Guide to Foreign Policy*. Princeton: Princeton University Press, 2019.

Hanson, Ann Ellis, and Monica H. Green. 'Soranus of Ephesus: Methodicorum princeps'. *Aufstieg und Niedergang der römischen Welt* 2.37 (1994): 968–1075.

Harrington, Carol. 'What Is "Toxic Masculinity" and Why Does It Matter?' *Men and Masculinities* 24.2 (2021): 345–52.

Harris, William V. *War and Imperialism in Republican Rome: 327–70 BCE*. Oxford: Oxford University Press, 1979.

Hartog, François. *The Mirror of Herodotus: The Representation of the Other in the Writing of History*. Translated by Janet Lloyd. Berkeley: University of California Press, 1988.

Hase, K. B. *Leonis Diaconi Caloënsis: Historiae libri decem*. Corpus scriptorum historiae Byzantinae. Bonn: Weber, 1828.

Havrilesky, Heather. 'Don't Call It "Toxic Masculinity". They're Sociopathic Baby-Men'. *The Cut*, 6 October 2017. https://www.thecut.com/2017/10/this-isnt-toxic-masculinity-its-sociopathic-baby-men.html.

Heartless Bitches International. 'Women Don't Want Nice Guys', 2002. https://www.heartless-bitches.com/rants/niceguys/predicate.shtml.

Heslin, P. J. *The Transvestite Achilles: Gender and Genre in Statius' Achilleid*. Cambridge: Cambridge University Press, 2005.

Hess, Amanda. 'How "Snowflake" Became America's Inescapable Tough-Guy Taunt'. *New York Times*, 13 June 2017. https://www.nytimes.com/2017/06/13/magazine/how-snowflake-became-americas-inescapable-tough-guy-taunt.html.

Hill, L. 'The First Wave of Feminism: Were the Stoics Feminists?' *History of Political Thought* 22 (2001): 13–40.

Hill Collins, Patricia. *Black Feminist Thought*. London: Routledge, 1990.

Hillard, T. W. 'On the Stage, Behind the Curtain: Images of Politically Active Women in the Late Roman Republic'. In Barbara Garlick, Suzanne Dixon and Pauline Allen, eds. *Stereotypes of Women in Power: Historical Perspectives and Revisionist Views*. Vol. 125. Contributions in Women's Studies. New York: Greenwood Press, 1992, 37–64.

Hindley, Clifford. 'Xenophon on Male Love'. *Classical Quarterly* 49.1 (1999): 74–99.

Hodkinson, Stephen. *Property and Wealth in Classical Sparta*. London: Duckworth, 2000.

————. 'The Episode of Sphodrias as a Source for Spartan Social History'. In Nicholas V. Sekunda, ed. *Corolla Cosmo Rodewald*. Gdansk: Foundation for the Development of Gdansk University, 2007, 43–65.

————. 'Sparta: An Exceptional Domination of State over Society?' In Powell 2018, 29–58.

Hölkeskamp, K.-J. *Reconstructing the Roman Republic*. Princeton: Princeton University Press, 2004.

Holland, Nancy J. 'Tyranny and Blood: Rethinking Creon'. *Philosophy and Literature* 41.1A (2017): 1–11.

Holloway, K. 'Toxic Masculinity Is Killing Men: The Roots of Male Trauma'. *Salon*, 12 October 2015. https://www.salon.com/2015/06/12/toxic_masculinity_is_killing_men_the_roots_of_male_trauma_partner/.

Holmes, Brooke. *Gender: Antiquity and Its Legacy*. London: I. B. Tauris, 2012.

Holmes, M. M., H. S. Resnick, D. G. Kilpatrick and C. L. Best. 'Rape-Related Pregnancy: Estimates and Descriptive Characteristics from a National Sample of Women'. *American Journal of Obstetrics and Gynecology* 175.2 (1996): 320–5.

Holt, Philip. 'Polis and Tragedy in the "Antigone"'. *Mnemosyne* 52.6 (1999): 658–90.

Holter, Øystein G. 'Social Theories for Researching Men and Masculinities: Direct Gender Hierarchy and Structural Inequality'. In Kimmel et al. 2004, 15–34.

Holzberg, N. 'Lesbia, the Poet, and the Two Faces of Sappho: "Womanufacture" in Catullus'. *Proceedings of the Cambridge Philological Society* 46 (2000): 28–44.

Hoof, L. van. 'Strategic Differences: Seneca and Plutarch on Controlling Anger'. *Mnemosyne* 60.1 (2007): 59–86.

hooks, bell. *Feminist Theory: From Margin to Center*. Boston: South End Press, 1984.

————. *The Will to Change: Men, Masculinity, and Love*. New York: Washington Square Press, 2004.

Hooper, Charlotte. *Manly States: Masculinities, International Relations, and Gender Politics*. New York: Columbia University Press, 2001.

Hope, V. 'Living without the Dead: Finding Solace in Ancient Rome'. In F. S. Tappenden and C. Daniel-Hughes, eds. *Coming Back to Life: The Permeability of Past and Present, Mortality and Immortality, Death and Life in the Ancient Mediterranean*. Montreal: McGill University Library Press, 2017, 39–70.

Hope, V., and J. Huskinson, eds. *Memory and Mourning: Studies on Roman Death*. Oxford: Oxbow Books, 2011.

Hubbard, Thomas K. 'Athenian Pederasty and the Construction of Masculinity'. In Arnold and Brady 2011, 189–225.

Humble, Noreen. 'Xenophon's View of Sparta: A Study of the *Anabasis, Hellenica* and *Respublica Lacedaemoniorum*'. PhD diss., McMaster University, 1997.

———. 'The Author, Date and Purpose of Chapter 14 of the *Lakedaimoniôn Politeia*'. In Tuplin 2004, 215–28.

———. 'Xenophon, Aristotle and Plutarch on Sparta'. In Nikos Birgalias, Kostas Buraselis and Paul Cartledge, eds. *The Contribution of Ancient Sparta to Political Thought and Practice*. Athens: Alexandria Publications, 2007, 291–300.

Huntley, Katherine, and Lisa McClain. 'Legitimately Ancient Ideas about Rape: The Roots of Todd Akin's Medical Beliefs'. *Blue Review*, 12 October 2012. https://thebluereview.org/ancient-akin-rape/.

Huskinson, J. 'Bad Deaths, Better Memories'. In Hope and Huskinson 2011, 113–25.

Hutchings, Kimberly. 'Making Sense of Masculinity and War'. *Men and Masculinities* 10.4 (June 2008): 389–404.

Hylen, Susan E. *A Modest Apostle: Thecla and the History of Women in the Early Church*. Oxford: Oxford University Press, 2015.

Ilberg, Johannes, ed. *Gynaeciorum libri iv, De signis fracturarum, De Fasciis, Vita Hippocratis Secundum Soranum*. Leipzig: Teubner, 1927.

Istituto di Studi Romani. *Africa Romana*. Milan: U. Hoepli, 1935.

Jacobson, H. 'Ovid's Briseis. A Study of *Heroides* III'. *Phoenix* 25.4 (1971): 331–56.

———. *Ovid's Heroides*. Princeton: Princeton University Press, 1974.

James, Sharon L. 'From Boys to Men: Rape and Developing Masculinity in Terence's Hecyra and Eunuchus'. *Helios* 25 (1998): 31–47.

———. *Learned Girls and Male Persuasion: Gender and Reading in Roman Love Elegy*. Berkeley and Los Angeles: University of California Press, 2003.

———. 'A Courtesan's Choreography: Female Liberty and Male Anxiety at the Roman Dinner Party'. In Faraone and McClure 2006, 224–51.

———. 'Teaching Rape in Roman Love Elegy: Part II'. In Gold 2012, 549–57.

———. 'Rape and Repetition in Ovid's *Metamorphoses*: Myth, History, Structure, Rome'. In Fulkerson and Stover 2016, 154–75.

Janka, M. *Ovid: Ars Amatoria. Buch 2: Kommentar*. Heidelberg: Winter Verlag, 1997.

Johnson, Marguerite. 'Guide to the Classics: Ovid's *Metamorphoses* and Reading Rape'. *The Conversation*, 13 September 2016. https://theconversation.com/guide-to-the-classics-ovids-metamorphoses-and-reading-rape-65316.

Johnston, Andrew C. 'Nostri and "The Other(s)"'. In Grillo and Krebs 2018, 81–94.

Jones-Lewis, Molly. 'Physicians and "Schools"'. In Georgia L. Irby-Massie, ed. *A Companion to Science, Technology, and Medicine in the Ancient World*. Chichester: John Wiley and Sons, 2016, 480–96.

Joshel, S. D. 'The Body Female and the Body Politic: Livy's Lucretia and Verginia'. In Amy Richlin, ed. *Pornography and Representation in Greece and Rome*. Oxford: Oxford University Press, 1992, 112–30.

Kahn, Madeline. *Why Are We Reading Ovid's Handbook on Rape? Teaching and Learning at a Woman's College*. Boulder: Paradigm, 2005.

Kaldellis, A. *Streams of Gold, Rivers of Blood: The Rise and Fall of Byzantium, 955 AD to the First Crusade*. Oxford and New York: Oxford University Press, 2017.

Kappas, A. 'Mysterious Tears. The Phenomenon of Crying from the Perspective of Social Neuroscience'. In Fögen 2009, 419–38.

Karner, T. 'Fathers, Sons, and Vietnam: Masculinity and Betrayal in the Life Narratives of Vietnam Veterans with Post-Traumatic Stress Disorder'. *American Studies* 37.1 (1996): 63–94.

Kaster, R. A. *Emotion, Restraint, and Community in Ancient Rome*. Oxford: Oxford University Press, 2005.

Keegan, P. M. 'Seen, Not Heard: Feminea Lingua in Ovid's *Fasti* and the Critical Gaze'. In G. Herbert-Brown, ed. *Ovid's Fasti: Historical Readings at Its Bimillennium*. Oxford: Oxford University Press, 2002, 127–53.

Keith, Alison. 'Lycoris Galli/Volumnia Cytheris: A Greek Courtesan in Rome'. *Eugesta* 1 (2011): 23–53.

Keith, Thomas. *Masculinities in Contemporary American Culture: An Intersectional Approach to the Complexities and Challenges of Male Identity*. New York: Routledge, 2017.

Kennell, Nigel. *The Gymnasium of Virtue: Education and Culture in Ancient Sparta*. Chapel Hill: University of North Carolina Press, 1995.

Kenney, E. J., ed. *P. Ovidi Nasonis Amores, Medicamina Faciei Femineae, Ars Amatoria, Remedia Amoris*. Corr. 1995. Oxford: Oxford University Press, 1961.

Kenty, Joanna. *Cicero's Political Personae*. Cambridge: Cambridge University Press, 2020.

Kessler, S. J., D. J. Ashenden, R. W. Connell and G. W. Dowsett. *Ockers and Disco-Maniacs*. Sydney: Inner City Education Center, 1982.

Kiernan, Ben. 'The First Genocide: Carthage, 146 BC'. *Diogenes* 51.3 (2004): 27–39.

Kierstead, J. 'Democracy's Humility: A Reading of Sophocles' *Antigone*'. *Polis* 34 (2017): 288–305.

Kimmel, Michael. 'Masculinity as Homophobia: Fear, Shame and Silence in the Construction of Gender Identity'. In Stephen M. Whitehead and Frank J. Barrett, eds. *Masculinities Reader*. Cambridge: Polity Press, 2001, 266–87.

————. *Manhood in America. A Cultural History*. New York: Oxford University Press, 2006.

————. *Angry White Men: American Masculinity at the End of an Era*. New York: Nation Books, 2013.

————. *Angry White Men: American Masculinity at the End of an Era*. 2nd ed. New York: Nation Books, 2017.

Kimmel, Michael, Jeff Hearn and R. W. Connell, eds. *Handbook of Studies on Men & Masculinities*. Los Angeles: Sage, 2004.

Kimmel, Michael, and Lisa Wade. 'Ask a Feminist: Michael Kimmel and Lisa Wade Discuss Toxic Masculinity'. *Signs: Journal of Women in Culture and Society* 44.1 (September 2018): 233–54.

King, Claire Sisco. 'It Cuts Both Ways: Fight Club, Masculinity, and Abject Hegemony'. *Communication and Critical/Cultural Studies* 6.4 (December 2009): 366–85.

King, Helen. 'Medical Texts as a Source for Women's History'. In Powell 1995, 199–218.

————. *Hippocrates' Woman: Reading the Female Body in Ancient Greece*. London and New York: Routledge, 2002.

Kinsley, Michael. 'Gaffes to the Rescue'. *Time*, 8 February 2007. http://content.time.com/time/magazine/article/0,9171,1587283,00.html.

Knox, P. E. *Ovid Heroides: Select Epistles*. Cambridge: Cambridge University Press, 1995.

Konstan, David. 'Aristophanes' *Lysistrata*: Women and the Body Politic'. In Alan H. Sommerstein, ed. *Tragedy and Comedy, and the Polis: Papers from the Greek Drama Conference. Nottingham July 1990*. Bari: Levante, 1993, 431–44.

————. 'Clemency as a Virtue'. *Classical Philology* 100 (2005): 337–46.

————. 'Understanding Grief in Greece and Rome'. *Classical World* 110 (2010): 3–30.

Koptev, A. 'From the Tarquin Kingship to the Republic: Three Versions of the Graeco-Roman Historiography'. In C. Deroux, ed. *Studies in Latin Literature and Roman History*. 16. Brussels: Latomus, 2012, 23–93.

Kraemer, Ross Shepard. *Unreliable Witnesses: Religion, Gender, and History in the Greco-Roman Mediterranean*. New York: Oxford University Press, 2011.

Krämer, H. J. 'Die Sagen von Romulus und Remus in der lateinischen Literatur'. In H. Flashar and K. Geiser, eds. *Synusia: Festgab für Wolfgang Schadewaldt zum. 15 März 1965*. Pfullingen: Neske, 1965, 355–402.

Krausmüller, Dirk. 'The Lost First Life of Athanasius the Athonite and Its Author Anthony, Abbot of the Constantinopolitan Monastery of Ta Panagiou'. In Margaret Mullett, ed. *Founders and Refounders of Byzantine Monasteries: Papers of the Fifth Belfast Byzantine International Colloquium, Portaferry, September 1999*. Belfast: Belfast Byzantine Enterprises, 2007, 63–86.

Krebs, Christopher B. *A Most Dangerous Book: Tacitus's Germania from the Roman Empire to the Third Reich*. New York: W. W. Norton, 2011.

Kupers, Terry A. 'Toxic Masculinity as a Barrier to Mental Health Treatment in Prison'. *Journal of Clinical Psychology* 61.6 (2005): 713–24.

———. 'Gender and Domination in Prison'. *Western New England Law Review* 39.3 (2017): 427–47.

Lakmann, Marie-Luise. *Der Platoniker Tauros in der Darstellung des Aulus Gellius*. Leiden: Brill, 1995.

Lamberton, Robert. *Plutarch*. New Haven: Yale University Press, 2001.

Lambrecht, Bill. 'Todd Akin Recalled in DC Dust-Up'. *St Louis Post-Dispatch*, 13 June 2013. https://www.stltoday.com/news/local/govt-and-politics/bill-lambrecht/todd-akin-recalled-in-dc-dust-up/article_b522d2ef-2175-53e4-8095-7e2cf37adfc7.html.

Lamers, Han, and Bettina Reitz-Joosse. *The Codex Fori Mussolini: A Latin Text of Italian Fascism*. London: Bloomsbury, 2016.

Landy, M. *Italian Film*. Cambridge: Cambridge University Press, 2000.

Langlands, Rebecca. *Sexual Morality in Ancient Rome*. Cambridge: Cambridge University Press, 2006.

———. *Exemplary Ethics in Ancient Rome*. Cambridge: Cambridge University Press, 2018.

Laqueur, Thomas. *Making Sex: Body and Gender from the Greeks to Freud*. Cambridge, MA: Harvard University Press, 1990.

Larbalestier, Justine. '"Legitimate Rape" and Other Craptastic Beliefs from the Olden Days'. *Justine Larbalestier* (blog), 20 August 2012. http://justinelarbalestier.com/blog/2012/08/20/legitimate-rape-and-other-craptastic-beliefs-from-the-olden-days/.

Lateiner, D. 'Tears and Crying in Hellenic Historiography: Dacryology from Herodotus to Polybius'. In Fögen 2009, 105–34.

Launey, Marcel, and Pierre Roussel. *Inscriptions de Délos*. Paris: Librairie Ancienne Honoré Champion, 1937.

Lauxtermann, M. D. 'John Geometres: Poet and Soldier'. *Byzantion* 68 (1998): 356–80.

———. *Byzantine Poetry from Pisides to Geometres: Texts and Contexts*. Vienna: Austrian Academy of Sciences Press, 2003.

Lawrence, S. 'Ancient Ethics, the Heroic Code, and the Morality of Sophocles' *Ajax*'. *Greece and Rome* 52.1 (2005): 18–33.

Lebow, Richard Ned. 'Thucydides the Constructivist'. *American Political Science Review* 95.3 (September 2001): 547–60.

Leen, Anne. 'Clodia Oppugnatrix: The Domus Motif in Cicero's *Pro Caelio*'. *Classical Journal* 96.2 (2000): 141–62.

Lefkowitz, Mary R. 'Influential Women'. In Averil Cameron and Amelie Kuhrt, eds. *Images of Women in Antiquity*. London: Routledge, 1983, 49–64.

Leisner-Jensen, Mogens. 'Vis Comica. Consummated Rape in Greek and Roman New Comedy'. *Classica et Mediaevalia* 53 (2002): 173–96.

Lenski, Noel E. *Constantine and the City: Imperial Authority and Civic Politics*. Philadelphia: University of Pennsylvania Press, 2016a.

———. 'Violence and the Roman Slave'. In Werner Riess and Garret G. Fagan, eds. *The Topography of Violence in the Greco-Roman World*. Ann Arbor: University of Michigan Press, 2016b, 275–98.

Lentano, M. '"Un nome più grande di qualsiasi legge". Declamazione latina e patria potestas'. *Bollettino di studi latini* 35 (2005): 558–89.

Levant, R. F. 'A New Psychology of Men'. *Professional Psychology Research and Practice* 27.3 (1996): 259–65.

Levin-Richardson, Sarah, and Deborah Kamen. 'Lusty Ladies in the Roman Imaginary'. In Ruby Blondell and Kirk Ormand, eds. *Ancient Sex: New Essays*. Columbus: Ohio State University, 2015, 231–52.

Ley, David J. 'The NoFap Phenomenon: There's Nothing New about This Fight against Self-Love'. *Psychology Today* (blog), 3 March 2015. https://www.psychologytoday.com/us/blog/women-who-stray/201503/the-nofap-phenomenon.

Libatique, Daniel. 'Ovid in the #MeToo Era'. *Helios* 48.1 (2021): 57–75.

Lidman, Satu. *Gender, Violence and Attitudes: Lessons from Early Modern Europe*. London and New York: Routledge, 2018.

Lilly, M. 'The World Is Not a Safe Place for Men: The Representations Politics of the Manosphere'. Master's thesis, University of Ottawa, 2016.

Link, Stefan. 'Education and Pederasty in Spartan and Cretan Society'. In Stephen Hodkinson, ed. *Sparta: Comparative Approaches*. Swansea: Classical Press of Wales, 2009, 89–112.

Lipka, Michael. *Xenophon's Spartan Constitution: Introduction, Text, Commentary*. Berlin: De Gruyter, 2002.

Littlewood, C. 'Seneca's *Thyestes*: The Tragedy with No Women?' *Materiali e discussioni per l'analisi dei testi classici* 38 (1997): 57–86.

Liveley, Genevieve. 'Teaching Rape in Roman Elegy: Part I'. In Gold 2012, 541–8.

Long, Thomas Lawrence. 'Akin Medievalism'. *The Long View* (blog), 20 August 2012. http://thelongview.tv/2012/08/20/akin-medievalism/.

Loraux, Nicole. *The Children of Athena: Athenian Ideas about Citizenship and the Division between the Sexes*. Translated by C. Levine. Princeton: Princeton University Press, 1993.

———. *The Experiences of Tiresias: The Feminine and the Greek Men*. Translated by P. Wissing. Princeton: Princeton University Press, 1995.

———. 'Thucydides and Sedition among Words'. In J. S. Rusten, ed. *Thucydides: Oxford Readings in Classical Studies*. New York: Oxford University Press, 2009, 261–92.

Lowe, Lisa. *Critical Terrains: French and British Orientalisms*. Ithaca, NY: Cornell University Press, 1991.

'LUCE', n.d. https://www.archivioluce.com/.

Ludwig, P. *Eros and Polis: Desire and Community in Greek Political Theory*. Cambridge: Cambridge University Press, 2002.

Lugones, Maria. 'Toward a Decolonial Feminism'. *Hypatia* 25 (2010): 742–59.

Lytle, Ephraim. 'Sparta? No. This Is Madness'. *Toronto Star*, 11 March 2007. https://www.thestar.com/entertainment/2007/03/11/sparta_no_this_is_madness.html.

Macciocchi, Maria-Antonietta. 'Female Sexuality in Fascist Ideology'. *Feminist Review* 1 (1979): 67–82.

MacDonald, Dennis R. *The Legend and the Apostle: The Battle for Paul in Story and Canon*. Philadelphia: Westminster, 1983.

MacDowell, Douglas M. *Spartan Law*. Edinburgh: Scottish Academic Press, 1986.

———. *Aristophanes and Athens: An Introduction to the Plays*. Oxford: Oxford University Press, 1995.

Machiavelli, Niccolò. *Discourses on Livy*. Translated by Harvey Mansfield and Nathan Tarcov. Chicago: University of Chicago Press, 1996.

Mack, Sara. 'Acis and Galatea or Metamorphosis of Tradition'. *Arion* 6.3 (1999): 51–67.

MacKinnon, Catherine A. *Towards a Feminist Theory of State*. Cambridge, MA: Harvard University Press, 1989.

Magdelain, A. 'Paricidas'. In *Du châtiment dans la cité. Supplices corporels et peine de mort dans le monde antique. Table ronde de Rome (9–11 novembre 1982)*, 549–71. Rome: École française de Rome, 1984.

Maire, Brigitte. 'Mustio et Soranos ou la conception de jumeaux hétérozygotes'. In Véronique Boudon-Millot, Véronique Dasen and Brigitte Maire, eds. *Femmes en médecine. Actes de la journée internationale d'étude organisée à l'université René-Descartes-Paris V, le 17 mars 2006 en l'honneur de Danielle Gourevitch*. Paris: De Boccard, 2008, 105–17.

Mak, Tim, and Katie Glueck. 'Romney, Ryan "Disagree" with Akin'. *Politico* (blog), 20 August 2012. https://www.politico.com/story/2012/08/romney-ryan-disagree-with-akin-079876.

Malinas, Yves, Paul Burguière and Danielle Gourevitch. 'L'anatomie gynécologique dans Soranos d'Ephèse'. *Histoires Des Sciences Médicales* 19 (1985): 161–7.

Manavis, Sarah. 'No Nut November: The Insidious Internet Challenge Encouraging Men Not to Masturbate'. *New Statesman*, 13 November 2018. https://www.newstatesman.com/science-tech/social-media/2018/11/no-nut-november-insidious-internet-challenge-encouraging-men-not.

Manne, Kate. *Down Girl: The Logic of Misogyny*. Oxford: Oxford University Press, 2017.

Manning, C. E. 'Seneca and the Stoics on the Equality of the Sexes'. *Mnemosyne* 26.2 (1973): 170–7.

Manuli, Paola. 'Elogio della castità. La "Ginecologia" di Sorano'. *Memoria* 3 (1982): 39–49.

Manuwald, Gesine. *Roman Republican Theater*. Cambridge: Cambridge University Press, 2011.

Marcello, Flavia. 'Mussolini and the Idealisation of Empire: The Augustan Exhibition of Romanità'. *Modern Italy* 16.3 (2011): 223–47.

Marcotte, Amanda. 'Overcompensation Nation: It's Time to Admit That Toxic Masculinity Drives Gun Violence'. *Salon*, 13 June 2016. https://www.salon.com/2016/06/13/overcompensation_nation_its_time_to_admit_that_toxic_masculinity_drives_gun_violence/.

Mardorossian, Carine. *Framing the Rape Victim*. New Brunswick, NJ: Rutgers University Press, 2014.

Marincola, John. 'Xenophon's *Anabasis* and *Hellenica*'. In Flower 2017, 103–18.

Marks, R. *From Republic to Empire: Scipio Africanus in the Punica of Silius Italicus*. Frankfurt am Main: Peter Lang, 2005.

Marturano, Melissa. 'Vim Parat: Patterns of Sexualized Violence, Victim-Blaming, and Sororophobia in Ovid'. PhD diss., The Graduate Center, CUNY, 2017.

———. 'Sororophobia in Ovid'. In Deacy et al. 2023.

Masterson, Mark. 'Studies of Ancient Masculinity'. In T. K. Hubbard, ed. *A Companion to Greek and Roman Sexualities*. Chichester: Wiley-Blackwell, 2014, 17–30.

———. *Man to Man: Desire, Homosociality, and Authority in Late-Roman Manhood*. Columbus: Ohio State University Press, 2014.

———. *Between Byzantine Men: Desire, Homosociality, and Brotherhood in the Medieval Empire*. London: Routledge, 2022.

Mastrocinque, A. *Lucio Giunio Bruto: Ricerche di storia, religione e diritto sulle origini della repubblica romana*. Trento: Edizioni La reclaime, 1988.

———. *Romolo: la fondazione di Roma tra storia e leggenda*. Padova: Libreria editrice Zielo, 1993.

Mattingly, David. *Imperialism, Power, and Identity*. Princeton: Princeton University Press, 2013.

Mattioli, Umberto. Ἀσθένεια e ἀνδρεία. *Aspetti della femminilità nella letteratura classica, biblica e cristiana antica*. Roma: Bulzoni Editore, 1984.

McAuley, Mairéad. 'Ambiguus Sexus: Epic Masculinity in Transition in Statius' *Achilleid*'. *Akroterion* 55 (2010): 37–60.

———. *Reproducing Rome: Motherhood in Virgil, Ovid, Seneca and Statius*. Oxford: Oxford University Press, 2016.

McCarter, Stephanie, and Jia Tolentino. 'The Brutality of Ovid: A Conversation on Sex, Violence, and Power in the Metamorphoses'. *Lapham's Quarterly*, 11 September 2019.

McClure, Laura. *Spoken Like a Woman: Speech and Gender in Athenian Drama*. Princeton: Princeton University Press, 1999.

McCoskey, Denise. *Race: Antiquity and Its Legacy*. London and New York: I. B. Tauris, 2012.

McCoy, Marsha. 'The Politics of Prostitution: Clodia, Cicero, and Social Order in the Late Roman Republic'. In Faraone and McClure 2006, 177–85.

McDonnell, Myles. *Roman Manliness: Virtus and the Roman Republic*. Cambridge: Cambridge University Press, 2006.

McGeer, E., Nicephorus Uranus and Nicephorus II Phocas. *Sowing the Dragon's Teeth: Byzantine Warfare in the Tenth Century*. Washington, DC: Dumbarton Oaks Research Library and Collection, 1995.

Mercati, Silvio Giuseppe. 'Note d'epigrafia Bizantina'. *Bessarione* 37 (1921): 136–62.

Merriam-Webster. 'No, "Snowflake" as a Slang Term Did Not Begin with "Fight Club"'. *Merriam-Webster Words We're Watching* (blog), n.d. https://www.merriam-webster.com/words-at-play/the-less-lovely-side-of-snowflake.

Messerschmidt, James W. *Hegemonic Masculinity: Formulation, Reformulation, and Amplification*. Lanham, MD: Rowman & Littlefield, 2018.

Meyer, P. *Die Haupturkunden für die Geschichte der Athos-Klöster*. Leipzig: J. C. Hinrichs'sche Buchhandlung, 1894.

Miles, G. B. *Livy: Reconstructing Early Rome*. Ithaca, NY: Cornell University Press, 1995.

Millbank, Lisa. 'Under Duress: Agency, Power and Consent, Part One and Two'. *A Radical Transfeminist* (blog), January 2012.

Millender, Ellen G. 'Kingship: The History, Power, and Prerogatives of the Spartans' "Divine" Dyarchy'. In Powell 2018, 452–79.

Miller, Matt. 'Sorry Chuck Palahniuk, "Fight Club" Did Not Invent the Alt-Right's Favorite Insult'. *Esquire*, 30 January 2017. https://www.esquire.com/entertainment/books/news/a52667/chuck-palahniuk-snowflake-alt-right-origin/esquire.com/entertainment/books/news/a52667/chuck-palahniuk-snowflake-alt-right-origin.

Moloney, M. E., and T. P. Love. 'Assessing Online Misogyny: Perspectives from Sociology and Feminist Media Studies'. *Sociology Compass* 12.5 (2018): 1–12.

Montoya Rubio, Bernat. 'La esclavitud como factor de corrupción en la historiografía de cultura helenística: hybris, tryphé y moral estoica'. *Dialogues d'histoire ancienne* 40.2 (2014): 155–77.

Moore, Lori. 'Rep. Todd Akin: The Statement and the Reaction'. *New York Times*, 20 August 2012. https://www.nytimes.com/2012/08/21/us/politics/rep-todd-akin-legitimate-rape-statement-and-reaction.html.

Morales, Helen. *Antigone Rising: The Subversive Power of the Ancient Myths*. New York: Bold Type, 2020.

Morley, Neville. *Classics: Why It Matters*. Medford, MA: Polity, 2018.

————. 'Sphinx'. *Sphinx* (blog), 2019. https://thesphinxblog.com/.

Morris, Rosemary. 'The Two Faces of Nikephoros Phokas'. *Byzantine and Modern Greek Studies* 12.1 (1988): 83–116.

Moss, Candida. 'The History of the Orgasm'. *Daily Beast*, 23 September 2017. https://www.thedailybeast.com/the-history-of-the-orgasm.

Mosse, George. *Nationalism and Sexuality: Middle-Class Morality and Sexual Norms in Modern Europe.* Madison: University of Wisconsin Press, 1985.

Murphy, Charles T. 'The Use of Speeches in Caesar's *Gallic War*'. *Classical Journal* 45.3 (1949): 120–27.

Murray, S. O. *Homosexualities.* Chicago and London: University of Chicago Press, 2000.

Myers, Nancy. 'Cicero's (S)Trumpet: Roman Women and the *Second Philippic*'. *Rhetoric Review* 22.4 (2003): 337–52.

Myketiak, Chrystie. 'Fragile Masculinity: Social Inequalities in the Narrative Frame and Discursive Construction of a Mass Shooter's Autobiography/ Manifesto'. *Contemporary Social Science* 11.4 (2016): 1–15.

Nagel, Joane. 'Masculinity and Nationalism: Gender and Sexuality in the Making of Nations'. *Ethnic and Racial Studies* 21.2 (January 1998): 242–69.

Nagle, Angela. *Kill All Normies.* London: Zero Books, 2017.

Nandini, B. P. 'Caput Mundi: Female Hair as Symbolic Vehicle of Domination in Ovidian Love Elegy'. *Classical Journal* 113.4 (2018): 454–88.

Narro, Ángel. 'The Cloud of Thecla and the Construction of Her Character as a Virgin (Παρθένος), Martyr (Μάρτυς) and Apostle (Ἀπόστολος)'. *Collectanea Christiana Orientalia* 16 (2019): 99–129.

Neel, J. *Legendary Rivals: Collegiality and Ambition in the Tales of Early Rome.* Leiden: Brill, 2014.

Nelis, Jan. *From Ancient to Modern: The Myth of Romanità During the Ventennio Fascista: The Written Imprint of Mussolini's Cult of the 'Third Rome'.* Brussels: Belgisch Historisch Instituut te Rome, 2011.

Nesbø, Ingeborg Heen. 'Nice Guys Masculinities in *The Great Gatsby* and *500 Days of Summer*'. Master's thesis, University of Oslo, 2021.

New York Times. 'Strawberry Generation'. *New York Times, Schott's Vocab: A Miscellany of Modern Words and Phrases* (blog), 30 November 2008.

Newell, Waller R. 'Tyranny and the Science of Ruling in Xenophon's "Education of Cyrus"'. *Journal of Politics* 45.4 (1983): 889–906.

Newmyer, Stephen. *Animals, Rights, and Reason in Plutarch and Modern Ethics.* New York: Routledge, 2005.

Nicholson, Rebecca. '"Poor Little Snowflake" – The Defining Insult of 2016'. *Guardian*, 28 November 2016. https://www.theguardian.com/science/2016/ nov/28/snowflake-insult-disdain-young-people.

Nilsson, Martin P. 'Greek Mysteries in the Confession of St Cyprian'. *Harvard Theological Review* 40 (1947): 167–76.

Nock, Arthur D. 'Hagiographica II. Cyprian of Antioch'. *Journal of Theological Studies* 28 (1927): 411–15.

Noret, Jacques, and Monachus Athanasius. *Vitae duae antiquae Sancti Athanasii Athonitae.* Vol. 9. Corpus Christianorum Brepols. Leuven: Turnhout, 1982.

Nortjé-Meyer, Lilly. 'Retrieving the Voices of Women Sages in the New Testament and Early Christianity'. *Journal of Early Christian History* 8.3 (2018): 1–6.

Nortwick, Thomas Van. *Imagining Men: Ideals of Masculinity in Ancient Greek Culture.* Westport, CT: Praeger, 2008.

Nussbaum, Martha Craven. *The Therapy of Desire: Theory and Practice in Hellenistic Ethics.* Princeton: Princeton University Press, 1994.

Nye, Robert A. 'Sexuality'. In Teresa A. Meade and Merry E. Wiesner-Hanks, eds. *A Companion to Gender History.* Malden, MA: Blackwell, 2004, 9–25.

Ober, Josiah. *Mass and Elite in Democratic Athens: Rhetoric, Ideology, and the Power of the People.* Princeton: Princeton University Press, 1989.

———. *Political Dissent in Democratic Athens: Intellectual Critics of Popular Rule.* Princeton: Princeton University Press, 2001a.

———. 'Thucydides Theoretikos/Thucydides Histor: Realist Theory and the Challenge of History'. In D. R. McCann and B. S. Strauss, eds. *Democracy and War: A Comparative Study of the Korean War and the Peloponnesian War.* Armonk, NY: M. E. Sharpe, 2001b, 273–306.

Ogden, Daniel. 'Homosexuality'. In Mark Golden and Peter Toohey, eds. *A Cultural History of Sexuality in the Classical World.* Vol. 1. London: Bloomsbury Academic, 2011, 1:37–54.

O'Gorman, Ellen. 'No Place Like Rome: Identity and Difference in the *Germania* of Tacitus'. *Ramus* 22.2 (2003): 135–54.

O'Hara, S. F. 'Patria Potestas: A Brief Re-Examination'. In T. W. Hillard, R. A. Kearsley, C. E. V. Nixon and A. M. Nobbs, eds. *Ancient History in a Modern University: Proceedings of a Conference Held at Macquarie University, 8–13 July, 1993.* Vol. 1: The Ancient Near East, Greece, and Rome. Grand Rapids, MI: William B. Eerdmans Publishing Company, 1998, 1:210–16.

Oliver, Jay H. 'Queer World-Making in Petronius' *Satyrica*'. PhD diss., University of Toronto, 2016.

Olson, Kelly. 'Masculinity, Appearance, and Sexuality: Dandies in Roman Antiquity'. *Journal of the History of Sexuality* 23.2 (2014): 182–205.

O'Malley, Harris. 'The Difference Between Toxic Masculinity and Being a Man'. *Good Men Project* (blog), 27 June 2016. https://goodmenproject.com/featured-content/the-difference-between-toxic-masculinity-and-being-a-man-dg/.

Opstall, Emilie Marlène van. *Jean Géomètre: Poèmes en hexamètres et en distiques élégiaques.* Leiden: Brill, 2008.

Ortega, Matt. 'Days without a GOP Rape Mention'. *Days without a GOP Rape Mention*, n.d. http://www.dayswithoutagoprapemention.com/.

Orwin, Clifford. *The Humanity of Thucydides*. Princeton: Princeton University Press, 1997.

Ostrogorsky, G. *History of the Byzantine State*. Translated by J. Hussey. 2nd ed. Oxford: Oxford University Press, 1968.

Pachoumi, Eleni. 'The Erotic and Separation Spells of the Magical Papyri and the Defixiones'. *Greek, Roman, and Byzantine Studies* 53.2 (2013): 294–325.

Palmer, Carl L., and Rolfe D. Peterson. 'Toxic Mask-Ulinity: The Link between Masculine Toughness and Affective Reactions to Mask Wearing in the COVID-19 Era'. *Politics and Gender* 16.4 (2020): 1044–51.

Parent, M. C., T. D. Gobble and A. Rochlen. 'Social Media Behavior, Toxic Masculinity, and Depression'. *Psychology of Men and Masculinities* 20.3 (2018): 277–87.

Parker, Victor. 'Sphodrias' Raid and the Liberation of Thebes: A Study of Ephorus and Xenophon'. *Hermes* 135.1 (2007): 13–33.

Parrish, Katie. 'Translation in the Age of #MeToo'. *Sewanee Features*, 7 September 2018. https://new.sewanee.edu/files/resources/055_22_general-convention-magazine_150.pdf.

Pascoe, C. J. *Dude You're a Fag: Masculinity and Sexuality in High School*. Berkeley: University of California Press, 2011.

Pascoe, C. J., and Tristan Bridges, eds. *Exploring Masculinities: Identity, Inequality, Continuity and Change*. Oxford: Oxford University Press, 2015.

Pauly, Madison. 'The War on Masks Is a Cover-up for Toxic Masculinity'. *Mother Jones*, 8 October 2020. https://www.motherjones.com/coronavirus-updates/2020/10/trump-masks-covid-toxic-masculinity/.

Pelling, Christopher B. R. *Plutarch and History: Eighteen Studies*. London: Classical Press of Wales and Duckworth, 2002.

Penrose, Jnr., Walter D. *Postcolonial Amazons: Female Masculinity and Courage in Ancient Greek and Sanskrit Literature*. Oxford: Oxford University Press, 2006.

Perusino, Franca. 'Violenza degli uomini e violenza delle donne nella Lisistrata di Aristofane'. *Quaderni Urbinati di Cultura Classica* 63.3 (1999): 71–8.

Petrarch, Francesco. *Petrarch's Secret*. Translated by William H. Draper. London: Chatto and Windus, 1911.

Petronius Arbiter. *Satyricon Reliquiae*. Edited by Konrad Müller. Berlin: De Gruyter, 2004.

Pharos. 'Neomasculine Site Argues for the Revival of Roman "Manly Character"'. *Pharos* (blog), 4 December 2017. http://pages.vassar.edu/pharos/2017/12/04/neomasculine-site-argues-for-the-revival-of-roman-manly-character.

Pinault, Jodie Rubin. 'The Medical Case for Virginity in the Early Second Century CE: Soranus of Ephesus, Gynecology 1.32'. *Helios* 19 (1992): 123–39.

Pittenger, Miriam R. Pelikan. *Contested Triumphs: Politics, Pageantry, and Performance in Livy's Republican Rome.* Berkeley: University of California Press, 2008.

Pleck, Joseph H. *The Myth of Masculinity.* Cambridge, MA: MIT Press, 1981.

Poletti, B. 'L. Junius Brutus, a Model and Predecessor for the Emperor Augustus. Some Remarks on Dionysius of Halicarnassus 4.71–75'. *Acta Antiqua Academiae Scientiarum Hungaricae* 55 (2015): 229–45.

Pomeroy, Arthur. 'Classical Antiquity, Cinema and Propaganda'. In Roche and Demetriou 2018, 264–85.

Pomeroy, Sarah B. *Goddesses, Whores, Wives, and Slaves: Women in Classical Antiquity.* Studies in the Life of Women. London and New York: Schocken Books, 1975.

Porter, Amber J. 'Compassion in Soranus' *Gynecology* and Caelius Aurelianus' *On Chronic Diseases*'. In Georgia Petridou and Chiara Thumiger, eds. *Homo Patiens: Approaches to the Patient in the Ancient World.* Leiden: Brill, 2016, 285–303.

Porter, James I., ed. *Constructions of the Classical Body.* Ann Arbor: University of Michigan Press, 1999.

Posadas, Jeremy. 'Teaching the Causes of Rape Culture: Toxic Masculinity'. *Journal of Feminist Studies in Religion* 33.1 (2017): 177–9.

Poucet, J. *Les Rois de Rome: tradition et histoire.* Brussels: Académie royale de Belgique, 2000.

Powell, Anton, ed. *A Companion to Sparta.* Hoboken: John Wiley and Sons, 2018.

———. 'Sparta and the Imperial Schools of Britain: Comparisons'. In Powell 2018, 723–59.

Powell, T. G. E. *The Celts.* London: Thames and Hudson, 1980.

Pratt, Norman T. 'The Stoic Base of Senecan Drama'. *Transactions and Proceedings of the American Philological Association* 79 (1948): 1–11.

Prenner, Antonella. *Mustione 'traduttore' di Sorano di Efeso.* Naples: Liguori, 2012.

Price, Jonathan J. *Thucydides and Internal War.* New York: Cambridge University Press, 2001.

Projansky, Sarah. *Watching Rape: Film and Television in Postfeminist Culture.* New York: New York University Press, 2001.

'Prosopographie der mittelbyzantinischen Zeit Online', n.d. https://www.degruyter.com/PMBZ.

Quiroga Puertas, Alberto J. *The Dynamics of Rhetorical Performances in Late Antiquity.* London: Routledge, 2018.

Raaflaub, Kurt A. *Equalities and Inequalities in Athenian Democracy.* Princeton: Princeton University Press, 1996.

————. *The Discovery of Freedom in Ancient Greece*. Chicago: University of Chicago Press, 2004.

Rabinowitz, Nancy Sorkin, and Fiona McHardy, eds. *Abortion to Pederasty: Addressing Difficult Topics in a Classics Classroom*. Columbus: Ohio State University Press, 2014.

Rabinowitz, Nancy Sorkin, and Amy Richlin, eds. *Feminist Theory and the Classics*. New York and London: Routledge, 1993.

Rademaker, Adriaan. '"Most Citizens Are Europrôktoi Now": (Un)Manliness in Aristophanes'. In Rosen and Sluiter 2003, 115–26.

Ranger, Holly. 'Why Are We Still Reading Ovid's Rapes?' In Deacy et al. 2023.

Rapp, Claudia. *Holy Bishops in Late Antiquity: The Nature of Christian Leadership in an Age of Transition*. Berkeley: University of California Press, 2013.

————. *Brother-Making in Late Antiquity and Byzantium: Monks, Laymen and Christian Ritual*. New York: Oxford University Press, 2016.

Re, Lucia. 'Italians and the Invention of Race: The Poetics and Politics of Difference in the Struggle over Libya, 1890–1913'. *California Italian Studies* 1.1 (2010): n/a.

Reay, Brendon. 'Agriculture, Writing, and Cato's Aristocratic Self-Fashioning'. *Classical Antiquity* 24.2 (2005): 331–61.

Reich, Wilhelm. *The Mass Psychology of Fascism*. Translated by Vincent Carfagno. London: Condor, 1933.

Reinhart, Morgan. '"Legitimate rape" in the Bible'. *Humanist* 72.6 (2012): 8–11.

Reynolds, L. D. *L. Annaei Senecae: Ad Lucilium Epistulae Morales*. Oxford: Oxford University Press, 1965.

————. *L. Annaei Senecae: Dialogorum Libri Duodecim*. Oxford: Oxford University Press, 1977.

Richer, Nicolas. 'Spartan Education in the Classical Period'. In Powell 2018, 525–42.

Richlin, Amy. *The Garden of Priapus: Sexuality and Aggression in Roman Humor*. New Haven: Yale University Press, 1983.

————. 'Emotional Work: Lamenting the Roman Dead'. In Elizabeth Tylawsky and Charles Weiss, eds. *Essays in Honor of Gordon Williams: Twenty-Five Years at Yale*. New Haven: Henry R. Schwab, 2001, 229–48.

————. 'Reading Ovid's Rapes'. In Amy Richlin, ed. *Arguments with Silence*. Ann Arbor: University of Michigan Press, 2014, 130–65.

————. *Slave Theater in the Roman Republic*. Cambridge: Cambridge University Press, 2017.

Ridley, R. T. 'To Be Taken with a Pinch of Salt: The Destruction of Carthage'. *Classical Philology* 81.2 (1986): 140–6.

Riggsby, Andrew M. *Caesar in Gaul and Rome: War in Words*. Austin: University of Texas Press, 2006.

Rimell, Victoria. *Petronius and the Anatomy of Fiction*. Cambridge: Cambridge University Press, 2002.

———. *Ovid's Lovers: Desire, Difference, and the Poetic Imagination*. Cambridge: Cambridge University Press, 2006.

Robin, Diana. 'Film Theory and the Gendered Voice in Seneca'. In Rabinowitz and Richlin 1993, 102–21.

Robson, James. *Sex and Sexuality in Classical Athens*. Edinburgh: Edinburgh University Press, 2013.

Roche, Helen, and Kyriakos Demetriou, eds. *Brill's Companion to the Classics, Fascist Italy and Nazi Germany*. Leiden: Brill, 2018.

Roisman, Joseph. *The Rhetoric of Manhood: Masculinity in the Attic Orators*. Berkeley: University of California Press, 2005.

Roller, M. 'Exemplarity in Roman Culture: The Cases of Horatius Cocles and Cloelia'. *Classical Philology* 99 (2004): 1–56.

———. *Models from the Past in Roman Culture: A World of Exempla*. Cambridge: Cambridge University Press, 2018.

Romm, James S. *The Edges of the Earth in Ancient Thought: Geography, Exploration, and Fiction*. Princeton: Princeton University Press, 1994.

Ronnet, Gilberte. *Sophocle, poète tragique*. Paris: E. de Boccard, 1969.

Rood, Tim. 'Panhellenism and Self-Presentation: Xenophon's Speeches'. In Robin Lane Fox, ed. *The Long March: Xenophon and the Ten Thousand*. New Haven and London: Yale University Press, 2004, 305–29.

Rosen, Ralph M., and Ineke Sluiter, eds. *Andreia: Studies in Manliness and Courage in Classical Antiquity*. Leiden: Brill, 2003.

Rosenmeyer, Thomas G. *Senecan Drama and Stoic Cosmology*. Berkeley: University of California Press, 1989.

Roth, Ulrike. 'Speaking Out? Child Sexual Abuse and the Enslaved Voice in the *Cena Trimalchionis*'. In Deborah Kamen and C. W. Marshall, eds. *Slavery and Sexuality in Classical Antiquity*. Madison: University of Wisconsin Press, 2021, 211–38.

Roy, Jessica. 'Analysis: "Cuck", "Snowflake", "Masculinist": A Guide to the Language of the "Alt-Right"'. *Los Angeles Times*, 16 November 2016. latimes. com/nation/la-na-pol-alt-right-terminology-20161115-story.html.

Ruzé, F. 'The Empire of the Spartans (404–371)'. In Powell 2018, 320–53.

Saha, J. 'Whiteness, Masculinity and the Ambivalent Embodiment of "British Justice" in Colonial Burma'. *Cultural and Social History* 14.4 (2017): 527–42.

Saller, R. P. *Patriarchy, Property and Death in the Roman Family*. Cambridge: Cambridge University Press, 1994.

Salter, Michael. 'The Problem With a Fight against Toxic Masculinity'. *The Atlantic*, 27 February 2019. https://www.theatlantic.com/health/archive/2019/02/toxic-masculinity-history/583411/.

Salzman-Mitchell, Patricia B. *A Web of Fantasies: Gaze, Image and Gender in Ovid's Metamorphoses*. Columbus: Ohio State University Press, 2005.

Sanna, M. V. 'Dal ius vitae ac necis di una lex regia al ius occidendi della lex Iulia de adulteriis : note e interrogativi'. *Iuris Antiqui Historia* 6 (2014): 11–36.

Sansone, David. *Plutarch: The Lives of Aristeides and Cato*. Warminster: Aris and Phillips, 1989.

Santoro L'Hoir, Francesca. *The Rhetoric of Gender Terms: 'Man', 'Woman', and the Portrayal of Character in Latin Prose*. Vol. 120. Mnemosyne: Bibliotheca Classica Batava: Supplementum. Leiden: Brill, 1992.

Sapsford, T. 'The Wages of Effeminacy? *Kinaidoi* in Greek Documentary Sources from Egypt'. *Eugesta* 5 (2015): 103–23.

———. *Performing the Kinaidos*. Oxford: Oxford University Press, 2022.

Sautel, J. 'Discours et récits dans les *Antiquités Romaines* de Denys d'Halicarnasse: différents niveaux d'énonciation'. *Pallas* 97 (2015): 51–67.

Schenk, Christine. *Crispina and Her Sisters: Women and Authority in Early Christianity*. Minneapolis: Fortress, 2017.

Schick, Irvin C. *The Erotic Margin: Sexuality and Spatiality in Alteritist Discourse*. London: Verso, 1999.

Schippers, Mimi. 'Recovering the Feminine Other: Masculinity, Femininity, and Gender Hegemony'. *Theory and Society* 36.1 (2007): 85–102.

Schmeling, Gareth. *A Commentary on the Satyrica of Petronius*. Oxford: Oxford University Press, 2011.

Schorn, S. 'Tears of the Bereaved: Plutarch's *Consolatio ad Uxorem* in Context'. In Fögen 2009, 335–66.

Schrock, Doug, and Michael Schwalbe. 'Men, Masculinity, and Manhood Acts'. *Annual Review of Sociology* 35 (2009): 277–95.

Schultze, C. E. '"The Sole Glory of Death": Dying and Commemoration in Dionysius of Halicarnassus'. In Hope and Huskinson 2011, 78–92.

Schwalbe, Michael. *Manhood Acts: Gender and the Practices of Domination*. Boulder: Routledge, 2014.

Schwartz, Dana. 'Why Trump Supporters Love Calling People "Snowflakes"'. *GQ*, 1 February 2017. gq.com/story/why-trump-supporters-love-calling-people-snowflakes.

Sciarrino, Enrica. *Cato the Censor and the Beginnings of Latin Prose: From Poetic Translation to Elite Transcription*. Columbus: Ohio State University Press, 2011.

Scipione l'Africano, dir. Carmine Gallone. ENIC, 1937.

Scott, James. 'The Ethics of the Physics in Seneca's *Natural Questions*'. *Classical Bulletin* 75.1 (1999): 55–68.

Scott, Joan W. 'After History?' *Common Knowledge* 5 (1996): 9–26.

Sculos, Bryant W. 'Who's Afraid of "Toxic Masculinity"?' *Class, Race and Corporate Power* 5.3 (2017).

Sears, Matthew A. 'Toxic Masculinity Fostered by Misreadings of the Classics'. *The Conversation*, 29 November 2017. https://theconversation.com/toxic-masculinity-fostered-by-misreadings-of-the-classics-88118.

Segal, Charles. *Tragedy and Civilization: An Interpretation of Sophocles.* Cambridge, MA and London: Harvard University Press, 1981.

Seider, A. 'Catullan Myths: Gender, Mourning, and the Death of a Brother'. *Classical Antiquity* 35 (2016): 279–314.

Seita, M. 'Una tragedia senza palcoscenico: Tarquinio il Superbo e i suoi familiari secondo Tito Livio'. *Bollettino di studi latini* 30 (2000): 485–513.

Sellars, John. *Stoicism*. London and New York: Routledge, 2014.

Sergent, B. *Homosexuality in Greek Myth*. Boston: Beacon Press, 1986.

Sharrock, Alison. 'Gender and Transformation: Reading, Women, and Gender in Ovid's Metamorphoses'. In Alison Sharrock, Daniel Möller and Mats Malm, eds. *Metamorphic Readings: Transformation, Language, and Gender in the Interpretation of Ovid's Metamorphoses*. New York: Oxford University Press, 2020, 33–53.

Shaw, B. D. 'Raising and Killing Children: Two Roman Myths'. *Mnemosyne* 54 (2001): 33–77.

Shay, J. *Achilles in Vietnam: Combat Trauma and the Undoing of Character*. New York: Athenaeum, 1994.

———. 'Killing Rage: Physis or Nomos – or Both?' In H. van Wees, ed. *War and Violence in the Ancient World*. Swansea: Classical Press of Wales, 2000, 31–56.

Sherman, Nancy. *Stoic Warriors: The Ancient Philosophy Behind the Military Mind*. Oxford and New York: Oxford University Press, 2005.

Sinha, Mrinalini. *Colonial Masculinity: The 'Manly Englishman' and the 'Effeminate Bengali' in the Late Nineteenth Century*. Manchester: Manchester University Press, 1995.

Sjöblad, A. *Metaphorical Coherence: Studies in Seneca's Epistulae Morales*. Lund: Lund Centre for Languages and Literature, Lund University, 2015.

Skinner, Marilyn B. 'Clodia Metelli'. *Transactions of the American Philological Association* 113 (1983): 273–87.

———. *Sexuality in Greek and Roman Culture*. Ancient Cultures. Malden, MA: Blackwell, 2005.

———. *Clodia Metelli: The Tribune's Sister*. Women in Antiquity. New York: Oxford University Press, 2011.

Slater, Niall. *Plautus in Performance: The Theater of the Mind*. London: Routledge, 2013.

Smiler, A. P. *Dating and Sex: A Guide for the 21st Century Teen Boy*. Washington, DC: Magination Press, 2016.

Smith, S. C. 'Brutus as Earthborn Founder of Rome (Livy 1.56)'. *Mnemosyne* 60 (2007): 285–93.

Smucker, Jonathan. *Hegemony How-To: A Roadmap for Radicals*. Oakland: AK Press, 2017.

Soloway, Jill. 'Jill Soloway on Donald Trump, Locker Rooms and Toxic Masculinity', 11 October 2016. https://time.com/4527277/jill-soloway-donald-trump-locker-rooms-toxic-masculinity/.

Somanader, Tanya. 'House GOP Unanimously Passes Anti-Abortion Bill That Redefines Rape, Raises Taxes, and Creates Rape Audits'. *Think Progress*, 4 May 2011. https://thinkprogress.org/house-gop-unanimously-passes-anti-abortion-bill-that-redefines-rape-raises-taxes-and-creates-rape-c616c17aa1c8/.

Sommer, Michael. 'Scipio Aemilianus, Polybius, and the Quest for Friendship in Second Century Rome'. In B. Gibson and T. Harrison, eds. *Polybius and His World: Essays in Memory of F. W. Walbank*. Oxford: Oxford University Press, 2013, 307–18.

Sommerstein, Alan H. *Aristophanes: Lysistrata*. Warminster: Aris and Phillips, 1990.

———. 'Sophocles and Democracy'. *Polis* 34 (2017): 273–87.

Soranus. *Soranus' Gynecology*. Translated by Owsei Temkin. Baltimore: Johns Hopkins Press, 1956.

Sowers, Brian P. 'Thecla Desexualized: The Saint Justina Legend and the Reception of the Christian Apocrypha in Late Antiquity'. In James H. Charlesworth and Lee M. McDonald, eds. *'Non-Canonical' Religious Texts in Early Judaism and Early Christianity*. New York: T&T Clark International, 2012, 222–34.

———. 'Historiolae: Narrative Charms in Magical Texts and Literature in Late Antiquity'. *History of Religions* 56.4 (2017): 426–48.

———. *In Her Own Words: The Life and Poetry of Aelia Eudocia*. Washington, DC: Center for Hellenic Studies, 2020.

Sowers, Brian P., and Kimberly Passaro. 'Christianity Re-Sexualised: Intertextuality and the Early Christian Novel'. In Allison Surtees and Jennifer Dyer, eds. *Exploring Gender Diversity in the Ancient World*. Edinburgh: Edinburgh University Press, 2020, 185–96.

Spencer, Diana. *Roman Landscape: Culture and Identity*. Vol. 39. Greece and Rome. New Surveys in the Classics. Cambridge and New York: Cambridge University Press, 2010.

Spivak, Gayatri Chakravorty. 'Three Women's Texts and a Critique of Imperialism'. *Critical Inquiry* 12.1 (1985): 243–61.

———. 'Can the Subaltern Speak?' In Carey Nelson and Lawrence Grossberg, eds. *Marxism and the Interpretation of Culture*. Basingstoke: Macmillan, 1988, 217–313.

Stadter, Philip. *Plutarch and His Roman Readers*. Oxford: Oxford University Press, 2015.

Stafford, Emma J. 'Masculine Values, Feminine Forms: On the Gender of Personified Abstractions'. In Foxhall and Salmon 1998, 43–56.

Stem, R. 'The Exemplary Lessons of Livy's Romulus'. *Transactions of the American Philological Association* 137 (2007): 435–71.

Šterbenc Erker, D. 'Gender and Roman Funeral Ritual'. In Hope and Huskinson 2011, 40–60.

Stewart, D. 'From Leuktra to Nabis, 371–192'. In Powell 2018, 374–402.

Stewart-Steinberg, Suzanne. 'Grounds for Reclamation: Fascism and Postfascism in the Pontine Marshes'. *Differences: A Journal of Feminist Cultural Studies* 27.1 (2016): 94–142.

Stone, Marla. 'A Flexible Rome: Fascism and the Cult of Romanità'. In Catharine Edwards, ed. *Roman Presences: Receptions of Rome in European Culture 1789–1945*. Cambridge: Cambridge University Press, 1999, 205–21.

Strasburger, H. 'Poseidonios on Problems of the Roman Empire'. *Journal of Roman Studies* 55 (1965): 40–53.

———. *Zur Sage von der Gründung Roms*. Heidelberg: Carl Winter, 1968.

Streete, Gail P. C. *Redeemed Bodies: Women Martyrs in Early Christianity*. Louisville, KY: Westminster John Knox, 2009.

Stringer, Rebecca. *Knowing Victims: Feminism, Agency and Victim Politics in Neoliberal Times*. New York: Routledge, 2014.

Strong, Anise K. *Prostitutes and Matrons in the Roman World*. New York: Cambridge University Press, 2016.

Sullivan, Denis. *The Rise and Fall of Nikephoros II Phokas: Five Contemporary Texts in Annotated Translations*. Vol. 23. Byzantina Australiensia. Leiden: Brill, 2018.

Sussman, Lewis A. 'Antony the Meretrix Audax: Cicero's Novel Invective in *Philippic* 2.44–46'. *Eranos* 96.1–2 (1998): 114–28.

Swain, Simon. *Hellenism and Empire: Language, Classicism, and Power in the Greek World, AD 50–250*. Oxford: Clarendon Press, 1996.

Talbot, Alice-Mary, and Denis Sullivan. *The History of Leo the Deacon: Byzantine Military Expansion in the Tenth Century*. Vol. 41. Dumbarton Oaks Studies. Washington, DC: Dumbarton Oaks Research Library and Collection, 2005.

Tarrant, Harold. 'Platonist Educators in a Growing Market: Gaius, Albinus, Taurus, Alcinous'. *Bulletin of the Institute of Classical Studies* 2 (2007): 449–65.

Taylor, Kris, and Sue Jackson. '"I Want That Power Back": Discourses of Masculinity within an Online Pornography Abstinence Forum'. *Sexualities* 21.4 (2018): 621–39.

Tereškinas, Arturas. 'Performing a Victim: Toxic Postsocialist Masculinities'. In V. Deliyanni, H. Naciri, A. Tereškinas, K. Bekkaoui and H. Reddad, eds. *Gender, Identities and Education*. Morocco: Sultan Moulay Slimane University, 2018, 139–48.

Thomas, John, and Angela Constantinides Hero, eds. *Byzantine Monastic Foundation Documents*. Vol. 1. Washington, DC: Dumbarton Oaks Research Library and Collection, 2000.

Thomas, Richard F. *Lands and Peoples in Roman Poetry: The Ethnographical Tradition*. Cambridge: Cambridge Philological Society, 1982.

Thomas, Y. 'Vitae necisque potestas. Le père, la cité, la mort'. In *Du châtiment dans la cité: Supplices corporels et peine de mort dans le monde antique, table ronde, Rome, 9–11 novembre 1982*, 499–548. Rome: École française de Rome, 1984.

Thomkins-Jones, R. 'Toxic Masculinity and Social Work'. *Social Worker 3* (2017): 1–3.

Thorsen, Thea. 'Intrepid Intratextuality: The Epistolary Pair of Leander and Hero (Heroides 18–19) and the End of Ovid's Poetic Career'. In Stephen Harrison, Stavros Frangoulidis and Theodore D. Papanghelis, eds. *Intratextuality and Latin Literature*. Berlin: De Gruyter, 2018, 257–2.

Tickner, J. Ann. *Gender in International Relations: Feminist Perspectives on Achieving Global Security*. New York: Columbia University Press, 1992.

Tomlin, R. 'The Curse Tablets'. In Barry Cunliffe, ed. *The Finds From the Sacred Spring: The Temple of Sulis Minerva at Bath, Vol. 2*. Oxford: Oxford University Press, 1988, 59–277.

Traina, Giusto. 'Lycoris the Mime'. In Augusto Fraschetti, ed. *Roman Women*. Chicago: University of Chicago Press, 2001, 82–99.

Treadgold, Warren. *The Middle Byzantine Historians*. New York: Palgrave Macmillan, 2013.

Treggiari, S. 'Home and Forum: Cicero between "Public" and "Private"'. *TAPA* 128 (1998): 1–23.

Trillin, Calvin. 'Three Republican Candidates Discourse on the Subject of Rape'. *The Nation*, 30 October 2012. https://web.archive.org/web/20150819235727/ https://www.thenation.com/article/three-republican-candidates-discourse-subject-rape/.

Tuplin, Christopher. *The Failings of Empire: A Reading of Xenophon Hellenica 2.3.11–7.5.27*. Stuttgart: Franz Steiner Verlag, 1993.

Turner, S. '"Only Spartan Women Give Birth to Real Men": Zack Snyder's *300* and the Male Nude'. In D. M. Lowe and K. Shahabudin, eds. *Classics for All: Re-Working Antiquity in Mass Cultural Media*. Cambridge: Cambridge Scholars Publishing, 2009, 128–49.

Veissière, S. P. L. '"Toxic Masculinity" in the Age of #MeToo: Ritual, Morality and Gender Archetypes across Cultures'. *Society and Business Review* 13.3 (2018): 274–86.

Vernant, Jean-Pierre. *Mythe et pensée chez les Grecs. Études de psychologie historique*. Paris: Maspero, 1965.

Versnel, H. S. 'Beyond Cursing: The Appeal to Justice in Judicial Prayers'. In Faraone and Obbink 1991, 214–43.

————. 'An Essay on Anatomical Curses'. In Fritz Graf, ed. *Ansichten griechischer Rituale: Geburtsags-Symposium für Walter Burkert*. Stuttgart: Teubner, 1998, 217–67.

Visser, Romke. 'Fascist Doctrine and the Cult of Romanità'. *Journal of Contemporary History* 27.1 (1992): 5–22.

Walcot, Peter. 'Greek Attitudes towards Women: The Mythological Evidence'. *Greece and Rome* 31.1 (1984): 37–47.

Walters, Jonathan. 'Invading the Roman Body: Manliness and Impenetrability in Roman Thought'. In Hallett and Skinner 1997, 29–44.

Walters, Suzanna Danuta. 'In Defense of Identity Politics'. *Signs: Journal of Women in Culture and Society* 43.2 (November 2017): 473–88.

Ware, Cellestine. *Woman Power: The Movement for Women's Liberation*. A Tower Public Affairs Book. New York: Tower, 1970.

Waterfields, Robin. *Herodotus: Histories*. Oxford: Oxford University Press, 1998.

Weissmann, Jordan. 'Is Robin Hanson America's Creepiest Economist?' *Slate*, 30 April 2018. https://amp.slate.com/business/2018/04/economist-robin-hanson-might-be-americas-creepiest-professor.html.

Welch, Rhiannon Noel. *Vital Subjects: Race and Biopolitics in Italy, 1860–1920*. Liverpool: Liverpool University Press, 2016.

Welwei, K.-W. 'Lucius Iunius Brutus: Zur Ausgestaltung und politischen Wirkung einer Legende'. *Gymnasium* 108 (2001): 123–35.

Wendt, Simon, and Pablo Dominguez Andersen. *Masculinities and the Nation in the Modern World: Between Hegemony and Marginalization*. New York: Palgrave Macmillan, 2015.

Whalen, Alexis. 'Resource Blog: Contemporary Views of Men's Views on Women's Anatomies'. *Dux Femina Facti* (blog), 24 February 2013. https://feminadux.wordpress.com/2013/02/24/resource-blog-contemporary-views-of-mens-views-on-womens-anatomies/.

White, Michele. *Producing Masculinity: The Internet, Gender, and Sexuality*. New York: Routledge, 2019.

Wiater, N. 'Writing Roman History – Shaping Greek Identity: The Ideology of Historiography in Dionysius of Halicarnassus'. In N. Wiater and T. A. Schmitz, eds. *The Struggle for Identity: Greeks and Their Past in the First Century BCE*. Stuttgart: Franz Steiner Verlag, 2011, 61–91.

Wikipedia contributors. 'Rape and Pregnancy Statement Controversies in United States Elections, 2012'. *Wikipedia, The Free Encyclopedia*, 2012. http://en.wikipedia.org/w/index.php?title=Rape_and_pregnancy_statement_controversies_in_United_States_elections,_2012.

Wilcox, Amanda. 'Sympathetic Rivals: Consolation in Cicero's Letters'. *American Journal of Philology* 126 (2005): 237–55.

————. 'Exemplary Grief: Gender and Virtue in Seneca's Consolations to Women'. *Helios* 33.1 (2006): 73–101.

Wilkins, Ann Thomas. 'Augustus, Mussolini, and the Parallel Imagery of Empire'. In Claudia Lazzaro and Roger Crum, eds. *Donatello among the Blackshirts: History and Modernity in the Visual Culture of Fascist Italy*. Ithaca, NY and London: Cornell University Press, 2005, 53–65.

Williams, Craig A. *Roman Homosexuality: Ideologies of Masculinity in Classical Antiquity*. Ideologies of Desire. Oxford: Oxford University Press, 1999.

———. *Roman Homosexuality*. 2nd ed. Oxford: Oxford University Press, 2010.

———. 'The Meanings of Softness: Some Remarks on the Semantics of Mollitia'. *Eugesta* 3 (2013): 240–63.

Willke, John C. 'Assault Rape Pregnancies Are Rare'. *Life Issues Connector*, 1999. http://www.physiciansforlife.org/assault-rape-pregnancies-are-rare/.

Willson, Perry. 'Empire, Gender and the "Home Front" in Fascist Italy'. *Women's History Review* 16.4 (2007): 487–500.

Winkler, John J. 'Laying down the Law: The Oversight of Men's Sexual Behavior in Classical Athens'. In John J. Winkler and David M. Halperin, eds. *Before Sexuality: The Construction of Erotic Experience in the Ancient Greek World*. Princeton: Princeton University Press, 1990a, 171–209.

———. *The Constraints of Desire: The Anthropology of Sex and Gender in Ancient Greece*. New York: Routledge, 1990b.

———. 'The Constraints of Eros'. In Faraone and Obbink 1991, 214–43.

Wiseman, T. P. *New Men in the Roman Senate, 139 BC–AD 14*. Oxford: Oxford University Press, 1971.

———. *Remus: A Roman Myth*. Cambridge: Cambridge University Press, 1995.

———. *Roman Drama and Roman History*. Exeter: University of Exeter Press, 1998a.

———. 'Roman Republic, Year One'. *Greece and Rome* 45 (1998b): 19–26.

———. *Unwritten Rome*. Exeter: University of Exeter Press, 2008.

Witzke, Serena S. '*Roe* v. *Wade*, the GOP, and Echoes of Augustus: Reproducing Fascism'. *Society for Classical Studies Blog* (blog), 25 June 2022. https://classicalstudies.org/scs-blog/switzke/blog-roe-v-wade-gop-and-echoes-augustus-reproducing-fascism.

Wohl, Victoria. *Love Among the Ruins: The Erotics of Democracy in Classical Athens*. Princeton: Princeton University Press, 2002.

Wortley, John, ed. *Ioannes Scylitzes: A Synopsis of Byzantine History, 811–1057*. New York: Cambridge University Press, 2010.

Wray, David. *Catullus and the Poetics of Roman Manhood*. Cambridge: Cambridge University Press, 2001.

Wyke, Maria. *The Roman Mistress*. Oxford: Oxford University Press, 2002.

Yagoda, B. 'Who You Calling "Snowflake"?' *Chronicle of Higher Education* (blog), 4 December 2016. https://www.chronicle.com/ blogs/linguafranca/2016/12/04/who-you-calling-snowflake/.

Zeitlin, F. I. *Playing the Other: Gender and Society in Classical Greek Literature.* Chicago and London: University of Chicago Press, 1996.

Zuckerberg, Donna. *Not All Dead White Men: Classics and Misogyny in the Digital Age.* Cambridge, MA: Harvard University Press, 2018.

Zumbrunnen, John. 'Realism, Constructivism, and Democracy in the History'. In Christine Lee and Neville Morley, eds. *A Handbook to the Reception of Thucydides.* Malden, MA: Wiley-Blackwell, 2015, 296–312.

Index Locorum

Index

EU representative:
Easy Access System Europe
Mustamäe tee 50, 10621 Tallinn, Estonia
Gpsr.requests@easproject.com

www.ingramcontent.com/pod-product-compliance
Lightning Source LLC
Chambersburg PA
CBHW070842300326
41935CB00039B/1349